THE IMPROVEMENT
OF HUMANITY

THE IMPROVEMENT
OF HUMANITY

EDUCATION AND
THE FRENCH REVOLUTION

by R. R. PALMER

PRINCETON UNIVERSITY PRESS
PRINCETON, NEW JERSEY

Library of Congress Cataloging in Publication Data will be found
on the last printed page of this book

ISBN 0-691-05434-7

This book has been composed in Linotron Galliard
Clothbound editions of Princeton University books are printed on acid-free paper,
and binding materials are chosen for strength and durability.
Printed in the United States of America by Princeton University Press
Princeton, New Jersey

CONTENTS

ACKNOWLEDGMENTS   vii

PRELIMINARY OBSERVATIONS   3

1. *REALITIES BEFORE THE REVOLUTION*   8

    The ABCs   9

    Colleges and Private Schools   12

    Higher Learning   30

2. *NATIONALIZATION*   37

    The Growth of Royal Authority   39

    Signs of the Enlightenment   48

    Writings of the 1760s on "National Education"   52

    Actual Changes, 1762-1789   59

    The State, the Church, and the Public Power on the Eve of the Revolution   70

3. *POLITICIZATION*   79

    Politics and Education   80

    Plans and Projects   85

    The Talleyrand Report and Its Critics   94

    Discord and Disarray   102

    Disendowment   112

4. *DEMOCRATIZATION: THE QUEST FOR EQUALITY*   121

    The Condorcet Plan   124

    The Disintegration of the Condorcet Plan   129

    The Ambiguities of *Education Commune*   139

    The "Parisian Democracy" of 1793   146

    Educational Demands of the Sections of Paris   155

    The Paris Plan of September 15, 1793   160

    Some Actualities   170

CONTENTS

5. *DEMOCRATIZATION: BUILDING THE BETTER WORLD*   177

     The Bouquier Law   179

     A National Language   183

     National Festivals and a New Civic Environment   190

     The Accelerated "Revolutionary Courses"   197

     The *Ecole Normale*: Democracy Confused and Confounded   208

6. *MODERNIZATION: THE PATHS OF PROGRESS*   221

     Idéologues and Intellectuals   222

     The Half-Revival of Condorcet   225

     The Law of 3 Brumaire of the Year IV   230

     The Public and the Private Sectors   236

     The Central Schools: Progressive Education   242

     More Democrats: The Debate of the Year VII   257

     And Idéologues: The Council on Public Instruction   268

7. *MODERNIZATION: COLLECTIVE POWER*   279

     The Last Public Discussion, 1800-1802   281

     Old Colleges or New Central Schools?   287

     The Law of 11 Floréal of the Year X   293

     The Napoleonic Lycées   299

     The Imperial University   306

     Monopoly and Competition   315

     The Higher Spheres   320

     CONCLUDING REFLECTIONS   329

     APPENDIX   333

     INDEX   337

ACKNOWLEDGMENTS

Since becoming interested in the history of education over a dozen years ago I have incurred obligations that I am glad to acknowledge. There have been various grants for release of my time, including a month in 1973 at the Rockefeller Center for Study and Research at Bellagio, Italy, a semester in 1973 from the John Simon Guggenheim Foundation, two periods of several months in 1973 and 1974 from the National Endowment for the Humanities, and three months in 1979 at the National Humanities Center in North Carolina. My thanks go to all these, and to Yale University for reduction of my teaching duties in the years before my retirement from its faculty. I am grateful also for the library resources at Yale, the University of Michigan, the Newberry Library, the New York Public Library, the British Library, and the inexhaustible libraries and archives of Paris. From all these some years ago came a small book of translation and commentary, *The School of the French Revolution: A documentary history of the College of Louis-le-Grand and its director, Jean-François Champagne*, published by the Princeton University Press in 1975. This work is now somewhat tardily followed by the present volume which surveys all levels and purposes of education in France before, during, and shortly after the French Revolution.

Historians may also recognize a more general debt to their own time. An awareness of present problems of education has shaped the ideas as distinct from the information in the present book. It was during the French Revolution that education was first linked with democracy, explicitly and by name. The problems of equality in education, the development of youthful talents, the reliance on education for social change, the role of intellectuals and political pressure groups, the connections between centralized government and the schools, the question of religious instruction, the formation of nationality, the hope of progress, and the use of schools for both the technical development and the moral strengthening of society are recurring themes on which the present and the past may illuminate each other.

There are many persons from whose help I have benefited, including

vii

former students, colleagues, and editors and others at the Princeton University Press. A word of special appreciation must go to my wife, both for research assistance at critical moments and for her support and understanding over many years in connection with this and other books.

R. R. PALMER

THE IMPROVEMENT
OF HUMANITY

PRELIMINARY OBSERVATIONS

L'éducation peut tout. "Education can do anything." The phrase was coined by Helvétius in his posthumous treatise *On Man*, published in French in 1773. It reduced to three words the point of his two-volume work, known in full as *On Man, his intellectual faculties and his education*, which presented a theory of human nature in which education became an almost universal corrective to human and social ills. Though considered simplistic and disputed in its own time, Helvétius' book echoed one of the main themes of the Enlightenment. A "sensationalist" or associationist psychology saw the contents of the mind as arising from sensations and from the association of ideas derived from the senses. The mind at birth was a kind of blank tablet to be written on, or clay yet to be molded. It followed that the behavior of individuals and of nations could be attributed to environment, whether of climate, social institutions, religion, the family, the schools, or the teachers and parents to whom children and young persons were exposed. A pervasive environmentalism gave new impetus to the study of society, or to what would become the social sciences including a science of education, in a general atmosphere of expectation for the improvement of humanity.

That "education could do anything" was therefore by no means the only message that Helvétius meant to convey. He insisted also that the most important part of education was the moral part, which should instill "virtue," or a set of desirable attitudes and habits. True morality, he said, had nothing to do with religion, and indeed a perverse morality was inculcated by priests. It followed that there must be "no priests or no true morality." Organized religion would have to disappear. Existing society must be transformed. The ignorant, he went on, suppose the world to be changing and immobile. The enlightened know that radical change can easily occur. To them "the moral world presents . . . the always varied spectacle of a perpetual revolution." Such were the powers of priestcraft and bad government that "any important reform in the moral part of education presupposes one in the form of government and of the laws." Or in other words, "the

3

philosopher perceives in the distance, whether near or far, the moment when the public power will adopt the plan of instruction developed by men of wisdom. Excited by this hope, the philosopher will concern himself in advance with undermining the prejudices that oppose the execution of this plan."[1]

Helvétius of course, who died in 1771, did not foresee the French Revolution as it actually happened. By perpetual revolution he probably had in mind no more than perpetual change. Yet he clearly looked forward to some kind of sweeping transformation, in which a new and better regime would undertake, by education, to improve the human material at its disposal. This is precisely what the successive governments of the French Revolution hoped to accomplish, and it is the main subject of this book.

After the Revolution, or in the years following the revolutionary climax, when the problem was to consolidate the post-Revolutionary First Republic, the philosopher Destutt de Tracy, in 1798, wrote a short tract entitled *What are the means to establish the moral outlook of a people?* He rejected the idea, which he said had been held even by Voltaire (and of course Rousseau), that moral sentiments were naturally implanted in the human mind, or would flourish spontaneously now that the bad influences of the old order had been removed. Moral ideas, he said, must be taught, must be implanted deliberately. Left to themselves, individuals would disagree or fall into error. Yet education in the sense of schooling was not enough. "Law-makers and government are the true preceptors for the mass of the human race, and the only ones whose lessons are effective." For example, the Revolutionary law authorizing divorce had produced happier marriages. So it was in education.

> The poor professor can repeat every day that decisions should be made according to reason . . . that reason alone will be enough to make him realize that it is in his own interest to do right. He will talk in vain. But let the legislator stop paying priests, and stop letting them interfere in education and civil matters, and in ten years everyone will think like the professor without his having said a word.[2]

It is evident that the pre-Revolutionary *philosophe* and the post-Revolutionary *idéologue* had much in common. Both thought education

[1] C. A. Helvétius, *De l'Homme, de ses facultés intellectuelles et de son éducation. Ouvrage posthume de M. Helvétius*, 2 vols. (London, 1773), 1: 398; 2: 417, 438-40.

[2] Destutt de Tracy, *Quels sont les moyens de fonder la morale d'un peuple?* (Paris, An VI). As reprinted in conjunction with his *Commentaire sur l'Esprit des lois de Montesquieu* (Paris, 1819), pp. 464-65. In his preface of 1819 Tracy declared he still believed as he did in 1798.

important, and most especially moral education; both saw the main obstacle to be in religion, and in their case the Roman Catholic religion of France; and both thought that education must be directed and reinforced by the powers of the state. In fact Destutt de Tracy, with the experience of the Revolution behind him, seems to have had more faith in legislation, and less in teaching, than Helvétius. In 1799 Tracy had a brief opportunity to apply his ideas, when he was appointed by the Minister of the Interior to a new Council on Public Instruction, to advise on the interminable problem of reform of the schools. We shall see what happened to him and his *idéologue* friends and to the plan that they drafted.

Helvétius and Destutt de Tracy were both intellectuals, hardly in touch with the common man. Helvétius was an altruistic millionaire of the Old Regime, Tracy a scion of the ancient nobility who joined in the Revolution, was imprisoned as an aristocrat during the Terror, and supported the Republic after the death of Robespierre. Both aspired to be benefactors of mankind. Probably neither ever set foot in an actual school during his adult life. Tracy was tutored at home, like many boys of his class, until he was sent to a regiment at the age of fourteen to complete his education as a cadet. Helvétius was for several years a student at the College of Louis-le-Grand in Paris, at the time before 1762 when it was still operated by the Jesuits. It is said that he read Locke's *Essay concerning the human understanding* while at Louis-le-Grand. In any case, as often happens with intellectuals, he looked back on his schooling and on his teachers with a distant disapproval and without much regard to changes since his own school days in the 1720s. The same can be said of most *philosophes* who wrote tracts on education—d'Alembert, Rousseau, Condillac, Mably, and various Physiocrats.

Others who were closer to the real educational scene also addressed themselves to educational questions. Both before and during the Revolution many actual teachers, or "professors" in the "colleges" (for boys from ten to eighteen or older), wrote tracts, devised projects, and sometimes tried to reform the institutions in which they worked. Various ministers and bureaucrats, and members of the Parlements or supreme law courts, became active educational reorganizers in the 1760s. The Assembly of the Clergy of France, in which the bishops met every several years, took up the subject very seriously. When Louis XVI convened the Estates-General for 1789, and invited the thousands of election districts to submit their comments on the state of the country, the resulting *cahiers de doléances* in many cases made suggestions for the schools. The archives of the Revolution are full of unpublished projects, and education was discussed in the successive Revolutionary assemblies. The voices of ordinary people were also heard, especially during the most radical phase in 1793. One of the most common demands of the *sans-culottes* was for education. These revolutionary democrats, or what some have called the popular masses, had their own ideas not only on schools for working people like themselves but on larger systems including higher education for the country as a whole. As the democratic pressures subsided, debate continued under the Directory, both in the legislative chambers and in the press. It ended only with Napoleon Bonaparte's lycées of 1802, and his Imperial University of 1808, by which time the public discussion of education, as of all public questions, came to a halt, to be resumed only after Waterloo.

It is desirable to combine an account of thinking about education with some description of actual educational institutions. The actualities of the past are more difficult to recover than the language of writers or the speeches of orators. Educational reformers do not always give a balanced picture of the schools that they propose to reform, and revolutionaries easily exaggerate the faults of a previous regime that they mean to replace. Opponents of a revolution, whether contemporary with it or looking back on it with repugnance, of whom there have been many ever since the French Revolution, may either idealize the institutions of the Old Regime unduly or do less than justice to the ideas and accomplishments of the Revolution itself. Historians may give a better account if they use sources of diverse origin and conflicting viewpoints, or if they find sources previously overlooked, or if they draw on materials that reflect something other than intention or opinion, such as records of actual enrollments and courses of study. There has in fact, in the past 20 years, been a good deal of research on the realities of education in France before, during, and after the Revolution. It is more possible than it used to be to treat philosophical discussion and institutional operations together.

A strategy is needed for coping with such a multifarious subject. It would be possible after half a lifetime to produce a work of inordinate length and complexity. A narrative approach, proceeding step by step, while possibly more faithful to reality, might obscure the very points that give importance to the inquiry. In the hope of combining relative brevity with close scrutiny and coverage of half a century, the method adopted in the following pages is meant to throw the strongest light on a few topics or themes.

Four themes are selected as being both true to the past and enlightening for the present. Each can be expressed in a word—nationalization, politicization, democratization, and modernization. Each can be detected throughout the whole period, yet they take on an especial significance in a roughly chronological sequence. The attempt at nationalization of education becomes noticeable in the 1760s. More acute politicization is evident early in the Revolution. Efforts at democratization mark the radical revolutionary phase in 1793 and 1794. Modernization, for want of a better word, may be said to mark the dominant trend after 1795. In the general compromise that Napoleon imposed on France between Revolution and anti-Revolution, or between the Republic and the Church, the educational system emerged more strongly marked by nationalization than by the three others and remained so for the next century. But education long remained politicized and it is obvious that democratization and "modern" movements have again commanded attention in our time.

A further preliminary word may be added. The thought that humanity could be improved by education, or that young human beings could and should be shaped by their surroundings, was of course hardly new in the eighteenth century. The *philosophes* themselves, the heralds of change, admired the ancient wisdom of China in this respect. The belief had a long history in the religious and humanistic tradition of Europe. It had been expressed by the Greeks and by Cicero and Quintilian. The Jesuits in particular, but also other Catholic and Protestant teachers since the Reformation, had set out to "mold" their pupils' minds. All agreed that sound education needed the support of the civil power.

If we ask what was so special in this regard about the French Revolution and the thinkers who preceded it there are various answers that may occur to us. For one thing, the new belief was more intense, even dogmatic, and endlessly restated. For another, it expected education to produce a general transformation of society. For a third, the virtue that it hoped to inculcate was primarily social, or even political, where earlier educators had aimed more at developing individual character. Both of course aimed at instilling right belief, which in the Christian context referred to religion and in the new thinking meant correct ideas about nature and the world. Charles Rollin, the famous rector of the University of Paris, a generation before Rousseau, insisted that education must develop the "heart" as well as convey knowledge, while the more secular view, despite all its stress on morality, was addressed more particularly to cognition. Finally, even among liberal Christians there was a residue of belief in original sin, or the idea that human beings if left to themselves would exhibit unpleasant characteristics, whereas the new thinkers were inclined to suppose that unpleasant characteristics were themselves the product of a faulty education.

7

CHAPTER 1

REALITIES BEFORE
THE REVOLUTION

No CAUTIOUS HISTORIAN would claim to capture "reality," and the word is used here only to mean actual educational institutions, as distinguished from critiques, proposals, and attempted reforms to be treated later. Thus understood, France was well equipped before the Revolution, at least for a preindustrial and predemocratic society. There was a great diversity of teaching establishments, imparting learning at all levels, and there was much variation between different parts of the country.

It is difficult to give a systematic description, if only because of the meaning of words. Many "public schools" existed, but in a sense of the word now surviving only in England. Where today, at least in the United States, an endowed school is considered private, in the eighteenth century in France and elsewhere it was public institutions that were endowed. Colleges and lesser schools received income from gifts, usually of land and buildings, made in the recent or distant past. Public schools were also supported by grants from town councils, which might then contract with a group of clergy to recruit the teachers and do the teaching. A few public institutions at higher levels were subsidized by the king. "Private" schools, *écoles particulières*, usually of low prestige and brief existence, were enterprises with no public support, no endowment, no charter, and no continuing governing board. They lived by fees or subscriptions. Toward the end of the Old Regime they multiplied rapidly, and their status was rising.

The terms "primary," "secondary," and "higher," as applied to education, were adopted during the Revolution and took on their modern meanings only in the nineteenth century. The schools we call primary were *petites écoles*—"petty" or "village" schools. Or writing might be taught by a writing master, with or without other subjects. The level that we call secondary was occupied by the "colleges." There were also *maisons d'éducation* conducted by *maîtres de pension*, where the "master" provided room and board, the *pension*, for boys to whom he gave primary or secondary instruction, or both, somewhat as the master of a trade might house and teach his apprentices. Girls' schools, less numerous, were often called convents, because religious sisterhoods provided both board and instruction. "Higher" education (confined to males) was dispensed in "faculties" of theology, law, and medicine in the old universities, and in newer schools of engineering, road-building, mining, and the military arts established by the royal government. The sciences, in the strict sense, were mainly pursued in the academies, outside the educational system, as in the rest of Europe.

THE ABCs

Little will be said here on the elementary schools in which reading, writing, and simple arithmetic were taught, along with moral precepts and respect for the church and the king. Louis XIV had issued various ordinances to require universal elementary schooling, in the hope of extirpating the Protestant heresy that he saw as a threat to his realm; but after Protestantism was outlawed in the 1680s and had apparently or theoretically disappeared, the royal government lost interest and occasionally even tried to shut down some of the "petty" schools. The church continued to favor universal elementary education, and the multiplication of printed catechisms and devotional books suggests that reading became more widespread. Bishops and priests hoped also, through schooling and religion, to raise the general level of civilized behavior by reducing crime, vagabondage, drunkenness, wife-beating, and tavern-brawling. Their successes along this line seem to have had economic consequences, by improving the work habits and productivity of the people and so instilling what has been too narrowly called a Protestant ethic.

Much research has been done recently on the common schools of the Old Regime, as a byproduct of a growing interest in the subordinated social classes.[1] It confirms a difference within France that was noticed as long ago as the 1820s and was clarified in an extensive

---

[1] See F. Furet and W. Sachs, "La croissance de l'alphabétisation en France, 18ᵉ et 19ᵉ siècle," *Annales E.S.C.* 29 (1974): 714-37; the maps on pp. 59-68 of F. Furet and J. Ozouf, *Lire et écrire: l'alphabétisation des Français de Calvin à Jules Ferry*, 2 vols. (Paris, 1977); D. Julia, R. Chartier, and M. M. Compère, *L'éducation en France du 16ᵉ au 18ᵉ siècle* (Paris, 1976), to which I am indebted for much of the following discussion.

survey conducted by Louis Maggiolo in the 1870s. The border between two different areas has become famous as the "Maggiolo line,"
which ran from Saint-Malo in eastern Brittany to Geneva in Switzerland, and so swept about a hundred miles south of Paris. The difference between these two parts of France can be seen in various quantitative measures: the number or density of elementary schools, and
the rate of literacy as shown by the ability of marriage partners to sign
their names at the time of marriage. North and east of the line the
schools were more numerous and closer together, and literacy higher,
than in the west and south, with exceptions for some of the western
and southern cities. Northeastern France, England, and the Netherlands showed about the same rate of literacy and together formed the
most literate zone in Europe, until overtaken by Scotland during the
eighteenth century and by Prussia somewhat later. The ability of spouses
to sign their names at marriage, usually only once in a lifetime, is of
course an inadequate measure of literacy in a meaningful sense. Its
advantage is that it embraces all social classes (thanks to the careful
keeping of parish registers) and that it is probably correlated with
more significant achievements. That is, in an area where more persons
can sign their names there should be more who can read and write,
and who make a habit of doing so. The same correlation may be supposed to operate chronologically; if the proportion of the population
signing their names increases, as it did in most of France from the
time of Louis XIV to the Revolution, the proportion of readers should
also have been growing. Since Maggiolo collected data for the two
five-year periods 1686-1690 and 1786-1790, the Maggiolo line "reveals, between the end of the seventeenth century and the Revolution,
the definitive breakthrough of the majority of peasants in the North
into the world of writing."[2] Literacy was more common, and schools
more accessible, in the towns than in the country, and artisans and
shopkeepers were usually able to read, however laboriously. The rates
for women were lower than those for men, though both rose steadily
during the eighteenth century. But only among the comfortable
bourgeoisie and cosmopolitan aristocracy could both husband and wife
be expected to read with facility.

A few figures illustrate the difference between North and South, and
between men and women. In Normandy, in the department of Cal-
vados, including its rural areas, in the years 1780-1789, 82 percent of
the men and 63 percent of the women signed their names at marriage,
but in the town of Caen the percentages were respectively 86 and 73.

---

[2] Julia, Chartier, and Compère, ibid., p. 108.

In the South, in the department of the Bouches-du-Rhône, only 30 percent of the men and 10 percent of the women were able to sign, but in the town of Aix-en-Provence the figure for men was 46 percent and for women 27 percent. All these figures had about doubled in the three or four generations since 1686-1690. The same rate of increase is shown for most parts of France by Maggiolo's cohort of 1816-1820, in which the marriage partners must have learned to write their names during the troubled years of the 1790s, a fact that suggests that the Revolution, with local exceptions, was neither constructive nor destructive in its impact on rudimentary literacy.

These simple generalizations are subject to various complications. It was in the old-fashioned towns that literacy was higher than in the country. In those few towns or parts of towns where early signs of industrialization could be seen, as in textile manufactures, the workers were less able to sign their names (and so less able to read) than were persons in the neighboring rural parishes. Such places were still the exception, however, and it was the traditional urban artisans and shop-keepers who formed the articulate working classes. Another variable lies in the fact that reading and writing were often taught separately, so that more might learn to read than to write, and in any case laboring people who were taught to write as children might lose this ability through having no use for it, while retaining some ability to read. In such cases persons unable to sign their names might not be totally illiterate, but in other cases the opposite might be true. In many parts of France, although standard French was used everywhere by the upper classes, ordinary people spoke only a *patois* or dialect in which little or nothing was printed. In the South the spoken language was Provençal or Occitan. In Brittany and Alsace it was respectively Celtic and German. An Alsatian child could learn to read German, but where the local spoken language had no accepted written form the schools were obliged to teach spelling, writing, and reading in standard French, imposing additional difficulties on the child, and with results that are hard to measure; but it is clear that the ability to sign one's name on a marriage register implies less knowledge of reading in a region where standard French was unknown to the mass of the people. The Church was generally willing to have preaching done in the local language or dialect; the royal government was more ambivalent. It was only with the Revolution that plans were adopted to require the schools to teach standard French everywhere throughout the country. Linguistic uniformity became an aspect of nationalization, or as the Revolutionaries would say, of "fraternity."

How rising literacy may have contributed to democratization is unclear. Louis XIV had called for universal elementary schooling, and so did Frederick the Great of Prussia. In England, the philanthropists like Hannah More who sponsored popular reading were no friends of equality or popular government. The Prussian General Code of 1794 required universal schooling at the very moment when the democratic revolutionaries in France found it hard to cope with the question. In 1789, when rural parishes drew up their *cahiers* for the Estates-General, only about one percent of them made any request for additional schools. The demand for basic schooling came from the towns or from middle-class friends of the peasantry, as when Dupont de Nemours penned a *cahier* in 1789 for a village near Paris. It may be that the effect of a rising literacy was to provide leaders with followers, or to enable wider segments of the population to understand what was said to them, or to make them more susceptible to persuasion, by the priest or the magistrate before and after 1789, or by pamphleteers, journalists, street orators, and speakers in popular assemblies during the Revolution. That is, the ability to read, or simply to recognize by ear words not often used in conversation, produced a mass of consumers for ideas that minorities formulated and expressed. In that sense, it was prerequisite not only to democratization but to modernization or politicization of any kind. It also strengthened the power of elites.

COLLEGES AND PRIVATE SCHOOLS

In a way almost incomprehensible today, the university might be the next step above elementary education. This is because a university, at its lowest level, contained a "faculty of arts" consisting of one or more "colleges." "I assume," said Diderot in a plan prepared for Catherine II of Russia, which in fact followed French practice quite closely—"I assume that whoever presents himself at the door of a university knows how to read, write and spell easily in his own language; I assume that he knows how to form the characters used in arithmetic."[3] Age, he went on, had nothing to do with admission to a "public school of the sciences." The difficulty, for our own understanding, is that a domain of secondary education had yet to be clearly defined. Despite the rigid institutional structure of the colleges, their boundaries were hazy. Some belonged to a university, but most did not. They taught boys of ten and young men of twenty, they offered both elementary and advanced

[3] "Plan d'une université pour le gouvernement de la Russie," in Diderot, *Oeuvres*, ed. Assézat, 20: 448. Not published until 1813.

instruction, and the teachers even of younger boys were called "professors," like those of the higher faculties of law, medicine, and theology. The uncertainty of what constituted secondary education was to plague the Central Schools after 1795; it makes more understandable the overlap between Bonaparte's *collèges secondaires, lycées,* and *facultés* after 1802; and it explains the peculiarities of the French system (until well into the twentieth century and in contrast to other countries) in which both secondary and higher establishments formed part of a generalized *université.*

The colleges were in any case the places in which most young men who had any schooling finished their studies and from which a minority went on to professional education. There are known to have been 347 colleges when the Revolution overtook them in 1789. They were old institutions, two-thirds of them having been founded before 1650. Their organization and methods dated from the educational revolution associated with the Renaissance and the Catholic Reformation. Half of them, known as *collèges de plein exercice,* offered an eight-year program of study, whereas the other half, the *collèges d'humanités,* confined themselves to a six-year program, in each case beginning with boys of about the age of eleven or twelve. In general, the colleges of *plein exercice* were older, larger, and located in the populous towns. The others, the *collèges d'humanités,* were smaller and more local, representing the geographical spread of education in the seventeenth and eighteenth centuries.

It has been argued that the ideal French college in the seventeenth and eighteenth centuries was a place of salutary confinement, designed to shield growing boys from the evils of the outside world, a "closed and supervised universe" conducted by clerics, and hence that it was a boarding school from which pupils could rarely emerge even to visit their families.[4] In fact, the overwhelming majority of students in the French colleges were day pupils. This was true even in Paris, which was exceptional in that its colleges attracted boys and young men from all over the country. Elsewhere, since almost every small town had its college, boys could easily live at home. Town boys with well-to-do parents, and those who came from small villages or rural estates, might board in town with less prosperous families, or with one of the teachers who took in a few boys to supplement his own livelihood. The pattern was changing rapidly, however, in the generation before the Revolution, as the outlines of the later boarding school began to take form. In 1762 hardly more than a tenth of the Jesuit colleges main-

---

[4] G. Snyders, *La pédagogie en France aux 17ᵉ et 18ᵉ siècles* (Paris, 1965), pp. 35-48.

tained *pensionnats*. In 1789 about half of the 347 colleges boarded some fraction of their pupils.[5] Boarders, or *internes*, were either *pensionnaires* who paid fees or (in smaller numbers) *boursiers* whose board and room were defrayed by *bourses* or scholarships. A similar development was taking place in England, where at Eton, for example, there was a distinction between the "collegers," boys living in the college "on the foundation," and the "oppidans," usually richer youths who boarded more comfortably in private houses.

By the eighteenth century there had come to be eight graded annual classes in the French colleges. The normal beginning class was called the Sixth, and those above it were numbered in reverse order, up to a "first" that was called Rhetoric, at which the *collèges d'humanités* terminated, while the *collèges de plein exercice* offered two additional years called Philosophy. Average age in grade was becoming more normalized throughout the country. For certain competitions among the colleges of the University of Paris it was prescribed, in 1784, that no student in the Sixth could be more than twelve years old; for the Fifth, no more than thirteen; and so on until for the Second no one could be over sixteen; but no limit was set for Rhetoric and Philosophy.[6] A student who completed his Philosophy received the degree of *maîtrise ès arts*. Many boys even in the colleges of *plein exercice* went no further than Rhetoric. The degree itself was of little importance, except for those who might wish to become teachers themselves, though it facilitated entrance to the faculties of law, medicine, and theology.

Of the 173 complete colleges that had the two years of Philosophy, 33 belonged to the faculties of arts in various universities. It was by entering one of these colleges that a boy might pass directly from elementary school to a university, as Diderot said. The University of Paris had 10 such colleges; Caen had three; other universities had only one or two. Most colleges were unaffiliated with any university, but between the university colleges and those nonuniversity colleges that offered the full eight-year program there was no great difference. The teachers were almost all members of the clergy, in a general sense, in that many were not priests but young men in minor orders, or *confrères* who wore ecclesiastical costume and remained celibate, but who were free to leave and often did so, like the tutors and theology students in American colleges at the time. A professor in Paris was paid from

[5] Julia, Chartier, and Compère, *L'éducation en France*, p. 215; they call the shift to boarding schools after 1762 *une mutation*.

[6] On the crystallization of age levels see ibid., p. 194, and for Paris see C. Jourdain, *Histoire de l'Université de Paris au 17ᵉ et au 18ᵉ siècle*, 2 vols., 2nd ed. (Paris, 1888), 2: 442.

2,000 to 2,500 livres a year, about the same as an infantry captain. Until 1762 the French Jesuits operated about 105 colleges, from which they were expelled in that year, so no one under forty years old in 1789 had ever been in a Jesuit college.

The colleges vacated by the Jesuits were taken over by other groups of clergy, but we must beware of the allegation, made by *philosophes*, that education was purveyed by "monks." It is true that it was purveyed by members of the unmarried Catholic clergy, but over half the colleges existing in 1789 were conducted by "seculars," that is, by clerics who belonged to no religious order. In such a college the principal and senior teachers might be ordained priests, but some classes would be taught by unordained ecclesiastics or even by an occasional layman. The principal teaching orders, the Oratorians and Doctrinaires, known as *congrégations séculières*, were neither monkish nor secluded from the world. The controlling groups of 340 colleges in 1789 are listed in the table that follows.[7] All 10 colleges of the University

Controlling group	8-year colleges (*plein exercice*)	6-year colleges (*humanités*)
Secular clergy	91	91
Doctrinaires (Pères de la Doctrine Chrétienne)	25	14
Oratorians	23	6
Benedictines	10	9
Other religious orders	21	44
Protestant pastors		1
Laymen	3	2
Total	173	167

of Paris were in the hands of secular clergy, as were two of those at Caen, but colleges in other provincial universities were run by one or another of the religious congregations. There had formerly been numerous Protestant colleges, which disappeared during the reign of Louis XIV; the Protestant case in the list above was in the principality of Montbéliard in eastern France, not fully incorporated into France until

[7] Derived from the table in D. Julia and P. Pressly, "La population scolaire en 1789: les extravagances statistiques du ministre Villemain," *Annales E.S.C.* 30 (November-December 1975): 1548:56. This article and Julia, Chartier, and Compère, *L'éducation en France*, are the source of most of the quantitative statements presented here.

the Revolution. A Protestant college at Strasbourg, where Protestant-ism had been tolerated since the annexation, was conducted by laymen.

There are many reasons for the predominance, even the monopoly, of the clergy in what we would call secondary education. For one thing, the authorities in the church insisted on it. Most families and many educational writers also regarded it as desirable. The clergy had for centuries been the traditional repository of bookish learning. The teaching fathers were expected to have a good moral influence on ad-olescents. It was convenient to turn over the problems of teacher re-cruitment, discipline, and curriculum to men who made such matters a specialty. Unmarried men, living at the school and sharing a com-mon table, could make do with small salaries. Laymen with families needed more money, and those who would make a lifetime occupation of dealing with other people's children were in any case hard to find. It was thought also that unmarried men, with no families of their own, had more time to spend with their pupils and became more attached to the college and more conscientious as teachers. Not until after the Revolution did teaching become a recognized profession for laymen.

In the plan of study there were significant changes in the decades before the Revolution.[8] With the expulsion of the Jesuits the stress on Latin somewhat abated, but it continued to be taught in the early years, and read in the later years, of the six- or eight-year program. It was increasingly valued both in itself and as an aid in the learning of French. There was more teaching of French, and Racine and other seventeenth-century authors became "classics," that is, readings thought suitable for use in the classroom.

Rhetoric, formerly concentrated on the study of rules laid down by Aristotle and Cicero, came rather to mean command of the spoken word, more a matter of elocution than of erudition. Its purpose was in part vocational, to prepare young men to be fluent advocates in a courtroom, convincing advisers in royal councils, or eloquent preach-ers if they later joined the pastoral clergy. For this reason families desired their sons to complete at least the Rhetoric class and cared less whether they went on to Philosophy. The values of personal presence, retentive memory, and pleasing expression were instilled also by the college theater, which produced performances for the public, and in which the Jesuits excelled, but which existed also in non-Jesuit col-leges, though occasionally frowned upon as pernicious. Rhetoric found another outlet in the annual ceremonies in which the school year ended,

[8] See Julia, Chartier, and Compère, *L'éducation en France*, chaps. 6 and 7; R. Taton, ed., *Enseignement et diffusion des sciences en France au 18ᵉ siècle* (Paris, 1964), pp. 13-168.

when selected students delivered orations before assemblies of teachers, parents, and public officials. Though ceremonial and usually platitudinous, these discourses gave practice in public speaking. Rhetoric, in short, was no mere decoration or disguise of thought. It meant verbal facility. That results were obtained is apparent even in some of the ephemeral pamphlets of the time, often written with great vigor and clarity, and in the long speeches in the Revolutionary assemblies, which, with all their grandiloquence and their stylized references to the Greeks and Romans, were often also (at least as we know them in published form) effective as exhortations, or denunciations, or arguments, or simply as expositions of complex financial or legal problems.

The sponsors of schools of a more modern kind, outside the colleges, often claimed it as an advantage that they taught more mathematics and less Latin or merely verbal arts. Yet a boy who entered the Sixth knowing no more than elementary arithmetic was unlikely to remain in such ignorance. Mazarin College at the University of Paris was especially known for a series of mathematics teachers, including the Abbé La Caille, and so was Beauvais College where Rivard began to teach in the 1740s. Both wrote textbooks going as far as quadratic equations, spherical trigonometry, conic sections, and differential calculus, and the frequent reprinting of such textbooks suggests that they were used in colleges other than their own. It was in the Paris colleges that the mathematicians d'Alembert, Condorcet, and Legendre received their introductions to mathematics.

The two years of Philosophy, offered only in the eight-year colleges, were devoted to metaphysics, moral philosophy, advanced mathematics, and increasingly to the natural sciences. They were generally taught in Latin, which by this time the student was supposed to understand easily. While there was still much discussion of Aristotle, the writings of Locke, Condillac, and others of the new empirical school were also read by the mid-century. Although there were conferences and disputations, instruction was primarily by lectures, giving a survey of the comparative merits of philosophical systems, and delivered by a *dictée*, with the student expected to write down exactly what the professor said. There was much criticism of the *dictée* as a waste of time, a survival of the Middle Ages when books had been rare, and a professional teacher writing in Diderot's *Encyclopédie* in the 1750s condemned it. It is curious to note, before this condemnation is taken at face value, that it was soon afterward regarded in America as an improvement. When John Witherspoon came from Scotland and introduced the Scottish Enlightenment at Princeton, he caused a stir by replacing the old recitations with dictated lectures, which his students tried to take down verbatim, as we know from the fact that his book, *Lectures on Moral Philosophy*, was reconstructed from the notes of his students, which were found to contain identical passages.

The natural sciences made a more difficult entry into the college curriculum. Apparently nothing but physics was taught, and then only in the second year of Philosophy, which most students never reached. Even so, it is estimated that 5,000 young men were studying physics in a given year in the closing decades of the Old Regime. In 1753 the French government established a chair in experimental physics for the Abbé Nollet at Navarre College in Paris. Nollet attracted many hearers to his lectures in addition to his students, so much so that the government provided him with a hall seating 600 persons. When the scientific instruments belonging to Navarre College were inventoried during the Revolution, the list contained 231 named and numbered items. Throughout France, in 1761, there were 85 colleges having a professor of physics, and the course lasted through the whole second year. From the confiscation of *cabinets de physique* during the Revolution we know that many belonged to royal and aristocratic persons, but that 15 belonged to professors, and 37 belonged to colleges. It is notable that 35 of these 37 colleges were not in Paris but in the provinces, and that, although the Oratorian fathers were thought to pay special attention to science, 32 of these 37 were not Oratorian. The collections were used for demonstrations, or for experiments performed by the professor, often for a larger public than his students alone. Students did not perform experiments themselves, but men having scientific collections sometimes took them from college to college throughout the country as traveling exhibits, using them in lectures and demonstrations to illustrate the vacuum, steam pressure, or electricity. One, as early as 1783, was so up-to-date as to demonstrate the principles of Montgolfier's balloon.

Since there were no elective studies, anyone completing the work of an eight-year college had studied physics. The situation for history was more uncertain. Its value was held to lie in giving concrete examples of moral and political principles. It presented cases of wise and unwise statesmanship, good and bad government, personal heroism and cowardice, the merits of different systems of government, and the rise and decadence of empires. It conveyed a kind of embryonic political science and provided examples for exercises in Rhetoric. Textbooks of modern history were written and presumably read. One by C.F.X. Millot was translated into eight languages. It was sufficiently esteemed in America for the English version to be reprinted at Worcester, Massachusetts, in 1789, containing two volumes of ancient and three of modern history, with a second American edition at Salem in 1796. Modern history was thus by no means ignored, but it was ancient history that was studied more fully, in connection with Latin, or in the reading of such Greek authors as Plutarch in translation.

Classical Greece and Rome focused the student's imagination on a world very different from the world of Louis XV and Louis XVI. It showed him an alternative value system and formed a background for judgment of his own time. It could do so even in America, where a translation of Rollin's *Roman History* was widely used in colonial colleges and is thought to have helped to shape the American idea of a republic and of the dangers of decay that a republic might face. In France a lesser *philosophe*, L. S. Mercier, complained that as a student the names of Brutus, Cato, and Scipio had followed him in his sleep. The study of Latin, he said seven years before the French Revolution, produced "a taste for republics." A boy enchanted by "the liberty and majesty of the Roman people" every day in his classroom found it hard to emerge from his school and "find himself once again a bourgeois of the rue des Noyers." "Yet it is an absolute king who pays professors to explain gravely the meaning of these eloquent declamations against the power of kings."[9] Teaching in the colleges was far from subversive, and it was intended to produce loyal and useful subjects; but it is obvious that students in the colleges learned much more than Latin.

It produced, so far as education does, one signer of the American Declaration of Independence, Charles Carroll "of Carrollton," as he called himself. As a Maryland Catholic, with limited educational opportunities at home, he was sent to France for his schooling. At the age of eleven he entered the English Jesuit college at Saint-Omer, and then at eighteen, in 1755, went on to Paris for the two years of Philosophy at Louis-le-Grand. He reports that at Saint-Omer the pupils presented a ballet, learned both to speak and read Latin, and studied modern literature and history. At Louis-le-Grand, in these final years of its time as a Jesuit institution, his studies included mathematics and physics and the philosophies of Aristotle and Thomas Aquinas, but also those of more modern writers who "stemmed from Locke." He then proceeded to law school at Bourges, where he says that he spent £130 a year, or about 2,000 French livres, so he must have been

[9] Louis-Sébastien Mercier, *Tableau de Paris*, 12 vols. (Amsterdam, 1782-1788), 1: 252-57. On Rollin's history in America see William Gribbin, "Rollin's Histories and American Republicanism," *William and Mary Quarterly* (October 1972), pp. 611-22. For authors read in the colleges, and the effects of reading them, see H. T. Parker, *The Cult of Antiquity and the French Revolutionaries* (Chicago, 1937), esp. chaps. 2-4.

regarded by his fellow students as a rich young American. Returning to America in 1764, he soon became involved in the movement for independence.[10]

The best recent estimate is that there were about 50,000 students in the colleges in the years preceding the Revolution, to which an unknown number of boys and young men in private schools would have to be added.[11] A figure of 50,000 represents only about one in 50 of the male population of the 11-18 age group. It was generally believed, however, even during the Revolution, that this number was quite enough—enough, that is, for persons receiving the kind of literary and scientific education that the colleges gave. As the Talleyrand plan of 1791 expressed it:

"It has been said a thousand times that among the crowd of students thrown by the thoughtless vanity of their parents into our old schools open free to everybody, a large number, on reaching the end of their studies, were no longer suited for the occupations for which these studies were preliminary, and had gained only an unsurmountable distaste for honorable occupations . . . and became an embarrassment to society."

Even the radically democratic plan of Michel Lepeletier, sponsored by Robespierre in July 1793, while providing for compulsory and universal elementary free schooling for both boys and girls, called for only one fiftieth of the boys to go on for study of *les belles-lettres, les sciences, et les beaux-arts*, or no more than had been in the colleges before 1789.[12]

The pre-Revolutionary colleges, while hardly open free to "everybody," as Talleyrand said, were in fact open to boys of various social classes and were to a large extent free in charging no tuition. After 1719 the royal government paid the salaries of the professors, about a hundred in number, in the 10 colleges of the faculty of arts of the University of Paris in return for an agreement that no tuition should

---

[10] Thomas O. Hanley, *Charles Carroll of Carrollton* (Washington, D.C., 1970), pp. 23-61.

[11] Julia, Chartier, and Compère, *L'éducation en France*, p. 190; and Julia and Pressly, "La population scolaire," p. 1522. L. B. Brockliss, "Patterns of attendance at the University of Paris, 1400-1800," *Historical Journal* (1978), pp. 503-44, attempts quantitative comparison of France and England, with uncertain results, considering the difficulty of comparing the Oxford and Cambridge colleges with the eight-year French colleges, most of which were outside the universities, though their terminal years would be germane to the comparison.

[12] For the quotation from Talleyrand see his *Rapport sur l'instruction publique, fait au nom du comité de la constitution de l'Assemblée Nationale* (Paris, 1791), p. 22. For the Lepeletier report see below, pp. 138-39.

be charged. In the provinces there might be either no fees or only nominal fees for instruction. The main cost was for room and board, but as already noted most students lived at home or in *pensions* that ranged from the economical to the expensive. If they lived in a college, the fee for board and room was usually 300 or 400 livres a year; but there were also scholarships or *bourses*. Most of the endowed funds of the colleges had been given to support such scholarships. In Paris in the 1780s there were over 700 scholarships for a college population of about 5,000.[13] The number for the whole of France is unknown. Scholarships were awarded on a basis in which intelligence, luck, local residence, family connections, and official favor were mixed. Diderot, in his recommendations to Catherine II, observed that scholarship boys were looked down on by others, and that therefore they should be kept for their own good in a separate house or college; the implication is that scholarship students were of lower social standing than those who paid their own fees. They might, however, include boys of noble families in reduced circumstances.

Some colleges were especially attractive to an aristocratic clientele, for example, La Flèche and Juilly. In Paris, the College of Louis-le-Grand was favored by distinguished families so long as it was a Jesuit institution, though both Helvétius and Voltaire also studied there. From 1762 until the Revolution Louis-le-Grand was reserved for scholarship students, of whom the most famous in later years was Maximilien Robespierre. For 120 of its scholarship students we know the occupation of their fathers. Among them were 20 men in government or finance (probably including some nobles), 16 lawyers, 11 doctors of medicine, 9 *négociants* or large merchants, 37 in shopkeeping and skilled trades, 15 in agriculture, and 12 miscellaneous.[14] A roughly similar distribution is found for the College of Avallon, a small town with a population of about 4,000 a hundred miles southeast of Paris. Such a college typically drew its students both from the town and from families living in smaller places or in the open country, and for Avallon it is possible to see the difference, for 1,113 students enrolled between 1711 and 1779.[15] (See the following table.) "Bourgeois" at this time

[13] See my article, "Le Prytanée français et les écoles de Paris, 1798-99" *Annales historiques de la Révolution française* (January-March 1981), pp. 123-52.

[14] H. Chisick, "Bourses et mobilité sociale à la veille de la Révolution: bourses et boursiers au Collège Louis-le-Grand, 1762-92," *Annales E.S.C.* 30 (November-December 1975): 1569.

[15] W. Frijhoff and D. Julia, *Ecole et société dans la France d'ancien régime* (Paris, 1975), p. 14. F. Dainville, analyzing the social origins of students in Jesuit colleges in northeastern France, found a distribution somewhat more heavily weighted toward the pop-

generally meant *rentiers* or persons "living nobly" on income from property.

It is evident that more of the affluent boys came from out of town, if only because they could afford to board privately or in the college, while local boys of shopkeeping and artisan families could also attend, if only because they could live with their parents. In general, given geographical accessibility, it seems that a family above the poverty level, not needing the labor of its children at an early age, could hope to have at least one son obtain an education.

Father's occupation	Percentage of town students (N=671)	Percentage of out-of-town students (N=642)
Nobles and seigneurs	7.9	12.0
"Bourgeois"	5.7	8.1
Upper and middle office-holders, lawyers, doctors	20.4	26.5
Lower officeholders and lesser liberal professions	19.7	24.0
Merchants and shopkeepers	29.1	19.6
Artisans	15.9	3.6
Farm owners and tenants	1.1	6.2
Day laborers	.2	.0
Total	100.0	100.0

While the very rich might rely on private tutors and foreign travel and the very poor receive no education at all, and while the proportion of well-to-do families sending sons to a college was higher than the proportion for the more numerous middling income groups, it appears from the evidence that the spread of social classes represented in a

ular side, remaining much the same for the whole period, with fathers who were (for 1736) about 10 percent nobles and bourgeois, 28 percent artisans and farmers, and the remainder merchants and officeholders (*Population* 10 [July-September 1955]: 478). Of 79 students at the small college of Lectourne in the later eighteenth century, 4 were nobles, 22 upper bourgeoisie, 40 middle and lower bourgeoisie, and 13 working class; see J. de Viguerie, *Une oeuvre d'éducation sous l'ancien régime: les Pères de la Doctrine chrétienne* (Paris, 1976), p. 596. For 35 colleges not operated by religious congregations see C. R. Bailey, "Municipal *Collèges*: Small-Town Secondary Schools in France Prior to the Revolution," *French Historical Studies* 12 (1982): 351-76.

French college before the Revolution was very large. The sons of noblemen and of tradesmen met in the same classroom. The sons of artisans, indeed, were less likely to finish the full course; we must remember that not all completed their Rhetoric, and even fewer Philosophy. One suspects, nevertheless, without knowing positively, that the social mingling of adolescents was greater in France than in England or Germany. If so, the fact throws light on one of the best known observations of Tocqueville, that Frenchmen before the Revolution were becoming more alike while separated by legal distinctions. It explains also how Frenchmen of diverse social origin could cooperate during the moderate phases of the Revolution. In addition to the bourgeois Diderot, Voltaire, Helvétius, and Robespierre already mentioned, the graduates of the 10 Paris colleges included the foundling d'Alembert, the great chemist Lavoisier who was a bourgeois while still in college, such noble youths as Turgot, Calonne, Condorcet, and Talleyrand, and two future cardinal archbishops of the highest aristocratic extraction, Rohan of diamond necklace fame, and Loménie de Brienne, the last "prime minister" of the Old Regime.

The question of upward social mobility is harder to explore with quantitative data. It is likely that upward mobility had been greater in the early seventeenth century, when many new colleges were being founded, and when the consolidation of the monarchy after the religious wars and the progress of the Catholic Reformation set up a rising demand for educated personnel. By a kind of sociological law, as the proportion of educated families in a population becomes larger, the greater is the pressure to use education as a means of preserving status for one's children, or at least to prevent their losing it. In the decades before the French Revolution this "consolidation of elites" was occurring in the upper, the upper middle, and the lower middle classes. The normal expectation in both professional and working-class families was for the son to remain in the father's occupation or in one closely akin to it. Yet there are significant signs of the use of education as a channel of upward mobility. The figures for Avallon show both tendencies. For example, of 135 students who finished the course at the College of Avallon and then went on to law school at Paris or Dijon, 83 were the sons of lawyers or officeholders, but 17 were the sons of merchants, shopkeepers, and artisans (the others being of miscellaneous parentage).[16] More sons of merchants, shopkeepers, and

---

[16] Frijhoff and Julia, *Ecole et société*, pp. 80-81. Viguerie, *Une oeuvre d'éducation*, p. 605, for the College of Avallon, found that 30 students remained in the same social status as their fathers, 10 rose above it, and 4 fell below it in their later careers.

artisans went on into theology than into law or medicine. The church remained the chief avenue of advancement for boys of this class, since its organization provided, below the levels of the bishoprics occupied by nobles, many intermediate positions for an ambitious or studious youth.

A typical college, in Paris or the provinces, thus had from 100 to 500 students of high and low birth, who paid fees or enjoyed scholarships and were enrolled as residential or day pupils. Rich boys could have better accommodations, and the socially prominent could scoff at their more humble classmates, but there was also an atmosphere of equality and of rivalry, which the college authorities tried to promote. Charles Rollin, rector of the University of Paris, in his *Traité des études*, insisted that all students must be treated equally. The advantage of "public education," he said, was that "the schoolboy becomes convinced that fortune and birth give no privilege, and that the only superiority to be recommended is that of merit and knowledge."[17] Another of the Paris professors insisted that nobles and commoners should be put to the same tests.

Competition and rivalry, or what was called *l'émulation*, were thought to have high educational value. In 1747 the Abbé Louis Legrand, author of a textbook in modern history, left a sum producing 3,000 livres a year to found a contest among the 10 Paris colleges, with prizes for a Latin oration, Latin verse, and Greek translation. The resulting *concours général* was held annually thereafter until the Revolution, with awards distributed in a grand public ceremony attracting hundreds of auditors. One of the first winners was the future minister of Louis XVI, Calonne, who took first prize for Greek translation and second prize for Latin verse. A few years later a group of professors complained that too much was made of this annual spectacle, that teachers were too eager to show off their best students, that some of the colleges outdid themselves to recruit bright boys who might become prize winners, that the time spent in preparation was so excessive, and the strain so great, that only the scholarship boys would compete. The atmosphere of strenuous exertion was praised by Diderot in his proposals to Catherine II. As an example for Russia he cited the practice in the Paris colleges, where *l'émulation* reigned, where a boy "works, studies and has a deadly fear of having to repeat a year," and where the unsuited were sternly weeded out. It was a good thing, said Diderot, for teachers to exhibit their best pupils in public assem-

---

[17] Rollin as quoted by G. Dupont-Ferrier, *Du Collège de Clermont au Lycée Louis-le-Grand*, 1563-1920, 3 vols. (Paris, 1921-1925), 1:477.

blies, and for colleges to reward their best students with medals, badges, and crowns, which might be lost to a rival in the following year; so that both pride and shame were used to provide motivation. It is also true that Diderot, in his impetuous way, said the opposite at about the same time. The famous *émulation*, he observed, meant that the teacher gave all his attention to his four or five best pupils, so that any parent able to do so should avoid the public colleges, and "if you are rich bring up your son at home."[18]

What actually happened in the classroom, in face to face exchange between teachers and students or among students themselves, is harder to recapture than the official plans of study. There were doubtless, as always, both dreary classrooms and lively ones. The *philosophes* generally projected an image of drill and memorization, of dry lectures and dull routine, and since they long remained the most widely read French writers of the period their image has tended to prevail. We can at least gather a few contrary observations from some of the teachers themselves. Charles Rollin, in listing the advantages of public schools over private education at home, remarked that a teacher was stimulated by having a numerous audience and became more excited, ardent, and convincing than in speaking to only a single pupil. The historians both of the Oratorians and the Doctrinaires insist that Philosophy was not taught by lectures only but also by directed readings, conferences, and disputations that turned into dialogues. "One person upholds a new idea, other restless and fiery spirits take up arms to destroy it. They attack each other, become heated, tear each other to pieces. The spark passes from one to another and becomes a general conflagration." This description was offered by a teacher who in fact disapproved of such dissensions on the ground that more enlightened textbooks would make them unnecessary, but its value as evidence is not lessened by his disapproval. The very students who petitioned for new methods in the Philosophy classes, early in the Revolution, admitted that their teachers had recommended the reading of Mably and Condillac, and that the teaching of Rhetoric had already been greatly improved.[19]

---

[18] On *émulation* see Snyders, *La pédagogie en France*, pp. 48-53; on the annual *concours* Jourdain, *Université de Paris*, 2: 265-73; for Diderot, see his "Sur l'école des cadets," in M. Tourneux, *Diderot et Catherine II* (Paris, 1899), p. 356, and his *Oeuvres*, 2: 451. The complaints of professors against excessive zeal are recorded by H. Bouquet, *L'ancien collège d'Harcourt et le lycée Saint-Louis* (Paris, 1891), pp. 408-409. See also P. Marchand, "L'émulation au collège de Lille, 1765-91," *Actes du Congrès national des sociétés savantes. Histoire moderne et contemporaine, 1970*, 1: 149-69. John Adams commented on "emulation" when his son John Quincy was in school in Paris: *Diary and Autobiography*, ed. Butterfield, 2: 301.

[19] C. Rollin, *De la manière d'enseigner* . . . [commonly known as the *Traité des études*]

25

Among the Revolutionaries there were some who looked back on their school days with satisfaction, and even nostalgia. Robespierre in 1793 remarked that the old colleges had been nurseries of republicanism in which the French had learned to love liberty. His youthful protégé, Marc-Antoine Jullien, who outlived him by 50 years and who had attended Montaigu College in Paris, reflected in 1801 on "public education, in which republican ideas germinated under the monarchy, and which offered in our colleges so many little states where rank and fortune gave no superiority, where independence and equality were the highest goals, and where the students, forever transported into an imaginary country, no longer lived in their own, but learned the eloquence of Cicero and Demosthenes."[20]

It was once believed, and taken as a sign of decadence in the colleges, that the number of students in what we would call secondary education was declining in the decades before the Revolution. The evidence was that some colleges that had formerly been very large became much smaller in the later years of the eighteenth century. This is indeed a fact, but the inference does not follow. Though at a decreasing pace, new colleges had been founded since 1650, and especially small and predominantly local ones, so that there is no reason to suppose that total enrollments had decreased. The closing decades of the Old Regime also saw a rising number of "private" schools.

A private school, as already explained, was one that was by definition not a college; that is, it had no endowment, no official or municipal support, and no long history. Such schools seldom preserved any records, so that it is impossible to know much about them. As for their teaching programs, they usually aspired to be more modern than the colleges and to offer more of what parents demanded. Some private schools were day schools, offering a more vocationally oriented course of study, with less Latin and literature, and more subjects useful for boys expecting to go into commercial and other practical work. Some were hardly more than *pensionnats* for students attending classes in a college. Still others were true boarding schools, appealing to parents who preferred not to keep boys beyond a certain age at home or

---

(Paris, 1732-1733), 4: 433; on the Oratorians, Taton, *Enseignement et diffusion*, p. 81; on the Doctrinaires, Viguerie, *Une oeuvre d'éducation*, p. 521; on the "general conflagration" J. A. Borrelly, *Système de législation* (Paris, 1768), p. 146, and see below, p. 59; on the students' petition of 1789, my *School of the French Revolution* (Princeton, 1975), p. 89.

[20] On Robespierre see below, p. 140. Marc-Antoine Jullien, *Appel aux véritables amis de la patrie* (Paris, 1801), p. 51, as quoted in H. Goetz, *Marc-Antoine Jullien de Paris (1775-1848): Der geistige Werdegang eines Revolutionärs* (Zurich, 1954), p. 66.

whose style of life made them unable to do so, or those who simply wanted more individual attention for their sons, with better living quarters and a more socially restricted atmosphere than the colleges provided.

A letter of David Hume gives us a glimpse of French upper class private schools in 1764. His friend, Sir Gilbert Elliot, requested him, while Hume was in Paris, to find a school for Elliot's two sons, aged twelve and thirteen. Hume visited four schools. One he rejected because it was located in too poor a part of the city. Another he dismissed as too expensive; here "a genteel agreeable" man already had two Russian princes among his pupils and would accept Elliot's boys for 5,000 livres a year. A third possibility was offered by a professor of Rhetoric at one of the Paris colleges, who would board the two boys but send them to the college for their studies, an alternative that Hume also excluded, knowing that Elliot preferred not to send his sons to a university, though Hume himself favored it. He selected, therefore, an establishment operated by an Abbé Choquart, on the outskirts of the city, near the Invalides, with access to open fields, possessing "instruments of experimental philosophy," and limited to 35 boys. Hume assured Elliot that his sons would hear nothing about religion and need never go to mass. The cost was 1,300 livres a year for each boy, with 500 more for the preceptor who would come with them, plus extra fees for masters of dancing, music, and art. The school was frequented by "youth of the best quality in France," including a nephew of Choiseul, one of Louis XV's ministers at the time. Elliot accepted Hume's judgment, and the two boys came to Choquart's school. One of them became the fourth baronet and later first earl of Minto.[21]

Choquart called his school the Pension Militaire, and Hume's letter throws light on a curious quasi-militarization that became fashionable in French education about the middle of the century. Hume found the boys wearing "a blue uniform with narrow silver lace." After hearing a drumbeat in the courtyard, he watched them go through the "Prussian exercise" with "muskets in their hands." At Sorèze, a Benedictine school, when a new building opened in 1759, the boys appeared in uniforms of royal blue, with crimson breeches and imitation gold buttons. Diderot in 1775 thought that the boarders in a college should wear a special costume to prevent their escape in the daily tumult when the day boys rushed out. The fashion spread to some of the university colleges. At Sainte-Marthe, a part of the University of

---

[21] *Letters of David Hume*, ed. Greig (Oxford, 1932), 1: 472-73, letter 254.

Poitiers, the students in 1781 wore a blue uniform with scarlet lining and silver buttons. When three professors of the Paris faculty of arts submitted a plan to the Constituent Assembly in 1790 they included military exercises (though not uniforms) among their recommendations. It is evident that when the French government set up its *écoles militaires* in 1776, and when Napoleon introduced uniforms into his lycées after 1802, they were following a trend already established. As early as 1762 the University of Paris protested against it. Foolish parents, said the University, were "seduced by a uniform and by a few military institutions and frivolous exercises that the wisdom of our fathers carefully has kept out of the public schools." The Abbé Proyart in 1785 denounced the craze for martial demonstrations in the private schools, which he feared had also infected some "colleges in our provinces." He attributed it to the fasionable new "philosophy."[22]

An altogether different kind of private school, designed more for a middle-class clientele, is revealed in a recent study of the city of Lille and the adjoining region of northern France.[23] In the two departments of the Nord and the Pas-de-Calais there are known to have been 44 private schools that opened between 1770 and 1789, of which only 29 were operating in 1789. They were therefore usually short-lived. They were also relatively expensive, charging on the average about 400 livres a year, where the two colleges in Lille charged only 100. They required a space large enough for 50 or 100 pupils, on which the proprietor found it difficult to pay the rent. They taught some Latin but also modern languages that the colleges ignored; they put more stress on the sciences, arithmetic, geometry, and botanizing excursions into the country; and they offered practical subjects such as bookkeeping and navigation. They were mainly patronized by merchant families that could pay the fees and whose sons expected to go into business. Though smaller than the colleges, they served at least as many students. Twelve private schools in 1789, within the city of Lille, had 535 pupils, while the two colleges in the town had respectively only 200 and 250. But the author of this study warns us against exaggerating their importance, insisting that the colleges were prospering also.

[22] J. Fabre de Massaguel, *L'école de Sorèze de 1758 au 19 fructidor An IV (5 Septembre 1796)* (Toulouse, 1958), p. 44; Diderot, "Plan d'une université," in *Oeuvres* 3: 526; J. Delfour, *Le collège de Poitiers après l'expulsion des Jésuites (1762-1795)* (Poitiers, 1917), p. 203; Palmer, *School of the French Revolution*, pp. 248-50; on the royal *écoles militaires* see below, pp. 66-69; Jourdain, *Université de Paris*, 2: 308; L. B. Proyart, *De l'éducation publique* (Paris, 1785), pp. 108-10.

[23] P. Marchand, "Un modèle d'éducation à la veille de la Révolution: les maisons d'éducation particulières," *Revue d'histoire moderne et contemporaine* 22 (1975): 552-62.

Since the density of schools and colleges in this region was greater than for almost any other part of France, it is probable that these findings are not altogether typical.

In still another category of "private" schools were the free schools of drawing, which originated in the provinces but of which the most famous was in Paris. The Paris school, opened in 1766 by a private citizen, J. J. Bachelier, received the title of Royal Free School of Design in 1767. Thus favored by the king, it attracted philanthropic donors, who by the time of the Revolution numbered 430, mostly upper class persons and including 73 women, from a duchess to an actress. The school was expressly intended for working-class youths, of whom about 1,500 came in turn for two days a week. They received instruction in such subjects as applied geometry, mechanical drawing, and stone-cutting, to qualify as skilled artisans in the building trades, furniture-making, ornamental woodwork, tapestry- and carpet-making, textile design, jewelry, and work as goldsmiths and silversmiths. The precedent of the Free School of Design was carried over into the Central Schools of the Republic, with significant modifications, as will be seen.[24]

It is impossible to give any quantitative estimate of the number or importance of private schools before the Revolution, but one sign of their multiplication can be seen in the number of books written against them and in defense of the colleges. An Abbé Gosse admitted that the 10 Paris colleges were inconveniently located, still crowded together in old buildings in the Latin Quarter at a time when Paris had expanded to harbor a population of 600,000. But he denied that the new establishments offered a solution, since they either taught trivial subjects at the expense of solid education or were too expensive, or too far from the Latin Quarter for those students who might wish to reach the colleges every day, especially in the winter. He therefore proposed that five of the 10 existing colleges should be redistributed into newer buildings throughout the city. He conceded also that philosophy and physics should be taught in French, not Latin, and said that most professors were of the same opinion, but added, somewhat lamely but significantly, that nothing could be done without the sanction of the government. The Abbé Proyart, who had taught in both a provincial and a Paris college, and whose attack on the military fad has been already mentioned, ridiculed the pretensions of private schoolmasters who claimed to have discovered new pedagogical meth-

[24] There is an excellent account of the *écoles gratuites de dessin* in Taton, *Enseignement et diffusion*, pp. 441-79. See also p. 254 below.

ods by which any subject could be made understandable to any child. Against Emile, that figment of Rousseau's imagination, said Proyart, the University of Paris could point to any number of its graduates in high offices of church and state. A councillor at the Parlement of Metz, Rigolet de Juvigny, wrote a diatribe against modern "philosophy," which he blamed for the expulsion of the Jesuits 25 years before, and which now advanced crazy ideas of replacing Latin with music, dancing, and gymnastic exercises, and was setting up newfangled *maisons d'éducation* with great fanfare of educational theory. The result, he said, would be a decadence of morals and learning and "an overthrow of the throne and the altar."[25]

HIGHER LEARNING

At the level of higher learning the institutions of the Old Regime were too numerous and diverse for any careful description to be attempted. There were 22 or 24 universities, depending on how they are counted.[26] All but two dated from before 1600, or even from the Middle Ages, and their organization and functions by the eighteenth century were obsolescent. In principle a university had three higher faculties—theology, law, and medicine—and a faculty of arts that was preparatory for the upper three. But not all universities had all three higher faculties, and the new university at Dijon was no more than a law school. A provincial faculty of arts, consisting of only one or two colleges, was hardly different from the more numerous nonuniversity colleges that included the two years of Philosophy. The degree of *maîtrise ès arts*, given at the end of Philosophy, was in principle a prerequisite for admission to a higher faculty; yet alternative ways of admission existed, so that the importance of the college was reduced.

[25] Abbé Gosse, *Exposition raisonnée des principes de l'Université* (Paris, 1788), pp. 107-24, 164-69; Proyart, *De l'éducation publique*, pp. 98-142; Rigolet de Juvigny, *De la décadence des lettres et des moeurs* (Paris, 1787), pp. 470-508. This last book has a preface by Dumouchel, rector of the University of Paris in 1787, who calls it the best reply the University could have to its detractors. No enemy of innovation, Dumouchel remained high in the educational system through both the Revolutionary and the Napoleonic years.

[26] On the universities, including their higher faculties, see the works cited above by Taton; Julia, Chartier, and Compère; and Jourdain, noting that the first edition of Jourdain's *Histoire de l'Université de Paris au 17ᵉ et au 18ᵉ siècle* (Paris, 1862) contains a large documentary appendix; see also the more recent article by J. de Viguerie, "Quelques remarques sur les universités françaises au 18ᵉ siècle," *Revue historique* (July-September 1979), pp. 29-50.

The universities were more devoted to teaching, or at least to the preparation and certification of the young for adult positions, than to exploration of the unknown or accumulation of new knowledge. But the teaching role of the faculties of theology had declined with the rise of diocesan seminaries for the training of priests. In Paris Saint-Sulpice was the educational seminary for the diocese, but the faculty of theology, known as the Sorbonne, remained formidable by the number and influence of its doctors and their collective powers in the determination of orthodoxy and censorship of books. There were in principle 22 faculties of medicine, but only five were important—those at Paris, Strasbourg, Montpellier, Reims, and Toulouse. They were to some extent centers of scientific inquiry because of their concern for pharmacology and materia medica, but the medical education that they offered consisted mostly of lectures and the writing of a thesis in Latin. The law faculties also gave lectures, which were not assiduously attended, since young men aiming at the law relied more on home study, on apprenticeship in a law office, or on lectures at the College of France. The higher faculties held somewhat formalistic examinations and awarded degrees, which served as marks of status and licenses to practice. Professors of law and medicine were laymen, usually married men who lived at home, without the communal arrangements of the faculties of arts and theology. They were also practicing lawyers or physicians, who took turns in teaching or devoted only part time to their lectures. Except for a few endowed chairs, they received no income from their professorships except for the fees for examinations. Neither teachers nor students took the formal instruction or the examinations very seriously. The award of the law degree, in particular, was subject to abuses and consequent complaints.

It is estimated that there were almost 4,000 students in theology, about 3,500 in law, and about 600 in medicine when the Revolution began in 1789. Theology students were of more modest social origins; those in law were overwhelmingly the sons of lawyers and officeholders, with some tendency as the years passed for the sons of merchants and shopkeepers to increase. Not all the theology students intended to become parish priests, nor all the law students to become lawyers, for it was possible to find more inviting appointments under either ecclesiastical or royal auspices. Some continued to be supported by their families and faded into a general *rentier* or leisured class. Any judgment of the quality of the pre-Revolutionary higher education must be ambivalent. Fine men undoubtedly came out of the seminaries; one graduate of Saint-Sulpice and refugee from the Revolution in 1792, Gabriel Richard, lived for over 30 years in America, becoming a leading citizen and priest in Detroit and a cofounder of the University of Michigan. There were conscientious lawyers in the Parlements of the 1780s, and it was men trained in the old law faculties that drafted the codes of Napoleon. Yet there was a preponderant belief in 1789, apparently well founded, that the higher faculties were stagnant, more so than the colleges, incapable of innovation and unwilling to meet modern needs. They were all swept away in the following years.

The most active intellectual life went on outside the universities, in institutions for the most part supported by the royal government. A short way of seeing these institutions as a whole is provided by a kind of budget for the year 1789, made public in the early months of the Revolution. It is reproduced in the first column of the appendix to this book, which gives corresponding (if not strictly comparable) figures for certain years of the Revolution and the Napoleonic empire.[27] Unfortunately the list for 1789 does not include such important establishments as the academies of painting and music, the military schools, the school of military engineering at Mézières, and the civil engineering schools of Mines and of Roads and Bridges, for all of which the costs were included in those of the Royal Household, the War Department, or other branches of government. It is clear that the monarchy at the close of the Old Regime was spending well over a million livres a year for educational, scholarly, and scientific purposes, but of this sum over 300,000 livres went to the Paris Faculty of Arts and so not for higher learning. To the higher faculties of the University the royal treasury granted very little. A million livres formed only a microscopic part of total royal expenditures, which according to the same source reached 531,533,000 livres in 1789. For comparison, 150 million livres were spent on the army, navy, and colonies, and eight million went to religious and charitable institutions. Almost half the total outlay was for the burden of debt service under which the Old Regime collapsed.

Highest in prestige, and most remote from education, was the Académie Française, the honorific and mainly literary establishment of 40 immortals, whose main collective function, apart from glorifying French culture, was the interminable task of preparing an authoritative dictionary of the French language.

---

[27] See the Appendix. Condorcet, no admirer of the old monarchy, estimated in 1792 that the "public treasury" had spent at least four million livres on public instruction under the Old Regime. J. Guillaume, *Procès-verbaux du Comité de l'Instruction publique de l'Assemblée législative* (Paris, 1889), p. 308. For a full, recent, and authoritative treatment of these institutions of higher learning see C. C. Gillispie, *Science and Polity in France at the end of the Old Regime* (Princeton, 1980).

More important was the Royal Academy of Sciences, founded by Colbert and Louis XIV, which served both as a center of scientific inquiry and as an agency consulted by the government on practical questions. About 20 of its members received stipends averaging 2,000 livres a year. It held frequent meetings at which papers were presented, it corresponded with foreign and provincial associates, it proposed new lines of investigation, it provided means of scientific publication for its own members and others, it awarded prizes, and it granted recognition to a few fortunate individuals by election to its own body. It also advised the government on new inventions to ascertain whether they were actually new and whether they deserved the kind of privilege, or monopoly, that amounted to a kind of patent. By exercising so many powers, issuing judgments, and hence making enemies as well as friends, it exposed itself to charges of elitism, and so was abolished in the Revolution, though it soon reappeared in a new form, as early as 1795, as a component of the new National Institute.[28]

The Academy of Inscriptions and Belles-Lettres, in which 15 members were paid by the government, was in principle engaged in historical and antiquarian research. Its functions paralleled or overlapped with other learned activities subsidized by the monarchy, as shown in the table in the Appendix for the sum of 198,150 livres, and which included inventories of medieval charters, publication of the *ordonnances* of the kings of France, a salary of 3,000 livres for the office of royal historiographer (once held by Voltaire, and in 1789 by Marmontel), des Essart's *Dictionnaire universel de police*, and a work on anatomy, with engravings, by the medical luminary, Vicq d'Azyr.

The academies of painting, sculpture, architecture, and music dated from the time of Louis XIV. Other academies founded later, from about 1730 until the Revolution, were intended for more scientific ends. The government attempted repeatedly to overcome the monopolistic and self-protective attitudes of the Faculty of Medicine, which insisted on recognition of exclusive powers that it had received in the Middle Ages. Thus a Royal Society of Medicine was created in 1778, with Vicq d'Azyr as its guiding spirit; it somewhat resembled the Academy of Sciences, in lesser degree; that is, it was more open than the old faculty to new discoveries, it advised the government on problems of hygiene or epidemics, and it gathered information from correspondents throughout the country. Academies were set up also for

[28] Roger Hahn, *The Anatomy of a Scientific Institution: The Paris Academy of Sciences, 1666-1803* (Berkeley, 1971); Joseph Fayet, *La Révolution française et la science, 1789-1795* (Paris, 1960).

surgery and for pharmacy, with associated teaching functions, and a college for veterinary medicine. For the College of Surgery the government built a new building with the best amphitheater in Paris in 1775. Thus surgery, pharmacy, and veterinary medicine, looked down on by the Faculty of Medicine, were emerging, like engineering, as separate modern professions, requiring special training under the supervision of qualified experts.

The Bibliothèque du Roi, dating from the fifteenth century, was a great repository of books and manuscripts open to the scholarly public for certain hours of the week; it became the Bibliothèque Nationale in the Revolution. Art students could study the royal collections in the Louvre, where various academies were lodged. The Royal Garden or Jardin des Plantes, containing specimens from all parts of the world, was famous as both a scientific and a teaching institution; it was renamed the Museum of Natural History in the 1790s. The Observatory consisted of a director and three advanced students, paid by the government, and engaged in astronomical and geophysical observations and calculations.

The Collège Royal, later known as the College of France, was older than any of the academies and offers perhaps the only case, during the closing decades of the Old Regime, of reform of an ancient educational institution that produced significant results.[29] It had been founded by Francis I as long ago as 1530 to promote the humanism of the Renaissance and had been purposely set up outside the University of Paris to overcome the conservatism of the faculties. Disrupted during the wars of religion, neglected in the seventeenth century, and exposed to the continuing hostility of the university, it consisted in 1770 of 19 chairs, financed by the royal treasury; but the professors were paid very little and had to take turns lecturing in three dilapidated rooms. The reform of 1772 provided them with better facilities and redefined the 19 chairs to accommodate more modern subjects. The new assignment of chairs remained unchanged through the Revolution, except for the abolition of canon law and of Hebrew and Syriac. The rearrangement of 1772 is given in the table that follows. By special arrangement a chair was also established in hydrodynamics. It will be

---

[29] Abel Lefranc, *Histoire du Collège de France depuis ses origines jusqu'à la fin du premier Empire* (Paris, 1893), pp. 264-66. An *Histoire de France depuis l'établissement de la monarchie jusqu'au règne de Louis XIV*, 33 vols. (Paris, 1760-1799), of which vols. 17 through 30 on the years 1767-1786 were written by the Abbé J. J. Garnier, contains an account of the Collège de France in vol. 25, pp. 537-63, from which much later information seems to be derived. Garnier was professor of Hebrew and *inspecteur* of the College during the years of its transformation and has been called its second founder.

seen that the shift was in general from Greek, Latin, and canon law toward the natural sciences, oriental languages, and modern legal studies. All the professors were laymen except the Abbé Garnier, professor of Hebrew, who was in fact the leading spirit in the reorganization. Fourteen of them held their chairs undisturbed through the most radical phase of the Revolution. The College awarded no degrees, gave no examinations, and charged no fees. The professors delivered public lectures at an advanced level, addressed to medical students, or to those who wished to carry their "philosophy" or physics beyond the offerings of the colleges, or to any interested adults. Garnier envisaged developing the College into a kind of graduate school. He observed in 1765 that "the young men who come here have finished their studies and are attracted only by love of the work; they are exactly the kind of students that we wish to have." How many attended any of the

Subjects	Number of chairs		
	In 1770	After 1772	
Latin eloquence	2	1	
Greek	2	2	
Greek or Latin philosophy	1	0	
Hebrew and Syriac	2	1	
Arabic	2	1	(in Arabic)
		1	(in Turkish and Persian)
Mathematics	2	2	(1 in geometry, 1 in astronomy)
Physics	1	3	(including 1 in experimental physics)
Medicine, surgery, pharmacy, botany	4	4	(in practical medicine, anatomy, chemistry, natural history)
Canon law	2	1	(in canon law)
		1	(in law of nature and of nations) law of nature and of nations)
History	1	1	1 (in history and moral science)
Poetry	0	1	
Total	19	19	

lectures is unknown, but they were numerous enough to be derided by Sebastien Mercier, a man of letters who disliked professors and who thought it ridiculous to see "men twenty-five or thirty years old going to hear a teacher talk about taste without having it."[30]

There was also in Paris before 1789 one significant private institution of higher learning, the Lycée des Arts, founded in 1781.[31] It enjoyed the eminent patronage of the king's brother but depended financially on gifts, subscriptions, and fees. Each year it offered several series of lectures, or courses, addressed to educated adults and delivered by such notables as Fourcroy in chemistry, Garat in history, and La Harpe in literature. The prospectus of 1785 observed that grown men did not enjoy attending lectures along with schoolboys, so that there was no place for them to go except the College of France, which, however, was reserved by custom for men. Both men and women were found in the lecture halls of the Lycée in the following years. A special room was provided for women, complete with a piano, as a gathering place while the lectures were not in progress. The fees were not low, being 100 livres for a seasonal subscription for men but only 50 for women. The Lycée, with its name changed to *Lycée republicain*, continued to draw audiences even during the Terror. Throughout these years, and in the educational plans of the French Revolution, the word *lycée* always referred to an institution of advanced instruction. When Bonaparte adopted the word for his officially supported schools at a high secondary level (the modern French "lycées") he forbade its use for any other purpose. The original Lycée then called itself the Athénée and remained alive under that name, as a private institution, for several decades.

[30] Abbé J. J. Garnier, *De l'éducation civile* (Paris, 1765), p. 148; Mercier, *Tableau de Paris*, 6: 213-17.

[31] C. Dejob, "De l'établissement connu sous le nom de Lycée ou Athénée," *Revue internationale de l'enseignement* 18 (1889): 3-38. The printed prospectus of 1785 and programs of lectures for the following years may be found at the British Library, Croker collection, R 374. See also Gillispie, *Science and Polity*, pp. 190-91, and Hahn, *Anatomy of a Scientific Institution*, "Lycée" in the index.

NATIONALIZATION

IT MAY BE SAID that French education was "nationalized" in the early and relatively moderate phase of the Revolution, from 1789 to 1791, with the sequestration of college endowments, the disruption of the teaching clergy, and the presentation of the Talleyrand plan to the National Constituent Assembly in September 1791. The Talleyrand plan was not adopted, and nothing was as yet really accomplished. It was clear, however, that the future of education in France would depend on reorganization by a new national government. This situation represented no radical break with the past but was the outcome of a long process, and to trace this process is the purpose of the present chapter.

What we are looking for under the heading of "nationalization" may be any one of several things, all the more elusive because the conception of the nation itself was not yet fully formed. One sign is in the tendency of a centralizing power, the monarchy, or of semi-centralizing powers such as the regional parlements, to encroach on the local or town governments in the management of schools. Another is the assertion of a "public" authority—the monarchy, the law courts, or in some cases the Catholic church as a national institution in a Catholic country—over institutions increasingly seen as "private." A third is in the desire to make educational facilities geographically more available, as well as more uniform, throughout the whole territory of France. Still another may be seen in demands that schooling should be more socially useful, as part of a process of nation-building at a time when the "nation" was coming to mean a more efficient form of the civil community. Finally, we see the phrase *éducation nationale* appearing as a slogan for reformers of all kinds in the 1760s, in the titles of tracts on education, and as a key to much of their argument, carried on eagerly for 30 years and triumphing in the Talleyrand report of 1791.

The process was not limited to France, and a quick comparative view offers a useful point of departure. Various European governments reorganized the universities and associated schools within their territories as a means of strengthening their states or "nations." The great exception was England, where Oxford and Cambridge, having survived attempts at reform by the republican regime of the 1650s, enjoyed a secure freedom from government in the eighteenth century, while generally decaying; and where the endowed or locally supported grammar schools, which corresponded somewhat to the French colleges, also remained free from central interference.

It was otherwise on the Continent. Charles III of Spain promoted reforms in the Spanish universities in the 1770s, and Pombal did the same for Coimbra in Portugal. In Piedmont, the monarchy in 1772 reorganized the University of Turin and its dependent colleges; it was later said, probably erroneously, that Napoleon modeled his Imperial University on the University of Turin. Joseph II attempted to reform Louvain without success. The prince-archbishop of Cologne founded a new university at Bonn, and his colleague at Mainz reconstructed his university in 1784, opening it even to Protestants and a few Jews as teachers and students. The term *nationale Erziehung* became common in the German states, including Austria, where a *Studienhofskommission* was established in 1773, and an *Oberschulkollegium* was created in Prussia in 1787. The founding of the University of Halle by the Prussian government in 1694, and of Göttingen by the electorate of Hanover in 1737, together with the upgrading of old Latin schools into *gymnasien* at the end of the century, represented the same trend toward state intervention. In Sweden the personal concern of Gustav III greatly strengthened the University of Uppsala. In Hungary, Maria Theresa proclaimed a *Ratio educationis* in 1777, to include all levels of study, and the diet of 1790-1791 addressed itself to *Educatio nationalis*. In Poland, from 1773 to 1793, in an attempt at national consolidation after the First Partition, a National Commission on Education acted as a kind of ministry, supervising the University of Cracow and some 60 other schools in a descending pyramidal structure. In Russia Catherine II obtained from Diderot a "plan for a university," meaning a whole system of schools, and Alexander I created a Ministry of Law and Public Education in 1803, which provided a complex organization with district chiefs and traveling inspectors. The German Christophe Meiners, publishing a book on the comparative history of European universities in 1804, found the new Russian arrangement the most highly centralized of all the centralizing efforts up to that date, not excluding those of the French Revolution.[1]

---

[1] C. Meiners, *Geschichte der Entstehung und Entwicklung der hohen Schulen unsers Erd-*

Even in America after the Revolution the use of schools for state- and nation-building was evident. New York created in 1784 a University of the State of New York, to have supervision over Columbia College and any new colleges that might be formed. This "university" is the ancestor of the New York Board of Regents. The states of Pennsylvania, North Carolina, and Vermont, in their first constitutions of 1776 and 1777, called for the establishment of "universities" as well as common schools. Leaders of the new republic also proposed a National University, to be situated in Washington and stand above the existing American colleges, in a much discussed project that never was realized.

THE GROWTH OF ROYAL AUTHORITY

If the development in France was not unique, neither was it recent. After the chaos of the religious wars, toward the close of the sixteenth century, reconstruction in education as in so much else took place on the initiative of the royal government. The University of Paris suffered more physical damage in the 1580s than at the height of the Revolution; several of its colleges were plundered by the Catholic League and its Spanish mercenaries (where in 1793 they were only obliged to quarter French volunteers); and some of the colleges, being deserted, were invaded by country people with their sheep and cattle or were turned into rooming houses. One of the first steps taken by Henry IV was to restore the University of Paris. In its already long history the previous reorganizations had always been attributed to the authority of the Pope. Now for the first time the secular power prevailed. The result was the statute of 1598, promulgated in 1600, which governed the University of Paris with occasional modifications for almost two centuries. It may be recalled that Oxford and Cambridge, having also suffered from the disorders of the Reformation, were reorganized by Queen Elizabeth at about this same time, and that her arrangements lasted in general well into the nineteenth century.

The statute of 1598-1600 consisted of 251 articles, of which 98 pertained to the faculty of arts and its colleges.[2] The preamble declared that

---

teils, 4 vols. (Göttingen, 1802-1805), 4: 219. For more recent work see R. Chartier and J. Revel, "Université et société dans l'Europe moderne: position et problèmes," *Revue d'histoire moderne et contemporaine* (1978), pp. 353-74.

[2] The text of the statute is published in the rare earlier edition of C. Jourdain, *Histoire*

the happiness of all kingdoms and peoples, and above all the well-being of the Christian Republic, depend on the right education for youth, which shapes rough minds to humanity, makes those that are sterile and unfruitful more suited and useful for the duties of the Republic, and promotes the worship of God, piety toward parents and country, and respect and obedience to magistrates.

Some of the words here in Latin—*populorum felicitas, humanitas, respublica, utiles*, and *patria*—had a similar yet different resonance in French a century and a half later, when the Christian Renaissance had given way to the Enlightenment.

The statute of Henry IV, with a few supplementary enactments, went into scrupulous detail. It defined the functions of the rector, deans, and heads of colleges; required all teachers to have the degree of *maîtrise ès arts* from Paris or another recognized university; ordered professors to wear the long robe and square cap in the classroom; and urged them to keep their fees low, with remission for needy students. It provided for graded instruction from the youngest to the oldest boys, with the professors "to examine all students diligently each year and distribute them individually into classes according to their comprehension."[3] It set up the two years of Philosophy, specifying which books were to be read, mainly Aristotle in 1600. It prescribed, probably in vain, that teachers and pupils speak only Latin within the college walls. It set up controls on the college funds, regulating the freedom of each college to lease, sell, and collect rents from its own property and setting rules for the *messageries*, of which more will be said. It ordered all private schoolmasters in Paris to send their boys over nine years old to classes in one of the university colleges. It required pupils to refrain from swearing, insults, and complaints; forbade them to wear swords or learn fencing; and specified corporal punishment for the unruly. All teachers, students, and employees had to be Catholics, and daily mass was prescribed along with catechetical lessons for the youngest boys. Thus, although separate Protestant schools were allowed for a while under the Edict of Nantes, the University of Paris and its colleges, like those elsewhere in France, remained Roman Catholic institutions. Means of enforcement of the statute were lodged in the king, his royal officers, and his Parlement of Paris. All this activity was of course not yet national, for the other French universities were

---

de l'Université de Paris au 17ᵉ et au 18ᵉ siècle (Paris, 1862), p. 3 of the *pièces justificatives*; and in *Recueil des lois et règlements concernant l'Instruction publique, depuis l'édit de Henri IV en 1598 jusqu'à ce jour*, 8 vols. (Paris, 1814-1827), 1: 1-60.

[3] Article 13, Jourdain, *Université de Paris* (1862), p. 4 of the *pièces justificatives*.

separately rehabilitated by combinations of royal officials, provincial parlements, and concerned local citizens, and meanwhile the international order of the Jesuits continued to expand, after a brief interruption, and in fact established 59 colleges in France in the years from 1600 to 1640, over half of all those it possessed in France when expelled in 1762. The Jesuits, however, continued to be excluded from the University of Paris.[4]

During the seventeenth century the king and the parlements, usually acting together, continued to assert their authority over education, though without much positive effect. The glories of the medieval University of Paris were never recovered. But a decree of 1629 forbade the sale of inheritance of professorships, so that universities and colleges were spared the venality of office that afflicted the French fiscal and judicial structure until the Revolution.[5] The government of Louis XIV attempted to codify the regulations for law and medical faculties for the whole kingdom. Law faculties added the teaching of statute and customary law to the old civil and canon law that they had taught since the Middle Ages. An edict of 1707, intended to apply to all medical faculties, prescribed a minimum number of courses, required three years of study after the *maîtrise ès arts* together with a period of hospital service for the student, and ordered each faculty to provide a chair in botany and a garden of medicinal plants.[6] Some in the government advocated more sweeping plans. Not only were learned and scientific academies actually founded under Louis XIV, and universal elementary schooling at least officially favored, but the royal administrators claimed authority over the hundreds of colleges that had grown up since the wars of religion. "One of the rights that sovereignty confers upon kings," as an adviser to Colbert noted,

> is the sole power of establishing academies in their Kingdoms. . . . The establishment of public schools and universities is all the more necessary since kings have a duty to take particular care of the education of their subjects. . . . Any communal group is illicit unless

---

[4] In addition to the statute see the discussion in C. Jourdain, *Histoire de l'Université de Paris au 17ᵉ et au 18ᵉ siècle*, 2 vols. (Paris, 1888), 1: 23-37. The figure for 59 Jesuit colleges is derived from the table on p. 187 of D. Julia, R. Chartier, and M. M. Compère, *L'éducation en France du 16ᵉ au 18ᵉ siècle* (Paris, 1976). The same table shows 18 out of 26 Oratorian colleges founded between 1611 and 1640.

[5] Isambert, *Recueil général des anciennes lois françaises depuis l'an 490 jusqu'à la Révolution française*, 29 vols. (Paris, 1820-1831), 16: 236.

[6] Isambert, ibid., 19: 195-202, 229; and on the largely unsuccessful attempts to regulate the medical schools, R. Taton, ed., *Enseignement et diffusion des sciences en France au 18ᵉ siècle* (Paris, 1964), pp. 172-74.

authorized by the prince. . . . Hence universities are deemed to be more lay than ecclesiastical institutions, and are considered as such when appointments are to be made.[7]

Such language and intentions anticipated what was to come later, but the government of Louis XIV was distracted by other ambitions, the parlements became torpid during his reign, and actual changes were slight. One most important development came from a "private" bequest. Cardinal Mazarin, dying in 1661, left the unprecedented sum of two million livres, together with his magnificent collection of books, to found a new college in the University of Paris. It was called the College of the Quatre-Nations because his purpose, for which he endowed 60 scholarships, was to bring young men from four areas annexed to France during the years when he had conducted the government—Catalans from Roussillon, Italians from the Alpine frontier, Germans from Alsace, and Flemings from the northern border—who after study in Paris would return to their homes so that, by gradual cultural influence, "these provinces would become French by inclination, as they are now by the rule of His Majesty." The new college, with its wealth, soon outgrew its 60 scholars and numbered hundreds of students from various parts of the kingdom. It enjoyed the advantage of occupying new buildings built for the purpose, which since the time of Napoleon have housed the Institute of France. Its very name reminds us that in the seventeenth century the word "nation" was seldom applied to France as a whole but referred to ethnic or linguistic groups without political significance or emotional connotation.[8]

The new College of the Quatre-Nations (also called Mazarin College) was so well endowed that it charged no fees for instruction (as distinct from fees for boarders) for any of its numerous students. The same was true of the Jesuit colleges, and in particular of the large College of Louis-le-Grand, which, though located in the heart of the Latin Quarter, had never been admitted to the university. Colleges of the Paris faculty of arts, except the Quatre-Nations, made a charge for instruction, as provided for in the statute of 1598, and so suffered a loss of students. The rector and others in the University devised a plan and appealed to the royal government for its cooperation.

The plan called for surrender of the *messageries* that had operated under supervision by the University since the thirteenth century. At that time, before so many other universities had been founded, the

---

[7] Jourdain, *Université de Paris* (1888), 1: 437.
[8] Ibid., 1: 396-98; 2: 52.

University of Paris had drawn students from great distances and from many parts of Europe. A system of messengers had grown up to convey letters, baggage, and funds for the students between Paris and their homes. The system also took on a banking role, in that there were men in Paris who made loans and advances to students. By 1700 the University was receiving an income of about 50,000 livres annually from the *messageries*, but this amount was not large enough to make fees for instruction unnecessary. Meanwhile a royal postal service was developing. The University and the government reached an agreement. The *messageries* were abolished, the students thereafter using the postal service instead, and the government granted to the University a sum equal to one twenty-eighth of the postal revenues each year. This amounted to about 130,000 livres in 1719, and rose to some 300,000 in the years preceding the Revolution. It sufficed to pay the salaries of professors in the Paris colleges, which thereafter offered *instruction gratuite*. The Paris professors prided themselves throughout the eighteenth century on teaching gratis, and so being less dependent on passing vogues or parental pressures. They became indirectly employees of the state, enjoying salaries of 2,000 livres or more as well as retirement pensions, and so were more favored than teachers in the provincial universities and colleges. The possession of assured incomes may also have made them less inclined to make innovations. Such at least was the view of some eighteenth-century reformers of education, such as d'Alembert, who claimed in the *Encyclopédie* that all enlightened persons disapproved of free instruction. For some, the payment of salaries by the state promoted academic freedom; for others it meant the freedom to vegetate.[9]

The introduction of *instruction gratuite* in 1719 was only a first step in an increasing involvement of the royal government, which continued progressively from the death of Louis XIV until the Revolution, in sporadic ways and without central planning, sometimes to reinforce traditional orthodoxy and sometimes for purposes of modernization, in some ways affecting the system of colleges and universities and in others acting outside it. The expulsion of the Jesuits in 1762 was the great turning point, but before its consequences are considered a mere listing of other and unrelated developments may be offered.

In 1721 the government set up and subsidized a group called the *jeunes de langue*, located in the College of Louis-le-Grand, composed of a few boys selected to learn the Turkish and Arabic languages, for future service in Constantinople and the eastern Mediterranean. In the

[9] On the *messageries* and the *instruction gratuite* of 1719, see ibid., 2: 161-74.

following years the king authorized new universities at Dijon and Pau, suppressed the old university of Cahors as too weak to be useful, and transferred the law faculty of the University of Nantes to Rennes, where it could function more effectively near the Parlement of Brittany. In the 1760s the government transferred the former Jesuit college of Pont-à-Mousson to Nancy, and strengthened the University of Perpignan by founding chairs in botany, anatomy, and experimental physics, to be supplemented by a botanical garden and a library. Outside the universities, it reorganized the College of France in 1772, as seen in the last chapter, and established new technical schools, for military engineering at Mézières in 1751, for civil engineering in the Ponts et Chaussées or "roads and bridges" in 1775, and for mining and mineralogy in 1783. In 1777 it created a Society of Medicine to supplement the more slow-moving medical faculty of Paris. It was also under royal protection, as has been seen, and against opposition in the medical faculty, that pharmacy and surgery were strengthened at this time. A new building for the College of Surgery was opened in 1775. At a less elevated level the government established three veterinary schools in the 1760s.[10]

A decree of 1749, reaffirmed in 1762 and 1785, revived older royal provisions for the control of mortmain. It provided that no new endowment or permanent foundation could be established, nor additions made to existing foundations, except with the approval of the government. Such endowments usually consisted in real property, and among the reasons given for the decree were to keep lands and buildings from going permanently off the market, to protect the rights of heirs to their inheritances, and to safeguard the tax revenues of the king. Another reason, however, was to protect the existing colleges, and maintain their quality, by preventing the multiplication of new ones that would be too small and ineffective.[11] This decree of 1749 was praised by Turgot when he contributed the article on *Fondations* to Diderot's Encyclopedia a few years later. A distrust of perpetual foundations was shared by French *philosophes*, Adam Smith, and perhaps many potential donors themselves. It was thought that as time passed they became carelessly administered, wasteful, and devoted to obsolete purposes. Small gifts continued to be made, such as endowments for prizes and

[10] On the *jeunes de langue* see G. Dupont-Ferrier, *Du Collège de Clermont au Lycée Louis-le-Grand, 1563-1920*, 3 vols. (Paris, 1921-1925), 1: 75 and 2: 347-436. On other matters in this paragraph see Taton, *Enseignement et diffusion*, and J. de Viguerie, "Quelques remarques sur les universités françaises au 18ᵉ siècle," *Revue historique* (July-September 1979), pp. 29-50.

[11] Isambert, *Recueil*, 20: 226-35, 323-28.

for a few scholarships, but the founding of whole colleges, which had slowed down ever since 1650, came almost to a halt after 1750. Of the 347 colleges existing in 1789 only 16 were established after 1750, and most of them were of the smaller or six-year type.[12] All the colleges except the Quatre-Nations occupied ancient buildings, for although the eighteenth century was a great period for the building of palaces, townhouses, country homes, government offices, and even churches, there was virtually no new construction of schools. By the time of the Revolution the colleges seemed to be, and in fact were, archaic. Innovation was not to be expected from new foundations; it must come either from "private" schools with uncertain resources or from the action of government.

As it was in the period of peace after the wars of religion that the French colleges enjoyed their greatest growth, so the royal government repeatedly intervened to protect them from religious turmoil. When Henry IV excluded Protestants from the universities it was to prevent discord within their halls. But as the Protestant schools allowed by Henry IV were gradually closed and then prohibited, the educational world was torn by ruptures associated with Jansenism, which is to say by disputes over the nature of Catholic orthodoxy. The lines were sharpened in 1713 by the papal bull Unigenitus, in which Jansenist principles were condemned. The royal government, by no means inclined generally to agree with the pope, and although its real preference was for silence, nevertheless undertook to enforce the bull, even to the point of calling it a law of the land. What had originated as a theological argument became a political issue. Favoring Unigenitus were the pope, the king, his ministers, most of the bishops, and very conspicuously, the Jesuits. Against it were certain theological thinkers, a few of the bishops, the Parlement of Paris in defense of the Gallican liberties, most of the provincial parlements, certain zealots made famous by the "convulsions" at a tomb in the cemetery of Saint-Médard, various crude spokesmen for a popular anti-Jesuitism—and many professors at the University of Paris. The teaching orders of the Oratorians and Doctrinaires, as well as the women's orders, were also thought to harbor Jansenist opinions. In the 1730s these very miscellaneous Jansenists were also called "Nationals" because they objected to the foreign authority of Rome, and some were even accused of "republican" sentiments because they were thereby resisting the royal will.

[12] D. Julia and J. Pressly, "La population scolaire en 1789: les extravagances statistiques du ministre Villemain," *Annales E.S.C.* 30 (November-December 1975): 1556.

The state, indeed, which was not yet the nation, was obliged—by its decision to give Unigenitus the force of law—to aim at ever firmer controls over educational institutions. It brought pressure on the Oratorians, Doctrinaires, and religious sisters who conducted girls' schools. Mostly, it had to contend with the University of Paris, which had always been hostile to the Jesuits and now openly opposed the bull. When the Faculty of Theology (the Sorbonne) was forced to submit, the opposition was headed by the Faculty of Arts, that is, by the professors in the 10 "undergraduate" colleges. The Paris police, after secret investigations, finding that the "little" schools, the convents, and the University itself were full of dissidents, reported that "public instruction in Paris is almost entirely corrupt and is leading toward a general revolution in religion," by which the strongest states might be "overturned."[13] The famous Charles Rollin, who had been rector of the University, had his house searched on suspicion of harboring a clandestine Jansenist press. Others were exiled to the provinces. In 1739 80 members of the Faculty signed a protest. The government, with more assistance from the police, forced their exclusion from the councils of the University. As Cardinal Fleury, the chief minister to the young Louis XV, wrote in warning to the Faculty of Arts: "The king, as father and protector of the University, has the right of special inspection over all its members." It was the royal duty to assure that youth was brought up "in the sentiments of submission that all Christians owe to the decisions of the Church."[14]

Jansenism nevertheless remained strong in the University, as in other segments of French society, and the attempts to crush it led to the notorious *billets de confession*. Bishops ordered that a dying person, before receiving the last rites, might be required to present a certificate showing that he had been confessed by an orthodox priest. The Parlement of Paris declared such a requirement to be unlawful on the ground that all Frenchmen had a right to the services of the Catholic faith. Many clashes and scandals followed. How the University was affected may be illustrated from the life and death of Charles Coffin. He had been rector when the *instruction gratuite* was introduced, then became principal of Beauvais College, and for years was active in opposition to the bull, being one of the 80 excluded from the University assemblies. He persisted in his stand, and when he died in 1749, having refused to obtain the required certificate, he was denied the last sacrament. His funeral was the occasion for a public demonstration, in

[13] Alan Williams, *The Police of Paris, 1718-89* (Baton Rouge, 1979), pp. 218-19.
[14] Jourdain, *Université de Paris* (1888), 2: 214.

which an angry and sympathetic crowd watched a long procession, as the casket was followed by the rector, four ex-rectors, and professors and students intoning dirges. One of Coffin's heirs tried to bring suit in the Parlement against the priest who had refused the sacraments. Sixty members of the Paris bar filed a paper declaring that a true legal case existed. The Parlement itself broke into factions. To quiet the uproar the royal government ordered the proceedings quashed.[15]

Feeling against the Jesuits mounted in both popular and learned quarters and among persons both in and outside the governments in many parts of Catholic Europe. They were accused of favoring a too permissive morality, of taking orders blindly from Rome, and hence of being poor citizens of their own countries. They were expelled from Portugal in 1759. The failure of one of their commercial operations accessory to their worldwide mission added to their unpopularity in France. A small resolute Jansenist group within the Parlement of Paris prevailed upon that body to order the Jesuits, in April 1762, to vacate their 40 colleges within the area of the Parlement's jurisdiction.[16] Provincial parlements took similar action. As parlements, Gallicans and Jansenists denounced the Jesuits, and as most of the French episcopate declared them to be necessary to education, the royal government sought to compromise; but in 1764 it ordered the expulsion of the order from France, though individual "ex-Jesuits" were allowed to remain with small pensions. In 1774 the order was totally dissolved by the pope (to be restored only in the general reaction of 1814). The collapse of Jesuit colleges in Poland, Austria, Spain, and elsewhere was a main reason for the wave of government reorganization of education throughout Europe. In France it left open the question of what to do with about 105 colleges, of which about 10 were attached through faculties of arts to various universities in the provinces. Thus almost a third of all the French colleges were affected.

In the furor against the Jesuits the actual conduct of their colleges, in either curriculum or discipline, does not seem to have been among the major complaints. In this as in other cases the problems of education reflected larger forces. These forces were such that, in the opportunity created by the expulsion of the Jesuits from their schools, the reforms and attempted reforms until the Revolution turned more on matters of administrative control than on the actual content of teaching.

[15] Ibid., 2: 281. Michaud, *Biographie universelle*, "Coffin."

[16] D. Van Kley, *The Jansenists and the Expulsion of the Jesuits from France* (New Haven, 1975).

SIGNS OF THE ENLIGHTENMENT

The downfall of the French Jesuits, though brought on by the older forces of Jansenism and Gallicanism, coincided in time with a rapid acceleration of the new, both in literary and intellectual circles and in the more pragmatic sphere of government action. The decade of the 1760s may in fact be seen as a turning point, which if it did not necessarily lead to the Revolution, gave ominous signs of the need for a new direction. The Enlightenment reached a climax with the publication of Rousseau's *Emile* and *Social Contract* in 1762 and of Voltaire's *Philosophical Dictionary* in 1764. The death of Jean Calas impelled Voltaire into his campaign to *écraser l'infâme*, to eradicate fanaticism, ecclesiastical power, and even Christianity itself in a passionate demand for judicial reform and religious freedom. As the Enlightenment developed a strongly antireligious wing the French bishops, notably in the Assembly of the Clergy of 1765, renewed their calls for censorship and warnings of disaster, setting up an antagonism that was to be very long-lasting. Meanwhile the royal government projected important reforms in taxation and in removal of controls on the grain trade, in the interests of a national market and economic development, but it operated in bureaucratic secrecy along the pattern of enlightened despotism, while the parlements and the *philosophes*, though often at odds, agreed on the demand for unrestricted publication of their views and together formed a new and rising force of public opinion. The parlements, after ejecting the Jesuits, made increasing claims to be representatives of the nation while opposing many of the reforms proposed by the government. A genuine constitutional confrontation of the 1760s resulted in 1771 in the temporary abolition of the parlements and their replacement by a judicial system that anticipated some of the Revolutionary innovations. The continuing conflict between the "despotism" of the king and the "aristocracy" of the parlements produced a dilemma that only the Revolution was to resolve.

Education was thus by no means the most urgent issue that agitated the 1760s, but it was a lively issue, made so in the short run by the need of operating the hundred ex-Jesuit colleges and in the long run by the whole trend of the Enlightenment to see in education the hope of a future society. Of known tracts on education, 32 were published in the three years from 1762 to 1765, a frequency not reached again until 1788-1790, when a further outburst of 32 pedagogical treatises marked the coming of the Revolution and the preparation of the Talleyrand report.[17]

[17] Julia, Chartier, and Compère, *L'éducation en France*, p. 208. On writings from 1760

The matter can be pursued along three lines: first, the changing atmosphere within the colleges themselves; second, the writings on the subject; and third, the measures taken by the civil authorities, that is, the royal government and the parlements, meaning in the present context mainly the Parlement of Paris, since not all the provincial parlements can be considered.

As for the atmosphere within the colleges, it has already been observed that after the expulsion of the Jesuits most of the colleges were conducted by secular clergy, or men who were not members of any religious order. There was a trend in the other direction in the 1770s, as will be seen, but by 1789 well over half the colleges were still "secular." In Paris, at least, and doubtless elsewhere, there was evidence of "secularization" in the broader sense of the word, meaning not the distinction between regular and secular clergy but between religion and the "world." Professors showed a desire to get outside their college walls, to mix in society, to go to entertainments in the city, and to be accepted as "citizens." They were not, however, widely welcomed in the salons of the day. The difficulty was as much social as intellectual. Most teachers were of modest birth, often having originated as scholarship boys. They might be awkward in the fashionable circles in which free intellectuals and *philosophes* moved. They were generally scorned as pedants. "Their whole tone is ridiculous, and insufferable in society," said Louis-Sebastien Mercier.[18] "Be sure not to let anyone from the University into the Academy," wrote Voltaire to d'Alembert in 1767.[19] Yet the professors seem to have enjoyed the attractions of Paris, for when the government reorganized La Flèche in 1776, and invited applications for three chairs there on highly favorable terms, no Paris professor applied.[20]

The bishops, although they deplored the loss of the Jesuits, saw an advantage in having secular clergy as teachers, since secular clergy were more amenable than the religious orders to discipline by the bishops. It was difficult, however, to find enough secular clergy, since in the atmosphere of the 1760s and 1770s the number of new ordinations

---

to 1789 see also H. Chisick, *The Limits of Reform in the Enlightenment: Attitudes toward the Education of the Lower Classes in Eighteenth-Century France* (Princeton, 1981).

[18] L. S. Mercier, *Tableau de Paris*, 12 vols. (Amsterdam, 1782-1788), 1: 252-57.

[19] Besterman, ed., *Complete Works of Voltaire*, 116: 340 and *Voltaire's Correspondence*, 67: 53. Voltaire was referring here to the French Academy, of which d'Alembert had been a member since 1754. The Royal Academy of Sciences admitted four professors in the Paris colleges: the physicists Nollet and Brisson, the mathematician Lacaille, and the astronomer Lemonnier. See Jourdain, *Université de Paris* (1888), 2: 421. Several professors of humanities were members of the Académie des inscriptions et belles-lettres.

[20] M. Targe, *Professeurs et régents de collège dans l'ancienne Université de Paris* (Paris, 1902), pp. 261-62.

was falling off. Sometimes it was argued that a college was better run by a religious order than by *isolés* or individual secular clerics. Unfortunately for this argument, the teaching orders that remained after the expulsion of the Jesuits were also increasingly secularized. Fewer young men wished to commit themselves to the priesthood. In the Oratorian colleges in 1740 the proportion of priests to *confrères* was one to two; by the 1760s it was less than one to four. In 1791 it was one to five; that is, the great change occurred in the mid-century.[21] The matter has been most fully explored for the Doctrinaires, as the Pères de la Doctrine chrétienne were called.[22] Originating in the religious warmth of the early seventeenth century, they had taken up teaching as a religious mission and by the mid-eighteenth century had almost 40 colleges in France. At first, young men entering the order had become priests at about the age of thirty; by the mid-eighteenth century they were postponing their ordination or avoiding it altogether. They showed a reluctance to be seen in the cassock and took to wearing wigs and being shaved by professional barbers while the expense accounts of their colleges showed mounting outlays for wines and the rental of carriages. They became a purely voluntary association, with members free to leave the order at will. Those remaining could keep in close touch with their families, dine in town, visit friends, inherit and dispose of property, and appear in law suits. Their religious vows, relaxed over the years, were abolished in 1776. "Thereafter the Doctrinaires were secular clerics without vows, like the Oratorians and Sulpicians." The same author remarks that the older spirit of Christian humanism had yielded to the spirit of the *Encyclopédie* while insisting that they remained men of generally irreproachable morals. It is not surprising that a majority of both the Doctrinaires and the Oratorians welcomed the Revolution. They had become organizations of teachers rather than religious communities. Many of them went on teaching as individuals

[21] Taton, *Enseignement et diffusion*, p. 68 and note on p. 71. At the Oratorian College of Juilly in 1770 there were only 3 priests to 20 *confrères*; ibid., p. 76.

[22] J. de Viguerie, *Une oeuvre d'éducation sous l'ancien régime: Les Pères de la Doctrine chrétienne en France et en Italie* (Paris, 1976). But see also W. Frijhoff and D. Julia, "Le recrutement d'une congrégation enseignante et ses mutations à l'époque moderne: l'Oratoire de France," in *The Making of Frenchmen: Current Directions in the History of Education in France, 1679-1979*, ed. D. N. Baker and P. J. Harrigan; a special issue of *Historical Reflections* (Waterloo, Ont., Canada, Summer-Fall 1980), pp. 443-58. The Benedictines, though more "monastic" than the Oratorians, also became a more specifically teaching order in the decades before the Revolution, specializing in upper class schools with "modern" innovations, as at Sorèze. See D. Julia, "Les Bénédictins et l'enseignement aux 17e et 18e siècles," *Sous la règle de Saint-Benoît* (Paris, 1982), pp. 345-400.

after their congregations were abolished in 1792. About 40 ex-Oratorians and 40 ex-Doctrinaires were still teaching in the Central Schools in 1799.

With these new attitudes on the part of the teachers went the changes that became evident after the mid-century in the content of teaching. In the strongest colleges, at least, more mathematics entered the program, and the two years of Philosophy saw the introduction of Newtonian and experimental physics while the philosophy of Locke and Condillac—with its sensationalist psychology and environmentalist implications, which *philosophes* presented as established truths—became at least topics for discussion. There were even theology students at the Sorbonne who began to express ideas typical of the Enlightenment. It was at the Sorbonne, in the 1750s, that the young Turgot delivered his famous discourse on progress, Loménie de Brienne (the future archbishop) aroused suspicions of infidelilty, and the Abbé de Prades caused a scandal with his thesis, *Jerusalem caelesti*. Prades had also written an important article for Diderot's Encyclopedia, and his thesis, like his article, used "modern" methods to prove the truth of the Christian revelation. There was, however, resistance to such modernizing. The doctors of the Sorbonne, who had at first given their approval to Prades's thesis, were obliged by public outcry to retract it. A similar case arose at Toulouse in 1769. An Abbé Audra published a modified edition of Voltaire's world history, the *Essai sur les moeurs,* and taught history at a college in Toulouse in a Voltairean spirit, which is to say a history that departed widely from the biblical pattern. A general outcry forced the Archbishop of Toulouse, who was none other than the free-thinking Brienne, to obtain Audra's resignation.[23]

We are left with the impression that an unknown but considerable number of teachers were inclined to the "enlightened" side on controversial questions, but that a combination of public opinion, religious feeling, and church authority stood in their way. The conservatism and routine mindedness of others should of course not be forgotten. But d'Alembert, in his highly critical article on "Colleges" in the *Encyclopédie*, was not especially hostile to their professors, many of whom, he said, would like to see improvements but were so blocked by various obstacles that only the government could put through the necessary changes.

[23] On Prades see my *Catholics and Unbelievers in 18th Century France* (Princeton, 1939), p. 123; on Audra, see Louis Trénard, "De l'*Essai sur les moeurs* à un manuel condamné," in *Etudes offertes à Sven Stelling-Michaud* (Geneva, 1975), pp. 161-78.

WRITINGS OF THE 1760S ON "NATIONAL EDUCATION"

Of all the writings on education in the 1760s the best remembered is of course Rousseau's *Emile, ou De l'Education*, published in 1762 and soon condemned both in Paris and at Protestant Geneva. He begins the book with one of his famous paradoxes—the best work on education is said to be Plato's *Republic*, and there is no real public education today because there is no *patrie*. "I do not regard as institutions of public education those laughable establishments called colleges." *Emile* has nothing to do with schools and is on education only in the extended and even infinite sense in which it merges into psychology, moral philosophy, and a theory of human nature. Rousseau defies or ignores existing society. He warns against the social mobility of which he was both the beneficiary and the victim. "In the social order, where all places are marked out, each person should be brought up to occupy his own place. If any individual brought up for his place leaves it, he is fit for nothing. In the natural order, all men being equal, their common vocation is the state of being human; and whoever is well brought up for this human state will not do badly in others." It is with this "natural" or ideal state that Rousseau is concerned. He thus describes at length how an imaginary boy is turned by an imaginary preceptor into a perfect man. "How to live is the trade I wish to teach him." The finished pupil would do well in any walk of life for which he had the talent or inclination.[24] Rousseau was ridiculed by contemporaries, who pointed out that a theory requiring a one-to-one ratio between an invented teacher and an invented student was not very helpful. His ultimate influence was immense, as seen later in theories of liberal or humanistic education, child psychology, self-fulfillment, the learning process, and much else. In his own time some of his principles were adopted by a few private schoolmasters and by tutors serving in upper class families, as when Mme de Genlis acted as governess to the children of the duke of Orleans, including the future king Louis-Phillipe. For "public" schools his *Emile* had no immediate application, except in such remarks as that true public education must rest on a sense of *la patrie*. This thought was developed further in his tract on the *Government of Poland*, in which the theme of nationalization became predominant. "It is education," Rousseau said there, "that must shape the minds of youth in the national mold." It was this sentence, not any-

---

[24] The quotations are from J.-J. Rousseau, *Emile, ou De l'Education*, 4 vols. (Amsterdam, 1762), 1: 13-18.

thing from *Emile*, that three reforming professors in the University of Paris chose as their epigraph for a plan of 1790.[25]

"National education" preoccupied all reformers after 1760. "The plans for 'national' education," in the words of Dominique Julia and Roger Chartier, "are indeed the symptom revealing the crisis of a whole culture"—the crisis of passage from the Old Regime to the modern state.[26] As for the *patrie*, a word that had occurred in the statute of 1598, it now meant for the most advanced thinkers, not so much the country of one's birth, as a country whose people were in possession of "rights"; hence the bold assertion that Frenchmen had no *patrie*.

The phrase "national education" was popularized by the *Essai d'éducation nationale* of Caradeuc de La Chalotais, published in 1763. This tract remains, except for *Emile*, the best remembered work on education of these years and the only one ever to be translated into English.[27] It was much praised by Voltaire, but when compared with other such writings it seems hardly the best, or most typical, in expressing what "national education" meant.

La Chalotais and two others of these reformers of the 1760s were members of parlements possessing some official authority. La Chalotais, royal attorney at the Parlement of Brittany, wrote his *Essai* at the request of that body, as a contribution to its plans for managing the ex-Jesuit schools in that province. He was a stormy character already famous for his thundering attacks on the Jesuits and was later embroiled in a long battle with the royal government in defense of the liberties of Brittany. A much younger man, Guyton de Morveau, of the Parlement of Burgundy, also published a plan of education, less hostile to the existing order than that of La Chalotais. He later became a prominent chemist, a member of the National Convention, and one of the founders of the Ecole Polytechnique. Most important of these three was Rolland d'Erceville of the Parlement of Paris, who, at the behest of that parlement, drafted plans and reports in the 1760s that were not published until 1783, and that dealt with the problems of

[25] The plan, never published, is translated in my *School of the French Revolution* (Princeton, 1975), pp. 237-59.

[26] Julia, Chartier, and Compère, *L'éducation en France*, p. 214. See also James Leith, "The idea of the inculcation of national patriotism in French educational thought," in *Education in the 18th Century*, ed. J. D. Browning (New York, 1979), pp. 59-77.

[27] La Chalotais's *Essai* was translated by F. de La Fontainerie in *French Liberalism and Education in the 18th Century* (New York, 1932), and by H. R. Clark (London, 1934). Strictly speaking, La Fontainerie also translated much of two works never published in their own time, Diderot's "Plan d'une université pour le gouvernement de la Russie" and the Turgot-Dupont "Memoire sur les municipalités," as well as excerpts from Condorcet's plan of education of 1792.

the 40 ex-Jesuit schools under the jurisdiction of the Paris parlement. Rolland consulted with the six universities of his parlementary district in preparing his reports and was active for years in the actual administration of the ex-Jesuit schools, especially Louis-le-Grand in Paris. He was guillotined in the Revolution to which Guyton de Morveau owed his later fame.[28]

Among *philosophes* Diderot played some mysterious role in the anonymous publication of a little book late in 1762, called simply *De l'Education publique*, which was almost certainly written by a professional teacher.[29] D'Alembert's article in the *Encyclopédie* has already been mentioned. Condillac, known for the radically empirical philosophy of his *Traité des sensations*, served for several years as tutor to the son of the Prince of Parma, for whom he composed 15 volumes of educational materials, but he never addressed himself to the problems of schools. The thoughts of Helvétius, as published posthumously in 1773, were quoted at the beginning of this book. Turgot, while in office in 1775, in conjunction with his secretary Dupont de Nemours, recommended a new system of education that they thought would change the country in 10 years; but they refrained from giving any details.[30] The Abbé Baudeau, a Physiocrat, in his journal *Les Ephémérides du Citoyen*, began a series of articles on "national education" that were carefully thought out but unfortunately never completed.[31] A view typical of the more extreme writers was expressed by the Abbé Mably in his treatise, *De la Législation*, written in the form of a dialogue

[28] Caradeuc de La Chalotais, *Essai d'éducation nationale, ou Plan d'études pour la jeunesse, par Messire Louis-René Caradeuc de La Chalotais, procureur-général du roi au Parlement de Bretagne* (n.p., 1763); L. B. Guyton de Morveau, *Mémoire sur l'éducation publique, avec le prospectus d'un collège suivant les principes de cet ouvrage* (n.p., 1764); Rolland d'Erceville, *Recueil de plusieurs des ouvrages de M. le président Rolland, imprimé en exécution des délibérations du bureau du collège de Louis-le-Grand des 17 juin et 18 avril 1782* (Paris, 1783). The Rolland *recueil* contains three kinds of documents: those pertaining to the disposition of Jesuit colleges in general, those pertaining to Louis-le-Grand in particular, and the *compte-rendu* or plan of study discussed below.

[29] See my article "A mystery explored: the *De l'Education publique* attributed to Denis Diderot," forthcoming in the *Journal of Modern History*.

[30] Turgot, "Mémoire sur les municipalités," in Schelle, ed., *Oeuvres de Turgot*, 4: 578-79. See also M. Bouloiseau, "Dupont de Nemours et l'éducation nationale," *Congrès national des sciences savantes. Histoire moderne et contemporaine* (1970), 1: 171-84. Bouloiseau traces Dupont's activity from his collaboration with Turgot in 1775 through publication of his *Vues sur l'éducation nationale* (Paris, An II), to his proposal to President Jefferson in 1800 for national education in the United States.

[31] Abbé Baudeau, "De l'Education nationale," in *Ephémérides du citoyen* for 25 November 1765, and 17 January, 7 March, 12 May, 4 August, and 15 August 1766.

between a philosopher and an English lord. "When I speak of public education, continued our philosopher, God preserve me from thinking of the colleges and universities established in Europe."[32]

To the practical discussion of schools more was therefore contributed by professors than by *philosophes*. All three persons suggested as the unknown author of *De l'Education publique*, for which Diderot wrote an introduction, were actual teachers, two of them, J.B.L. Crevier and D. F. Rivard, senior professors in the Paris faculty of arts, and the third, Dieudonné Thiébaut, a young ex-Jesuit who later taught in Prussia and still later in the Central Schools of the French Republic. Crevier also published a reply to La Chalotais, and Rivard a plan for a teachers' college.[33] A certain Père Navarre, of the order of the Christian Doctrine, won a prize at the Floral Games of Toulouse for his essay in reply to the question proposed: "What would be the plan of study most advantageous to France?"[34] The Abbé Garnier, professor of Hebrew at the College of France, published an interesting book, *De l'Education civile*, in 1765, in which he argued that the College of France might become a kind of graduate school drawing students from existing "undergraduate" colleges.[35] A young teacher at the ex-Jesuit college of Aix-en-Provence, J. A. Borrelly, published in 1768 a *Système de législation* that was in fact concerned exclusively with education as a means of "forming useful and virtuous subjects for the State."[36]

Virtually all these writings, whether by *parlementaires*, *philosophes*, or *professeurs*, call for action by an enlightened government, and many praise the action already taken by the monarchy after the fall of the Jesuits. They envisage a uniform education throughout the whole of France so that no region should be neglected. They propose the preparation of schoolbooks under government supervision. Teachers' training institutions are recommended, such as the Jesuits had had for their own neophytes. Some of the writers, and especially La Chalotais, thought that good teachers must be laymen and fathers of families; Rolland as

[32] Abbé Mably, *Oeuvres complètes de Mably* (Paris, 1797), 18: 136.

[33] J.B.L. Crevier, *Difficultés proposées à M. de La Chalotais* (Paris, 1763); D. F. Rivard, *Mémoire sur la nécessité d'établir une maison d'institution pour former des maîtres* [late 1762]. Crevier, Rivard, Thiébaut, and Borrelly are discussed in my article cited in note 29 above.

[34] Le Père Jean Navarre, de la Doctrine chrétienne, *Discours qui a remporté le prix par le jugement de l'Académie des jeux floraux en l'année 1763, sur ces paroles: Quel serait en France le plan d'étude le plus avantageux* (n.p., 1763).

[35] J. J. Garnier, *De l'éducation civile* (Paris, 1765), esp. pp. 148-50 and 172.

[36] J. A. Borrelly, *Système de législation, ou moyens que la politique peut employer pour former à l'état des sujets utiles et vertueux* (Paris, 1768).

a practical administrator wanted more laymen but was willing to settle for clerics; Diderot's anonymous collaborator thought that all teachers should be celibate members of the secular clergy. Several, and perhaps the *professeurs* more than the *philosophes*, called for improvements in the education of girls. All of them thought that the curriculum was too "literary," and they demanded more attention to science and history; they also complained that too much time was spent on Latin, although they generally held that Latin was valuable and often quoted a few Latin words as if to suggest that they were not speaking from ignorance.

All wanted to produce more useful members of society, a doubtless perennial aim of schooling, which in this case meant to be more abreast of modern knowledge, proficient and reliable in one's vocation, and a good *citoyen* for *la nation* and *la patrie*. It is in this connection that we hear much grandiose reference to the Greek and Latin classics, and indeed to China. "Why," asked Navarre, a priest himself of the Christian Doctrine,

> should our children not learn from their teachers to be not only sociable beings and Christians, but also citizens? Why should not literary education serve to multiply the prodigy of political virtues? Why should so many arid and unfruitful studies neglect the sublime study of duties to one's country? Why in France, as at Lacedemon and Athens and in China, should our colleges not become schools of patriotism? *For the king and for France* are two sentiments that education should unite and incorporate, so to speak, in the hearts of French youth as they are now in the national constitution.[37]

Father Navarre was competing in an oratorical contest, but more prosaic uses of *citoyen* and *constitution* by others at the time suggest the continuity from the Old Regime to the Revolution.

On the whole, our planners were open to a criticism launched by Crevier against La Chalotais. It was an error, said Crevier, for La Chalotais to argue both that education should adjust youth to the customs of the country and that it should be used to shape or mold new customs, or *moeurs*. The same question was of course to arise later, during the Revolution. Actually, said Crevier, education should instill "an order of duties independent of the laws and constitutions of states."[38]

There was less agreement on who or how many should be educated,

[37] Navarre, *Discours*, p. 24.
[38] Crevier, *Difficultés proposées*, p. 30.

or on the kinds of education that the various social classes should receive. It may be recalled that about 50,000 boys and young men were in the French colleges before the Revolution, and several more thousands in "private" schools; that students came from a wide range of social classes; and that, in the colleges, they followed the same program of study. For some reformers this constituted a defect in the existing order. Rousseau seems to have expressed this opinion in saying that each person, in the "social" order, should be educated for his own place. For others, notably La Chalotais and Baudeau, their thinking about education was combined with a kind of manpower planning. Their intent was not so much to restrict schooling or defend privilege as to produce a smoothly functioning society. France, said La Chalotais, already had too many priests and clerics, far too many judges and officeholders, too many writers and literary people—and too many students aiming at such careers. Even the common people, farm workers, and artisans "are sending their children to colleges in small towns where living is cheap."[39] This is all socially useless. *Multorum manibus egent res humanae, paucorum capita sufficiunt.* "Human affairs need the hands of many, but the heads of few." It would be better for the working class not to learn to read at all. In any case, contentment is better than social mobility. "It is for the Government," said La Chalotais, "to make each citizen happy enough in his condition (*état*) for him not to be forced to leave it." Radical by temperament, he saw the improved future society as a more pleasant form of the existing order—nobles would be more peaceful and refined, women more intelligent and better mothers, seigneurs more indulgent to tenants, rentiers less grasping, army officers more serious, judges wiser, curés more helpful to parishioners, and businessmen more informed about foreign markets.[40]

Baudeau, the Physiocrat, was more explicit. He would firmly prohibit all private schools and private tutors and have everyone from the royal family to the paupers participate in "national education." He conceived, however, of five different kinds of schools for five different social classes. All girls should also be educated in schools according to their class, though not with boys. Even the poorest should learn to read and write (remember that our peasants are now proprietors and *citoyens!*), and so be liberated from dependence on lawyers and a scribbling literate elite. For the children of shopkeepers and artisans a few other subjects, including drawing, should be added. For what Baudeau

[39] La Chalotais, *Essai*, pp. 26-27.
[40] Ibid., pp. 134-38.

calls the "bourgeoisie," whose sons aim at second-level positions in the church and the law courts, or at medicine and the arts, he seems to have in mind something like the existing colleges, reformed and modernized, and limited to this class. This leaves the two highest of the five classes, at the top the royal family and great noble personages, and second the ordinary nobles and *gentilhommes*. These two formed the ruling class, and he argues at length, and rather persuasively, that the ruling class should be educated by itself. After all, what did a simple professor know about the life and problems of important men? To mix upper and lower class boys in the same school only made the former arrogant and the latter insecure. Some upper class boys might indeed go on from their own schools to the University to prepare for the magistracy or the church. Others, however, must acquire a sterner code, learn to command and obey, to understand large affairs, to become tough enough to make hard decisions and carry heavy responsibilities, to know how to conduct themselves in public, go without sleep, undertake arduous journeys, and avoid the false pride that might come from mixing with boys of lower status from the age of ten or twelve. Baudeau's plan, far more than La Chalotais's was a plan of "national" education in offering something for everybody.[41]

Baudeau explicitly rejected the principle of "a public school open to all, as are our colleges today."[42] In a pre-democratic society the issue was neither very salient nor directly joined. But the *parlementaires* Guyton de Morveau and Rolland d'Erceville certainly disagreed with Baudeau and La Chalotais on this matter, and the professional teachers insisted on having the colleges open to boys without regard to family background. Crevier, a Paris professor and a Jansenist, attacked La Chalotais most sharply. His *Essai*, said Crevier, was no plan of national education but only a proposal for a reduced number of colleges for a small elite. It left out 19 out of 20 million Frenchmen. Social classes should mix in school. "Talents and genius bring together what social conditions keep apart. Any citizen born for the sciences, whether the son of an artisan or a farmer, should be seated beside the gentleman if by his talents he deserves to occupy the same place."[43] The unknown author of *De l'Education publique*, another teacher, was of the same opinion. "The children of the poor," he said, "are none the less the country's children [*enfants de la patrie*], from whom come our artisans, farmers and soldiers. In any case, God looks with the same kindness on the poor man's cabin as on the rich man's panelled walls; and his

[41] Baudeau, *Ephémérides*, 17 January and 7 March 1766.
[42] Ibid., 4 August 1766.
[43] Crevier, *Difficultés proposées*, p. 37.

supreme Providence has no regard for our little distinctions of rank and birth in the distribution of talents."[44] This sentence was quoted with approval by Borrelly in his *Système de législation* a few years later. The State, said Borrelly, should rest on "the union of minds and hearts among all its citizens. Uniformity of teaching and education is the surest way to establish it."[45] And Guyton de Morveau: "Since the schools are open to all they must be made useful to all" and must provide education without regard to a boy's future occupation or that of his father.[46]

Such thoughts led directly into the question of scholarships. Baudeau would provide scholarships for "poor gentlemen" and pointed to the new Polish Collegium Nobilium as an example. Others were concerned that scholarships should be awarded only for merit. Borrelly, quoting Diderot's collaborator, worried that without aid a talented poor boy might continue to "creep in obscurity."[47] Guyton de Morveau expressly differed with "a modern philosopher" (probably La Chalotais) who said that not all talents should be educated because not all could be socially useful. He observed that the soundness of the French monarchy depended on avenues of upward social mobility and was echoed by the professorial writers in defense of *instruction gratuite* and student aid.[48] Several thought that the income from superfluous church properties might be used for this purpose.

The talent that they wished to encourage was never defined but was thought of in pragmatic terms. Like Adam Smith, and in keeping with the philosophy of the *tabula rasa*, our authors were inclined to believe that all persons were much alike at birth, and that differences arose from the effects of family and other surroundings in early childhood, and from the habits, tastes, inclinations, and learning developed during the process of education, resulting in a combination of qualities that enabled the individual, by early adulthood, to excel in a particular kind of work. The idea of inborn, untrained, or irrepressible genius was more the product of a later romantic era.

Actual Changes, 1762-1789

We turn from the ideas of writers to a consideration of what actually happened, including changes set in motion by the public authorities—

[44] *De l'Education publique* (n.p., 1762 or 1763), pp. 159-60.

[45] Borrelly, *Système de législation*, pp. 51-53.

[46] Guyton de Morveau, *Mémoire*, pp. 54-58.

[47] Borrelly, *Système de législation*, pp. 106-107.

[48] Guyton de Morveau, *Mémoire*, pp. 42-51.

the king, the parlements, and the church. Each in its way had plans for national education. The king with his ministers and the church with its periodic Assembly of the Clergy were in effect national institutions. The parlements or sovereign courts were about a dozen in number, all enjoying equal status under the monarchy, and each having a jurisdiction limited to its own province, except for the Parlement of Paris, whose territory embraced various provinces in the remaining half of the kingdom. In matters of education the parlements acted along generally parallel lines, and when not defending their provincial liberties they thought in broadly national terms. In general, in the quarter-century before the Revolution, these public authorities tended to deadlock each other. The parlements at first seized the initiative, in alliance with some of the royal ministers, but were set back by the episode of the "Maupeou parlements" from 1771 to 1774. From 1775 there was a tendency for the Church hierarchy to offset their influence. The proliferating ideas of the 1760s, so far as they really went beyond existing practice, had hardly been realized at the time of the Revolution.

Scarcely had the Jesuits vacated their schools when the Parlement of Paris, on 3 September 1762, issued an order requiring the universities within its zone of jurisdiction—those of Paris, Reims, Bourges, Poitiers, Angers, and Orleans—to submit reports on the colleges (not merely the ex-Jesuit colleges) within that zone.[49] These were to contain proposals for the improvement of studies and for possible connections to be established between the colleges and the universities. The royal government, faced with the loss of about 1,250 Jesuit teachers in some 105 colleges, followed with an important edict in February 1763 that applied to the whole of France.[50] The Parlement of Paris appointed a commission of four of its own members to carry out its order of September 1762. The chief commissioners were L'Averdy and Rolland d'Erceville, but the former soon became the king's controller-general of finances and so involved in other more pressing business that Rolland d'Erceville became and remained the main agent of the

[49] This important *arrêt* of the Parlement was omitted by Isambert but may be found in the Rolland *Recueil* (note 28 above). It was published by the Jansenist *Nouvelles ecclésiastiques* in its number for 7 December 1762. The themes of the rest of the present chapter are treated also by D. Julia in "Les professeurs, l'église et l'état après l'expulsion des Jésuites," in Baker and Harrigan's *Making of Frenchmen*, pp. 459-81, and by Jean Morange in J. Morange and J. F. Chassaing in *Le mouvement de réforme de l'enseignement en France, 1769-1798* (Paris, 1974), pp. 9-95.

[50] Isambert, *Recueil*, 22: 389-91, published the preamble but not the enacting articles, which may be found in the Rolland *Recueil*.

Parlement in matters pertaining to the schools. Although the decade of the 1760s was one of severe stress between the royal officials and all the parlements of the kingdom on constitutional and fiscal questions, they cooperated closely in their policies on education. The result was a series of parlementary and royal actions along several overlapping lines.

One such line was a defense of the existing order. With the departure of the Jesuits and the ferment of discussion in the 1760s went an increase in the number of persons setting up private schools. The University of Paris complained to the Parlement as early as 1762. "We see everywhere in the city and its environs," said the University,

> men without qualifications, and often without ability, who by their own private authority dare to take the titles and discharge the functions of teachers of youth, open their homes to the public and there conduct schools and boarding establishments (*pensions*). . . . These charlatans, in prospectuses that they are careful to scatter through the city, the court and the provinces, loudly announce that they are the inventors of new methods of education, shorter, easier and more agreeable than those employed by the University.[51]

As private schools continued to spring up the Parlement acted. It issued a court order in 1779, repeated in 1784 (and apparently never enforceable) requiring any *maître de pension* in a town having a college to send his pupils over nine years old to classes in the college. Such *maîtres* were restricted either to teaching poor boys gratis or to giving only elementary lessons in reading, writing, and Latin grammar to the youngest while merely supervising the studies of older boys who received their instruction from authorized professors. Another court order forbade anyone to operate a Latin school without having the *maîtrise ès arts*. That such regulations went back to Henry IV's statute of 1598 only suggests how commonly they were disregarded.[52]

Parlement and king, however, were more innovative on a number of matters. One was the reorganization of the Jesuit College of Louis-le-Grand, which now became a part of the University of Paris for the first time. A second was the disposal to be made of all Jesuit colleges in France. A third, which in fact subsumed the second, was set forth in the sweeping royal edict of February 1763. It embodied ideas of

---

[51] Jourdain, *Université de Paris* (1888), 2: 307-308, prints the text of the University's protest to the Parlement.

[52] Isambert, *Recueil*, 26: 137, 28: 402; Jourdain, *Université de Paris* (1862), p. 261 of the *pièces justificatives*; C. R. Bailey, *French Secondary Education, 1763-1790: The Secularization of the French ex-Jesuit Colleges* (Philadelphia, 1978), p. 34.

the Paris parlementary commission, and it concerned all colleges that were *not* part of any university in the realm. The preamble announced the intention of dealing with the university colleges at a later date, which never came to pass.

At the new Louis-le-Grand a plan was at last realized that had often been discussed within the University of Paris without results. While there were 10 fully active colleges within the Paris faculty of arts, there were also 28 "small colleges," representing foundations made since the thirteenth century for the support of poor scholars. Income from these endowments had been eroded by time, inflation, mismanagement, or misuse, so that some colleges had only handfuls of students and others offered no instruction at all. The income of these decayed colleges was now combined with the income, buildings, library, and scientific equipment of the ex-Jesuit Louis-le-Grand. Many small scholarship funds were thus concentrated into a pool, and the new institution, still under the name of Louis-le-Grand, became a college primarily for scholarship students. Scholarships, or *bourses*, since professors' salaries were paid by the state, were used for board and room for students, and the new Louis-le-Grand, unlike its Jesuit predecessor, was entirely residential. The students came from many parts of France. The control of its funds, under the Parlement and especially Rolland d'Erceville, was so efficient that the number of its scholarships rose from 196 in 1763 to almost 500 in the years before 1789. Of these 500 students almost 200 were young men who lived in the college while going out to study in the higher faculties of law, medicine, or theology, and about 300 were distributed in the classes and age levels from the youngest up through Philosophy. Louis-le-Grand was neither a "secondary" nor a "higher" institution but combined elements of both. It was also the only one of the 10 Paris colleges to remain open even during the Terror and so to have a continuous history into the following century.[53]

The plan was at first to make it into a teacher training establishment, from which replacements for the departing Jesuits would go out to colleges throughout the country. It never became such, and its graduates went into many walks of life, but it did develop a small program of teacher training. The need for such training was expressed in tracts by several professors at the University in the 1760s such as D. F. Rivard and the Abbé Pellicier; but the action came with another royal decree in 1766, which established the *agrégation* in the faculty of arts.

[53] On Louis-le-Grand see my *School of the French Revolution*; see also Bailey, *French Secondary Education*, and Dupont-Ferrier, *Du Collège de Clermont au Lycée Louis-le-Grand*.

Sixty subsidized places were created, to be filled by open and competitive examinations, and to involve a year of further study beyond Philosophy, for which the students at Louis-le-Grand were allowed to extend their scholarships for a year. Twenty of the 60 were to prepare for teaching in the youngest classes in Grammar, another 20 for Rhetoric and the Second and Third, and 20 for Philosophy, which is to say Logic and Physics. While pursuing their studies they were to act when called upon as assistants or substitutes for the professors or take part in oral examinations and in disputations with students. At the end of their training they were to be qualified for professorships in the University of Paris, or more widely "in any one of the colleges of our realm approved in our edict of February 1763."[54]

The *agrégation* represented a step in nationalization both by its royal enactment and in aiming at a standard for the whole country. It aroused strong objection among some members of the Paris faculty of arts, even those like Rivard who favored change. They argued that with recruitment by competition and special training the heads of colleges would lose their freedom in making appointments, and that a college head's judgment of teaching ability, and of acceptability on moral and religious grounds, was more important than mere scholastic achievement as shown in examinations. Some objected that the new procedure would favor laymen as teachers, since the decree mentioned no requirements for clerical status, except in excluding the regular clergy. The *agrégation*, in fact, was pushed through by the government over protests from the faculty. The same was true of a regulation on scholarships issued in 1767. This measure provided that the scholarships newly combined in Louis-le-Grand should be equalized in value and that candidates must pass an examination and do well in their studies for two years before becoming entitled to their scholarships for their whole course of study. The regulation was drawn up by certain professors in conjunction with royal officials, but it was so strenuously objected to by conservatives in the faculty that the government had to step in to force its adoption.[55]

---

[54] The best account of the *agrégation*, its purpose and impact, and of the reasons for opposition to it, is in D. Julia, "La naissance du corps professoral," *Actes de la Recherche en Sciences Sociales*, no. 39 (Paris, 1981). See also my *School of the French Revolution*, pp. 49-52; Jourdain, *Université de Paris* (1888), 2: 344-68; Jourdain, *Université de Paris* (1862), for numerous documents on the *agrégation* and the opposition to it; and the first chapter *Centenaire de l'Ecole Normale* (Paris, 1895), "Les boursiers de Louis-le-Grand après l'expulsion des Jésuites," since the Ecole Normale Supérieure traces its origin to these actions of the 1760s.

[55] Jourdain, *Université de Paris* (1888), 2: 375-78; Julia, "Les professeurs, l'église et l'état," pp. 460-62, 481.

The *agrégation* of 1766 met with a modest measure of success, with over 200 young men receiving it between 1766 and the Revolution. Many of them, especially those preparing to teach in the lower grades, proved to be laymen and to be distinguished for scholastic performance, as shown by the fact that many who qualified for the *agrégation* had in earlier years won prizes in the *concours général*. The *agrégation* was thus a step toward the professionalization of teaching outside such teaching orders as the Oratorians and Doctrinaires. It disappeared in the Revolution, but by 1800 certain writers on education, in criticizing the Central Schools, looked back to it as a desirable credential that had been lost. It was restored by Napoleon in 1808, and with subsequent development it became the well-known French *agrégation* of later times.

Meanwhile the Parlement and the royal officials were busily carrying out both the parlementary order of September 1762 concerning all colleges in its territory and the royal edict of February 1763 concerning "colleges not dependent on universities" throughout the kingdom. The edict provided for local control of colleges according to a uniform national pattern. Each college received a tripartite board, consisting of the chief royal officer of the neighborhood, the bishop or his deputy, and certain local notables and town councillors. In towns having a parlement a member of that court was to represent the royal authority. The purpose of the legislation was to study problems raised by "the multiplicity of these colleges, the obscurity of some and the inadequate revenues of others," as well as "faults in administration that require an entire reform" or "consolidation with other colleges that are more useful and better established."[56] Hence all colleges were ordered to submit reports on their financial and other circumstances immediately to the government. Little of this ambitious program was carried out. The boards did become active but were engaged in routine administration, including the preservation or expansion of college property, control of expenditures, selection of teachers, discipline of teachers and students, and supervision of instruction.

It is difficult to generalize on what happened, in consequence of the edict of February 1763, in several hundred colleges under a dozen parlementary jurisdictions. We shall concentrate on the territory of the Parlement of Paris, which included 40 ex-Jesuit colleges and somewhat over 100 colleges all told. Among these, Louis-le-Grand was an exception by its size, its wealth, its designation as a scholarship institute, and the close scrutiny that the Parlement, located less than a mile

[56] Isambert, *Recueil*, 22: 391.

away, was able to give it. A comprehensive study has been made by an American, Charles Bailey, who has minutely examined developments in the 40 ex-Jesuit colleges under the Paris jurisdiction. These institutions presented special problems for their boards and for the Parlement, since there were Jesuit debts that had to be paid and pensions for individual Jesuits above a certain age. Otherwise, and always allowing for exceptions, Bailey's study may be taken to suggest the impact of the February Edict on colleges as a whole, at least within the domain of the Parlement of Paris.

The greater uniformity aimed at in the February Edict was never achieved. Exceptions had to be made for some colleges conducted by the religious congregations. There continued to be rich and poor colleges, large and small ones, from La Flèche with 500 students and 42,000 livres a year to Sens with only 100 students and 2,900 livres. Each local board faced a different financial problem, since the college revenues came from varying mixtures of municipal grants, private gifts, student fees, subsidies from bishops or other ecclesiastics, loans, urban rentals, and rural properties subject to the complications of "feudal" land law. There could be arguments over teachers' salaries and the expenses of proposed repairs or improvements. Our author concludes that the boards were nevertheless quite successful in handling their finances and did as well as could be expected with the difficult problem of finding teachers, most of whom turned out to be of the secular clergy. In some towns there was a desire for more lay teachers; in others, parents would have preferred to turn over the college to one of the teaching orders. Disputes might break out on a board between the representatives of the church, the king, and the local population. In some places there were lingering pro-Jesuit sentiments and objections to "Jansenism." Occasionally there would be small-town factionalism over the policies or competence of the college principal, or over the dismissal of an unsatisfactory teacher, especially since the February Edict prescribed certain procedures before a dismissal could take place. A board might have difficulty also in the punishment or expulsion of a troublesome student if he was the son of a locally influential family. In short, judging from the 40 establishments that he studied, Bailey concludes that by the time of the Revolution the colleges were in "a highly confused and somewhat depressed state," though not as bad as has been often said, and in any case the boards carried on until 1790.[57]

A further line of real innovation, as distinct from mere plans and projects, was the establishment of new *écoles militaires*. This program

[57] Bailey, *French Secondary Education*, passim, with conclusions at p. 108.

was carried out by the royal government, and in fact by the War Department, without participation by the parlements and in some cases against their opposition.

The building in Paris still called the Ecole Militaire was built in the 1750s to house 500 "young gentlemen," in fact boys who entered as early as nine years old and remained for five years, and were then sent to the regiments as sublieutenants to complete their education. The purpose was to produce a more professional army by making the service more of a learned profession, or as the preamble of 1751 expressed it, to overcome the prejudice that a good soldier was made only by valor, not by study. Entrants to the school had to provide written proof of four generations of nobility, and this requirement was later taken as a sign of aristocratic exclusiveness, though not many sons of commercial or legal families wanted a military career, and the working class was hardly in a position to expect commissions. It has recently been shown that the four-generations rule was aimed mainly against newly ennobled families, usually rich people whose sons hoped to cut a figure in society in a dress uniform rather than work in the field with troops, and who were therefore thought not to make good officers.[58] In any case, the big school in Paris was judged to be unsuccessful and too lavish and expensive. It was decided to send these junior cadets to already existing colleges throughout the country and then assign them, at the age of sixteen, mostly to the regiments but in a few cases to the Ecole Militaire in Paris for further training.

The royal government selected 10 such schools as *écoles militaires*, all of them conducted by religious orders, six by Benedictines, three by Oratorians, and one by the small order of Minimes at Brienne in eastern France, to which Napoleon Bonaparte went in 1778 as a boy of nine. An eleventh was soon added, the College of La Flèche, a former Jesuit institution that was now assigned to the Doctrinaires. It was intended for boys anticipating careers in the church or civil government, and who received royal scholarships for this purpose; but it was administered in the same way as the others and is generally counted as one of the *écoles militaires*. The government paid the schools a fee (*pension* or *bourse*) of 700 livres for each student. During the 1780s,

[58] D. D. Bien, "La réaction artistocratique avant 1789: l'exemple de l'armée," *Annales E.S.C.* (1974), pp. 522-30, and "The Army in the French Enlightenment," *Past and Present* (November 1979), pp. 68-98. Bien's argument pertains more generally to the four-generation rule in the Ségur law of 1781, but it is equally relevant to the *écoles militaires* in particular. On the *écoles militaires* see also Julia, Chartier, and Compère, *L'éducation en France*, pp. 217-21; Taton, *Enseignement et diffusion*, pp. 523-36; and above, pp. 27-28.

of 3,000 young men entering the line regiments as officers, about 500 had begun as these *élèves du roi*.[59]

It was significant that the government chose only schools run by religious orders. It is therefore thought that their selection expressed some kind of reaction against the secularizing or progressive tendencies of the time. This may be doubted when we remember that all colleges were manned by clergy of one kind or another, and than even religious persons in the 1770s believed that the teaching orders were in a state of decay.

The reasons for the choice are made clear in a planning document found in the archives of the Ministry of War. This document expresses no more than the usual concern for religion. The planner stressed finances; the king would simply get more for his money by the proposed program than by setting up his own schools in the provinces or by bringing the boys all to Paris. Mainly, he recommended the teaching congregations, and especially the Benedictines, because their programs of study were modern. Sorèze, a Benedictine institution not far from Toulouse, he pointed out, already taught not only Latin and Greek but also four modern languages, mathematics, music, dancing, and horseback riding. Since its reorganization in about 1759 it had given up the strict sequence of annual classes, paid little attention to student age, and allowed elective studies according to the student's intended career. It had also introduced student uniforms and a few simple quasi-military formations for its purely civilian clientele.[60]

Both the planning document and the final edict, while requiring four generations of nobility in the royal cadets, wanted to mix them with boys of less eminent parentage. His Majesty intended, said the edict, "by mixing them with other classes of citizens . . . to give them the precious advantage of public education, which includes making their characters more flexible, suppressing the pride that a noble youth may easily confuse with high station, and learning to consider all orders of society from a just point of view." Hence all students in the school were to be treated alike, wear the same uniform, be under the same rules, and sit in the same classrooms.[61] Each school received up

[59] Bien, "La réaction aristocratique," p. 516.

[60] J. Fabre de Massaguel, *L'école de Sorèze de 1758 au 19 fructidor An IV (5 septembre 1796)* (Toulouse, 1958), which also publishes the anonymous planning document in an appendix, pp. 209-11.

[61] For the royal decree, Isambert, *Recueil*, 24: 307-11, 505-20. For number of students and ratios of royal cadets, W. Frijhoff and D. Julia, "Les grands pensionnats de l'Ancien Regime à la Restauration," *Annales historiques de la Révolution française* (January-March 1981), p. 168, where it is shown that in 1787 for all the *écoles militaires*

to 60 royal cadets but was required to have at least an equal number of other pupils. In fact, Sorèze had over 400 students, Tournon almost 300, and in all the *écoles militaires* except Brienne the cadets were a minority of the student body.

A curious sidelight is thrown on these *écoles militaires* by the recollections of Samuel Breck, an American who was at Sorèze from 1783 to 1787.[62] He was the son of a Boston merchant who had become acquainted with the admiral in command of the French fleet at Boston during the War of Independence. The admiral recommended Sorèze, and young Breck was sent there to learn French for its future value in business. His recollections, written down over 40 years later and doubtless tinged with nostalgia, were all highly favorable. The Benedictine fathers had caused him no embarrassment about his Protestant and Puritan background and were in any case assisted by many lay teachers. Not everyone needed to study Latin, and those who did not, called the *pas-Latins*, included many sons of French West Indian planters and boys from towns in France, as well as the king's scholars. They were put to studying mathematics, engineering, topography, and drawing. The king's scholars and the others mixed readily together; Breck revealed no class consciousness in this matter and made no mention of the word "noble" in this connection. As he recalled it, the school proved that Latin and non-Latin students could get along together very well in the same college—a point being vigorously debated in the United States in the 1820s. He thought, too, that the fee of 700 livres "was exceedingly cheap," calling it the equivalent of $137. It may be added that Sorèze also made Breck's character more "flexible," for in later years, as a prominent Boston merchant, he was one of those who enabled the Frenchman, Jean Cheverus, to become the first Roman Catholic bishop of Boston. He remarks that, from his sojourn in France and later visits, he had outgrown his childhood New England prejudice against popery.

These *écoles militaires*, in short, were not military schools at all, a fact that is hardly surprising since their use as such pertained only to boys under sixteen years old. They were regular colleges containing small units of a kind of junior ROTC. They reflected the rising concern of the government for professional education, as in establishing the schools of mining, engineering, and roads and bridges; the placement of teacher

---

together about a fifth of the students were royal cadets and three-fifths were noble, and at Sorèze one tenth were royal cadets and somewhat over two-fifths were noble. They were clearly upper class schools.

[62] Samuel Breck, *Recollections of Samuel Breck* (Philadelphia, 1877), pp. 61-78. The recollections were written in 1830.

trainees in the large College of Louis-le-Grand; the financing of art students at the French Academy in Rome; and the temporary use of La Flèche for a few "poor gentlemen," subsidized by the king, as a training center for civilian branches of government.

The interest of the *écoles militaires* for present purposes lies in suggesting what happened when they came under supervision by the central government. Having 11 such schools, the government wished "to assure uniformity of methods of instruction," especially since the royal cadets from all the schools were to take the same examinations, by which it would determine to which branch of the service each fifteen-year-old would be sent, or whether he should proceed to the Ecole Militaire in Paris. Hence also the government would choose persons to write textbooks that the schools would be required to use. An inspector from the Ministry of War visited each school once a year—a visit that Samuel Breck says was dreaded by both teachers and pupils. Each year the inspector-general, surveying the results of the competitive examination of the king's students, would award gold medals to the most successful teachers—a provision that reappeared in the law of Floréal of the Year X creating the lycées in 1802. Since the law also required that all students be treated alike, and since the royal cadets were a minority, it would seem that such regulations would produce massive changes in the colleges concerned; but in truth the matter has not been sufficiently studied with this point in mind.

For whatever reason, the government did in fact choose only schools operated by religious orders in setting up its *écoles militaires*. It is a fact also that, although almost all the hundred-odd Jesuit colleges had been turned over to secular clergy in 1762 and 1763, about a third of them by 1789 had been reassigned to the Oratorians, Doctrinaires, Benedictines, Josephites, Chanoines du Saint-Sauveur, and other such organized groups. The question therefore arises, always remembering that over half the colleges in 1789 were in the hands of secular clergy, of whether the government was yielding to pressures brought by the church in matters of education, or whether there was some kind of ecclesiastical resurgence, vaguely analogous to an "aristocratic resurgence," in these closing years of the Old Regime.

The answer seems to be that the continuing favor enjoyed by the teaching orders arose not so much from episcopal demands, or from any rise in religious concern, as from the merits of their schools as schools. In many towns having an ex-Jesuit school the townspeople favored transfer to one of the non-Jesuit congregations. When the Assembly of the Clergy declared that an organized body of men could run a better school than an assemblage of individuals, whether secular clergy or laymen, they expressed a view that was credible then, and is credible today. The fact that so many Oratorians and Doctrinaires went on teaching in the Central Schools of the Republic and the Bonapartist lycées, after their orders were abolished, suggests both their dedication as professional teachers and the good repute that they continued to enjoy.

THE STATE, THE CHURCH, AND THE PUBLIC POWER ON THE EVE OF THE REVOLUTION

Plans and projects, of course, and the general climate of thinking about education were to be as important as institutional background when the Revolution came. And Rolland d'Erceville, along with his colleagues in the Parlement of Paris, not only administered the ex-Jesuit schools and implemented the royal edict in February 1763, but also formulated a plan that went beyond such actual operations.

Rolland assembled the reports from the six universities, as called for in the parlementary order of September 1762, and consulted with some of their professors, whose number and identity unfortunately remain unknown. Probably most of them were at the University of Paris. He prepared a digest of the ideas thus obtained, along with his own, in a *compte-rendu* to the Parlement of Paris in 1768. Revised and published in 1783, this *compte-rendu* has been remembered by historians as Rolland's plan of study, but it seems to have been little noticed in its own day.[63]

The Rolland plan is of interest not only in expressing ideas held in the Parlement of Paris and among members of the universities who favored change but also in anticipating the main features of the Napoleonic university of 1808. What had long been needed, Rolland said, was a plan that "would impress upon public education the precious character (too long neglected) of NATIONAL EDUCATION."[64] He was aware of the European trend noted at the beginning of this chapter; he praised Maria Theresa's *Ratio educationis* for Hungary and thought

[63] Rolland d'Erceville, *Compte-rendu aux chambres assemblées par M. Rolland, des différents mémoires envoyés par les universités sises dans le ressort de la Cour, en exécution de l'arrêt des chambres assemblées du 3 septembre 1762, relativement au plan d'étude à suivre dans les collèges non-dépendants des universités. Du 13 mai 1768.* This is a component of the *Recueil de plusieurs ouvrages* in note 28 above. Jourdain, *Université de Paris* (1888), 2: 379, believed that the ideas in Rolland's plan originated in the universities.

[64] Rolland, *Compte-rendu,* p. 8. The words EDUCATION NATIONALE are set in small capital letters in the original.

that Peter the Great, by "national education," had brought Russia out of barbarism quite rapidly in recent times. Since the Parlement of Paris had jurisdiction in only half of France, he urged his colleagues to request the king, that is the central government, to take the necessary action.

The plan found that many colleges were too small or were attempting to offer more in advanced teaching than they were able to deliver. It therefore recommended that some colleges should be shut down or merged with others, and that all should exist in an explicitly defined system, so that a few should be reduced to an elementary level, others restricted to the six annual classes concluding with Rhetoric, and still others recognized as full eight-year institutions offering the two years of Philosophy. The latter would include all university and certain non-university colleges. The advantages would be twofold: terminal schools would be available at various levels for boys having different educational needs or ambitions, and the quality of instruction would be enhanced by concentrating the best teachers of advanced subjects in fewer schools of large size. The system was to be uniform throughout the country so that a boy anywhere might find an appropriate school, and none should suffer the disadvantage in adult life of a strange accent or unduly provincial behavior. It was important also that "great talents" not be lost to society. Less time should be given to the study of Latin and more to the modern sciences and modern history and literature. Better books were needed for students and better training for teachers. Laymen, if qualified, were preferable as teachers, and secular clergy were acceptable, but it was unwise to have schools conducted by religious orders. Responsibility for national education should lie not with quasi-independent "orders" but with the state acting in the interests of the nation.

These ideas were commonly found among the more serious writers on organized education in the 1760s. Rolland's plan went further in proposing a means of execution. It divided the country into educational districts each of which was centered in a university. In a few of these, in the half dozen largest cities, the three higher faculties should be fully developed, but all should have at least a faculty of arts. Each district should have its own teacher training center, modeled on the *agrégation* recently set up in the University of Paris. Both the six- and the eight-year colleges should develop closer contacts with the university of their area, which would reciprocate by assisting the colleges, recommending textbooks, providing teachers, and periodically sending visitors from its own faculty on tours of inspection. The colleges in turn would superintend the elementary schools. The Rolland plan thus

71

projected a kind of educational pyramid, resembling those being designed elsewhere in Europe. But Rolland was vague on what to put
at the top of his pyramid, stipulating only that it should be in Paris,
which, by becoming a center for a whole network of communication
between universities and colleges, would enable all Frenchmen to learn
"good taste" and participate in the "treasures of science." It was Turgot and Dupont de Nemours, in another connection, who privately
advised Louis XVI to create a "council of public instruction having
direction over the academies, universities, colleges and lesser schools."[65]
And we have just seen how the government superintended its *écoles
militaires*.

That the Rolland plan reflected views that were current in the universities themselves, as Rolland claimed, is confirmed by a remarkable
memoir drawn up at the University of Poitiers in 1789 for submission
to the Estates-General. It was written by the rector and a former rector, both of the Faculty of Theology. Poitiers was one of the five
provincial universities within the area of jurisdiction of the Parlement
of Paris, and the two authors may have been among the professors
that Rolland had consulted 20 years earlier. In their introduction to
the memoir they used one of Rolland's phrases, wishing "to impress
the precious character of *national education*" on "public education,"
and the whole document parallels the Rolland *compte-rendu* very closely.
It also shows significant differences, with a far greater role to be played
by the clergy.[66]

The memoir begins by announcing that education in France had
always been a joint concern of the monarchy and the church, and that
universities had arisen in the first place, in the Middle Ages, as a means
of controlling the same kind of proliferation of questionable schools
that was a problem in the 1780s. Such schools might become "open
doors to the spirit of novelty and error." The memoir proposed, in
effect, an educational monopoly. "Education can be made truly national only by restricting the teaching function to teachers recognized
by the nation and invested with an authority emanating from the nation and responsible to it."[67] (Or as the Declaration of the Rights of

[65] Note 30 above.

[66] "Mémoire de l'Université de Poitiers pour les Etats-Généraux de 1789," published
without comment or explanation in *Revue internationale de l'enseignement* 1887 (2), 14:
209-40. The phrase *éducation nationale* is here found in italics. See also Boissonnade,
Histoire de l'Université de Poitiers (1432-1932) (Poitiers, 1932), pp. 116, 270. The University of Angers held much the same ideas as Poitiers. See B. Bois, *La vie scolaire en
Anjou pendant la Révolution, 1789-99* (Paris, 1929), pp. 36-41.

[67] "Mémoire," p. 213. L. Grimaud, *Histoire de la liberté d'enseignement* (Paris, 1944),

Man, adopted by the Constituent Assembly in August 1789, expressed it: "No body and no individual may exercise authority that does not emanate from the nation expressly.") The authors of the Poitiers memoir were particularly critical of the teaching orders, among which the Oratorians and Doctrinaires were explicitly named. Such "orders" or "congregations," they complained, existed as separate bodies apart from the university system; each went its own way, and some of their teachers, even of advanced subjects, lacked the appropriate university degrees.

Like the Rolland plan, the Poitiers memoir proposed a uniform nationwide system in which the country was divided into educational districts (Napoleon's future "academies"), each centered on a university and each having two levels of colleges, a six-year type going no further than Rhetoric, and an eight-year type going through Philosophy (Napoleon's *collèges communaux* and *lycées*). Each university should visit, inspect, and supervise its subordinate colleges. Each would have a teacher training program for its district, and all teachers even in the six-year colleges must have taken the *maîtrise ès arts* at a university. All universities and their degrees should have equal status. Possibly a few six-year colleges might be left with the teaching orders, but the eight-year colleges must be conducted by "secular ecclesiastics." Even more radical, in the Poitiers proposal, was the demand that all eight-year colleges be incorporated into universities, or in other words that the faculties of arts should monopolize the teaching of the two years of Philosophy to young men about eighteen years old. The radicalism of this idea is evident when it is recalled that there were 173 eight-year colleges in 1789, but only 22 universities. The authors of the Poitiers memoir, well aware that in such a reorganization many towns would lose their *collèges de plein exercice*, proposed an elaborate program of scholarships, in which a boy after study at his local college would be enabled to leave home and proceed to a university town to complete his education. Such a plan, if it had ever been introduced, would have marked a distinction between "secondary" and "higher" education, or adumbrated the pattern that had developed in England, where the studies of late adolescence were concentrated in the colleges at Oxford and Cambridge.

For the rest, the Poitiers memoir was full of useful and specific ideas. Each university, and each faculty within it, should have its own income from its own endowment in land or other property so that tuition

---

found the idea of an *éducation nationale* to produce *l'homme social* so common that various *cahiers* of the clergy in 1789 expressed it.

could be free. The scandal of meaningless degrees should be ended and requirements tightened. Salaries should be high enough to eliminate fees for examinations. Reliable retirement pensions would attract and hold able men. Equality of teaching and of degrees throughout the country would promote student mobility. There should be less use of dictated lectures and more free discussion by the professor with recommended readings for the students. Other proposals were less in the modern trend, for the memoir insisted on the value not only of Latin and Greek but of Hebrew and Syriac, and urged also that all existing privileges of the universities be respected, including tax exemptions for professors, corporate legal jurisdiction over teachers and students, and in short "all the privileges that are accorded to the order of the clergy to which the universities have always been assimilated."[68]

What we see in this long document, drafted by two theologians for the University of Poitiers, is that the idea of national education was not necessarily anticlerical. By "national education" its authors meant a territorially uniform, geographically equal, pedagogically effective system of public schools. They expected the clergy to supply it, although in their assault on the teaching orders they revealed a fissure within the clergy itself. They believed that in France the church was as much a national institution as the state. For them, the clergy represented the interests of the French people as much as the royal officials and the parlements did. Writing in April of 1789, they saw the church and the monarchy as partners in a coming reorganization of France. Taking religious and political loyalty for granted, they expressed no special concern for either religious instruction or the production of citizen patriots. The memoir was audacious in some ways, strongly defensive in others. It projected a complex hierarchy of colleges and universities, all in close correspondence within their respective districts, and all using similar methods in pursuit of similar goals; but it seems not to have occurred to the authors that their plan would inevitably require a central coordinating authority. Like Rolland d'Erceville, they built a pyramid but put nothing at the top.

If teachers were clerics, and universities and colleges were "assimilated to the clergy," then there was one institution that might claim to occupy the summit, the Assembly of the Clergy of France. This gathering, which met in Paris every few years, was composed of delegates from all the dioceses in the country (except those annexed since 1562), and while it included representatives of the lower clergy, it was dominated by the bishops. Its chief function was to vote a grant of money to the king in lieu of the taxes from which church properties were exempted. But it concerned itself with other matters, including warnings against "bad books," and was especially busy from 1765 until its last meeting in 1788. Its permanent administrative staff was headed by two agents-general, one of whom for a few years was the young Abbé de Périgord, or Charles-Maurice de Talleyrand, future bishop of Autun, member of the Constituent Assembly, and foreign minister to Napoleon.

The bishops repeatedly objected to the system of local boards and other consequences of the February Edict of 1763. They were not so averse to a degree of centralization, national uniformity, or educational improvements under supervision by the church. They had defended the Jesuits as long as possible and continued to recall the advantages of the Jesuit system, in which a central management had maintained the structure and discipline of a hundred colleges and had selected, trained, assigned, promoted, and transferred the teaching personnel, or even removed poor teachers by assigning them to other duties within the Jesuit order. The Assembly deplored the dispersion of authority among hundreds of local boards in which, they thought, the bishops' deputies had too little influence, and the town notables—though well intentioned—were inexperienced and able to devote only part of their time to the colleges. A good college depended on the quality and spirit of its teachers.

> But how to find these advantages in men of every condition—ecclesiastics, regular clerics, laymen, married men, unmarried men—brought together by chance or necessity rather than by a wise selection, who follow neither the same principles nor the same method . . . and who hold to their employment only from self-interest, until they find another that may be easier and more convenient?

Or how could poor teachers be dismissed, when their legal protection was such that the sovereign courts themselves could with difficulty remove them? In addition, of course, the bishops pointed to the dangers of secularism, "philosophy," and free-thinking.[69]

The Assembly of the Clergy therefore appealed to the king, in 1772, "to return to the bishops the principal powers of inspection over the education of youth." Otherwise they foresaw "perhaps a total ship-

---

[69] *Collection des procès-verbaux des Assemblées générales du Clergé de France*, 9 vols. (Paris, 1767-1780). In vol. 8, pt. 2, for the assembly of 1765 see pp. 1433 and 479-82 of the second pagination; for the assembly of 1772, pp. 687-90; for the assembly of 1775, pp. 771-79.

wreck of morals and religion."[70] The Parlement of Paris retorted that the bishops wanted "a revolution in education."[71]

The Assembly persisted and in 1780 instructed its agents-general to prepare a circular to be addressed to all the bishops in France. The two agents, and perhaps chiefly Talleyrand, drafted a questionnaire in nine specific questions, asking information from each diocese on the number and kinds of colleges within its borders, the training and assignment of teachers and principals, the "faults" in the plans of studies, the "disadvantages" resulting from the February Edict of 1763, and suggestions for improvement. The bishops' replies, the agents said, by assisting the Assembly at future meetings in its deliberations on education, would enable it "to accomplish, or at least to prepare, a revolution of such importance."[72] Here again we note the pre-Revolutionary use of the word "revolution" to mean simply a general and presumably peaceable changeover. In any case the bishops' replies were so fragmentary and slow that nothing happened. Both the clergy and the government were too beset with other problems to give sustained attention to education—for example, the Assembly of the Clergy voted 46 million livres in 1780 and 1782 to assist the government in the American War of Independence, and another 18 million in 1785 to help it avert bankruptcy. When the real Revolution came, it is possible that Talleyrand drew on this experience of 1780-1782 in preparing his report of 1791; but even this is doubtful, in view of the quantity of plans, projects, and proposals, published and unpublished, with which he and his committee were inundated in 1790 and 1791.

But if the bishops were slow to respond, and the Assembly unable to act, at least two books were published in which the questions raised by Talleyrand were discussed. One was by the Abbé L. B. Proyart, who had taught at Louis-le-Grand and was now head of a college in the Auvergne. His solution was to make the current regulations of the University of Paris into a uniform code for the whole of France.[73] By this he meant not the statute of Henry IV but the system of rules and procedures as they had grown up in the eighteenth century. He would

[70] *Procès-verbaux*, 8: 688.

[71] Quoted by A. Sicard, *L'ancien clergé de France* (Paris, 1912), p. 441.

[72] *Procès-verbal de l'Assemblée général du clergé de France . . . en l'année 1780* (Paris, 1782), pp. 1151-52; L. Greenbaum, *Talleyrand statesman-priest: The agent-general of the clergy and the church of France at the end of the Old Regime* (Washington, D.C., 1970), pp. 154-55.

[73] L. B. Proyart, *De l'éducation publique et des moyens d'en réaliser la réforme projetée dans la dernière assemblée générale du clergé de France* (Paris, 1785), pp. 134-40. See also F. Eyrard, *Observations sur l'éducation publique, pour servir de réponse aux questions proposées pars les agents-généraux du clergé de France* (Paris, 1786).

thus have a national standard for mealtimes, class hours, recreation periods, prayers, dates of vacations, books to be read in each annual grade, rules for "emulation" and award of prizes, training of teachers, and duties of principals. He was especially concerned that boarding students should have well ventilated and wholesome quarters to eat and sleep in, under a national inspector, and that the day pupils who formed the great majority in the provincial colleges should have adequate common rooms for their use when they were not in their classes.

Everything seemed to tend, whether coming from royal officials, parlements, the church, the universities, *philosophes*, Physiocrats, or individually inspired reformers, in the direction of a centralization and indeed bureaucratization of the education system. The question was where the central authority for "national education" should lie, whether lodged in the government, the church, or some institution protected against political and ecclesiastical pressures, as Condorcet was to hope, and as even Napoleon was to declare when he established the Imperial University. For all parties the reasons for centralization were of the best—not centralization as an end in itself but a desire to correct abuses, raise standards, improve quality, reduce faculty inbreeding, prevent intramural dissensions, get better schoolbooks, assure fairness in examinations, overcome provincialism, and produce a homogeneous culture by equal treatment of all parts of the country.

Since national centralization proved to be the wave of the future, we may ask who, if anyone, opposed it. Evidence on this side is more scanty. It is in the nature of ambitious programs of reform to be publicized, whereas criticism may be confined to private complaints. Undoubtedly many heads of private schools, which were clearly increasing in number, and against which spokesmen for the universities so often railed, objected to attempts to subordinate them. At least one teacher complained later, during the Revolution, that although he had the *maîtrise ès arts* he could not open his *maison d'instruction* before going through unpleasant red tape with the University of Paris and paying a fee for four louis.[74]

The bishops would resist centralization under the state. The royal officers and the parlements competed with each other, and both would resist centralization under the clergy. The Oratorians and Doctrinaires could hardly wish to become instruments of either the universities or the bishops. Many intellectuals, disgusted with the colleges, favored

---

[74] M. Fontaine de Fréville, *Essai d'un projet d'éducation nationale pour les hommes par M. Fontaine de Fréville, chef d'une maison d'éducation, président du comité de la section du Roule* (Paris, 1791), p. 9n.

private tutoring at home. Probably most professors in the universities were too set in their ways (or too uninterested) to share in the organizational dreams of the Poitiers memoir or the Rolland plan of study.

We can cite one "enlightened" person who was also a liberal in a nineteenth-century sense, Lamoignon de Malesherbes. His cousin, C. F. Lamoignon of the Parlement of Paris, requested his support for the plans of the Parlement as published in 1783 by Rolland d'Erceville. "Education should be under the inspection of the public power," said Lamoignon, "because it should by wholly directed toward public utility and the good of the State, and should not suffer from the variable views of private administration."[75] We see emerging here a sharpening distinction between public and private, in which only the state is assumed to act in the public interest.

Malesherbes, who as a royal official in the 1750s had been permissive toward *philosophe* publications and was to defend Louis XVI in 1793, strongly disagreed with his cousin. To have a highly centralized system of education, he replied, might be desirable in Poland, where everything remained to be done; a country like France, with many existing schools and a large educated class, had no need of it. It was best to have many different free and competing schools, with different plans of study, locally supported, and with parents left free to choose. Everyone should learn to read and write, as in the American colonies, England, and parts of Germany, and boys should be prepared for future occupations according to vocational and regional needs; there would also be no harm in providing better and more expensive schools for families willing and able to pay the cost. Malesherbes concluded by denouncing the universities for their self-protective and monopolistic ambitions, for their fear of the new private schools and efforts to suppress them, and for bureaucratic schemes of official reports, periodic inspections, and hierarchic dependency.[76]

Malesherbes's reply to Lamoignon was never made public. Yet there were surely many others who would agree. Even in 1793, when the demands of revolution and war favored centralization under a national state in every sphere, there were those even among the Jacobins who called for diversity, competition, and freedom for private schools in matters of education.

[75] Quoted by Julia and Pressly, "La population scolaire," p. 1524.
[76] This reply of Malesherbes to Lamoignon, "Mémoire sur les études de la jeunesse et sur l'Université," was published by P. Grosclaude, *Malesherbes, témoin et interprète de son temps* (Paris, 1961), pp. 452-61. See also *Mémoires de Marmontel*, ed. M. Tourneux (Paris, 1891), 3: 78-81.

CHAPTER 3

POLITICIZATION

"ENFANTS de la patrie, le jour de gloire est arrivé!" With this evocation of the Marseillaise, in August 1793, at the climax of revolution, war, and invasion, the president of the Department of Paris, Citizen Dufourny, greeted an eager assembly of the prize-winning students of the 10 ancient colleges of the University of Paris. For half a century there had been such a ceremonial closing to the school year, but the old was now enlivened by the new. The place was now the hall of the Jacobin society, which had lent its premises for the occasion. The audience now included, besides the usual professors and officers of the University, a deputation from the National Convention, delegates from the sections of Paris, judges in the law courts, and various municipal dignitaries. The galleries were filled with the mothers and fathers, friends and relatives, of the youngsters from twelve to eighteen years old who had excelled in their studies.

"It is only for your talents," said Dufourny, "that these crowns are conferred amid the acclamations of citizens and at the hands of the Nation." Do not shudder, he went on,

> that your brows will be encircled for a moment with crowns. They are not the crowns of pride, nor the crowns of tyranny; they are the crowns awarded for emulation, for the talents by which republics have been established and are distinguished. But you will have learned from your reading of ancient authors that republics are not founded on talents alone, that talents without virtue only make men very dangerous. . . . There are those among you that are destined to increase the happiness of the French people, restore the human race fully to its rights, and in the end bring universal peace.
>
> *Enfants de la patrie*, you are the last of French youth to suffer the misfortune of developing your talents surrounded by prejudice. A free Nation owes all its members the truth. . . . The French Nation, the free Nation, will give this great example to the earth.

The speaker was often interrupted and obliged to repeat himself, because the words *enfants de la patrie, liberté, égalité,* and *république* "were no sooner pronounced than the students broke into transports of joy, the certain signs of the republican virtues in their hearts." As quiet descended after Dufourny's address, the head of the deputation from the Convention presented a crown of oak leaves to each in turn of the 84 prize winners, from the oldest in Rhetoric down to the youngest in the Sixth. There was one regrettable omission: the prize for Latin eloquence that had been awarded since 1749, and converted this year into one for a discourse in French on how to teach history in a free country, was not awarded, "none having fulfilled the purpose of the contest."[1]

Taken together, the speech and the event provide a parable for the interplay between education and the French Revolution. Ideas not un-known to the colleges of the Old Regime, such as emulation, talent, virtue, and the value of Greek and Latin authors, now received a new emphasis and merged with a detestation of kings and a new message of national and universal liberation. The time had come, in the world as in the schools, to replace the prejudice of the past with the truth of the present and future. The excitement in the hall of the Jacobins reflected the atmosphere in Paris and much of the rest of the country at the very moment when the great Committee of Public Safety was taking form, and the measures were being adopted that would repel the combined counter-Revolutionary intervention of Austria, Prussia, Spain, and Great Britain. Unfortunately, the inability to award a prize for the teaching of history in a free country had its darker symbolism also, for in the short run, at least, the efforts to revolutionize education and to educate for revolution were almost equally lacking in positive results. It was easier to destroy than to create; there never was another such annual ceremony for the University of Paris, and by October the 10 colleges whose best students were so honored in August were closed—except for Louis-le-Grand, renamed Equality College.

POLITICS AND EDUCATION

It was observed at the beginning of this book that four themes would be followed, under the cumbersome labels of nationalization, politici-

---

[1] The proceedings of this assembly, with names of the prize winners, were published at the time and are reprinted in the first edition of C. Jourdain, *Histoire de l'Université de Paris au 17ᵉ et au 18ᵉ siècle.* (Paris, 1862), pp. 281-84 of the *pièces justificatives.* On the *concours général* see above, p. 24.

zation, democratization, and modernization. The first, in the sense both of nation-making and of central controls, so evident for many decades, continued unabated into the Revolution, as will be seen without the need for further explicit comment. The themes of democratization and modernization will be taken up later. At present, we must bring together a variety of developments that can be called aspects of politicization.

The most obvious was the attempt to use education as a means of founding a new polity, or a new society in which the powers of government and limitations on such powers were seen as the predominant issues. This meant that the national community was perceived as a body of citizens possessing certain rights, at first under a constitutional monarchy, then after September 1792 as citizens of a republic. It meant also that education must refer not only to the formative years of childhood and youth but also to the older generation. Schooling and adult education were part of the same problem, since the older generation had to be reeducated; hence we find that in all the planning and legislation of the Revolutionary years the arrangements for schools always went with arrangements for *fêtes*, patriotic festivals, national holidays, and public rallies and demonstrations—what seems to a modern reader incongruous or utopian was in fact a necessary and reasonable program under the circumstances. Education, which later liberals hoped might be a substitute or a preventive for revolution, was in fact part of the revolutionary process itself.

More concrete, and easy to document, is the fact that provisions for education were seen as part of the constitution. In the first Revolutionary constitution, drafted between the summer of 1789 and September 1791, and coming after the famous Declaration of the Rights of Man and the Citizen, there was a Title I listing the "fundamental provisions guaranteed by the constitution." To rehearse the list would be to summarize the Revolution itself, but on education it declared that "There shall be created and organized a system of Public Instruction, common for all citizens, and free for those subjects of knowledge that are indispensable for all men." Whether "all men" was meant to include women was a matter on which the Revolutionaries differed. Some luminaries from Mirabeau to Bonaparte, and including Brissot and Saint-Just, with echoes from Rousseau and ancient Sparta, thought that girls should be taught at home, but the more usual belief of the Revolutionaries (as of conservatives) was that girls should go to school at least at the elementary level. We note, too, that the very next clause among these fundamental provisions of 1791 called for *fêtes nationales* "to preserve the memory of the French Revolution, encourage fraternity among citizens, and attach them to the constitution, their country, and the laws."[2]

The Constituent Assembly, showing the importance it saw in education, assigned it to its committee on the constitution, which produced what is called the Talleyrand plan. The Legislative Assembly, elected in 1791 under the new constitution, immediately appointed a Committee on Public Instruction, whose most notable product was the Condorcet plan, which was never adopted, nor even discussed until after the Legislative Assembly and the first constitution had both vanished in the uprising of August 1792. The National Convention, assembling in September 1792 shortly after the dethronement of Louis XVI and charged with the task of writing a new and republican constitution, also immediately appointed a Committee on Public Instruction. In 1793 the Convention produced the document remembered as the Constitution of the Year I (promulgated but never put into effect), which affirmed in its declaration of rights: "Instruction is the need of all. Society should favor by all means in its power the progress of public reason, and make instruction available to all citizens." The discussions of education in conjunction with the constitution of the Year I are dealt with later, under "democratization."

The one Revolutionary educational plan that actually went into effect, commonly known as the Daunou plan or the law of 3 Brumaire of the Year IV (October 1795), was drafted by the same committee of the Convention (the Committee of Eleven) as drafted the constitution under which the Directory operated. This constitution of the Year III contained six articles on education, less democratic than those in the constitution of either 1791 or 1793. The extensive discussion of education in 1798, in the legislative chamber called the Council of Five Hundred, was led by a joint Commission on Public Instruction and Republican Institutions. In the "neo-Jacobin" movement of 1799 the small group of extreme democrats who led it called their secret executive a "committee on public instruction." When Bonaparte wished to justify his own program a few years later, he delivered this dictum to his council of state: "So long as one does not learn from childhood whether to be republican or monarchist, Catholic or non-religious, the State cannot form a Nation."[3] It was a sentiment that his Revolution-

[2] Texts of the constitutions can be conveniently consulted in J. Godechot, ed., *Les constitutions de la France depuis 1789* (Paris, 1970), in which the present quotations may be found on pp. 36-37, 82, and 133-34.

[3] Pelet de la Lozère, *Opinions de Napoléon . . . recueillies par un membre du Conseil d'Etat* (Paris, 1833), p. 154.

ary predecessors shared, however different the inferences that they might have in mind. Educational and constitutional matters were inseparable.

It must always be remembered also, and must arouse admiration for the quality of the debates, that they took place under bewildering conditions of distraction, interruption, postponement, and confusion with other more pressing issues. When the Talleyrand report was presented in September 1791, the Constituent Assembly was preoccupied by arguments over Louis XVI's acceptance of the constitution, disputes over the rights of citizenship for free blacks in the colonies, demands for the annexation of Avignon, which meant more trouble with the Pope, and the knowledge that its own powers would soon expire. It therefore suspended debate and postponed the question to the incoming "first legislature." Condorcet presented the plan drafted for this legislature in April 1792, on the very day of the declaration of war on Austria. When the Convention began discussion of the plan in December 1792, it was entangled by arguments over temporary military successes in Belgium and the trial of the king for betrayal of the country in time of war. When it returned to the subject in the summer of 1793, it was shaken by recent insurrection and the mounting disturbance among the working classes. When it enacted the law of Brumaire of the Year IV, in 1795, it had just escaped the threat of royalist revolt in the Vendémiaire uprising and knew that it would give way to the régime of the Directory on the very next day. At no time was there any calm or sustained concentration on purely educational questions.

A suppressed kind of politics, no doubt, had been at work under the Old Regime, as in the attempts to eliminate Jansenism from the colleges, or the maneuvers leading to the expulsion of the Jesuits, or the efforts, often behind the scenes, to strengthen or to weaken the impact of the royal edict of February 1763. What made for politicization in and after 1789 was the outburst of open discussion and acknowledged quarrels. Secrecy, discretion, deference, and private communication had formerly characterized government business. Now affairs of state suddenly became public. Everywhere there were persons who wished to act as citizens and patriots, be accepted as spokesmen for the national will, engage in controversy, make proposals, go to meetings, and make speeches. Education like everything else was caught up in a new political ethos.

The periodical press before 1789, so far as it was legal, had been restricted in the number and quality of its organs and generally bland in content. Beginning in 1789 hundreds of new *journaux* were launched. These "journals" were part newspaper, part propaganda, and part polemics. They appeared daily, weekly, or irregularly; some were ephemeral, several lasted for years, some had few readers, others 10,000-20,000. Given the technology of the day, and the small investment required, a quite ordinary person could edit a journal or find a publisher for a book or pamphlet. As the Revolution progressed, the government itself subsidized some such journals, not as official publications but by subscribing to multiple copies for circulation among its own employees and in the army. The dignified *Moniteur universel*, one of the first great European dailies, limited itself to dispatches from abroad and to reporting debates in the assemblies and eventually those in the Paris Jacobin club. That the Constituent, Legislative, Convention, and legislative councils under the Directory all admitted reporters to their halls was itself "revolutionary" in eighteenth-century Europe. Most journals, however, were less devoted to news than to editorial opinion, didactic essays, denunciation, name-calling, exposure of conspiracies, and the vice of "calumny" or slander of which they were accused by their adversaries and were in fact sometimes guilty.

Partisanship was intense, both in the press and in the legislative halls. It was evident in the distasteful habit of imputing the worst motives to opponents, and the best to oneself and one's friends, and in presenting all differences of opinion as conflicts between prejudice and enlightenment. It was asserted that before the Revolution the church had promoted superstition, and that kings had tried to keep their peoples in ignorance. Religious sentiment, where it resisted this or that Revolutionary development, was denounced as fanaticism. To the more conservatively minded the Revolution itself seemed fanatical, from Edmund Burke in 1790, or J. F. La Harpe's book of 1797, *Du fanatisme dans la langue révolutionnaire*, on through Taine's monumental history of the 1880s, and into the twentieth century. It is true that so long as the Revolution lasted the voices of moderation were stilled. Activists in all coups saw moderates as the friends of their enemies. Fanaticism did exist, if we mean by it an obsessive belief driven by strong emotion and a willingness to sacrifice all else to a single goal, whether to preserve or advance the Revolution or to defeat and reverse it.

But in this inflamed partisanship there were no political parties, only fluid groupings of momentarily like-minded people. Education was never a party question. Through the decade of the 1790s there was general agreement among Revolutionaries on universal elementary education, though those in power after 1795 did not think that it should be compulsory or that the central government should pay for it. There was general agreement that the universities should be suppressed and their functions taken over by separate special schools; this idea was neither revolutionary nor fanatical, for it was debated elsewhere on the

Continent, even in Germany before the German university as conceived by Wilhelm von Humboldt prevailed after 1800. There was general agreement, except for handfuls of anti-intellectuals, that the glories of French high culture should be preserved and indeed made more glorious by the Revolution. Differences on specific points were not differences between Jacobins and Feuillants (or constitutional monarchists) in 1791, nor between Girondins and Montagnards in 1793. Members of such groups might be found on any side of almost any educational question.

One result was that the discussion of education, in all the confusion, did usually revolve about real educational problems. It is not necessary to adopt the tone of some later histories, which presented these developments during the French Revolution as a kind of prologue or rehearsal for the triumphant public school systems of later times. It is enough to say that, with two exceptions, almost every kind of educational problem, including some not solved in the twentieth century, was anticipated in France in the 1790s. The two exceptions are that no one in the French Revolution supposed that universal education should go beyond the age of twelve or fourteen, or that it should be paid for with taxpayers' money, as distinct from public funds from the income of national property. Enough other questions remained—basic literacy, vocational training, sifting and selection of talents, reward of merit, scholarships, recruitment for higher learning, professional schools, the place of religion if any, cognitive versus moral values, central versus local controls, public versus private schools, monolingualism versus bilingualism, integration of ethnic groups, differentiation by social class, civic and patriotic formation, training and payment of teachers, financing by fees, government grant or endowment, and in general the hope for an improvement of humanity that underlies education even in stable times and was especially lively in the French Revolution.

PLANS AND PROJECTS

So far as the present chapter has a chronological concentration it is for the early years of the Revolution from 1789 to 1792. We shall try, as before, to deal with both ideas and actualities. We can trace ideas from the *cahiers* of 1789 through numerous unofficial publications to official plans. As for actualities, the existing schools and institutions of learning continued to operate, though under increasing difficulties. The Constituent Assembly in fact repeatedly ordered them to remain open until a new system should be adopted. In this precarious state the teachers and heads of schools had no way of anticipating the future but were well aware that almost all plans called for radical change, including the abolition of much that existed.

The *cahiers* of 1789 were in effect a gigantic survey of public opinion on the eve of the Revolution. The king, in calling for elections to the Estates-General, had requested every electoral assembly in the kingdom to prepare a statement of its *doléances*, or grievances, together with suggestions for possible reforms. There were several hundred "general" *cahiers*, drawn up by the clergy, the nobility, and the Third Estate in each principal electoral district, and over 30,000 "preliminary" *cahiers*, drawn up in the subordinate local assemblies of rural parishes, towns, and occupational groups. Such a mass of material can only be properly summarized by statistical methods, which have indeed been brought to bear on the subject, but final comprehensive results have not been reported.[4] Many historians over many years have nevertheless explored the *cahiers*, so that some fairly firm statements can be made.

On the whole, on matters of education, the *cahiers* made the same complaints as writers of the preceding years, and to go into detail would be to repeat what was said in the last chapter. It was the literate elements that had the most to say. Hardly one in a hundred of the rural parish assemblies expressed a desire for more schools.[5] At the higher level of the "general" *cahiers*, where the First, Second, and Third Estates each drafted its own statement, and where the Third Estate was represented by the educated bourgeoisie, there was no great difference between them, that is, no divergence of views between the clergy, nobility, and bourgeoisie. It may be recalled that the sons of nobles and bourgeois had often attended the same colleges, and it may be noted that before the Revolution, in contrast to what happened afterward, most priests had begun their education in these same col-

---

[4] Statistical studies of the *cahiers* have been carried on at the Ecole des hautes études en sciences sociales in Paris, and by Gilbert Shapiro of the University of Pittsburgh. The latter has developed a data bank that may be consulted by application to him and from which the following are derived: G. Shapiro, J. Markoff, and S. Weitman, "Quantitative Studies in the French Revolution," *History and Theory* 12 (1973): 163-91; and G. Shapiro and P. Dawson, "Social Mobility and Political Radicalism: The Case of the French Revolution," in *The Dimensions of Quantitative Research in History*, ed. W. Aydelotte et al. (Princeton, 1972), pp. 159-91.

[5] From the Ecole des hautes études figures as low as 0.3% and 0.1% are reported for rural areas in northern France. See D. Julia, R. Chartier, and M. M. Compère, *L'éducation en France du 16ᵉ au 18ᵉ siècle* (Paris, 1976), p. 43. A letter to me from Professor Shapiro, with enclosed tables, shows 3.6% of parish *cahiers* making mention of "public education."

leges also. There was little outspoken anticlericalism or distrust of the clergy as teachers, but it was occasionally suggested that income-producing properties of the church, beyond what was needed for a modest support of religion, might be converted to the financing of colleges and elementary schools.

In all three orders a demand for "national education" could be heard to include elementary schooling for the populace. The clergy was if anything more inclined than the nobility or Third Estate to call for such national education but less inclined to suppose that state control must follow.[6] The clergy seems to have assumed, like the memoir of the University of Poitiers written at the same time, that the Catholic church in France was as much a national institution as the government.

The colleges were blamed for spending too much time on Latin, though some knowledge of Latin was valued, and for not attending sufficiently to modern scientific and practical subjects. It was the faculties of law and medicine that received the most unfavorable comment, with demands for more strict professional training, more serious examinations, and more competent, honest, and reliable doctors and lawyers. Various *cahiers*, especially in the Third Estate, called for more equality of access to education through competitive tests or examinations instead of private patronage or official privilege. There was concern for the discovery and development of talent and for the equalization of opportunity as between town and town, or between different provinces. It has been pointed out that such demands would require a regulating bureaucracy, and that bureaucracy may result from popular wishes as much as from the ambitions of bureaucrats.[7]

[6] It is well to revive attention to the remarkable work of Beatrice Hyslop, *French Nationalism in 1789 according to the General Cahiers* (New York, 1934), written long before statistical studies became common among historians and accomplished before the era of grants, computers, and research assistants. Reading several hundred *cahiers*, she counted how many of each estate showed an emphasis on certain subjects. The following table is derived from nine of the 49 tables in her book. It shows, by number of *cahiers*, how each estate urged action on a category as she defined and interpreted it.

Educational Demand	Clergy	Nobility	Bourgeoisie	Total
"some measure of national education"	41	31	35	107
"*étatisme* in education"	24	40	70	134

[7] J. Markoff, "Governmental Bureaucratization: General Processes and an Anomalous Case," *Comparative Studies in Society and History* 17 (1975): 479-509, is a sociological study using the *cahiers* to show that bureaucracy may arise, not only from forces within

In any case, as events became more clearly revolutionary in the summer of 1789, the *cahiers* drafted in the preceeding April lost their importance. Our attention shifts to books and other materials published for general circulation. One convenient list of such items, recording them by year, reveals a significant change during the course of the Revolution.[8] From 1789 through 1791 almost all items on this list were books or tracts written by private persons outside the Constituent Assembly. The number fell off in 1792. In 1793 and 1794 almost all items (over a hundred) were the separate printings of speeches and reports in the National Convention. That is to say, so far as published discussion is concerned, the public was offering its advice to the assembly in 1789–1791, but in 1793-1794 the published discussion was more nearly monopolized by the assembly itself, or by what had become the Revolutionary establishment. This is not to say that the quality of the discussion in the latter years was inferior.

To the statement that the writings of 1789-1791 came from persons outside the Assembly there is one notable exception—no less a person than Mirabeau.[9] Known as a moderate in the terms of 1790, working to resist the drift to the left and to set up a strong constitutional monarchy, he nevertheless prepared some radical advice for the Assembly on education. The Assembly must realize that "if all was to be reconstructed, all must be demolished." It should not go into detail but "only concern itself with education to the extent of removing it from powers and bodies that might deprave its influence." The reference apparently was to the religious teaching orders and to private schools that might harbor royalist sentiments. In any case "the colleges and academies should be subject only to magistrates that are truly representative of the people, that is, elected and frequently renewed by them," and specifically to the authorities of the 83 new departments into which France was now subdivided. In *l'éducation gratuite*, or free instruction, Mirabeau saw one of the abuses of the Old Regime. It was an error to regard "free and public instruction as one of the great-

---

the government or bureaucracy but also from people outside the government desiring more equity in recruitment, examinations, promotions, and so forth.

[8] F. Buisson, *Dictionnaire de pédagogie et d'instruction primaire, première partie* (Paris, 1882), 1: 201-207.

[9] Mirabeau, *Travail sur l'éducation publique trouvé dans les papiers de Mirabeau l'aîné, publié par P.J.G. Cabanis, docteur en médecine* (Paris, 1791), pp. 5-73; see also M. Staum, *Cabanis: Enlightment and Medical Philosophy in the French Revolution* (Princeton, 1980), pp. 125-30. These views of Mirabeau—as of Talleyrand, Condorcet, Lanthenas, Romme, Le Peletier, Fourcroy, Calès, Lakanal, and Daunou—may be found in C. Hippeau, *L'Instruction publique en France pendant la Révolution* (Paris 1881). Note, however, that Hippeau did not include the *projets de loi* that accompanied several of these *rapports*.

est benefactions of kings," but an error that might have to be tolerated, provided that teachers should not be independent enough to oppose "national views." Boys should be educated for public affairs while also learning both Greek and Latin. Girls, with their more delicate nature, and destined only for private life, needed no schools beyond those for elementary reading, writing, and arithmetic. There should be an organized teaching body, national festivals, and one great central institution of higher learning.

These ideas of Mirabeau were found in his papers after his premature death in April 1791, apparently as notes for a speech to be made in the Assembly. They were published by his assistant, Cabanis, the future Idéologue, a few months later. Probably Cabanis added a few thoughts of his own. These reconstructed writings of Mirabeau had no particular influence at the time, nor did they express anything very unusual, but they were remembered a century later as one of the more puzzling texts left by the great ancestors of the Revolution.

It is more interesting to dip into the ideas of less famous persons. About 60 published efforts are known for the years 1789, 1790, and 1791, and handwritten contributions addressed to the committee on the constitution now repose in the archives.[10] What follows is a sampling of 16 of these works, numbered in parentheses in the notes. Two took up the special subject of the education of girls, which some of the others dealt with more incidentally.[11] Two were by lawyers, Raymond de Varennes of Angers and P. L. Lacretelle of Nancy and Paris. Lacretelle, who had *philosophe* friends, offers a painful example of the wordy abstraction for which the Revolution has been excessively blamed. He begins by asking what national education means. "After going back to the eternal nature of things to recompose our social organization [i.e. the constitution of 1789-1791] we must exhaust all the resources of reason to refashion men in that purified and perfected state to which

[10] Archives Nationales, F[17] 1310, dossiers 6-10. A. G. Camus, a member of the Constituent Assembly, who became the first director of the National Archives, wrote a summary in 1792 of the work of the Constituent in education, with a list (incomplete) of books and tracts submitted to it. Camus's summary is printed by J. Guillaume, *Procès-verbaux du Comité de l'Instruction publique de l'Assemblée législative* (Paris, 1889), pp. iv-xvii.

[11] (1) *Mémoire sur l'éducation des filles par M. Bachelier, de l'Académie de peinture* (Paris, 1789). The author had been the founder of the royal free school of drawing at Paris in the 1760s, mentioned on p. 29 above. (2) *Annales de l'éducation du sexe, ou Journal des Demoiselles, par Mme Mouret, descendante de La Fontaine, et auteur du Plan d'Éducation pour le Sexe présenté à l'Assemblée Nationale*, (Paris, 1790). Mme Mouret's *Annales* seems not to have lasted beyond the first number. The full titles given here for these and the following works convey something of their flavor.

nature leads them, but from which ingrained habits keep them away. That is what everyone understands, and everyone wants, in demanding national education."[12]

The remaining dozen of our authors were less vague, and were in fact all teachers by profession. Four were at the University of Paris: Jean-François Champagne, whose remarkable career in education lasted until his retirement in 1810; Yves-Marie Audrein, who gave up teaching, was elected to the Convention, and became a constitutional bishop in Brittany, where he was murdered by counterrevolutionaries in 1800; and two men of whom nothing is known but their surnames, La Cour and Degranthe.[13] Five were professors at colleges in the provinces. Two of these were Oratorians: Joseph Villier of Angers, and P.F.C. Daunou, who had taught in the colleges at Troyes and Soissons and for whom the Revolution was to open up a notable career.[14] The other three provincial professors were a certain J. F. Major of Bar-le-Duc, J. Courdin of Montpellier, and an Abbé Auger, who had taught at Rouen and collaborated in his tract of 1791 with an Oratorian, a Paris professor, and "other persons."[15] The remaining three of our peda-

[12] (3) Raymond de Varennes, *Idées patriotiques sur la méthode et l'importance d'une éducation nationale, pour assurer la régéneration de la France* (Paris and Angers, 1790). On Raymond see B. Bois, *La vie scolaire et les créations intellectuelles en Anjou pendant la Révolution, 1789-1799* (Paris, 1929), pp. 136, 144-47. (4) P. L. Lacretelle, *De l'établissement des connaissances humaines et de l'instruction publique dans la constitution française* (Paris, 1791), p. 2.

[13] (5) Champagne, professor at the College of Louis-le-Grand, in conjunction with two other professors in the Paris colleges, the brothers Guéroult, prepared a plan that is now in the Archives Nationales F[17] 1067, no. 1223, and is translated in my *School of the French Revolution* (Princeton, 1975), pp. 237-59. This plan was presented to the Constituent Assembly, and in its provision for redistribution of scholarship funds it was amplified by a document apparently in the files of the Committee on the Constitution, which in turn seems to have influenced the wording of the Talleyrand report. This intermediate document is an anonymous "Observations sur les fondations existantes à Paris pour l'éducation publique," in Archives Nationales, F[17] 1317[B] dossier 1. (6) *Mémoire sur l'éducation nationale française par Y. M. Audrein, vice-gérant du Collège des Grassins, presenté à l'Assemblée Nationale le 11 décembre 1790* (Paris, 1791). (7) *Ecoles nationales propres à former des hommes, des citoyens et des Français, par M. de La Cour* (Paris, 1790). (8) *Projet d'un plan d'éducation nationale suivant la nouvelle division du royaume en 75 ou 85 départements, par M. Degranthe, au Collège de Louis-le-Grand* (Paris, 1789).

[14] (9) J. Villier, *Nouveau plan d'éducation et d'instruction publique dédié à l'Assemblée Nationale, dans lequel on substitue aux Universités, Séminaires et Collèges des institutions plus raisonnables . . . propres à former des Négociants instruits, des bons marins, des militaires, des ecclésiastiques respectables, des magistrats éclairés, etc.* (Angers and Paris, 1790), and see Bois, *La vie scolaire*, pp. 136-42. (10) [Daunou] *Plan d'éducation présenté à l'Assemblée Nationale au nom des instituteurs publics de l'Oratoire* (Paris, 1790).

[15] (11) *Tableau d'un collège en activité par M.J.F. Major, professeur au Collège de Bar-le-*

gogues were private teachers: someone known only as "Arnauld, *instituteur*," a certain Fontaine de Fréville, and L.J.J.L. Bourdon de la Crosnière, who after 1792 called himself plain Léonard Bourdon and became one of the extremists that Robespierre branded as "ultra."[16]

One is impressed by the thoughtfulness and the careful detail to be found in these writings and by their ambitious scope. The authors share in the euphoria of the first years of the Revolution. They seem to imagine themselves as legislators, and several conclude their exposition with a *projet de loi*, or parliamentary bill, summarizing their proposals under successive titles and articles, as if for enactment by the Assembly. Almost all assume the need for a single total plan, in which everything should be properly interrelated to produce a uniform system throughout the country. In this they carry out the implications of the educational writers of the 1760s, the royal edict of February 1763, the report of Rolland d'Erceville to the Parlement of Paris, the views expressed in the Assembly of the Clergy of 1780, and the memoir of the University of Poitiers in April 1789. They offer a grand design in which educational and learned institutions of all kinds are arranged at three, four, or five levels (varying from one writer to another) rising from elementary local schools to a great scientific center at the top.

All believe that education should be "national," in the new Revolutionary sense of being subject to the national sovereignty, but without necessarily implying centralized control, since the new departments and local governments are assumed to represent the national will of a free people as well as the authorities in the capital. The Assembly in 1790 and 1791 was busily reshaping the diversity of the Old Regime into a hierarchy of communes, cantons, districts, and 83 departments, and rearranging all public bodies (electoral assemblies, law courts, tax-collecting agencies, and the church under the Civil

---

Duc, suivant son projet sur l'instruction publique adressé le 15 octobre au Comité de Constitution, Bar-le-Duc (1790). (12) *Observations philosophiques sur la réforme de l'éducation publique dédiée à MM les Administrateurs du Département de l'Hérault par J. Courdin, professeur de physique à Montpellier* (Montpellier, 1792). (13) *Organisation des écoles nationales rédigée par M. l'Abbé Auger, de l'Académie des Inscriptions et Belles-lettres, d'après des conférences tenues chez M. Gossin, député de Bar-le-Duc, avec M. Paris de l'Oratoire, M. Cérisier, professeur émérite de l'Université de Paris, et d'autres personnes* (Paris, 1791).

[16] (14) *Education. Plan proposé aux représentants de la Nation par M. Arnauld, instituteur,* (n.p., n.d. [1790]). (15) *Essai ou projet d'éducation nationale pour les hommes, par M. Fontaine de Fréville, chef d'une maison d'éducation, président du Comité de la Section du Roule . . . caporal-volontaire de l'armée parisienne* (Paris, 1791). (16) L.J.J.L. Bourdon de la Crosnière, *Mémoire sur l'instruction et sur l'éducation nationale. Avec un projet de décret et règlement constitutionnel pour les jeunes gens . . . suivi d'un essai sur l'éducation des héritiers presumptifs de la couronne* (Paris, l'an second de la liberté, 1790).

Constitution of the Clergy) in such a way that their operating units coincided with the boundaries of these local administrations. Our writers call for the same rearrangement in education. As each canton was to have its justice of the peace, and each department its bishop, so there would be echelons of schools, from communal establishments teaching reading and writing, through cantonal, district, and departmental schools up to the highest in Paris.

Most of our dozen professorial writers and the two lawyers, speak only of "regeneration," but some call for outright abolition. "All universities, colleges, boarding schools, and houses of public instruction," says the Abbé Audrein of the University of Paris, "are and will be suppressed."[17] Neither Audrein nor anyone else meant literal abolition; they assumed that the same buildings would be used and many of the same teachers would remain, redirected and reeducated to act in the service of the nation. On the existing college endowments, all deplore that some colleges should be rich and others poor, but they differ in their suggestions for corrective action. Two or three seem to favor the sale of such properties, with the suggestion that colleges should be supported by fees or from public funds; but most would prefer to confiscate and pool the endowments while reserving them for education, equalizing them among colleges, and in some cases turning them over to the departments to determine the use of the income. Most take up the related question of *bourses* or scholarships. They generally hold that, at least above the elementary level, families able to do so should pay fees, but that scholarships should also be provided, equalized in amount and in geographical distribution, and awarded competitively for scholastic achievement and promise. One suggests honorary scholarships for well-to-do boys able to pay.

Our writers seem to have in mind what would be called the comprehensive school in the twentieth century, that is, the principle that children of all social classes should receive their earliest schooling in the same schools. They refer to it as *éducation commune*, which was to take on a different meaning in the more radical phase of the Revolution. As the Abbé Auger put it, rich and poor should be "mixed together so as to learn very early that virtues and talents make the only real difference among men" so that "citizens of all classes should be obliged to send their children to the national elementary schools."[18] Bourdon de la Crosnière would "bring together in common the children of all citizens without exception, for them to have their appren-

[17] Audrein, (6), p. 91.
[18] Auger, (13), p. 11.

ticeship to life together, at the expense of the Nation."[19] Or J. F. Major of Bar-le-Duc: "It will perhaps be said that the former nobility will not send their children to the national colleges." Let the very rich, then, keep their private tutors. For ordinary nobility the law should forbid private schools. In the national schools noble young men would be "enlightened"; they would in fact "stamp their unfortunate prejudices underfoot and become the most zealous defenders of the Constitution."[20] This was surely optimistic, but we may recall somewhat similar hopes under the Old Regime and observe that compulsory democratic education was not invented by the *sans-culottes* of 1793. Yet our writers are not extreme equalitarians. They want equality of opportunity, not of results. They would have a strict sifting at ages variously given as from twelve to fifteen so that exceptional talents may be trained for the benefit of society. Dumouchel, the rector of the University of Paris, in officially representing the University before the Assembly in January 1791, observed that the Revolution was already using "the very inequality of virtues, talents and services to uphold civil and legal equality."[21]

While urging a national plan, some of our authors explicitly warn against monopoly and regimentation. La Cour proposes two colleges in each town so that they may compete with each other. Degranthe suggests that half the teachers in the whole country be formed into an organized body and the other half be left as private individuals so that parents may have a choice. Daunou, speaking for the Oratorians, made a similar suggestion: each local government should decide whether it wished to assign its elementary school or college to individual teachers or to a "teaching society." Almost all the writers favor some degree of religion in the curriculum. Several take issue with Rousseau for his low opinion of the education of girls. According to Audrein, most girls could indeed look forward only to domestic cares and labor on the farm, but others would "be obliged to take more part in the life of society," and for these the Nation should provide education "on the same foundation as for boys and men."[22] None, however, favored the schooling of boys and girls together beyond early childhood.

A further catalogue of miscellaneous proposals, made by one writer or another, could readily be drawn up. Schools should move from the crowded town centers into the suburbs or open country. There was

---

[19] Bourdon, (16), p. 122. See also F. Stübig, *Erziehung zur Gleichheit: Konzepte der "éducation commune" in der französischen Revolution* (Ravensburg, 1974), p. 457.

[20] Major, (11), p. 19.

[21] *Archives parlementaires*, 1st ser., 22: 92.

[22] Audrein, (6), pp. 6-7.

no reason why the Paris colleges should be confined to the old and decaying Latin Quarter. There should be more physical education. Boys should learn how to bear arms and defend their country. Men who had not attended national schools should never be entitled to public office. There should be more teaching of modern languages, agriculture, and commercial subjects. All students in a school should be treated alike; to have private apartments or private arrangements is "for the discipline of the college what public prostitution is for the morals of the capital."[23] Schools should be small models of free and democratic government; students should live under rules that they have themselves made or consented to and serve on committees for the maintenance of discipline. Old practices were bad. Yet some old practices were good. We find mention of the *agrégation* of 1766 as a model for teacher training and praise for the *concours général*, with its annual prize-giving ceremony, as an incentive to "emulation."

It is against this background of vigorous discussion that the Talleyrand report and later official pronouncements can best be seen. It is well to remember that most of what was said by politicians during the Revolution had already been said by professors in the institutions that were to be reformed.

THE TALLEYRAND REPORT AND ITS CRITICS

Tallyrand, reporting for the committee on the constitution, read its proposal to the Constituent Assembly on September 10 and 11, 1791.[24] In view of his later eminence in very different activities, and doubts concerning his actual principles, it is of interest to ask to what extent he was the real author, or whether he spoke for some kind of subcom-

---

[23] Ibid., p. 39.

[24] The report was followed by a *projet de loi*, or bill, submitted to the Assembly on September 25, and both were published in the *Moniteur* at the time and may be found in the *Archives parlementaires*. The *rapport* and *projet* came out as a book in 216 pages, plus tables, published late in 1791, of which one of two copublishers was Dupont de Nemours. This raises the question of whether Talleyrand may not have consulted with Dupont in preparing the report, since Dupont was a member of the Constituent Assembly and had involved himself in educational questions with Turgot in 1775, in Poland in the 1780s, and in the drafting of several *cahiers* in 1789. Marc Bouloiseau, however, after working on Dupont papers both in France and at the Eleutherian Mills Historical Library in Pennsylvania, found no evidence of such consultation. On the authorship see A. Aulard's article, "Talleyrand," in *Nouveau dictionnaire de pédagogie et de l'instruction publique*, ed. F. E. Buisson (Paris, 1911), p. 1956. It is strange that the Talleyrand report seems never to have been translated completely into English.

mittee. There is no evidence of the existence of any such subcommittee, although we may suppose that he discussed the matter with various colleagues in the Assembly. Talleyrand claimed the authorship for himself in 1795, when, hoping to return from the emigration, he wished to show that he had been a good patriot in the style of 1791. No one else ever claimed to have written it. He himself had real qualifications, having conducted the inquiry on education for the Assembly of the Clergy a decade before. In his memoirs written 40 years later he said that he had used materials submitted by Lavoisier, Laplace, Condorcet, and other luminaries, but the report makes no mention of them nor of the writings by lesser persons, such as those surveyed above, except for one on girls' education by a Mme Guyard. In any case the merit of the report lies not in its originality but in the sophistication and amplitude with which it expresses much prevailing opinion. One concludes, with Talleyrand's biographers, that there is no reason to deny him the credit for what is a great document in the history of education.

The report begins with a Revolutionary flourish, noting the "barbarism," "nullity," and "innumerable vices of what has hitherto been called instruction," and declaring education to be essential for the maintenance of the new constitution and of liberty and equality. It was necessary to liberty because unlettered persons would always be vulnerable to charlatans and impostors or dependent on a learned elite. It was necessary to the equality recognized by the constitution because "this equality of rights would have little reality, or be little felt, given so many inequalities of fact, if education did not constantly attempt to restore the level, and at least weaken the harmful inequalities that it cannot destroy."[25] A total reconstruction was urgent because schools were collapsing in the political turmoil of the moment. It was also feasible because "one of the most striking characteristics of man is his capacity for improvement, and this characteristic, observable in the individual, is even more so in the species."[26]

Society, said Talleyrand, is a "vast workshop." "It is not enough that all should work in it; each must be in his place."[27] Education was a chief means for preparing all persons for their most useful roles. The greatest of all "economies" was the *économie des hommes*, that is, manpower planning. Five principles followed. There must be some education for everybody. There must be no privileged educational estab-

---

[25] *Rapport* (Paris, 1791), p. 4.

[26] Ibid., p. 7. "Capacity for improvement" is here a translation for *perfectibilité*, which seems to have a less visionary connotation than the English "perfectibility."

[27] Ibid.

lishment; any proper person must be free to open a school. Education must be universal in the sense that all subjects must be taught somewhere. It should be for both sexes. It should also exist for all ages, not merely for youth.

The educational system, even in its most recondite parts, said Talleyrand, was meant to serve society as a whole. It did not follow that society owed the same kind or amount of education to everybody. What did follow was that society owed to "talent" the means for its development. Since young talent would in the future become a benefit to all members of society, society should encourge it by removing difficulties in its way. This meant that, with careful selection at each level to distinguish true talent from vague or mistaken ambitions, society should provide financial aid, as necessary, to smooth the passage from the most elementary to the most advanced and most specialized institutions. The criteria in this selection should not be single examinations or essays, which were subject to much uncertainty, but the reports of teachers on the student's performance for at least an entire year.

The plan set forth four different levels, corresponding to the levels of government. For the lowest it introduced the term *primaire*, which in subsequent Revolutionary usage always referred not to any elementary school but only to an elementary school conducted by the state. Boys and girls would be admitted together to the same schools at the age of seven. At this level instruction would be free, but it would not be compulsory, since the family itself might carry on simple teaching. The primary schools would offer instruction in what was "necessary for everybody to know": reading and writing in the national language, simple computation, land measurement, local geography, elements of morality and religion, and principles of the constitution, along with some physical exercise.

Next came the "district" schools, so named because there would be one in each of the districts, usually about half a dozen in number, into which each department was divided. Boys might enter these schools as young as nine years of age and remain until about sixteen. The district schools would in effect be the regenerated colleges of the Old Regime and would serve the same purpose, to produce the educated class of French society. They would teach the art of reasoning, mathematics, physics and chemistry, languages, history, literature, and moral philosophy. Each school would have 10 professors, with each professor somewhat specialized in his subject. Instruction would be by "course" rather than by "class." That is (in contrast to the usual pre-Revolutionary situation), each professor would teach his own subject to pupils coming to him for that purpose, instead of teaching all subjects to all pupils in an annual class. This substitution of courses for classes was considered an important reform and was put into practice in the Central Schools after 1795.

The French, during their Revolution, unlike later revolutionaries in other places, were not conscious of a pressing need for modernization in the sense of catching up with a more advanced or more civilized country. The Talleyrand report expressed no demand for a larger educated class than already existed. Nor did it offer quantitative estimates of the number of students to be expected at the several levels. It assumed that the great majority of children needed only primary schooling, after which the girls would acquire the household arts at home, the boys learn skilled trades, or both begin to help with agricultural labors. It would be "a real madness, or a cruel kindness, to make them all go through the several levels of an instruction that would be useless and hence harmful to most."[28] Since the district and higher schools were intended for a minority they should charge a fee. Those who attended them expected their education to lead to lucrative careers. It would be wrong, according to Talleyrand, for society—that is, the taxpayers, most of whom were of very limited incomes—"to give for nothing the means of entering occupations which so far as successful would be very rewarding for those who embraced them."[29] Free instruction above the primary level would therefore be limited to those talented but impoverished youths who received scholarships.

In a kind of appendix Talleyrand indicated what should happen to girls of the age at which some of the boys went to the district schools. He had said that education should be available for both sexes and was aware of a problem. "That half the human race should be excluded by the other half from all participation in government, that they should be natives in fact but foreign by law to the soil where they were born, that they should be owners of property but without influence or representation, are political phenomena which in abstract principle seem impossible to explain."[30] He nevertheless offered explanations. The public good and the general happiness, he said, as well as the rule that all persons should occupy their most useful places in the great social workshop, required that women superintend private life and enjoy the

[28] Ibid., p. 16. And see above, p. 20.

[29] *Ibid.*, p. 22. Pages 18-24 are devoted to the question of *gratuité de l'instruction*, on which Talleyrand remarks that "the best minds are divided." Pages 84-88 take up *bourses* for the talented poor.

[30] Ibid., p. 118.

advantage of removal from "the tumult of affairs." Not everything needed to be learned in school, and what a girl needed to know, after a short primary schooling, could best be learned at home from an attentive father and mother. Nevertheless, for unusual cases, or for girls without family support, each department should maintain a certain number of schools to replace those hitherto conducted by religious sisters. He was thinking not of the middle or upper classes but of orphans and girls who might expect to remain unmarried or to labor along with a future husband, for these schools would give instruction to girls "in the useful arts, and provide them with the means of an independent subsistence by the product of their work."[31]

Above the district level were to be schools called "departmental," somewhat inaccurately, since not all departments were to have them. They were designed to prepare for the learned professions, in which the Talleyrand plan surprisingly included only the three traditional professions of theology, law, and medicine while adding military science. These schools in effect replaced the three higher faculties of the old universities. The universities themselves simply disappear in the plan, where the word "university" never occurs, and the departmental schools are conceived of as separate and unrelated institutions, each devoted to hardly more than vocational training. The schools of religion are to teach practical theology, preaching, and pastoral duties. For those of medicine the chief innovations are to require teaching in the French language and to combine medicine, surgery, and pharmacy. For those of law it is said that mystery is removed from the law by the new constitution and the prospect of codification. For both law and medicine it is prescribed that qualification should depend on strict examinations, not on the number of years of study, and no academic degrees are awarded, since what the public wants in these professions is not a "gild" but a certification of knowledge. The military schools, besides the obvious subjects, will teach the principles of the constitution and the rights and duties of man so as to produce a citizen army. For these four kinds of professional schools it would clearly be absurd to have one in each department. To have them of adequate strength and size it would be enough to have six military schools, 10 law schools, and four principal medical schools, with departments allowed, if they wished, to provide for subsidiary medical training, including obstetrics, in connection with their best local hospitals. In this arrangement there was no great difference from the Old Regime.

At the apex Talleyrand placed a National Institute, to be located in

---

[31] Ibid., p. 122.

Paris, where all the sciences, arts, and literary studies would be pursued at their highest reaches by the most learned men in France. Unlike the Institute established in 1795, which became permanent, Talleyrand's Institute was to be engaged in teaching as well as research. It would train young men for scholarship and the sciences and would also develop new knowledge, with professors chosen for their fame or achievements, not for their skill in explaining what was already known. In reality, the Institute would be a reorganization of what already existed. The plan called for the abolition of all academies (French Academy, Academy of Sciences, Academies of Painting, of Music, of Inscriptions and Belles-Lettres, etc.), the suppression of chairs at the College of France and the Jardin du Roi, and the merger of all these bodies—along with the Bibliothèque Nationale and societies concerned with engineering and agriculture, with their funds, facilities, and personnel—into the new National Institute. It would cost no more, said Talleyrand, than was already being spent.

The Constituent Assembly, as already noted, took no action on its committee's report, except to recommend it for consideration by the incoming Legislative Body. The plan received a mixed reception in the press. The militantly counterrevolutionary *Ami du roi* dismissed it with contempt.[32] The moderate *Ami des patriotes* (moderation meant calling for "order" in September 1791, while accepting the Revolution hitherto) lavished high praise on the Talleyrand plan, which, it observed with satisfaction, would educate for productive work rather than for mere social position and accept the inequality of talents as a good thing for the general benefit of society.[33] The Left was divided. Brissot, an advanced Jacobin in 1791, in his *Patriote français*, echoed by Camille Desmoulins in the *Révolutions de France et de Brabant*, expressed cautious approval while both claimed that Talleyrand had obtained his best ideas from their friend, Bourdon de la Crosnière.[34] Brissot, however, rejected the whole idea of schools for girls, who he thought could be quite adequately instructed by their mothers, while Desmoulins insisted on the need for girls' schools but deplored Talleyrand's demand for religious instruction, which Talleyrand explicitly desired to be Catholic, so that, said Desmoulins, "a Protestant, Jewish or Mohammedan father" could never send his child to such a school.

---

[32] *L'Ami du roi*, September 13, 1791, pp. 2-3.

[33] *L'Ami des patriotes, ou le défenseur de la constitution*, no. 48 (1791), pp. 499-516.

[34] *Patriote français*, September 11, 12, 14, 26, and 27, 1791, pp. 312-14, 323-24, 370-75, and *Révolutions de France et de Brabant*, no. 93 (1791), pp. 1-21 and no. 95, p. 29. The *Courier de Provence*, no. 342 (1791), pp. 105-108, echoed Brissot in objecting to girls' schools.

Only a pure and agreed upon morality should be taught in public institutions, since "all religions are the work of imposture, crime and ambition."

The extreme Left was even more negative. Marat's *Ami du peuple* made no mention of the plan at all, being more concerned in September 1791 with plots and conspiracies and insisting that the whole new constitution should be junked. Hébert ignored it in his *Père Duchesne*. Prudhomme's *Révolutions de Paris* echoed the denunciations of the rightist *Ami du roi*.[35] In a medley of radical affirmations it declared that education would never remove inequalities, that the poor needed jobs not schools, that poor children were obliged to work in the fields and could learn what they needed at home during the long winter evenings, that morality could be learned from nature (supplemented by the gospels) and philosophy from a simple book like Descartes's *Discourse on Method*, that there was no need for lawyers or law schools nor for medical schools because hospitals were sufficient, that if girls should go to school the convents were good enough (this was sarcasm), and that the great fault of the plan was that four-fifths of the French people had nothing to gain from it—that it was, as a later generation would say, "elitist."

Much of this journalistic comment was "political" and would be heard again with respect to the later plans of Condorcet and others. Other criticisms were less ideologically motivated. A group of elementary teachers published a tract in which they argued that Talleyrand's provision for primary schools was wholly inadequate.[36] By his own reckoning, they said, each teacher in Paris would have 1,200 pupils. At the level of higher education the plan was seriously questioned by professors at the University of Strasbourg, who commissioned one of their colleagues, Isaac Haffner, to write a book stating their views.[37] Strasbourg, though in France, was a university on the German model. Haffner criticized the Talleyrand plan by comparing its provisions, at the level of the departmental schools and the National Institute, with the German university as it had developed since the founding of Göttingen half a century before. He had studied at Göttingen and Leipzig and knew the German system well.

---

[35] Prudhomme, *Révolutions de Paris*, September 10-17, 1791, pp. 465-76.

[36] *Observations sur le rapport que M. de Talleyrand-Périgard, ancien évêque d'Autun, a fait à l'Assemblée Nationale . . . suivies d'un plan d'instruction primaire, nationale, par les maîtres de pension de Paris* n.p., 1791). Fourteen persons signed as collective authors.

[37] I. Haffner, *De l'éducation littéraire, ou essai sur l'organisation des hautes sciences* (Strasbourg, 1792). And see Guillaume, *Procès-verbaux . . . Assemblée legislative*, pp. 184-85.

Haffner expressed concern that the University of Strasbourg would lose its identity in the general movement of national homogenization. He pointed out that the Talleyrand plan made no provision for higher scientific or learned studies except at the Institute in Paris, and that it dispersed the professional schools into separate establishments, essentially trade schools, distant from one another and from the center of true scientific inquiry. In short, it annihilated the universities. In Germany, he explained, and in particular at Strasbourg and indeed at any good university, all the arts and sciences and professional subjects were brought together in one place, where they mutually stimulated each other, with medical students and professors able to learn from biologists and those in law from historians. In France, said Haffner, the title of "professor" was used even by dancing masters. In Germany a professor was a learned man, respected for the profundity of his knowledge and concern for adult students. He was chosen by his colleagues for known achievements, usually by promotion from junior ranks, and not by some kind of public and theatrical competition; and he enjoyed life tenure, which, while subject to obvious mistakes, was needed to attract and hold able men. The students at German universities were not treated as minors. They were free to choose the professor with whom they wished to study and to move from one university to another as they wished. Haffner objected also to Talleyrand's plan for the award of scholarships at the highest level, that is, the removal of scholarship funds from the control of existing towns and universities, and their conversion into a nationalized program of student aid in which talented youth would be brought only to Paris. The provinces would become sterile, he prophesied, and young men interested in scientific and scholarly work would have less opportunity than before. As a Protestant at a Protestant university, Haffner was ready to admit that the Catholic universities of "the interior of France" might require reform. Let them be reformed, he said, not destroyed. And let the University of Strasbourg remain as it was.

Haffner's book remained unnoticed, although 50 copies were sent to the Committee on Public Instruction of the Legislative Assembly. It anticipated the criticisms that the French themselves made a century later, when the German university had become the cynosure of the learned world and the French were again trying to reform their arrangements for higher education. The Talleyrand report, seemingly stillborn, was in fact the embryo from which the post-Revolutionary educational system of France was to develop.

CHAPTER 3

DISCORD AND DISARRAY

As proposals were offered on all sides for a better educational system, the existing system began to go to pieces. The Revolution politicized education in actuality as well as in planning, in daily operations as well as in ultimate goals. Many teachers and students were strong adherents of the new ideas, but others were not, so that the polarization of the country was reflected internally within the walls of every establishment.

Edmund Burke's assertion, made in 1791, that the French Assembly meant to reform education along the lines of Rousseau, that "insane Socrates" and "professor of vanity," was of course absurdly incorrect.[38] But the educational world was agitated and in the end transformed by two of the most fundamental steps taken by the Assembly. Both of these affected the church. As early as November 1789 the Constituent Assembly, with Talleyrand as its chief spokesman, declared all property of the church to be "at the disposal of the Nation," that is, sequestered or nationalized. The intention was to raise funds to pay off the debt under which the monarchy had collapsed. The result was a massive transfer of property from institutional to private hands, since the former church properties were sold to individual buyers over a period of years. Land and buildings constituting college endowments, though at first excepted, were eventually included in these sales. Hence the colleges lost their endowments. In July 1790 the Assembly enacted the Civil Constitution of the Clergy, which was not meant at first to be antireligious but only to reorganize the Catholic Church in France as a kind of moral auxiliary of the newly designed constitutional order. It provided, for example, that each new administrative *département* should have its bishop, and that parish priests should be elected by the same voters as elected other local officials, with all clergy to be salaried by the state. Many of the clergy at first accepted this Civil Constitution, seeing it as a natural adaptation of the Gallican tradition to the principles of the Revolution. But the pope rejected it, as did almost all the French bishops and many of the more devout laity, who therefore came to oppose the Revolution itself.

Faced with subversion, the Assembly required an oath of all clergy, including those who were teachers. The impact on the schools was devastating and became more so as the probability of war rose during

[38] *Works of Edmund Burke*, 9. vols. (Boston, 1839), 3:306-307. This is Burke's "Letter to a member of the National Assembly," dated at Beaconsfield, January 1791, long before the Talleyrand report on education.

the winter of 1791-1792, when it seemed that the Austrians and the French émigrés, with the secret support of Louis XVI, would invade France, overthrow the new government, punish those involved in the Revolution, and restore the Old Regime. Local governments and Jacobin clubs conducted purges of their colleges as of other bodies. Under such pressures some teachers took the oath, some refused it, some took it with reservations, some took it and recanted, and some abandoned their clerical orders, proclaimed themselves good patriots, became laymen, and in some cases married. These last, called apostates then and later, were often reputable men. The case of J. B. Dumouchel may be cited. A man of fifty, a priest, a professor at the University of Paris and its last rector, a deputy of the clergy to the Estates-General and one of the clerics who first joined with the Third Estate in June 1789, in short a committed revolutionary, he took the oath to the Civil Constitution but gave up teaching and became constitutional bishop of the Gard; he then abdicated his holy orders, married, taught in the Central Schools, and ended his career as head of the bureau of public instruction in Napoleon's ministry of the interior.

It is a question whether any student radicalism existed of the kind that the nineteenth and twentieth centuries were to know. There was no distinctive student movement, and no generation gap, since in the circumstances of real revolution, where "the revolution" was not a mere ideological cry, the adult population was as radicalized as the youth. It was even said that "the insubordination begun by the teachers themselves lost no time in communicating itself to their pupils."[39] Youth clubs with fervently patriotic principles grew up in many towns in association with the local Friends of the Constitution, as the Jacobins were called until 1793, when they became the Friends of Liberty and Equality. Students at the University of Paris printed a leaflet, "The Death Agony of the University," with quotations from Helvétius, demanding that priests be eliminated from the teaching body and corporal punishment be abolished, but such ideas were not uncommon in 1790. The revolutionary sentiment of students was often hard to distinguish from patriotic excitement or youthful exuberance. For example, early in July 1790 a swarm of students from the other colleges invaded Navarre College in the Latin Quarter, demanding that the Navarre students join them in going to the Champ de Mars to help in preparation for the Fête de la Fédération that was to occur there on July 14, the first anniversary of the fall of the Bastille. The Navarre students protested that they had gone to the Champ de Mars the day

---

[39] Said in February 1792; see p. 882 of the document cited in note 46 below.

before for this very same purpose. A fracas followed, which was calmed down by a professor Degranthe, mentioned above as one of the many who published plans for educational reform. The invading students departed, and those of Navarre College remained peacefully at their studies, preparing for the *concours général*.[40]

In general, the colleges, lesser schools, higher faculties, and learned academies remained open until the extreme phase of the Revolution in 1793. Meanwhile, however, they fell into chaos. It is impossible to generalize because the strength of political forces varied from place to place. In some places the local governments struggled desperately to keep their schools open, in others they in effect closed them through intimidation of teachers and parents. For the country as a whole education suffered more from civil struggles and the zeal and fury of local authorities than from national legislation.

The Committee on Public Instruction appointed by the incoming Legislative Assembly in October 1791 included men of standing and experience suited to their task. The most prominent was Condorcet, perpetual secretary of the Academy of Sciences and long known for his potentially revolutionary opinions. Others were the naturalist Lacépède and the archaeologist Quatremère de Quincy; Lazare Carnot, an engineer who would become the "organizer of victory" two years later; Gilbert Romme, who had been preceptor to the son of Count Strogonov in St. Petersburg; and two who were ordinary professors, Audrein of the Paris faculty of arts, and Arbogast, a mathematician from Strasbourg. As one of its first actions the committee undertook an ambitious survey of education at all levels for the whole of France. Each of the 527 districts, the subdivisions of the departments, was to report on the number of its elementary schools, colleges, and private and advanced establishments; the number of their teachers, students, and scholarships; their real and movable property; and their categories of income and expense. It is not surprising, since these local governments were still in the process of consolidation under conditions of revolutionary confusion, that less than half of them replied, and that the replies were incomplete. The grand national statistical compilation

---

[40] A. Coutin, *Huit siècles de violence au Quartier Latin* (Paris, 1969), gathers examples from the Middle Ages to 1968 but scarcely mentions the French Revolution. Little has been written on youth clubs, several of which however are described by Michael Kennedy, *The Jacobin Clubs in the French Revolution* (Princeton, 1982), pp. 98-106. Reference above is to *L'Université à l'agonie, ou projet de réformer incessament l'éducation . . . Lettre d'un jeune étudiant de l'Université de Paris à ses confrères* (n.p., n.d. [1790]), and to *Réponse des étudiants du collège de Navarre aux reproches que leur ont fait des étudiants de quelques autres collèges* (Paris, 1790).

desired by the planners of a new France never materialized. The historian may regret it more than contemporaries.[41]

It was often observed at the time, even by revolutionaries themselves, that a whole generation was growing up in ignorance, indiscipline, and bad habits. There can be no quantitative estimate for the disruption in elementary schools. We can know only that some simple schoolmasters bravely carried on and that others fled, disappeared, or were driven away. But school attendance is not the only means by which children may learn reading and writing, and many were apparently taught by a grandparent, a friendly neighbor, or surreptitiously by a refractory priest. There is some significance in the statistics assembled by Maggiolo for persons marrying in the years 1816-1820, and hence mainly then in their twenties, of an age to have learned reading and writing during the most troubled years of the Revolution. These young men and women showed about the same degree of literacy as would be expected had the Revolution not taken place.[42]

The learned academies continued to function until 1793, as will be seen. The higher faculties of the universities went through increasingly difficult years until they too disappeared in 1793. The University of Strasbourg, which had many foreign students (including Metternich), saw its enrollment drop from 182 in 1788 to 73 in 1790 and to none in 1793, when in a kind of linguistic terror against the German language several of its professors, including Issac Haffner, were interned. The faculties of theology suffered from the rising anticlericalism, the loss of students, and the fact that the Assembly planned to replace them with diocesan seminaries. The theological faculty of Paris, the Sorbonne, was suppressed in April 1792, and its old building remained unused until 1821, when it was assigned to the faculties of letters and sciences of the new regime. A law of March 1791, abolishing all guilds and similar corporations, and opening all trades and professions to all persons on payment of a fee, was interpreted to mean that no university degrees would be needed for the practice of law and medicine. For several years there was thus no difference between authorized and unauthorized practitioners. Young men ceased attending lectures and submitting to examinations. Law students had an additional disincentive in the belief that all future laws would be different

---

[41] E. Allain, "L'enquête scolaire de 1791-1792," *Revue des questions historiques*, n.s., 6 (1891): 143-203, and his *L'oeuvre scolaire de la Révolution* (Paris, 1891; or Burt Franklin reprint, New York, 1969), pp. 343-45. Also, Guillaume, *Procès-verbaux . . . Assemblée législative*, pp. xxii-xxiv, 28-34.

[42] See above, p. 10, and M. Gontard, *L'enseignement primaire en France de la Révolution à la loi Guizot (1789-1833)* (Paris, 1959), pp. 81-188.

from those of the past, and that with rational codification the citizens would have little need for lawyers anyway. By 1793 young men were streaming into the army—or going into hiding or joining counterrevolutionary guerillas if otherwise minded—and the universities, while never exactly abolished, simply faded out of existence.

Let us concentrate on the colleges, of which, as already seen, there are known to have been 347 in France in 1789. About half were conducted by unaffiliated secular clergy, on whom it is hard to obtain numerical data, although we know that 38 professors in the 10 colleges of the Paris faculty of arts took the civil oath, and 28 refused it.[43] These recusants were forced to leave. Various actions of the Paris departmental authorities, such as closing of the college chapels and prohibition on new appointments to scholarships, caused further bad feeling and confusion.

The other half of the French colleges were operated by religious orders, the *congrégations séculières*, whose members took no permanent vows and remained uncloistered. Monasticism and binding vows were abolished early in the Revolution, but the question of the *congrégations séculières* was debated until the "second" revolution of August 1792. The most important of these congregations were the Oratorians and the Doctrinaires.

We have already seen how these two groups had been penetrated by the modern enlightened ideas since about 1760, and how they were largely composed of young men, or *confrères*, who were free to depart from the order at will. In 1791, almost two thirds of the Doctrinaires were under forty years old, and a third under thirty. "From 1789 to 1792 a majority took an active part in the revolutionary movement."[44] Some of them were launched by it into important civilian careers, notably Lakanal, who was elected to the Convention and became one of its educational planners, and Laromiguière, the future *idéologue* and philosopher. The Oratorians in 1790 had 236 priests, of whom only about 90 were actually teaching in the colleges, and 394 *confrères*, of whom half were younger than thirty. Only 51 of the priests took the oath to the Civil Constitution of the Clergy. On the other hand, only 60 members signed an appeal to the pope against the measures taken by the revolutionary assembly. When the head of the order proposed a public declaration describing the Oratory as a useful national institution that ought to be preserved, 269 members voted against it.

---

[43] O. Delarc, *L'église de Paris pendant la Révolution française*, 3 vols. (Paris, 1897), 1:376-81.

[44] J. de Viguerie, *Une oeuvre d'éducation sous l'ancien régime: les Pères de la Doctrine chrétienne* (Paris, 1976), p. 630.

In July 1790 some of the Oratorians elected a committee to consider revision of the statutes of the order. Its most active member was Daunou, then a *confrère* twenty-nine years old. The "Plan of Education" that he published went beyond the committee's intentions; never mentioning the Oratory by name, it proposed instead a new educational system for the whole of France. Although it allowed both for individual teachers and for "teaching societies" (such as the Oratory), these societies would lose all the attributes of organized bodies. They could hold no general assemblies. They would be forbidden to possess income-producing property, and their members would be salaried by the state. Not only would members take no vows (as was already the case), they would live under no collegial rules except for mealtimes and the closing hours of the college gate. They would be allowed to marry, but if married could not live in the college. Students would wear a "national uniform" and take part in military drills. The plan of study was somewhat traditional, beginning with languages and proceeding through rhetoric to conclude with philosophy and physics, with the remarkable provision that day pupils might be excused from the study of languages with consent of the parents. Especially to be noted is that each college would be subject to the local government of its civil department or district, which would collect student fees, pay salaries, appoint teachers, and conduct inspections. Nor could any teacher be transferred from one college to another against his will.[45]

In Daunou's plan the "teaching societies" evaporated. The young Oratorians for whom he spoke had more confidence in elected public authorities than in the heads of private organizations. It was the Revolutionary or pristine democratic faith. In the following years some of the Oratorians disappeared into anonymous civilian life, about 40 are known to have been teaching in the Central Schools in 1799, and a few became famous or infamous, including three prominent terrorists of 1793 (Fouché, Lebon, and Ysabeau), and Daunou himself, who like Lakanal became one of the educational planners of the Convention. Daunou went on to be head of the National Archives under Napoleon, and Fouché his minister of police.

These conditions within the secular congregations were well known

---

[45] P.F.C. Daunou, *Plan d'éducation présenté à l'Assemblée Nationale au nom des instituteurs publics de l'Oratoire* (Paris, 1790); P. Lallemand, *Histoire de l'éducation dans l'ancien Oratoire de France* (Paris, 1889), pp. 190-205; W. Frijhoff and D. Julia, "Le recrutement d'une congrégation enseignante . . . l'Oratoire de France," in *The Making of Frenchmen: Current Directions in the History of Education in France, 1679-1979*, ed. D. N. Baker and P. J. Harrigan; a special issue of *Historical Reflections* (Waterloo, Ont. Canada, Summer-Fall 1980), p. 457.

to the Committee on Public Instruction when it considered the matter in the winter of 1791-1792. The Committee valued and wished to retain the Oratorians and Doctrinaires as teachers. Noting that the heads of these orders were losing their authority, and that members who had taken the oath were already under the protection of the civil administration of the departments, it concluded that the orders could be dissolved without loss. In the thinking of the Committee, as generally during the Revolution, no "order" or "body" (i.e. interest group) should stand between *l'individu* and *la patrie*. The income-producing properties of the orders would be confiscated and added "to the funds available for public instruction." Teaching positions would be made open to all young men having the appropriate talents, including former Oratorians and Doctrinaires, who would qualify by their own abilities without the privilege of membership in an order.[46]

The Committee adopted this program in February 1792, but the legislation was not passed until the following August, when a mass of revolutionary enactments followed on the fall of the monarchy, the collapse of the Legislative Assembly, and the rise of more popular revolution. At that time all secular congregations and similar bodies were suppressed, including not only the Oratorians and Doctrinaires but the Josephists, Lazarists, and others who conducted colleges; the Brothers of the Christian Schools and others who provided elementary teaching; and numerous women's congregations that were thought to "spread the poison of fanaticism into the utmost ramifications of society."[47] Exception was made only for certain men's and women's orders, especially the Gray Sisters, engaged primarily in poor relief and hospital service. Teachers of all kinds were dispersed. Those who continued to teach as private individuals were forbidden to wear clerical costume.

A few examples of particular colleges may convey the general atmosphere.

Sainte-Marthe College, a part of the University of Poitiers, was conducted by members of the secular clergy. When several of them refused the oath, the authorities of the department of the Vienne replaced them; but a group of students led a rebellion against the new teachers, sufficiently serious to be discussed in Paris by the Constituent Assembly, which voted to uphold the department. In these rapid changes of

---

[46] "Rapport du Comité d'Instruction Publique sur les congrégations séculières," dated February 10, 1792, overlooked by J. Guillaume in editing his volume on the Legislative Assembly, and hence published by him in an appendix to vol. 6 of his *Procès-verbaux du Comité de l'Instruction publique de la Convention Nationale* (Paris, 1907), 6:881-88.

[47] *Ibid.*, 6:885.

personnel the revolutionary sentiment became more heated. With the declaration of war in April 1792 the students rushed forward to make patriotic gifts to the nation, surrendering the silver crosses that they had won as prizes in exchange for crosses of lead or iron, and the professor of physics, a man named Sabourain, became the new principal. A firm revolutionary, he published a prospectus for the school year 1792-1793, proposing "to bring the axe of reform into public instruction." The college would become "a little republic," and the students would be "the inventors of what they are to learn." According to the historian of the college Sabourain might have done great service to the cause of education, for he was a capable man, but "unfortunately he was interested in politics, and politics proved fatal to him." He fell victim to an intrigue in the local Jacobin club, of which he was a member. Falsely accused of conspiring with the counterrevolutionary Vendéan insurgents, the patriot principal died on the guillotine in 1794. The college stumbled on and was replaced in 1795 by the newly organized Central School of the department of the Vienne.[48]

The town of Angers, a hundred miles to the north, possessed a college run by a group of Oratorians. They took the oath "almost unanimously" in 1791. Although the college revenues declined from 12,000 to 5,000 livres from 1789 to 1792, and although the Oratorian order like all secular congregations was suppressed in August, the school year 1792-1793 opened favorably because of strong support from both the municipal and the departmental officers. The college still had seven professors, all former Oratorians. One of them was the president of the local Jacobin club. Nothing seemed really to change until the Vendéan rebellion. By March 1793 four of the professors were in the army to defend the Republic. The Vendéans nevertheless occupied the town. In Paris the Convention decreed the famous *levée en masse* against civil war and foreign invasion. Professors and students rushed to the colors. "Thus ended the Oratorian college at Angers."[49] Three years later the Central School of the Maine-et-Loire opened in the same building with almost the same teachers.

The Oratorians at Lyon had a more difficult time. Lyon was the largest city in France except Paris and was a busy center of commerce, banking, and silk manufacture. Its most important college had been taken over by the Oratorians from the Jesuits after 1763. Influential merchants had urged for many years that the college should reduce its

[48] J. Delfour, *Le collège de Poitiers après l'expulsion des Jésuits (1762-1795)* (Poitiers 1917), pp. 71-118. The text of Sabourain's prospectus is on pp. 215-18.

[49] B. Bois, *La vie scolaire en Anjou pendant la Révolution, 1789-99* (Paris, 1929), pp. 103-108.

emphasis on Latin and literature and give more attention to scientific and practical subjects. Hardly was the new municipal government formed, early in the Revolution, when it fell into disputes with the Oratorians over the management of the college property, the content of studies, and the appointment of teachers. Accused of Jansenism and poor civic spirit, the Oratorians presented themselves as defenders of humanistic learning against mere vocational training. The municipality ejected the Oratorians and turned the college into an "institute," to have nine professors teaching not only a bit of Latin but also applied arithmetic, business practice, experimental physics, public law, and civic morality. The institute was short-lived, for a true class struggle broke out in 1793 in this already semi-industrial city. First the working-class militants took over, only to be overcome by the revived strength of the mercantile bourgeoisie, which in turn was crushed by forces sent from Paris. Lyon suffered more from the Terror than almost any other city in France, with almost 2,000 "federalist" rebels shot to death by order of revolutionary courts. Recovery was slow in the crippled city, but the Central School of the Rhône was opened in 1796, with a program recalling the abortive institute of 1793.[50]

Two Benedictine colleges, Sorèze and Pontlevoy, were *écoles militaires* of the kind described in the last chapter. They resembled each other in that both were primarily residential schools with a teaching body composed both of Benedictine fathers and laymen. Both also, like Louis-le-Grand in Paris, were among the French colleges (whose number is unknown) that never closed at any time during the Revolution. Their role as *écoles militaires* lasted until 1793, for although the royal cadets were of noble birth many of them remained in their schools well into the Revolution, and the successive revolutionary assemblies continued to pay for their scholarships until the noble royal cadets became an anachronism under the Republic; so that the *écoles militaires* were abolished and the scholarships civilianized. It will be recalled that the cadets were in any case only a minority in their respective schools.

At Sorèze, 12 of the Benedictines refused the oath flatly, five took it with qualifications, and only four took it without reservation and remained at the school in 1791. Of these four, three became active in the local Jacobin society, and one was elected its president. The majority who refused the oath hardly did so from monastic zeal. Only one chose to continue in the communal life; he retired to an abbey in

[50] L. Trénard, *Lyon de l'Encyclopédie au préromantisme*, 2 vols. (Paris, 1958), 1:304-22 and 2:460-70; S. Charléty, *Histoire de l'enseignement secondaire dans le Rhône de 1789 à 1900* (Paris, 1901). And see n. 66 below.

Spain. One became a lieutenant of Hussars, one a bookseller in England, and one the principal of another school, where he turned into an enthusiastic partisan of the *gouvernement révolutionnaire* of the Year II of the Republic. Another turned up years later as an inspector-general of public instruction under Napoleon. When the American Samuel Breck revisited Sorèze in the 1790s, he found that one of his old teachers had died in the September Massacres, and one had become a young "dandified gentleman."[51]

The survival of Sorèze was the work of Dom Ferlus (later Citizen Ferlus), one of the four Benedictines that took the oath. He struggled successfully with the scarcities, requisitions, suspicions, and denunciations of the year of the Terror. He managed to hold his pupils and find new teachers as vacancies developed so that he still had 400 students and 60 teachers in 1796. He was less successful in preserving the college property. Sorèze had been a wealthy school before the Revolution. The value of its farm lands and other rental properties sold to various local inhabitants reached about 250,000 livres. Ferlus managed, after several years of trouble with competitors, to buy for himself the college buildings and one tract of income-producing land for a sum of 119,500 livres, partly paid for in cash, partly in installments payable to the state. Sorèze thus became a "private" school, envied by the Napoleonic university for its quality, and attacked during the Restoration for its liberalism, but surviving and prospering into the twentieth century.[52]

Pontlevoy had a more troubled existence than Sorèze. A feud developed early in the Revolution between the lay and clerical teachers, with the latter complaining that the former no longer accepted their subordinate status as mere employees. The lay teachers in fact (since Pontlevoy was a very small place) were the main organizers of the local Friends of the Constitution—or Jacobins. With such friction, and then with the requirement of the oath in 1791, the Benedictines drifted away and the lay teachers took over the school. The disgruntled clerics wrote to parents urging them to withdraw their sons from the revolutionized establishment. Enrollments declined sharply, and the departmental authorities, eager to keep the school open, hit on a compromise. They found three Benedictines who had taken the oath and made one of them, Dom Garrellon, the director of the school. Operations went on for a year or two under this mixed management of lay

[51] J. Fabre de Massaguel, *L'école de Sorèze de 1758 au 19 fructidor An IV* (Paris, 1958), pp. 128-32. On Samuel Breck, see above, p. 68; the present quotation is from p. 171 of his *Recollections*.

[52] Fabre de Massaguel, *L'école de Sorèze*, pp. 51-57 and 68-70.

teachers and "constitutional" or ex-Benedictines. As general conditions worsened—with inflation, high prices, unpaid salaries, and declining income—the harried director, Garrellon, began to impose economies, one of which was to increase the teaching hours of the lay teachers. A rebellion of the lay teachers against the three ex-Benedictines followed. The departmental authorities took the side of the lay teachers (who now called themselves *sans-culottes*) and dismissed the three ex-Benedictines late in 1793. It also forbade parents to remove their sons unless they could present a certificate of *civisme*. The students became virtual prisoners, since the National Guard was sent to prevent their departure. This measure was intended partly to keep the school open, but partly also as a means of holding the students as hostages, in the belief that many parents were secret sympathizers with Vendéan rebels and the forces of a royalist restoration, a belief probably true enough since Pontlevoy was (or had been) an upperclass school.

The new director, Chappotin, proved to be very adaptable. Attacked as a moderate in 1793, he proved the opposite by abandoning his priesthood and turning the college chapel into a temple of reason. Attacked as a royalist after Thermidor, he had his pupils participate ostentatiously in all republican holidays and festivities under the Directory. He was on such good terms with the government that he was able, like Ferlus at Sorèze but more easily, to purchase the school for himself and so make it into a "private" institution. By 1802, following the prevailing shifts in opinion, the college of Pontlevoy was offering a modified pre-Revolutionary curriculum, complete with Bible study and a chaplain, and boasted of eight ex-Benedictines on its faculty, of whom three were married. It was next converted to an *école secondaire* in Napoleon's system, and Chappotin became an officer of the Imperial University. He was only ousted in the general ecclesiastical reaction of 1823.[53]

DISENDOWMENT

The Revolutionary years were as disruptive to the economy of the educational system as to its personnel. Colleges and elementary schools saw their usual sources of income disappear. How much was lost by

---

[53] W. Frijhoff, "L'école militaire de Pontlevoy pendant les premières années de la Révolution (1790-93)" and D. Julia, "Le collège de Pontlevoy sous la direction de Pierre-François Chappotin (1793-1824)," *Actes du 103ᵉ congrès national des sociétés savantes, Nancy-Metz 1978, section d'histoire moderne et contemporaine* (Paris, 1979), pp. 23-64.

abolition of the tithe is impossible to say, but many colleges and schools collected tithes until 1789, since part of their income was in the form of ecclesiastical benefices. The same uncertainty hangs over the elimination of seigneurial dues; the impact depended on the situation of each educational institution, on whether it was a payer or receiver of such dues, and on the proportion of such income to its other sources of revenue. At Louis-le-Grand the receipts from tithes and seigneurial dues, before their abolition, represented about one-eighth of its income from property and *rentes*. So far as *rentes* (in effect, the interest on money) arose from debts owed by the monarchy and other official bodies of the Old Regime they were transformed by the Revolution into a national debt, which the Revolution did not expressly repudiate; but payment of *rentes* became very erratic, and most of the principal was in fact lost in the consolidations of the debt under the Directory. Local elementary teachers had sometimes been supported before the Revolution by income of the *fabrique*, the property belonging to parish churches, which was sequestered like all church property in November 1789. Bishops and the canons of cathedral chapters had also subsidized both lower schools and colleges, either from their private fortunes since some of them were wealthy, or from revenues of the dioceses, some of which were richly endowed. Town governments had also contributed to the support of education, but the towns lost much of their older form of revenue with the abolition of the *octroi*, or fees leveled on articles of consumption as they entered the town.

Many of these losses were temporary in that they were later replaced by new kinds of income. It was a main feature of the French Revolution to effect a conversion of older to more modern "bourgeois" forms of property, as of income, taxation, and fiscal procedures. During the Revolution the schools suffered, like others, from confusion, uncertainty, impoverishment, scarcities, inflation, occasional fraud, or simply the incompetence of officials in newly invented roles for which they had little preparation. But even in the worst years, as already seen, some towns came to the aid of their colleges. In the year and a half preceding October 1795 the National Convention authorized the payment of over five million francs in support of the Paris colleges and various special schools, but it is doubtful how much actually reached these recipients during this time of turmoil.[54] As the Revolutionary innovations took on more permanent form, which is to say after 1800, the public educational system came to be financed by fees paid by parents, by new local taxes under a national plan, and to a small extent

[54] See the Appendix.

by grants from the national treasury. There was less *instruction gratuite* than there had been under the Old Regime.[55]

More lasting, and affecting mainly the colleges, was the loss of endowments, that is, of income-producing property given in perpetuity since the later Middle Ages to particular institutions for particular purposes. Examples already cited are the huge bequest of Cardinal Mazarin of two million francs to establish the College of the Quatre-Nations and the smaller bequest of the Abbé Legrand to found the *concours général* in the University of Paris. With the disappearance of these endowments came a change in the definition of public education. Before the Revolution a public school might have endowed funds, large or small, while depending also on municipal or royal subventions, voluntary giving, and fees. After the Revolution the public system meant a system controlled by the state, though not fully paid for by it until well into the twentieth century, and hence dependent on fees especially at the secondary level, with almost no advantage from private benefactions. Since no one makes gifts to the state, philanthropy after the Revolution went to "private" schools, which after the mid-nineteenth century meant schools associated with the Catholic Church.

It is difficult to estimate the aggregate capital value of the educational endowments lost in the Revolution. A report made by Joseph Cambon to the Legislative Assembly in April 1792 offers a starting point.[56] He announced that the value of the *biens nationaux* ordered

[55] My article, "Free Secondary Education in France before and after the Revolution," *History of Education Quarterly* (Winter 1974), pp. 437-52, was unfortunately written before the publication of D. Julia and P. Pressly, "La population scolaire en 1789: les extravagances statistiques du ministre Villemain," *Annales E.S.C.* 30 (November-December 1975): 1516-61. The figures and percentages in my article are invalidated by Julia and Pressly's findings, but the conclusions concerning scholarships and the decline of free education seem to be unaffected.

[56] Jospeh Cambon, *Tableau des besoins et des resources de la nation, présenté à l'Assemblée par J. Cambon* (Paris, 1792), reprinted in the *Archives parlementaires*, 1st ser., 42:79-103. No one of course supposed that Cambon's figure of 2,225,638,237 francs was correct to 10 digits; it was a summation of detailed reports from the districts. It referred only to the *biens immeubles* (land and buildings, excluding the *droits incorporels*, which must have been *rentes*, etc.) among the *biens nationaux* of "first origin." That is, the property later confiscated from émigrés is not counted and is in any case irrelevant to education. Six weeks after Cambon's report the Committee on Public Instruction was informed by the Committee on the Domain that the *revenus affectés à l'instruction publique* amounted to five million francs, which at five percent would suppose a capital value of 100 million. In addition, buildings in Paris *affectés à cet objet* were estimated at 13 million. Guillaume, *Procès-verbaux . . . Assemblée législative*, p. 303. American readers may note with curiosity, and to gain a sense of comparative magnitudes, that Cambon

for sale by the Constituent and Legislative assemblies was 2,225,638,237 livres, of which two-thirds had already been sold. But the assemblies had suspended the sale of properties of hospitals, charitable and educational establishments, the Order of Malta, and a few others. The value of these *biens nationaux ajournés* Cambon set at 431,322,422 francs. Unfortunately there is no means of knowing the proportion represented by education in this figure. If it was only an eighth it would be 50 million francs.

Or we can approach the question of capital value from what is known about income. The University of Paris and its component colleges were said by the departmental authorities of Paris in 1791 to have an annual endowed income, from *rentes* and from rural farms and urban rentals, of 1,336,175 francs.[57] Supposing a return of five percent, the capital value would be well over 20 million for Paris alone. Possibly typical of the provinces was the College of Vienne in Dauphiny. It enjoyed 33,000 francs a year from real property before 1789, all of which was sold for a capital sum reported as 800,000 in specie, or 1,150,970 in paper money.[58] The Oratory had an endowed income of 600,000 francs a year, almost all used to sustain its 30 colleges.[59] The capital value would be over 10 million. A wealthy college before 1789 might have 50,000 francs a year of endowed income, indicating a capital value of one million, but we do not know how many of 347 colleges were "wealthy." Nor do we know how many colleges had no endowment at all. On the whole, however, an aggregate total of 50 million seems improbably low.

It was enough to make one understand some surprising remarks made by Roger Martin, a professor of physics both before and after the Revolution, who in 1798 was a deputy in the Council of Five Hundred, the lower house of the legislature. Taking the lead in an extended debate on education, he was trying (unsuccessfully) to persuade his colleagues to be more generous in supporting it with public money. A firm but moderate partisan of the Revolution, he neverthe-

---

stated the amount of the debt owed by the United States to France, and hence among its "resources" in 1792, to be 51,116,924 francs. Note, too, that although the word "franc" did not replace "livre" until 1796, it involved no change in value and is used here and henceforth for clarity.

[57] A. Tuetey, *Répertoire général des sources manuscrites de l'histoire de Paris pendant la Révolution française*, 11 vols. (Paris, 1890-1914), 6:205, no. 1683. J. F. Champagne in 1790 gave an estimate of 1,300,000 francs: see my *School of the French Revolution*, p. 256.

[58] C. Faure, *Recherches sur l'histoire du Collège de Vienne en Dauphiné* (Vienne, 1932), pp. 276 and 230.

[59] Guillaume, *Procès-verbaux . . . Convention*, 6:883.

less compared the current situation unfavorably with what had gone before.

"Under the old regime," he said,

> there had spread among us a kind of national munificence for all that concerned public instruction; a host of philanthropic establishments [*établissements de bienfaisance*] offered children even of the least comfortable class the first elements of instruction and even of a more developed education; free places or *pensions* intended for the needy, but often usurped by intrigue, provided great resources for talents without fortune; several universities and a crowd of colleges, most of them well endowed, offered free instruction everywhere.

It was only, he said, when education prepared for lucrative careers, as in law and medicine, that payment of significant fees had been required. His picture was somewhat roseate but would hardly have been persuasive to his audience had it been false. The men in the Five Hundred had been educated in the very colleges to which he referred.[60]

The Constituent Assembly, in exempting the property of educational institutions from immediate sale, did not leave it under the control of the former owners. Income from such property was collected by officials of the newly instituted national domain, who were to pay it out to schools and colleges having a claim on it after appropriate bureaucratic procedures. Disputes thus arose between colleges and local administrators of the domain, who in some cases were indifferent to the collection of rents, dilatory in payment to colleges, or guilty of favoritism or profiteering in the management of so much real estate. Among the Revolutionary leadership the prevailing thought during the first three years was to preserve the "adjourned" properties as a kind of national fund. There was widespread agreement that the old foundations were undesirable, that they represented the dead hand of the past, that they were anachronistic, inefficient, selfserving, and wasteful, and that they were an impediment to rational planning and renovation. None of these objections need obtain, however, if the existing foundations were merged into a common fund of property belonging to the nation, from which reformed educational and charitable institutions could be supported. It is for this reason that Condorcet in

---

[60] Roger Martin, *Rapport général fait par Roger Martin sur l'organisation de l'instruction publique. Séance du 19 brumaire. An VII* (Paris, 1799), pp. 21-22. The Five Hundred ordered it printed and postponed discussion. It was barely summarized in the *Moniteur*, 23 Brumaire of the Year VII. See pp. 259-60 below.

his plan of 1792, like Talleyrand in 1791, could argue that his newly projected educational system would cost no more than the old.

After war began in April 1792, and with the radicalization of the Revolution the following August—accompanied by internal rebellion, civil struggle, inflation, and the disorganization of tax receipts—the pressure mounted to raise funds by the sale of the properties whose sale had been suspended since 1789. It was evident in any case that the existing arrangements were unsuccessful. The colleges complained repeatedly to the Committee on Public Instruction of failures to receive their due income. The college properties were suffering from neglect; some had already been sold in disregard of the law. The teaching orders with their managerial skills were dissolved; every college had to contend alone with the bureaucrats of its neighborhood. Enlightened opinion had long opposed permanent foundations in principle and deplored them in practice. Complete nationalization offered a ready answer.

On March 8, 1793, Joseph Fouché, who had been head of the Oratorian college at Nantes when elected to the Convention, made public a report of the joint committees of public instruction and finance. Adopting their proposal, the Convention ordered the sale of "properties forming the endowments of colleges, scholarships and other establishments of public instruction, under whatever name they may exist."[61] The college buildings themselves and the lodgings of teachers and students were excluded; unsold, they still belonged to the nation. Farm lands, pastures, wood lots, urban lands, and buildings belonging to the colleges were sold off until the sales were again stopped in 1797. During these four years the old endowments melted away. Public education became an affair of the state. "Here in reality ended the educational old regime," as Albert Duruy observed a century later.[62]

It may be added that the furnishings, silverware, scientific collections, libraries, and other movable possessions of the colleges also to a large extent disappeared, sometimes into "cultural depots" for safekeeping against marauders, sometimes removed by departing professors, sometimes appropriated or indeed stolen by unknown hands. When Central Schools were established in some of the former college buildings, beginning in 1795, they often found their new quarters fairly empty. The College of Louis-le-Grand lost about 35,000 books, most of which were later recovered and eventually went into the library of

[61] *Archives parlementaires*, 59:710-11. *Moniteur, réimpression*, 15:652.

[62] A Duruy, *L'instruction publique et la Révolution* (Paris, 1882), p. 63. See also below, pp. 285-87, for later discussions of endowment for education.

the modern University of Paris. All told, counting those taken from religious houses, émigrés, and condemned persons, about 12 million books were confiscated in the Revolution. Some of them were added to the old royal library to form the Bibliothèque Nationale. There were also plans to use them to establish public libraries throughout the country, but little was accomplished nor perhaps was much lost, since old volumes in Latin, or dealing with theology, heraldry, obsolete science, or metaphysics, were of slight interest to the reading public. A curious sidelight was the attempt to create a vast union catalogue for the whole of France. After five years of serious bibliographic effort it was given up as impossible.[63]

Here again the example of a few colleges may convey a general impression. The College of Epinal in the Vosges enjoyed an income of 13,928 francs from real property, inherited from its earlier Jesuit phase and administered since the 1760s by one of the bureaus described in the last chapter. The Revolution proved to be more destructive to college endowments than the expulsion of the Jesuits had been. Most of the property was sold as early as 1790, in contravention to the law suspending such sales. Parcels of land described as *gagnages* (pastures) and a *seigneurie* were sold to persons described as *cultivateurs* (substantial farmers), a farm tenant, a widow, a candlemaker, a justice of the peace, and a bailiff in the law court. A remaining property, a small house in town, was bought in 1796 by a professor in the Central School. The college building itself, after briefly serving as the prefecture under Napoleon, eventually became, shorn of its possessions, a boys' school again.[64]

The College of Rennes in Brittany had nine pieces of rural property sold for a value of 31,138 francs before 1796. Two of these were farms purchased by merchants. By 1800 five buildings in town, valued at from 45,000 to 81,000 apiece, had been sold to five different persons, one of them a gendarme, the others of unspecified occupations. Five other buildings, remaining unsold, were assigned to the local hospital in 1803, by which time the Bonapartist educational system was supposed to be paid for by national scholarships, local taxes, and parental fees.[65]

Two ex-Jesuit colleges at Lyon, one of them the Oratorian college already mentioned, were receiving in 1789 an income of 43,856 francs

---

[63] P. Riberette, *Les bibliothèques françaises pendant la Révolution 1789-95* (Paris, 1970).

[64] L. Schwab, *Documents relatifs à la vente des biens nationaux. District d'Epinal (Vosges)* (Epinal, 1911), p. 22 and index.

[65] A. Guillon and A. Rebillon, *Documents relatifs à la vente des biens nationaux. Rennes* (Rennes, 1911), pp. 109-10, 474-78, 649.

from real property plus 11,560 of *rentes* owed mainly by the city of Lyon. The income was enough to make possible free instruction without subsidy from the city, though fees were paid by the *internes* for their board and room. During the spring of 1793, when the mercantile bourgeoisie and working-class leaders were struggling for control, the outlying rural properties of the colleges, mainly vineyards, were purchased for a total of about 1,300,000 francs by a silk manufacturer and various merchants and notaries. Then came the rebellion against Paris, the siege, the Terror, and the reimposition of the authority of the National Convention, during which the sales abated. In 1795 and 1796 the urban properties of the former colleges went up at auction; about 20 buildings fetched three million francs. The buyers included persons of more modest social position than those who had invested in vineyards. Among them were a furrier, a grocer, a hatter, and a dyer, but the prices they paid suggest that they were no simple artisans. On the other hand, not much can be deduced from the prices, which were wildly inflated before the Revolutionary paper money was repudiated early in 1797. When a furrier bought a house at 18 rue Turpin for 715,500 francs that had yielded an income of only 3,400 francs in 1790, we can make a number of inferences—that the old college properties had been carelessly administered, that the furrier had a sizable business in furs, and that the sales prices of the *biens nationaux* in 1796 offer shaky ground for an estimate of the value of the lost endowments.[66]

The 10 "undergraduate" colleges composing the faculty of arts of the former University of Paris were combined in 1798 into an establishment called the Prytanée français, to which all their property sequestered in 1789 was deemed to belong. The annual revenue amounted to about 800,000 francs, of which almost 600,000 came from urban rentals and rural farms and about 200,000 from *rentes*. By 1798 about two-thirds of the real estate had been sold. Most of it was rural land lying outside the city of Paris. Who the purchasers were is unknown. For the Paris properties a list of 63 purchasers exists. It includes 10 bakers; five wine merchants; four each of carpenters, gardeners, and booksellers; three masons; two locksmiths; two merchants; two office workers; and so forth, together with a "man of letters," a "geographer," a lawyer, a doctor, and an architect. In short, the Paris properties of the pre-Revolutionary colleges went into the hands of the professional and lesser bourgeoisie, some of whom probably became

---

[66] S. Charlety, *Département du Rhône. Documents relatifs à la vente des biens nationaux* (Lyon, 1906), pp. xviii, 22-23, and note 50 above.

the owners of shops and living quarters that they had occupied as tenants of the colleges. Probably much of the rural land was bought by well-to-do city people.[67]

The nationalization and politicization of education during the Revolution, like the Revolution as a whole, were thus a compound of perfervid idealism with material advantage, of the nationalization of institutions with turbulence and confusion, in which a new elite possessing money and property replaced the older elites of noble birth, the royal court, and the ecclesiastical hierarchy. We turn to the third of our six-syllabled abstractions, most obvious in 1793 and 1794 during the Terror—democratization.

[67] See my article, "Le Prytanée français et les écoles de Paris, 1798-99," *Annales historiques de la Révolution française* (January-March 1981), pp. 123-52.

CHAPTER 4

DEMOCRATIZATION:
THE QUEST FOR
EQUALITY

THE MOST DEMOCRATIC PHASE of the French Revolution, according to many historians, came in the two years from the insurrection of August 1792 to the death of Robespierre in July 1794. The August uprising led within a few weeks to the dethronement of Louis XVI, the collapse of the constitution of 1791, the disbanding of the Legislative Assembly, the September Massacres, the election of the National Convention, and the proclamation of the Republic. It may seem paradoxical to call these two years democratic, for they were also the period of the Terror, the revolutionary tribunals in Paris and elsewhere, some 20,000 executions by the guillotine or firing squad, the height of the radicalized Jacobin clubs, and the dictatorship of the Committee of Public Safety. During most of this time foreign armies were operating within the borders of France, and the country was torn also by a civil war. To repel the invaders the Convention called into being an army of a million men, by far the largest ever yet seen in Europe, and differing from other armies in being recruited from all social classes, and fired by political and patriotic excitement. To raise and maintain such an army the governing authorities made appeals for popular support. For example, what remained of "feudal dues" was abolished without compensation, systems of price control and requisitioning were enacted, and the new constitution of 1793 provided for universal male suffrage while adding equality to the list of human rights. The constitution, however, understandably in the circumstances, was suspended for the duration of the war. The Convention declared the

121

government to be "revolutionary until the peace." The Revolutionary Government, as the regime called itself after October 1793, was by definition extraconstitutional and expected to be temporary. Its function was to win the war but also to protect and advance the Revolution until the new order was secure. Thus was born the theory of revolutionary dictatorship, looked back on with admiration or nostalgia by the more militant Left of later times.

But the two years in question were democratic in senses that can be generally accepted. Middle and upperclass leaders celebrated the virtues of equality. Real members of the working class, such as artisans, mechanics, and small shopkeepers, along with their wives and adult children, became a political force with which the leadership had to reckon. These popular revolutionaries were the "sans-culottes." They gathered in the "primary assemblies" of the "sections" of large cities (electoral districts left from the first constitution) and in "popular societies" (local political clubs) throughout the country. They were extremely active especially in 1793. Another reason for accepting the term "democratic" is that the Revolutionary leadership (as well as frightened conservatives) called it such. Robespierre used the word frequently in a great speech of February 1794 on the Principles of Political Morality, in which he made his famous equation between Virtue and Terror. He attempted also to uphold representative democracy against the direct democracy that the sans-culottes clamored for. "Democracy," he therefore said, "is a state in which the people, as sovereign, guided by laws of their own making, do for themselves what they can do well, and by their delegates what they cannot." And he went on to affirm: "Democracy is the only form of state which all the individuals composing it can truly call their country, and which therefore can count on as many interested defenders as it has citizens. . . . The French are the first people in the world to establish a true democracy, by calling all men to enjoy equality and the fullness of civil rights; and that, in my opinion, is the real reason why all the tyrants allied against the Republic will be defeated."[1]

Attempts at democratization in education must be seen against this background. They foreshadowed the future while having little immediate effect. Nor were they totally different from the past; the Talleyrand report had already proposed universal free elementary schooling,

---

[1] *Moniteur*, February 7, 1794. The general atmosphere and developments for the period of this and the following chapter are evoked in my *Twelve Who Ruled: The Year of the Terror in the French Revolution* (Princeton, 1941, 1958), originally subtitled *The Committee of Public Safety in the French Revolution*.

and most pre-Revolutionary writers on education (with La Chalotais as the best remembered exception) had called for widespread knowledge of reading, writing, arithmetic, morality, and religion among the common people, as had professional teachers and the church. Nevertheless, the demand for equality in education, as well as a concern for the difficulties and ramifications that went with it, was mostly fully expressed during these climactic years.

The National Convention could give only episodic attention to matters of education. But its Committee on Public Instruction worked continuously and assiduously, meeting almost every day. In addition to being charged with such problems as development of the metric system and the preservation of confiscated works of art and libraries, it developed a series of plans for the future of schools and institutions of higher learning. The minutes and associated documents of this committee filled six oversized volumes when published a century later.[2] Its proposals on educational matters came to the floor of the Convention for full discussion only at fairly long intervals, first in December 1792, then during the summer of 1793, again in December of that year, and sporadically through 1794 and 1795. For convenience we can see two phases in the efforts of these three years of the National Convention, a first phase in which the chief concern was for equality, and a second phase in which, while equality remained a goal, there was a mounting concern for an education that would produce actual results. The two phases form the principle of division between this chapter and the next. For all phases our sources consist mainly of the plans themselves, a few pieces of legislation, speeches made in the Convention, and petitions submitted to it by the sans-culottes and others who pressed for action. We shall therefore be dealing more with ideas than with actual conditions. The preceding chapter has described these conditions—bewilderment, frustration, closing of some schools, and perplexities of others as personnel and income were disrupted—that formed a chaos in which far-reaching plans were propounded.

"Phantoms soaring over ruins," as the disgusted Guizot called these plans many years later; or should we call them, in the words of a more

---

[2] J. Guillaume, *Procès-verbaux du Comité d'Instruction publique de la Convention Nationale*, 6 vols. (Paris, 1891-1907), with a two-volume index, undated but later. These superbly edited, annotated, cross-referenced, and indexed volumes are valuable also for Guillaume's introductions to the separate volumes, which taken together make up a detailed running history of the subject. The documents include relevant speeches in the Convention, reports, petitions, and so forth, and selections from the periodical press of the time.

celebrated writer, the prophetic voice of the wide world dreaming on things to come?

THE CONDORCET PLAN

The Condorcet plan, as it is always called (and Condorcet was the author, though the committee at first insisted on its collective responsibility), was brought up for discussion in the Convention in December 1792.[3] Some members of the Committee, including Condorcet and Romme, had belonged to the committee of the same name of the preceding Legislative Assembly, in which the plan had originated; it had been laid before that Assembly in April, but the outbreak of war and mounting crisis of the Revolution had made consideration impossible. Now in December, although the Revolution faced another crisis in the trial of the king, the Convention devoted several sessions to the plan. For more than a year, in fact, the terms of discussion were set by the Condorcet plan, including the objections to it, its burial, and its partial revival.

As for Condorcet himself, he was a man of almost fifty in 1792, an eminent mathematician and philosopher, the last of the *philosophes*, and the herald of social science. Noble by birth, even a marquis, he was one of the first to declare himself a republican before the Republic. Secretary to the Royal Academy of Sciences since 1773, he had been the friend, disciple, and biographer of Turgot and had written tracts in praise of the American Revolution. He is best remembered for his *Sketch of the Progress of the Human Mind*, with its historical and futuristic panorama of human improvement, written while he was in hiding before his death in prison in 1794. In that book he saw "equality of fact" as the final victory of the "social art."

The Condorcet plan, like Talleyrand's, presented a kind of table of organization for national education at all levels and for the whole country. It differed from the Talleyrand plan in important respects. One difference was that Condorcet excluded the teaching of religion

---

[3] The Condorcet plan, often reprinted, is best consulted in Guillaume's volume for the Legislative Assembly, *Procès-verbaux du Comité d'Instruction publique de l'Assemblée Législative* (Paris, 1889). With Condorcet's own exposition of the plan are included here the preliminary discussions, the *projet de loi* submitted to the assembly (pp. 188-246), and the *Aperçu des frais que coutera le nouveau plan d'instruction publique* (Paris, 1792), pp. 304-309). Condorcet's exposition, with others of his writings on education, has been translated by Keith Baker, *Condorcet: Selected Writings* (Indianapolis, 1976), as well as by La Fontainerie (see above, p. 53n.), but these translations do not include the *projet* or the *aperçu des frais*, which add significant details.

from the national system; those who wanted it were to obtain it in their preferred places of worship. Other differences were more matters of degree. The Condorcet plan showed more concern for problems of equality. It was to assure equality between Catholics, Protestants, and others that Condorcet argued that the schools should be religiously neutral. Where Talleyrand had proposed that elementary education should be free, Condorcet wanted free instruction at all levels, with all teachers to be paid from public funds. Condorcet also, more than Talleyrand, argued for decentralization outside Paris, which is to say for equality of treatment for all parts of France. He emphasized the cognitive rather than the moral side of education, which must above all else impart the "truth"; hence he gave great weight to the scientific, technical, and vocational subjects on which future progress must depend. There was to be complete freedom for the teaching of these subjects, and Condorcet took pains to shield the educational system against all outside pressures, whether religious, political, or simply propagandistic. He disliked the idea of republican catechisms and civic indoctrination. He distinguished between *l'instruction*, which developed knowledge and skills, and *l'éducation*, which was designed to form character and commitments. He expected that with right knowledge the desired virtues would naturally emerge. Sheer enlightenment would be enough.

"In short," he said, "the independence of instruction is in a way a part of the rights of the human race. Since man has received from nature a perfectibility whose limits, if indeed they exist, are expanding well beyond what we can yet conceive . . . what power would have the right to say: Here is what you must know? Here is the boundary where you must stop?"[4]

Concretely, Condorcet envisaged five levels of instruction where Talleyrand had had only four. First came 31,000 primary schools, open to both boys and girls from ages six to eleven. Above the primary level the plan made no provision for girls, as Talleyrand had attempted to do, for although Condorcet personally believed and said that women should have the same educational advantages as men, he refrained from putting so controversial an item in his project. Above the primary schools he introduced a new level that he called *secondaire*; it was the first use of the word, which did not yet have its later meaning. There would be at least one *école secondaire* in each of the over 500 districts into which the departments were divided. In them about a tenth of the boys would receive further instruction for three years, with em-

---

[4] Guillaume, *Procès-verbaux . . . Assemblée Législative*, p. 223.

phasis on artisan skills for town boys and on agriculture for the sons of such peasants as could spare the labor of their male children after age eleven. Condorcet thought of these primary and secondary levels as "universal," teaching what was useful to everybody.

Next came about 110 *instituts*, a word that the Committee adopted deliberately to replace the term *collèges*. They would for the most part occupy the existing college buildings. It was expected that they might have some 80,000 students and offer a four-year course to boys aged from fifteen to eighteen. They would replace the Philosophy and Humanities years of the old colleges, while the "secondary" schools replaced the old grades from the Sixth through the Third. There would thus be far more teenage pupils than before the Revolution or for a long time after it, but the institutes would be fewer in number than the old colleges. From Condorcet's own figures it is evident that there would be an average of some 700 students in each institute, a figure far higher than for the old colleges. Few of his critics noticed this anomaly or the housing problems that it would produce. No plan made during the Revolution envisaged any program of new building for education.

Above the *instituts* would be some 10 *lycées*, one in Paris and the others in principal cities throughout the country. They would both teach and carry on scientific and scholarly work at the highest level. They would replace the 22 existing universities, whose disappearance is assumed in the plan, which never mentions the word "university" except to compare the *lycées* with the "great universities" of England, Germany, and Italy. So advanced and specialized was the work of the *lycées* that a proportion of only one in 1,600 of the male population, as the student body, was deemed sufficient for the needs of the country.

At the fifth and highest level, above the 10 *lycées*, Condorcet projected a National Society of Arts and Sciences. He thus created a top for his pyramid, where such a top had been vague or missing from the pyramidal schemes of Rolland, Talleyrand, and others. This top, or summit, was to be the most disputed and troublesome element in Condorcet's program.

The National Society, though located in Paris, would have half its members residing in the rest of the country out of deference to the principle of regional equality. It would also have foreign corresponding members, as a means of upholding standards and maintaining international repute. The number of members was strictly limited, so as to assure the highest qualifications, and the Society would choose its own members and their successors, so as to avoid encroachment by outside or nonintellectual influences. The membership was divided into four classes, representing the main branches of human knowledge, and each with subsections representing the relevant specialties. The classes and their numbers were projected as shown in the table that follows.

Class	Paris residents	Regional residents	Foreign members	Total
I. Mathematical and physical sciences	48	48	8	104
II. Moral and political sciences	30	30	8	68
III. Applications of science to the [industrial and practical] arts	72	72	12	156
IV. Literature and fine arts	44	44	12	100
Total	194	194	40	428

The prestige of First Class went to the mathematical and physical sciences, which included botany and zoology as subsections. A place was made for traditional work in literature and the beaux-arts. But the largest class was for the applied sciences, from which the well-being of humanity was expected to grow. The great innovation, having no precursor before the Revolution, was the class in Moral and Political Sciences, whose sub-sections included *science sociale*, public law, political economy, and history, which were also expected to contribute to bringing a better world into being.

These same four divisions of subject matter governed the curriculum in both the *instituts* and the *lycées*, which is to say that the content of teaching in the old colleges and universities was thoroughly revolutionized. Each institute, for example, was to have four professors of mathematics and sciences, three of moral and political sciences, three of applied sciences (teaching comparative anatomy, military arts, and "the general principles of arts and trades"), and four of literature and fine arts (teaching the theory of the fine arts, "general grammar," Latin, and a modern language). Pupils had the option of taking any two or more courses at one time. The rigidity as well as the content of the old course of study was thus abandoned. The *lycées*, each with its more numerous professors of more specialized subjects, represented an equally drastic transformation of the old universities with their faculties of law, medicine, and theology. Medicine became simply one of the applied sciences, law one of the moral and political sciences, while theology was abolished.

The National Society was to do no teaching itself but have supervision over teaching at the subordinate levels. Each class in the Society would appoint each year three of its members to serve as a "directorate of instruction," which would appoint professors in the *lycées* in that class and deal with the other problems that the *lycées* might have encountered. The same principle was extended downward. Professors in the *lycées*, within their several classes, would have the same powers of appointment and supervision in the *instituts*. Those of the *instituts* would draw up short lists of persons qualified for positions in the secondary and primary schools, but as a concession to local interests the town council would then make its choice from this list for its secondary school, and family heads could choose from the appropriate list for their local primary school. The purpose throughout was to assure adequate knowledge in the teachers, in the belief that experts qualified at each level were the best judges of teachers in the next level below.

Running through this elaborate mechanism was a deep concern not only for equality but also for reconciling equality with high quality, while recognizing the fact that not all persons could receive the same kind and duration of education, either for their own good or for the good of society. "Equality of minds and of instruction are chimeras," said Condorcet. "We must try to find a way to make this necessary inequality useful."[5] How did he square this circle? The universal schooling prescribed for the primary level would promote equality by protecting all persons from being imposed on by the learned; it would enable them to make intelligent choices of public officials in a system of universal male suffrage; it would help them to understand that the most enlightened persons were the most to be trusted with public powers; it would treat all parts of France alike; and it would enable bright boys to show their abilities at an early age and so be encouraged by their teachers to obtain the further education that was possible only for a few. Inequality of education was justified by the fact that talents were in fact unequal, that some occupations required far more education than others, that those who received additional schooling received it not for their own benefit but for the benefit of society and particularly of the less educated, and by the provision of student aid to the talented poor. Poor youths needed support for their living costs as well as the freedom from fees for instruction that all were to enjoy.

[5] Ibid., p. 202. Added by Condorcet in 1793.

There should therefore be 3,850 scholarships paid for by the nation. Each year the primary schools of each department would select a certain number of boys for secondary schooling, the secondary schools a certain number for the institutes, and the institutes for the lycées. There would be equality of opportunity for youths of equal talent, whether rich or poor, and this, combined with equalization among geographical areas, would "be useful in laying an unshakable foundation for national unity."

Social utility, individual self-advancement, and national unity would be promoted also by a program of continuing education. Primary and secondary teachers would give lectures on Sundays, open to the public but designed especially for adolescents who were obliged to work on the farm or find paid employment. Professors in the institutes would give public lectures at least once a month "to report on discoveries in the arts and sciences." The whole population would thus benefit from the progress of knowledge.[6]

When doubt was expressed on whether the country could afford such a comprehensive program, especially with its universal *instruction gratuite*, Condorcet replied that it would cost no more than was already being spent before the Revolution. He estimated the cost of the plan at 24,400,000 livres a year. But before the Revolution, by his calculations, the colleges had had some eight million a year of their own incomes, the "public treasury" had spent at least four million on education, many towns and villages had granted subsidies, and various charities and small foundations had supplied funds, to which the proceeds of some of the confiscated church lands might if necessary be added. The total would at least equal the cost of the plan. In addition, some five million formerly spent "on the part of instruction that is not universal" could be transferred to "general common instruction," that is, to support primary and secondary schools.[7] Education would be not only nationalized but democratized.

THE DISINTEGRATION OF THE CONDORCET PLAN

About 20 persons spoke on the Condorcet plan in the Convention in December 1792, and almost all of them opposed it. The great equalitarian was accused of elitism, and the *philosophe* was found to neglect

[6] Ibid., p. 211. Added by Condorcet in 1793.
[7] Ibid., p. 308.

the need for moral and civic training.[8] Signs of party divisions were beginning to appear in the Convention; they were inflamed at this very moment by debates leading to the trial of Louis XVI, and would become acute six months later with the expulsion of the group known as Girondins.

Robespierre, as spokesman for the emerging Mountain, the victorious Jacobins of 1793, dismissed the Condorcet plan as "not worth discussing." He did so in the journal he was then editing, his *Lettres à ses commettants*, in an article expressing his usual combination of high principle and political animosity.[9] He began with a plain Rousseauist declaration: "Man is good as he comes from the hands of nature; no one who rejects this principle should ever undertake to educate (*instituer*) man. If man is corrupt, it is to the vices in social institutions that the disorder should be imputed. ... If social institutions have depraved man, it is social institutions that must be reformed." But who should have the moral right, the wisdom, or the power to make the needed reforms? Who could dare to educate human beings, *à instituer l'homme*? The present government, he said, was corrupt, self-seeking, and untrustworthy. (The ministries were at this time held by Girondins.) It was absurd to have a ministry of the interior already disbursing "enormous sums" to shape public opinion, and such a ministry would control education if the Condorcet plan should be adopted. And he concluded: "Snatch the reins of power from the hands of immorality and hypocrisy, and you will then be worthy of entering on the great work of public instruction." What Robespierre thought of state control of education a few months later, with the Mountain in power, will soon be seen.

The question was thus politicized, yet there was no clear party division. Neither Robespierre nor any other prominent member of the Mountain spoke up in the Convention against the Condorcet plan. In fact, the Mountain supplied in the person of Gilbert Romme the only speaker who defended the plan in these debates of December 1792. Most of those who opposed it were moderates as then defined. Condorcet himself was to die as a Girondin, but three of his most vocal opponents would be guillotined as Girondins also. It is to be noted, in addition, that although several speakers expressed anti-intellectual sentiments, none was uneducated; several had obtained law degrees,

---

[8] Keith Baker, *Condorcet: From National Philosophy to Social Mathematics* (Chicago, 1975), pp. 293-320; Roger Hahn, *The Anatomy of a Scientific Institution: The Paris Academy of Sciences* (Berkeley, 1971), pp. 159-225.

[9] M. Robespierre, *Oeuvres complètes de Robespierre, vol. 5, Les journaux ... édition critique préparée par Gustav Laurent* (Gap, 1961), pp. 207-11.

two had been Prostestant pastors, and one was an important merchant from Bordeaux.

It is possible to see in the attacks on the Condorcet plan, beyond the inflamed language of revolutionary clichés, a troubled discussion of perennial educational problems.

It was feared that the proposed National Society of the Arts and Sciences would be like an "academy"—the French Academy and the academies for the sciences, painting, and other artistic and scholarly activities of the Old Regime. These had been (or indeed were, being still alive) exclusive corporate bodies, choosing their own membership, setting their own standards, passing judgments of merit, and conferring or withholding honors. Objection to these academies had developed well before the Revolution, which of course intensified it. The painter David had already founded a Commune des Arts for independent painters. Artisans and ingenious inventors had long complained against the Royal Academy of Sciences; they were now sansculottes with organizations of their own. "Free" and "private" societies had multiplied since before 1789. The pre-Revolutionary Lycée des Arts now functioned as the Lycée Republicain. A new Lycée des Arts, formed during the Revolution, aimed more at serving working-class interests and had working-class members. There were also, since 1789, the Société Philomatique, the Société d'Histoire Naturelle, and others. These new societies now stood as symbols of liberty and equality against the aristocracy and despotism of the academies, which were in fact soon abolished, at the height of the sans-culotte movement in August 1793.

Condorcet, as secretary of the Royal Academy of Sciences for the past 20 years and a member of the French Academy for 10, was himself a symbol of the old order. He was vulnerable both to the suspicions of artisans and to assault by disaffected writers, intellectuals, and discredited scientists like Marat. His National Society, as he proposed it, would in fact be a corporate and self-enclosed body, more powerful than the old academies in having powers over a whole system of national education that the academies had never had. He knew the arguments against academies and tried to anticipate them, but without success.

The whole apparatus of "institutes, lycées and a National Society," cried Durand-Maillane, a lawyer, "would form a formidable corporation." "After having shaken off the yoke of tyrants and rid ourselves of priestly domination . . . it is strange that, on the pretext of science and enlightenment, it is proposed to the nation to confer, at its own expense, a permanent and particular status on one class of its citizens.

And what citizens? Those most able to dominate public opinion by guiding it, for there is a superstition about what are called men of learning, as there used to be about kings and priests."[10] Durand-Maillane raised a stir in the hall by avowing his own Catholic faith, but the same sentiments were shared by the Protestant Jeanbon Saint-André: "Is it after overturning the hierarchy of priests that you are going to create a hierarchy of the learned?" It would be "a true corporation, a new clergy, armed by yourselves with a dangerous influence, a group of masters, a gild." And further: "The Republic is not required to produce savants."[11] Or to quote Durand-Maillane again: "The French people, to be happy, have no more need of science than what is necessary to arrive at virtue"; and virtue had nothing to do with talent or success in studies, for it was simply "the love of country and observance of the laws."[12]

All believed in "national education," but some distinguished it from "public instruction." The need for instruction might vary, but everyone must have *éducation* in the new Revolutionary sense. Education formed the spirit, instruction only the mind. Education, said the Protestant pastor and future Girondin, Rabaut Saint-Etienne, required "circuses, gymnasiums, armed exercises, public games, national festivals, the fraternal concourse of all ages and sexes, the touching and imposing spectacle of a human society gathered together." It demanded "common institutions, so well known to the ancients, which brought it about that on the same day, at the same instant, among all citizens, of all ages and in all places, all should receive the same impressions, by the senses, by imagination, by memory, by reasoning, by all human faculties, by that enthusiasm that we may call the magic of reason."[13] On all this the Condorcet plan was nearly silent.

Several speakers, including two future Girondins, found Condorcet (and the Committee on Public Instruction) too indifferent to the attainment of genuine equality. There should be compulsory common

---

[10] Guillaume, *Procès-verbaux . . . Convention*, 1:xvii, 124, 126.

[11] Ibid., 1:278, 275. This speech by Jeanbon Saint-André was written in December 1792 in opposition to the Condorcet plan, but it was not delivered; it was printed in June 1793 in opposition to the Sieyès-Daunou-Lakanal plan. The reader may be reminded of the phrase said to have been spoken at the time of Lavoisier's death: "The Republic has no need of savants." The authenticity of this quotation was examined by J. Guillaume in 1900 in *Révolution française*, 38:385-99. In any case Saint-André's words quoted above, "la République n'est pas obligée de faire des savants," may be understood to mean that men of learning may be produced by agencies other than the state.

[12] Ibid., p. 124. *Science* in French at this time, here translated as "science," sometimes meant something more like "knowledge."

[13] Ibid., p. 231.

schooling. All children, said the merchant from Bordeaux, J. F. Ducos, should be required to attend primary school together at least for a few years. "So long as, by instruction in common, you have not brought together the rich and the poor, the powerful and the weak, so long as, to employ an expression of Plutarch's, you have not put all children of the country on one track and molded them to one form of virtue, it is in vain that your laws will proclaim a sacred equality; the Republic will always be divided into two classes, the *citoyens* and the *messieurs*."[14] Saint-André, Rabaut, and J. B. Leclerc, another lawyer, said much the same.

For J.B.C. Masuyer, a lawyer and judge from eastern France, the regional equality and decentralization in the Condorcet plan were delusive. The plan provided too few institutes and too few lycées, so few that only privileged localities and persons would benefit. "If you want to avoid the double patriciate of wealth and privileged education, make it easier for all citizens without distinction to acquire all forms of knowledge, or else grant it to none."[15] Or as another "moderate," Bancal des Issarts, expressed it: "Either suppress your lycées or give one to each department."[16] What would happen to education at the high level contemplated by Condorcet for the lycées, if scattered among 80-odd departments, Bancal did not say. The notion had been expressed that what not all could enjoy, none should have.

What was to be done with the old colleges, many of which were still operating? The Condorcet plan would abolish them and replace them with "institutes." "If you do not organize public instruction at all levels," said Romme, defending the plan, "the colleges will rise again from their ruins . . . and these creations of error and prejudice will poison the schools of new creation at their birth."[17] But some critics thought that the state-supported national system should apply only at the primary level. They would leave intermediate and higher levels to private initiative. These men were not opposed to learning, despite their anti-intellectual outbursts; they had in mind the two Lycées and other *sociétés libres* and private schools already existing in Paris, and it must be remembered that the decision to sell off the college endowments was not made until the following March. They wanted the primary schools to be universal, even compulsory, for all classes, and devoted to the formation of a unified nation of patriotic republicans and fraternal democrats, especially in time of war. The idea of

[14] Ibid., p. 191.
[15] Ibid., p. 143.
[16] Ibid., p. 252.
[17] Ibid., p. 216.

éducation commune was to surface again in the sans-culotte summer of 1793. It had been anticipated by these bourgeois Girondins. But although there was real agreement in the Convention on the need for universal and free primary schooling, there was also so much confusion of debate on other issues—the National Society, the lyées and institutes, the fate of Louis XVI, and the temporary conquests in Belgium—that no legislation even on primary schools was enacted. The issue was simply postponed.

Events moved rapidly in the following months. Louis XVI was executed on January 21; those who had not voted for the death penalty came under suspicion of "moderatism." As the war turned against the French, the defection and flight to the enemy of the Girondins' favorite general, Dumouriez, threw a cloud of doubt over his erstwhile friends. In March the Committee on Public Instruction finally agreed, apparently with reluctance, with proposals of the Committee on Finance for sale of the "adjourned" national properties, as a means of financing the war; the two committees obtained the decree from the Convention for liquidation of the college endowments. The Convention decreed also that the salaries of professors and scholarships for students should be paid by the Nation. Civil war broke out in the West. Revolutionary fervor mounted in Paris. Those who warned against the radicalism of Paris, or gave evidence of fear or disdain for the lower classes, found themselves branded as enemies of the people. From May 31 through June 2 an enormous crowd of armed insurrectionists besieged and invaded the hall of the Convention, demanding the expulsion of members who had become offensive to the sans-culottes. Thirty were arrested and imprisoned; these and their supporters are the Girondins of history. Meanwhile the Convention had created a Committee of Public Safety, to which it granted emergency powers and which gradually became a steering committee for the Convention and executive head of the government agencies. On May 30, the day before the great insurrection, the Committee of Public Safety ordered the Convention to establish "a primary school in every place of 600 inhabitants" and the Committee on Public Instruction to draft a new "plan of public instruction."[18]

This Committee was dominated after the insurrection of May 31 by three men who, though good revolutionaries, had vaguely clerical antecedents: the Abbé Sieyès, known as the great theorist of national sovereignty, and two young men who had been professional teachers,

---

[18] A. Aulard, ed., *Recueil des actes du Comité de salut public de la Convention Nationale*, 28 vols. (Paris, 1889-1955), 4:353, 378.

P. D. Daunou, of the former Oratory, and Joseph Lakanal, of the former Congregation of the Christian Doctrine. Daunou's plan of 1790 has already been mentioned; it had favored "teaching societies" but accepted the disbanding of the Oratory as a significant organization and would have placed the colleges more fully under the civil authorities. The new plan of the Committee, that is the Sieyès-Daunou-Lakanal plan, was soon denounced as a subterfuge to revive the abolished *congrégations séculières* and restore a clerical influence in education. There is really no evidence of any such intent. None of the three planners was exactly a cleric. They seem rather to have incorporated what they supposed to have been the wishes expressed by the Convention in the preceding December.

The new plan, presented on June 26, 1793, went into great detail on "education" as distinct from "instruction." As a part of "education," school children and adult women would learn music and dancing so as to take part with men in national festivals, of which no fewer than 40 were specified. There would be festivals for Visible Nature, for the French Revolution (July 14), and for the Fraternity of the Human Race (New Year's Day); and at the village level festivals for the opening of the fields, for youth, for marriage, for motherhood, and "for the animals who live with man"—at which even the Convention laughed.[19]

In "instruction" the main novelty was that the national system under public control would have only one level instead of Condorcet's five and Talleyrand's four. This one level would provide universal and free education in the primary schools. To have the intermediate and higher levels in a national system, in the view of the new planners, would produce a sluggish bureaucracy, a privileged corporation, self-satisfied in its ways and resistant to new ideas. "I ask you," said Daunou, "whether public professors, always sure of their salaries, will not in general be less zealous than free and private professors who are more directly interested in the success of their teaching?"[20] He added that any attempt to control them would become unbearable. "Let instruction at this level, like commerce, be honored but not undertaken by the State." Under a regime of freedom "you will see opening up, in effect, secondary schools, institutes, courses, lycées and academies; you will have

---

[19] Guillaume, *Procès-verbaux . . . Convention*, 1:507-16; the quotation is on p. 514.

[20] Daunou and Sieyès defended the plan in separate writings, Daunou in an *Essai sur l'instruction publique* (Paris, 1793), and Sieyès in the short-lived *Journal d'instruction sociale par les citoyens Condorcet, Sieyès et Duhamel*, 6 numbers (June-July 1793). Daunou's *Essai* is reprinted by Guillaume, *Procès-verbaux . . . Convention*, 1:581-607 (for the quotation see p. 599); Sieyès's journal articles by Guillaume, ibid., 1:567-78.

summoned all sciences, arts, opinions, methods, industries and talents to the fruitful activity of a great competition."[21] Allowing for the usual discount on oratory, this view was by no means utopian. For 30 years there had been an increase not only of independent learned societies but also of private schools for boys and young men, some of them fashionable boarding schools such as David Hume had visited in Paris in 1764, others more middle-class establishments like those at Lille, where 12 private schools in 1789 had more students than the two old colleges of that city. A "private" sector had in fact arisen as a progressive force against the more conservative "public" system (in the pre-Revolutionary sense) of universities, faculties, and colleges.[22]

It may seem that Sieyès, Daunou, and Lakanal were irresponsible in relying on private institutions in June, when the old colleges had lost their endowments as recently as the preceding March, and when the Convention had already agreed to support the dispossessed professors and scholarships from public funds. Expropriation of the colleges could only inhibit private giving for education in the future. The trio seem, however, not to have regretted the loss; at least Daunou now claimed that with all the free instruction and endowed scholarships of the Old Regime the poor had had little chance for education. Nor would the poor benefit from a state-supported system. "A system in which the State carries the cost of higher schools will never be more than a way of making the poor man pay to make the rich man more learned."[23] Sieyès wanted a liberal system of state-supported scholarships to send promising youths to private schools. Daunou, while allowing for such student aid, was also (in 1793) more radical. Equality would never come out of educational institutions, he announced; it could come only from legislation controlling private property and inheritance, redistribution of the tax burden, price regulation, and public works. It was the poor and not the lettered class that should be subsidized. With real equality all talent would find its place, and a free system of education, free in the sense of independence from the state, would flourish.[24]

The Sieyès-Daunou-Lakanal plan did provide, however, for a Central Commission to oversee the primary schools as well as certain other public institutions such as libraries and museums. The recently triumphant party in the Convention, the Mountain, seized upon this feature to discredit the whole proposal as well as its authors. They raised the

[21] Guillaume, *Procès-verbaux . . . Convention*, 1:602, 599.
[22] See above, pp. 26-30, 36, 61, 131.
[23] Guillaume, *Procès-verbaux . . . Convention*, 1:605.
[24] Ibid., 1:570, 605.

same charges of elitism, corporatism, privilege, and bureaucracy that had been hurled against Condorcet and that Sieyès and his two colleagues had also raised. With the Committee on Public Instruction thus discredited, Sieyès and Daunou simply disappeared from the political stage for over a year, although Lakanal contrived to remain.[25]

Maximilien Robespierre now entered the debates on education for the first time, though his role would be brief. On June 18, while the Convention was preparing a new republican constitution, he persuaded it to include *une instruction commune* among the rights guaranteed to all citizens. He obtained also the creation of a new Commission on Public Instruction in addition to the existing Committee of the same name. He himself was elected to this Commission (also called the Commission of Six), as were Lakanal, the humanitarian Abbé Grégoire, and Léonard Bourdon, now a militant of the Mountain, who operated a school in Paris of which more will be said. While the rebuffed Committee continued to busy itself with work on the metric system and the preservation of national monuments the new Commission took up the task of educational planning.

It may be parenthetically remarked that in the world of real life, as distinct from the world of planning and speech-making, the Convention at this same time granted 307,552 francs to the 10 colleges of Paris. On August 4 it sent a delegation to the prize-giving ceremony held at the Jacobin Club for students of the Paris colleges, as described at the beginning of the last chapter. The next day the young prize winners were invited to appear in the hall of the Convention itself, where the presiding officer received them with a little speech: "The enemies of the Revolution have accused the National Convention of wishing to annihilate letters. The flattering welcome that it now extends to you is the best answer to such calumnies." Nevertheless, by action of the Department of Paris, nine of the 10 Paris colleges were closed down a few weeks later.[26]

With the Condorcet plan never adopted, and the alternative Sieyès-Daunou-Lakanal plan rejected, the new Commission was in a position to make a fresh start but was drawn for several weeks into a troublesome digression, which proved to be temporary but which had a certain long-range significance. This was the question of *éducation commune*. It was brought up by Félix Lepeletier, who demanded the right

[25] Curiously, Sieyès in defending against the charge of academic aristocracy asserted that the proposed Central Commission would be merely a "ministry" subordinate to legislative authority. This is possibly the first suggestion of a "ministry" of public instruction, which did not exist in France until 1824. Ibid., 1:575.

[26] Ibid., 2:196, 230-31.

to appear before the Convention to read a plan of education composed by his late brother, Michel, a member of that body, during the debates on the Condorcet plan six months before but neither delivered orally nor printed at that time. The Lepeletiers were of a sixth-generation noble parlementary family, the Lepeletiers de Saint-Fargeau; and Michel, the elder brother, had been one of the richest men in France with an annual income estimated at over half a million livres. Both brothers had moved along at a rapid pace with the radicalization of the Revolution. Michel had been a member of the Convention and had voted for the death of Louis XVI. For this he was assassinated by a royalist a few days later. Michel Lepeletier thus became a fallen hero, and when Marat was also assassinated in June, at the very moment now under consideration, both the Jacobins and the sans-culottes demanded solemn honors for Marat and Lepeletier as martyrs of liberty. Félix Lepeletier made it his business to glorify his deceased brother. He pressed for the adoption of his plan in 1793, then became a founding member of Babeuf's Conspiracy of Equals in 1796, and was active among the neo-Jacobins of 1799, in both of which groups the demand for *éducation commune* was revived. He lived to publish Michel's works in 1826, thus launching the Lepeletier plan into one of the tributaries of the nineteenth-century revolutionary movement.

Robespierre, by a stratagem, obtained a copy of Michel Lepeletier's hitherto unknown discourse, and it was Robespierre that read it aloud in the hall of the Convention on July 13, while Félix had to content himself with reading it to the Jacobin Club a little later. Robespierre, speaking for the Commission of Six, strongly endorsed the Lepeletier plan and introduced a bill for its adoption by the Convention on July 29. Lepeletier had in fact approved of most of the Condorcet plan, accepting its four levels of primary schools, secondary schools, institutes, and lycées. He was no absolute equalitarian, for his plan, like Condorcet's, was meritocratic and *sélectionniste*. Making the usual distinction between education and instruction, he observed that instruction, though offered to all, would "become the exclusive possession of a small number of members of society because of differences in occupations and talents," but that education must be "common to all and universally beneficial."[27] Lepeletier therefore proposed that only one in 50 boys in the lowest schools should go on to the next stage, and thereafter only half from each stage to the next higher, culminating in the lycées. But Lepeletier also thought that much of this could wait,

[27] The Lepeletier plan, with Robespierre's prefatory remarks, is printed by Guillaume, ibid., 2:34-61; this quotation is from p. 35.

and that universal "national education" in elementary schools should be provided immediately.

His idea was that instead of the *écoles primaires* as hitherto proposed there should be *établissements d'éducation nationale*, or state boarding schools, in which children of all social classes should be brought together to live apart from their families. Boys and girls should be placed separately in such institutions at the age of five. Here they would of course learn the elements of reading, writing, and arithmetic but would also strengthen their bodies and characters under a régime of "austere discipline," observing regular hours under strict surveillance, sleeping on hard beds, wearing coarse garments, and eating only wholesome foods. They would also perform simple tasks within the establishment, and in neighboring fields and on the roads, partly to develop habits and skills of work but also to contribute to the costs of their education. At the age of twelve for the boys and eleven for the girls, they should "be returned to their parents or guardians and to the various useful occupations of society in the diverse trades and in agriculture," except for those chosen for higher schools. This procedure would be mandatory. "Fathers, mothers or guardians who neglect to fulfill this duty will lose their rights of citizenship and be subjected to a double rate of direct taxation for as long as they withhold the child from *éducation commune*."[28]

THE AMBIGUITIES OF *Éducation Commune*

The Lepeletier plan is remembered, rightly enough so far as elementary schooling is concerned, as the most radically democratic and equalitarian of all the educational plans generated in the assemblies of the French Revolution. *Éducation commune* has been presented as a distinctive idea of the sans-culottes.[29] It is likely, however, that in its form as expressed by Lepeletier it had more appeal for intellectuals than for the real popular masses or actual working class. It must be emphasized also that the Lepeletier plan was never adopted by the Convention, most of whose members were too practical, or too "bourgeois," or too steeped in a sentimental feeling for parenthood and the family to contemplate the forcible separation of children from their mothers and fathers. What the Convention did was to adopt a modi-

[28] Ibid., 2:163, from Robespierre's *projet de décret* embodying the Lepeletier plan.
[29] F. Stübig, *Erziehung zur Gleichheit: Konzepte der "éducation commune" in der französischen Revolution* (Ravensburg, 1974), esp. pp. 144-376.

fied and optional version of the plan in August, which it then rescinded in October.

There were many ambiguities in the idea of *éducation commune*, and a reading of the speeches in the Convention is enough to show that not all speakers in using the phrase meant the same thing. The phrase had several levels of meaning.

That it was desirable to have boys of different social classes meet in the same classroom, and be treated alike, was an idea by no means unknown to the Old Regime. It had then applied to the colleges and to the minority of adolescents who attended them. Many colleges had in fact been quite mixed. If some writers, such as Baudeau, had favored segregation by social class, others, such as Charles Rollin, the Abbé Crevier, Guyton de Morveau, and the royal ministers who set up the *écoles militaires*, had favored a system in which boys of different social background were brought together. Both Robespierre and Danton, in urging *éducation commune* in 1793, were reminded of their experience in their own colleges, in whose communal atmosphere they thought that ideas of equality had been promoted.[30]

The idea of "common education," or "education in common," was broadened by the Constituent Assembly to apply to younger children at the elementary level, and to all such children—"a public instruction common to all citizens, and free for those parts of instruction indispensable for all men"—and was stipulated for both boys and girls in both the Talleyrand and the Condorcet plans. The thought here seems to have been that a primary level for all should *precede* a secondary level for the few who needed it, or whose further schooling was needed by society, not that the primary and secondary should be separate tracks from the start, as came to be the case in the nineteenth century. It thus anticipated a principle that reappeared in the twentieth century, that all persons should have acquired together a common or national fund of experience, and a mutual acquaintance and respect, at an early age, before going their separate ways in different occupations in later life. During the Revolution this idea was reinforced by plans for national festivals, by which adults would be brought together for the same purpose of social or national solidarity.

A further step was the addition of the principle of obligation, or that schooling for a certain number of years should be compulsory. This was much discussed though never effectively adopted. Here again there were uncertainties of meaning. For some, who would allow pri-

---

[30] See above, pp. 21-24, 58, 67; and on Robespierre and Danton, Guillaume, *Procès-verbaux . . . Convention*, 2:278, n. 2; 3:xliii, n.3.

vate schools to exist alongside the public or national system, the parents would simply be required to send children to a school of their choice. What they rejected was private tutoring at home. For others, no private schools should be allowed, and parents would be required to send children to the national *écoles primaires*, where they would meet and work together in the classroom and share in the same physical exercises and civic activities while living with their parents. This was probably the most common view among sans-culottes and Montagnards during the most intensely revolutionary months of 1793, but we have seen that certain persons designated as Girondins had expressed it in December 1792, and indeed the Abbé Auger, Léonard Bourdon, and J. F. Major had favored compulsory attendance at the national schools in 1790.[31] An odd variant was proposed by a certain Jean-Gervais Labène, who worked on the great abortive bibliographical project in 1793. He thought that children might receive "instruction" anywhere, at home or in any school, but that for "education" all parents and teachers should be required "to send their pupils to the public grounds twice a day, from ten in the morning until noon, and from four to six in the afternoon," there to receive an intensive civic formation in common.[32]

We reach the point of extreme equalitarianism when *éducation commune*, in addition to being universal, free, and compulsory, is conducted by the state in boarding schools away from the family, as in the Lepeletier plan. There was much logic in Lepeletier's position. He expressed genuine concern for the plight of the very poor. Some parents, he said, were too poor, or too ignorant, or too distressed even to send their children for a few hours a day to a local schoolroom. The state should relieve them, and save their children from lives of futility, by assembling, housing, feeding, and teaching poor children in communal establishments. He had come to share in the Revolutionary passion for equality. The rich and the poor should therefore be treated alike. The family was the great self-perpetuating obstacle to real equality. All children should therefore, for their own good, be removed from their families and made to live together as soon as feasible during their formative years. The older generation were the bearers of the wrong ideas of the past. The younger generation should therefore be protected from retrogression. There was the logic of theoretical environmentalism; if children were formed by their surround-

[31] See above, pp. 92-93.

[32] Jean-Gervais Labène, *De l'éducation dans les grandes républiques* (Paris, An III). BN. R 22931.

ings, it followed that surroundings must be carefully designed. And there was the political logic of guidance and planning; if the Revolutionary leaders were to produce a truly free and enlightened society, they must begin with the children. "A truly national, truly republican education, equally and effectively common to all, is the only kind of education capable of regenerating humankind."[33]

The ambiguities even in the extreme version of *éducation commune* are illustrated by the career of Léonard Bourdon, who in July 1793 joined Félix Lepeletier as a forceful spokesman for the Lepeletier plan. He was also one of the most rabid of the Mountain, always to the left of Robespierre, so that when Robespierre turned against the "ultras" Bourdon took alarm, joined with other extremists against him, and was present at his arrest on 9 Thermidor of the Year II. In the weeks after Robespierre's death, as a Thermidorian of the Left, to give assurance to his "ultra" friends, he helped to bring about the curious episode of the Pantheonization of Marat. He took part in the popular uprising of Germinal of the Year III in March 1795, for which he was arrested and spent a few months in prison. During all this revolutionary activity he also conducted a school. In educational efforts from 1788 to 1798 he kept repeating the same ideas, of which *éducation commune* was one, but which described an institution that varied from an upperclass boarding school to an orphan asylum.

As early as 1780, if we may believe Bourdon's own words, he acted as a kind of consultant to the Benedictine fathers on the management of their *écoles militaires* such as the one at Sorèze, for which he had made various liberal recommendations, such as reducing the severity of the teachers, increasing the "confidence" of the students, and motivating the latter to "a love of good order and work." With these claims to experience, in 1788, Bourdon de la Crosnière, as he now called himself, obtained from the royal government its protection for a new school to be called the Société Royale d'Emulation. It would charge an annual fee of 3,000 livres (at a time when the king paid only 700 livres apiece for his noble cadets at the *écoles militaires*), and so was designed, as Bourdon explained, for "those whose birth and fortune call them to high position." This arrangement was upset by the Revolution, in which Bourdon soon became heavily involved.[34]

In 1791 he projected a new school that he hoped would attract the sons of members of the Paris Jacobin Club. He proposed to charge

[33] Guillaume, *Procès-verbaux . . . Convention*, 2:37.

[34] [L.J.J.L. Bourdon de la Crosnière], *Plan d'un établissement d'éducation nationale, autorisé par arrêt du conseil du 5 octobre 1788, sous le titre de Société Royale d'Emulation* (Orleans, 1788); the quotation is from pp. 11-12.

them 1,000 livres a year—a sign that many Jacobins of 1791 were financially comfortable, and indeed there were four nobles on the committee of the Jacobin Society that examined Bourdon's proposal, including the first husband of Josephine Bonaparte and a young man who became the future King Louis-Philippe. The school would teach both practical and cultural subjects; it would train its pupils to "depend on things, not on persons"; it would be administered by joint committees of teachers and students, who would live under laws of their own making; and despite the high fees it would contain workshops in which boys would learn skilled manual trades and be paid for their efforts—"the only means perhaps of making instruction attractive by the incentive of a legitimate wage for work, and to lay the foundation of an education that will become truly national only in so far as it becomes common." The Paris Jacobins approved of Bourdon's proposed establishment as an experimental school, or pilot study, for a future nationwide system, a few days after the postponement of the Talleyrand plan in the Constituent Assembly; and they circulated it with their endorsement to other Jacobin clubs throughout France.[35]

Bourdon went ahead and organized a school that he called the Society for French Youth, located in the former priory of Saint-Martin-des-Champs in Paris. Beginning with 50 pupils in 1792, it was enlarged the next year when the Convention ruled that it should take in war orphans, for each of whom the War Ministry paid 1,000 livres a year. It soon came about that three-quarters of the pupils were paid for by the government. The school became an expensive social benefit, limited to a few. It had 204 pupils in April 1795, after which it was closed in consequence of Bourdon's arrest for involvement in the attempted insurrection of Germinal.

It was the actual existence of this school, his Society of French Youth, that Bourdon cited as an argument in supporting the Lepeletier plan in the Convention in the summer of 1793. What he now had in mind was affirmative action for the eradication of class differences. Lepeletier's *maisons d'éducation*, he said, were much better than mere *écoles primaires* because if a child went to school only a few hours a day "the rich child will get practical lessons in pride, aristocracy and despotism from his parents, while the poor child becomes the pupil of superstition and prejudice."[36] He also argued that the Lepeletier system, while

---

[35] A. Aulard, ed., *La Société des Jacobins*, 6 vols. (Paris, 1889-1897), 2:167-72; 3:172-79.

[36] *Discours sur l'institution commune, par Léonard Bourdon . . . prononcé dans la séance du 30 juillet 1793* (Paris, 1793), p. 2; reprinted in Guillaume, *Procès-verbaux . . . Convention*, 2:179.

instilling equality, would not be unduly costly, because the industry of the children themselves, from the age of seven, would suffice to pay for their upkeep within three years, and in five years could yield "double the cost." Nevertheless Bourdon, as well as Robespierre, in the face of resistance in the Convention, agreed to a compromise by which the state boarding schools would be optional, with parents free to send their children to ordinary primary schools if they preferred. It would be the poor who would at first benefit from this arrangement, they thought; but the boarding schools would be so attractive that families of all classes would eventually use them. The Convention did in fact enact this optional version of the Lepeletier plan but rescinded it a few weeks later.

In October 1797, under the Directory, Bourdon submitted a *pétition sur l'éducation commune* to the Council of Five Hundred, urging it to open a school on the model of his Society of French Youth, closed over two years before, but which he said had operated successfully for three years. The new school would have the same methods and purposes as its predecessor and would begin as a school for war orphans; it would also pay for itself through the labor of the pupils, within a period that Bourdon now estimated at 12 years. Since the school would be self-financing, it could readily be replicated into a national system. But Bourdon failed to get any action, and the doubt remains on whether his *éducation commune* was an idealistic plan to bring the advantages of an expensive boarding school to the general population, or was a practical arrangement for using child labor to finance a system of public elementary schools.[37]

Meanwhile Félix Lepeletier took a more positively radical tack than Bourdon. Not being a member of the Convention, he sent it a letter in August 1793, insisting that the state boarding schools of his brother's plan must be mandatory for all social classes. Since he was not yet ready to wipe out the rich as a class through abolition of private property, like the later Babeuf group, he argued that *l'éducation commune forcée* was the only way to make them accept equality. The state board-

---

[37] *Pétition au Conseil des 500 sur l'éducation commune par Léonard Bourdon*, 4 Brumaire of the year VI, with accompanying documents in Archives Nationales, AF III 109, nos. 3, 4, and 5. These include a printed report of 1794, drawn up shortly after the death of Robespierre, by a committee charged with examining Bourdon's school: *Rapport des députés nommés par la Commission des Arts pour assister aux exercices de l'Ecole Republicaine connue sous le nom de Société des Jeunes Français.* The workings of the school are well described in this report of 1794. There is a good chapter on Bourdon and his school in Stübig, *Enziehung zur Gleichheit*, pp. 433-88. See also A. Léon, *La Révolution française et l'éducation technique* (Paris, 1968), pp. 131-34.

ing schools would be *la révolution du citoyen prolétaire*.[38] Rich boys would learn in them that wealth itself was worthless and even dangerous to its possessors. By laboring alongside others in the school workshops, they would even contribute to the maintenance of their less fortunate classmates. "You will establish, by mandatory common education," he told the Convention, "a fraternity among citizens and an equality that can only be developed in the age of innocence by institutions for youth, but whose traces last until the winter of old age."[39]

When Babeuf organized his famous Conspiracy of Equals in 1796 Félix Lepeletier was among the first members of the secret committee aiming at the overthrow of the Directory. Babeuf and a few others, though not all their followers, saw the abolition of property as the best corrective to social inequities, but other features of his plan received more publicity in his journal, the *Tribun du peuple*, and in an *Analyse de la doctrine de Babeuf* that was posted in the streets in Paris. The *Analyse* declared that "*l'éducation doit être commune.*" Babeuf called Michel Lepeletier's plan "sublime" and went farther than Lepeletier into an unconditional equalitarianism. He published in his journal a "Manifesto of the Plebeians." "Education is a monstrosity when it is unequal," said the Manifesto. "Superiority of talents and industry is only a chimera or a decoy that has already unduly served the plots of conspirators against equality." "In a human society"—or a "humane society"?, the French *humain* having both meanings—"it would always be necessary either to have no education at all or for all individuals to be able to have it equally."[40] And when Philippe Bounarroti, Babeuf's companion of 1796, published his book on the Conspiracy of Equals many years later, he noted that the insurrectionary committee of 1796 had wanted education to be "National, in Common, and Equal," with children kept apart from "parental sway," living under arrangements "simultaneously administered to all children under the same discipline."[41]

[38] *Lettre du citoyen Félix Lepeletier aux membres de la Convention*, reprinted in Guillaume, *Procès-verbaux . . . Conventions*, 2:235. Italics in the original.

[39] Ibid., 2:238.

[40] Babeuf's views are conveniently assembled in M. Dommanget, "Babeuf et l'éducation," *Annales historiques de la Révolution française* 162 (October-December 1960): 488-506 and 163 (January-March 1961): 35-46. For fuller texts see Dommanget, *Pages choisies de Babeuf* (Paris, 1935), which reprints long extracts from the *Tribun du Peuple*, including the "Manifeste des plébéiens" on pp. 250-64. See also Dommanget, *Les grands socialistes et l'éducation* (Paris, 1970), pp. 82-84, 130-32, and my *Age of the Democratic Revolution*, 2 vols. (Princeton, 1964), 2:235-44.

[41] See Bronterre O'Brien's translation of Buonarroti, *Babeuf's Conspiracy for Equality* (London, 1836), pp. 203, 208-209.

It is normal to see in Babeuf's conspiracy a somewhat distant precursor to communism, though no modern communist state, with possible exception for certain years in Maoist China, has carried his educational equalitarianism to such lengths. An admiring historian, Maurice Dommanget, has praised Babeuf for his highly developed class theory of education, holding that the possessing class uses its own education as a means of impressing and dominating the poor while refusing to allow the poor enough education to learn to perceive their rights. Babeuf himself, at his trial, insisted that what he aimed at was no more than simple democracy. His statements on education can indeed be taken as formulas for extreme democratization carried to the point of absurdity. They did not accurately reflect what the rank and file of sans-culottes or democrats of 1793 really wanted.

There was a mainstream in demands for democratized education beside which mandatory boarding schools can be seen as no more than a Leftist deviation. It was expressed in another plan that was never adopted but is significant because of the social identity of its sponsors. This climax of the democratic movement took the form of a petition to the Convention, submitted on September 15, 1793, "by the Department of Paris, the rural districts, the commune, and the sections and popular societies meeting jointly." The plan revived important elements of the Condorcet plan, and in the words of James Guillaume "this triumph of the Encyclopedic spirit was due to the initiative of the Parisian democracy."[42] Before describing the plan of September 15, let us examine the groups that devised and supported it.

THE "PARISIAN DEMOCRACY" OF 1793

It is not to be supposed that democracy in the France of 1793 signified endorsement by a majority of large numbers of voters. Both the Commune of Paris (the municipal government of the city) and the Department of Paris (renamed the Department of the Seine in 1795, and comprising the area of the city and 16 adjoining rural cantons) were administered by elected councils, but the elections were held in public and could be noisy and even dangerous, so that, when allowance is also made for the apathy that exists even in time of revolution, the number of actual voters could be very small.

[42] Guillaume, *Procès-verbaux . . . Convention,* 2:xxx. Guillaume was a late nineteenth-century socialist; preference for the term "popular masses" reflects a more recent Marxist orientation.

The council of the Department, as elected in January 1793, was in principle chosen by 989 qualified electors, but at no meeting of the electors were more than half of them present. Several members of the Department council in 1793 held office by less than a hundred votes.[43] The council of the Commune, or governing body of the city, was elected by voters meeting in the primary assemblies of the sections of Paris. In 1793 all adult men residing in the sections were qualified to vote. But attendance at the section assemblies varied in general from five to 15 percent of those qualified. One of the largest figures for attendance of which there is any record is for 678 present at the Section des Sans-Culottes on June 19, 1793. This section, in a poor neighborhood on the Left Bank, had a population of about 15,000 and some 4,000 qualified voters, so that 678 represents about 16 percent of the qualified. In other sections and at other times the attendance was much lower. Nevertheless, to have excited gatherings of several hundred enthusiasts meeting almost continuously and simultaneously all over the city made for an extremely busy political life.[44]

This political life was democratic in that it was carried on by very plain people. Not only the royal authorities and old-style aristocrats, but the liberal noblemen and members of the upper bourgeoisie who had figured prominently in the early phase of the Revolution, were swept away in the insurrection of August 10, 1792—the "second" revolution. Who were these plain people, or sans-culottes and their supporters, who made up the Parisian democracy of 1793?

The Department council consisted of 36 members, elected or re-elected in January, but exactly half of them had been members of the more strictly revolutionary provisional council set up during the uprising of the preceding August. Of the other half, several had been leaders in their sections at that time. The Revolutionary credentials of the Department in 1793 were thus well established. Twenty of the 36 were either skilled artisans, such as an engraver, a clockmaker, and a painter of miniatures, or else small manufacturers, shopkeepers, merchant furriers, merchant hatters, and so forth. Three were office workers or employees of government. Others were in occupations presup-

---

[43] Sigismond Lacroix, *Le Département de Paris et de la Seine pendant la Révolution (février 1791 à ventôse An VIII)* (Paris, 1904), p. 171.

[44] Albert Soboul, *Les Sans-culottes parisiens en l'An II: mouvement populaire et gouvernement révolutionnaire: 2 juin 1793-9 thermidor An II* (Paris, 1958), pp. 585-99 and the tables on pp. 1091-1104. These tables are omitted from both English translations of Soboul's book, both of which are very much abridged. Soboul's book is mainly about the Paris sections and the tensions between them and the national Revolutionary Government.

posing some degree of learning: two engineers, two teachers, an architect, a lawyer, a geometrician, and a *chimiste-manufacturier*, who was none other than Nicolas Leblanc, known as the inventor of the process for making artificial soda. Two were farmers from the rural districts of the department. Only one had a more dubious occupation, a *colporteur de journaux*, or hawker for the Revolutionary press. There was only one lawyer, and only one described as being *sans profession*, who was retired at the age of sixty-seven.[45]

We know something also of the personnel of the Commune, from a list of 144 citizens elected by the sections, in July 1793, to serve as notables from whom the 48 members of the council of the Commune were to be selected.

About 80 of these 144 can be classified in the general category of economic production, including several *négociants* or larger business men and the usual artisans and small merchants of a preindustrial society. Among the more learned were nine doctors, eight lawyers, five teachers, and two each of engineers, professors, "men of letters," and clergy. Ten persons were described as artists, painters, or sculptors. Nine were apparently government employees. Seven were simply called "citizens," and three seem to have had no occupation at all. That the Commune was more radical than the Department was probably because it had, through election by the sections, more leisured persons, more talkative lawyers, and more intellectuals, though not more of the real working classes, proportionately, than the Department.[46]

It was in the 48 sections that the ordinary people of Paris were most clearly to be found. The sections had originated in 1790, under the first Revolutionary constitution, as subordinate jurisdictions of the Paris municipality. At first only "active" citizens, or somewhat over half the adult males, had been qualified by paying a certain level of taxes to attend the section assemblies. With the second revolutionary upheaval of August 1792 this distinction disappeared, and virtually all adult men were admitted to attend and vote. But many section leaders of 1793 had been "active" citizens since 1790, so that what happened in 1792 was not a total displacement or overthrow of the rich by the poor but a process in which the more affluent ceased to come to the assemblies, while more of the laboring poor streamed in. There is no doubt that the section assemblies were small images of the "popular masses," mainly at the artisan level, who were assisted, however, if not exactly led, by persons who were by no means plebeian. All called

---

[45] Lacroix, *Département de Paris*, pp. 229-31 and 441-79.

[46] *Liste générale des 144 citoyens élus et agréés par les quarantehuit Sections, pour former le Conseil-général de la Commune* (Paris, 13 July 1793). BN. Lb⁴⁰ 1322.

themselves sans-culottes in 1793, but the sans-culottes were not a class in a Marxist sense. Some were wage workers and others were employers of labor, on a small scale at the workbench and in retail shops, usually in a setting where the master or shopowner worked together with his employees in the same round of daily labor. It was from talking with such employers that journeymen, servants, and day laborers obtained many of their Revolutionary ideas. What all had in common was a desire for more equality, or rather a strong resentment of inequality, a detestation of "aristocrats." It was a dislike and suspicion of those who wore more fashionable clothing, used more polite language, engaged in less irksome labor, ate better meals, and were free from worry about the next day's income. The true sans-culotte was inclined to believe that even the National Convention could not always be trusted, and to think that the people themselves, and not their representatives, must take action in time of revolution, war, and invasion.

Each section assembly did its business through committees. It would have a civil committee to arrange and conduct the meetings, publicize the laws, issue ration cards, and maintain contact with the Commune and the Convention. There would be a revolutionary committee, originally called a surveillance committee, which engaged in patrols, house searches, pursuit of suspects, and exposure of counterrevolutionaries. A few sections seem to have had committees on public instruction, of which nothing is known. It was through such committees that the more educated of the sans-culottes provided leadership for their more unlettered or wholly illiterate fellows. Statistics are impossible for some tens of thousands of militants in the turbulence of revolution, but an analysis can be made for some 1,311 persons active in the section assemblies. By far the majority of these 1,311 were merchants, shopkeepers, artisans, and wage employees. But 40 percent of members of the civil committees, and 17 percent of the revolutionary committees, were members of liberal professions, retired persons, or persons living on the income from property. "The *sans-culotterie*," as Albert Soboul has said, "was indeed a coalition of heterogeneous social elements."[47]

With the rise of the Committee of Public Safety as the executive organ of the Convention, and the gradual formation of the Revolutionary Government, the higher political leadership began to suppress spontaneous revolutionism from below. In September 1793 the Convention ordered that meetings of the Paris sections should be limited to two a week. This led to a multiplication of *sociétés populaires*, which

[47] See my review article, "Popular Democracy in the French Revolution," *French Historical Studies* 1 (1960):458, and Soboul, *Sans-culottes*, p. 449.

as voluntary associations, unlike the legally constituted sections, were outside the scope of the new law. The membership of the popular societies was much the same as of the section assemblies; the same people on some days of the week would meet as a club, and on the two permitted days would gather in the same place as an assembly.

Women may have found it easier to take part in the popular societies than in the section assemblies. But women were always much in evidence among the sans-culottes, since the assemblies were not very exclusively conducted; it was also mainly the women that formed lines at the bakers' doors; and they shared in denouncing suspects, demonstrating on the floor or in the galleries of the Convention, and pushing forward in the great armed insurrections. There were also several revolutionary women's clubs, of which the most famous was the Citoyennes Républicaines Révolutionnaires. Since women could be quite revolutionary in other ways, only the most militant joined such clubs. Their clubs made an especial issue of education, both for developing women's education and for schools for their children.[48]

Other means of expression for the Parisian democracy were provided by several organizations that arose during the Revolution to meet the demands of artists and artisans. These two categories, both called *artistes* in French, were much alike or at least overlapped. They perceived themselves and were perceived by the upper classes as skilled practitioners of their several trades, *les arts et metiers*. They ranged from such a man as David, already a famous painter and a member of the National Convention, to more lowly mechanics and inventors, some of whom tried to keep abreast of the latest scientific ideas.

For artists and artisans the Revolution meant liberation from the government controls of the Old Regime, generally administered through the academies as a means of developing talent, recognizing achievement, and assuring high quality. There were naturally many who disagreed with decisions made by the academies or who believed themselves to have been overlooked or insufficiently recognized. Such groups had helped to block the Condorcet plan in 1792 because its proposed National Society seemed like an academy under a new name. They were important in bringing on the legal abolition of all academies in August 1793. They contributed also to some features of the petition of the following September 15, already noted as the high point in the attempted democratization of education.

Disaffected painters and sculptors, led by David, had organized a

---

[48] See Jane Abray, "Feminism in the French Revolution," *American Historical Review* 80 (1975):52.

Commune des Arts in 1790 in protest against the Academy of Painting and Sculpture. This "commune" provided a place to which any
artist could bring his work for exhibition and sale. Workers in the
mechanical, metallurgical, and chemical trades were more concerned
with the Academy of Sciences, which had had the power to judge
inventions and to grant or withhold the legal privilege that protected
the rights of the inventor. Men who worked with their hands, often
disdaining theory and drawing on the lore of their own trades, had
long complained that when they brought a new contrivance before the
Academy they were scorned or embarrassed for their lack of knowledge of physics or mathematics. In 1791 the Constituent Assembly
withdrew certifying powers from the Academy by enacting a new patent law. It created a Bureau des Brevets et Inventions, with a board
on which half the members should be drawn from the Academy, and
half should be actual artisans. Other artisans at the same time organized a Société du Point Central des Arts et Métiers.

The most important such body was a new Bureau de Consultation
des Arts et Métiers, which received the authority to determine the
merit of new inventions and to issue patents. Here too the membership included both established and even famous scientists, such as Lavoisier, and artisans engaged in developing new processes and machines. With a government grant of 300,000 francs made in 1791, the
Bureau encouraged men working on such diverse projects as a stocking
machine, a spring balance, a gun lock, a compass to facilitate the taking
of longitude at sea, a device for producing screws, and a steam-driven
pile driver. As for Lavoisier, who was to die on the guillotine in 1794
because of his involvement in the pre-Revolutionary tax farm, he was
an enlightened and open-minded reformer, who hoped to save the
Academy of Sciences from extinction, and so to protect the interests
of high science, by granting more participation to artisans in matters
on which their technical knowledge could be useful and should be
respected. He failed, because at the most radical phase of the Revolution no amount of conciliation was enough, and because of the distrust in all social classes for all privileged corporate bodies of the Old
Regime.[49]

[49] There is an excellent discussion of these artisan groups in Roger Hahn, *The Anatomy of a Scientific Institution: The Paris Academy of Sciences, 1666-1803* (Berkeley, 1971),
pp. 185-238, to which the present discussion is much indebted. See also C. C. Gillispie,
in *Critical Problems in the History of Science*, ed. M. Clagett (Madison, Wisc. 1962), pp.
273-78, and Gillispie's *Science and Polity at the End of the Old Regime* (Princeton, 1980),
p. 122. These American historians of science have done more than the French to bring
out the importance of the artisan groups in 1793. For details on individuals and partic-

Similar views brought about the formation of the Lycée des Arts in 1792. The older Lycée, founded in 1781, has already been mentioned as one of the "private" institutions that sprang up shortly before the Revolution. It still existed, concealing its former princely association under the name of Lycée Republicain from 1792 until 1803, when it became the Athénée. Both Lycées offered courses of public lecturers chiefly in the natural sciences, though the older one is chiefly remembered for the lectures on literature given by J. F. La Harpe after he turned against the Revolution. Many of those who lectured at the Lycée des Arts, such as the scientists Fourcroy, Berthollet, Darcet, Jussieu, and Vicq d'Azyr, also taught at the older Lycée or were members of the Bureau de Consultation.

The new Lycée des Arts occupied extensive quarters in the buildings and gardens of the Palais-Royal, called the Palais-Egalité in 1793. It differed from the older Lycée in being more concerned with the applied sciences and in opening its doors more readily to workingmen. It acted as a kind of mechanics' institute, granting 400 "free places" for attendance at its lectures. In conjunction with the Bureau de Consultation, it assisted artisans in obtaining patents, gave financial assistance for legal costs, provided them with a hall to exhibit their machines, and arranged contacts with entrepreneurs who might wish to market their inventions. It gave aid, for example, to a maker of pianos who devised improvements in the manufacture of cannon. In five years the Lycée des Arts granted awards for about 600 such improvements and inventions.[50]

One of the most active in the Lycée des Arts was J. H. Hassenfratz, a chemist of moderate repute, who had worked in Lavoisier's laboratory, and was in touch with the scientific work of Berthollet and Guyton de Morveau. He later became one of the founders and a professor at the Ecole Polytechnique, and author of a four-volume work on the

---

ular awards see Charles Ballot, "Procès-verbaux du Bureau de Consultation des Arts et Métiers," *Bulletin d'histoire économique de la Revolution* (1913), pp. 15-160.

[50] On the two Lycées see Hahn, *Anatomy of a Scientific Institution*, passim (see index) and Charles Dejob, "De l'établissement connu sous le nom de Lycée et d'Athénée et de quelques établissements analogues," *Revue internationale d'enseignement* 18 (1889):3-38, and Dejob, *L'Instruction publique en France et en Italie an 19ᵉ siècle* (Paris, 1894), pp. 123-245, which despite the title is on the two Lycées. See also M. Crosland, *The Society of Arcueil: A View of French Science in the Time of Napoleon I* (London, 1967), pp. 184-85. The index to Guillaume, *Procès-verbaux . . . Convention*, will lead to supporting information on both the Lycée des Arts and the Bureau de Consultation. The *Oeuvres de Lavoisier*, 6 vols. (Paris, 1862-1893), 6:559-69, contain a description of the Lycée des Arts perhaps written by Lavoisier and in any case with corrections in his own hand, with details on the subjects to be taught.

mining and processing of iron. As the son of a tavern keeper, and having been a carpenter and a surveyor in his youth, he could mix more easily with ordinary workmen than could most of his scientific colleagues. At the height of the Revolution he was one of the aggressive democrats of the Mountain. Like Léonard Bourdon, he took part in the unsuccessful popular uprising of March 1795, after which he went for a while into hiding. He then gave up politics, but in 1793 he thought of himself as a sans-culotte.

It is generally held, and is probably true, that most sans-culottes were conservative in their economic ideas—that they resisted the rise of capitalism and industrialism, preferred their familiar methods in their traditional crafts, hoped more for a more equal distribution of wealth than for increased production, and by equality meant a society in which there should be no rich, and all should be content with a modest living or even be virtuously poor. Such a picture seems less than fair to the artisan groups now under consideration. It is admittedly difficult to distinguish in such groups between the influence of real working people and that of more educated and middle-class persons. The same is true of the personnel of the Department, the Commune, and the sections. In any case, the artisan groups showed a more positive attitude toward modern developments in matters of education. The pressure for a more modern form of vocational and technical schooling came from artisans and their friends and was expressed by Hassenfratz as their spokesman.

It must be recalled that the Sieyès-Daunou-Lakanal plan, presented to the Convention on June 26, put a particular emphasis on *fêtes nationales* or national festivals to celebrate such events as the fall of the Bastille and such principles as the fraternity of the human race. On June 30 Hassenfratz singled out Sieyès in a violent attack on the plan at the Jacobin Club. On July 5 he presented a petition to the Convention, signed by himself and 14 others, of whom 11 are known to have been inventors who received aid from the Bureau de Consultation. The petitioners regretted that the Sieyès-Daunou-Lakanal plan, in its preoccupation with public festivals, "sacrifices the instruction of the present generation to concern itself with the generation to come." They deplored its neglect of the arts and trades. They asserted that under the monarchy all encouragements had gone to "the aristocracy of human knowledge and for improvement of the sciences and fine arts" and not to "manufactures, arts and trades," so that France's neighbors had won out in foreign markets by producing at lower cost.[51]

[51] Hassenfratz's speech at the Jacobins is reprinted by Guillaume, *Procès-verbaux* . . .

Hassenfratz also published a brochure to the same effect. "The most essential part of public instruction is being neglected," he wrote, "that is, the development of the national industry and education in the arts and trades, which is being replaced by festivals." Festivals are "a beautiful metaphysical idea" and may have been suited to the ancients.

> But among a commercial, manufacturing, agricultural people, surrounded by industrious other peoples, let us take care that while we occupy ourselves with the organization of festivals our neighbors are not organizing their industry and destroying our manufactures and commerce.
> It is not by festivals that the English had come to have a great preponderance in the political balance of Europe.
> It is not by festivals that the United States of America are becoming a flourishing people.[52]

Some two weeks later Hassenfratz presented another petition to the Convention, this one from the Lycée des Arts, signed by himself and ten others, including Berthollet and Vicq d'Azyr. Robespierre had read the Lepeletier plan to the Convention only a few days before, and members were entering upon the discussion of *éducation commune*. The petition of the Lycée des Arts makes no mention of *éducation commune*. It urges the Convention to supplement "the primary schools that you are going to decree with a particular instruction for agriculturalists, artisans and workers." It expresses what may be called a concept of productivity. "A main source of wealth is in the advantageous exchange of the products of labor. . . . One obtains the same production at a lower price by improving the arts, trades and agriculture and by developing the physical and moral qualities of the workers." The petition therefore urged the formation of evening and Sunday classes, "the establishment of primary schools for the arts and trades, the augmentation of the national industry and all developments of which it is capable."[53]

In short, in Hassenfratz, the Lycée des Arts, and the Bureau de Consultation we detect a trend in the democratic movement which, in matters of education, favored economic and technical progress rather than training for membership in a future form of society.

Convention, 1:525-26. For the petition of July 5, ibid., 2:426-28. Unknown to Guillaume, 11 of the 14 names on this petition may be traced through Ballot's index to the proceedings of the Bureau de Consultation, cited above.

[52] Ibid., 1:578-80.
[53] Ibid., 2:428-29.

EDUCATIONAL DEMANDS OF THE SECTIONS OF PARIS

The chief centers of democratic fermentation were the sections of Paris. From August 1792 until September 1793 they were in "permanent session"; that is, their halls remained open without adjournment for their assemblies, committees, and individual activists to come and go at will. The sections passed resolutions, exchanged delegations, pursued suspects, drew up petitions to the Convention, threatened merchants and shopkeepers as prices rose, organized demonstrations, and recruited the men and women who took part in the great insurrections. In all this agitation they generated a good deal of paper, both in print and in manuscript, so that their activity is abundantly documented. The bibliography of printed sources for the Revolution contains over a thousand items originating in the sections alone. The catalogue of manuscript sources lists hundreds of entries for the sections solely for the year 1793. Many more were found by Albert Soboul in his massive work on the sections of Paris.[54]

Our problem is to find out what the *sectionnaires* wanted in the matters of education. The difficulty is that most documents originating in the sections were obviously written by highly literate persons. Only occasionally do we find one with the misspellings or grammatical oddities that suggest truly working-class authorship. Far more often we note references to Plutarch or Plato, the conspiracy of Cataline, the heroism of Brutus, or other echoes from the colleges of the Old Regime. But so far as such references are only ornamental, mere flourishes added to substantial and relevant demands, there is no reason to doubt that the authors expressed the wishes of their less classically educated associates.

As for *éducation commune*, in the full sense embracing Lepeletier's state boarding schools, those sans-culottes who supported it were more likely to be journalists and intellectuals than persons of more usual occupations. As a German scholar has concluded "the Lepeletier plan on the whole found surprisingly little response in the papers of the

---

[54] M. Tourneux, *Bibliographie de l'historie de Paris pendant la Révolution française*, 5 vols. (Paris, 1890-1913), 2:255-74, nos. 7840 through 9036; A. Tuetey, *Répertoire général des sources manuscrites de l'histoire de Paris pendant la Révolution française*, 11 vols. (Paris, 1890-1914), 9:613-15 of the index; and Soboul, *Sans-culottes*, and his *Les papiers des sections de Paris* (Paris, 1950). J. R. Vignery, *The French Revolution and the Schools: The educational policies of the Mountain* (Madison, Wisc., 1965), is mainly on the debates in the Convention and at the Paris Jacobin Society and rightly emphasizes that there was no single "Jacobin" policy despite the legend of Jacobin centralization.

Paris sections."[55] Support came rather from the *enragé*, Jean-Théophile Leclerc, who praised the Lepeletier plan in writing in Marat's *Ami du peuple* after Marat's death. Why should the Convention, he said, "be afraid to force parents to bend under the level of equality by sending their children without distinction into common houses of education?"[56] It may have been this same Leclerc who initiated a petition in the Sections des Lombards, which was circulated and signed in eight other sections. It demanded *éducation forcée et gratuite*, and the fact of its date, August 23, at a time when the Lepeletier plan had just been under discussion suggests that the nine sections intended to support this plan; but compulsory free education by no means necessarily implied Lepeletier's compulsory boarding schools.[57] A deliberation of the Section des Sans-culottes, in March 1794, demanded that "instruction be equal for all children in the Republic," that all children be brought together in all departments and fed and clothed in the same manner, and that "all houses of instruction be exactly alike." But over half of this document is concerned with what would soon be called "ideology"—the children should learn of "things and existent beings before learning the conventional signs that represent them," and "all objects should be classed in the order most suitable for impression on the children's memory, not only to convey their exact image but in a way to make the children sense the relationships and differences between objects, and with man." We have here the thoughts of an intellectual or an educational theorist, not of the common people of Paris.[58]

Another proposal by a "citizen of the Section of the Tuileries" goes even beyond Lepeletier. Children in this plan will indeed live at home. But the youngest infant, "as soon as born, belongs to the state more than to his parents and should be watched over even while in his parents' home. And by whom? By everyone, for a republican belongs to all. He will be watched by the commune, by the section, by the neighbors," who will report to the authorities the names of parents who bring up their children improperly. Even the baby should be exposed to danger, like Hercules who played with snakes in his cradle,

---

[55] Stübig, *Enziehung zur Gleichheit*, p. 297. She notes two cases on pp. 294-95 where the phrase *éducation commune* occurs in section documents of November 1793.

[56] Soboul, *Sans-culottes*, p. 499, quoting the *Ami du peuple* of August 17, 1793.

[57] Guillaume, *Procès-verbaux . . . Convention*, 2:400-402, and Archives Nationales, F[17] 1005[A] no. 790. It may be significant that only nine sections signed, since the Section des Lombards ordered it to be "communicated to the forty-seven other sections."

[58] *Extraits des registres des délibérations de l'Assemblée générale de la Section des Sans-culottes, du 10 ventôse, l'an deuxième de la République française une et indivisible.* BN. Lb[40] 2131 (2). See also Stübig, *Enziehung zur Gleichheit*, p. 301. Coming in February 1794, this document reflects the "Hébertist" resistance to the Revolutionary Government.

or Achilles plunged into the sea by his mother, Thetis. The small child should go barefoot and bareheaded night and day—"it was by hardening the head in the open air, according to Herodotus, that the Egyptians developed the skulls that blunted the swords of the Persians." At the age of seven all boys, rich and poor, while continuing to live at home, would go to school from seven in the morning to seven in the evening. They would wear the same clothes and eat the same plain food, to include occasionally a little unseasoned meat. They would learn to swim, throw the javelin, and spend stormy nights outdoors. They might do without books, as in Sparta, and should learn to write on slates so as to save the expense of pen and paper. In history they should learn about human progress, not about kings, and come to admire heroes of Liberty, who knew "how to live like Aristides, fight like Miltiades, and die like Cato." It is to be noted that this learned effusion came from an individual citizen, not from the Section des Tuileries as such.[59]

The sections should not be judged by such freakish idiosyncrasies. In the summer of 1793 they poured out a stream of demands in which significant ideas on education were mixed in a chaos of other genuine concerns. These months saw the most radical crisis of the Revolution. Peasant rebellion raged in western France and urban revolts in the provincial cities, while real counterrevolutionaries, royalist plotters, and foreign spies lurked in Paris, with the Austrians invading through the northeastern frontier and by September the British in occupation at Toulon. Food shortages and rising prices made life in Paris uncertain. Whether the popular agitation was due more to economic causes or to political hopes and fears remains a much debated but finally unanswerable question.

We begin our more normal series with a petition to the Convention drafted jointly by four sections on the Left Bank—those called Panthéon-français, Observatoire, Sans-culottes, and Finistère. Panthéon-français included much of the Latin Quarter and had various professors in the colleges active in its affairs. The other three sections were poor quarters of the Faubourg Saint-Marcel. The petition was dated about May 20, shortly before the mass uprising that forced the Girondins out of the Convention. It was menacing in tone. Put an end, it said to the Convention, to your puerile quarrels and shameful dissen-

---

[59] *Vues générales sur l'éducation à donner aux garçons dans la République française*, with the phrase *par un citoyen de la section des Tuileries* at the end. Mention of the *décadi* dates it after September 1793, and it may be another evidence of "Hebertist" opposition. It is doubtless at the Bibliothèque Nationale, but the copy used here is at the British Library, Croker collection F 233.

sions. Never forget that "the French people has its eyes on you." The people will soon rise and demand an accounting. Write our new republican constitution. Decree a maximum on the price of necessities. Create government jobs "for fathers of families and elderly patriots, especially those whose trades have been made sterile by the revolution." Take a vote by open roll call to outlaw the fugitive and traitorous family of Bourbon-Capet; set a price on their heads; "let a sum of 200,000 livres be the reward for any citizen that brings in the head of one of those scoundrels."

The point is that in all this fury education was not forgotten. The petitioners ask that "when you have completed the constitution, you concern yourselves with a Code of National Education in conformity with its principles, and with the establishment of public festivals to give them life." No further details, however, were offered.[60]

The threatened uprising occurred when tens of thousands of the *sectionnaires* besieged the Convention on May 31. They forced out the Girondins and put the Mountain into the shaky seats of power. The Committee on Public Instruction, as already explained, then produced its Sieyès-Daunou-Lakanal plan, which the Montagnards refused to accept. The sections continued to agitate.

The Section Panthéon-français petitioned again on June 27, this time specifically on education.[61] The petition was drafted by the secretary of the section assembly, Antoine Sérieys, described in the biographical dictionaries as a *littérateur français*. He held a job sorting confiscated manuscripts earlier in the Revolution and later became a professor of history. The petition called for a "common and republican education" and "a democratic instruction, the gospel of liberty." Schools would be "a barrier against the prejudices of the priesthood and nobility." Nobles and priests, unless married, should be driven from public office. Untutored sans-culottes were not yet capable of replacing them. Education therefore should be designed to qualify the plain citizen to take positions in government. We wonder whether it would be too much to think that these denizens of the old university quarter had a particular interest in white-collar jobs and government employment.

A more purely working-class demand is seen in an address to the

---

[60] *Pétition des sections réunies de l'Observatoire, du Finistère, des Sans-culottes et du Panthéon-français faisant partie du ci-devant Faubourg Saint-Marcel, pour être présentée à la Convention Nationale.* BN. Nouv. Acq. 2702 folio 232. See also Soboul, *Sans-culottes,* pp. 37 and 497, and Stübig, *Enziehung zur Gleichheit,* pp. 258-60.

[61] *Section du Panthéon-français. Assemblée générale du 27 juin 1793 . . . Pétition. . . .* BN. Lb⁴⁰ 2028. See also Soboul, *Sans-culottes,* p. 498; Stübig, *Enziehung zur Gleichheit,* p. 280; and *Nouvelle biographie générale,* "Sérieys."

Convention from three sections in the Faubourg Saint-Antoine, a heavily artisan district on the Right Bank. Certain irregularities in the French suggest a popular authorship. We respectfully await the new law on education, these sections declare—"we are assured of finding there the means by which the farmer, that nourishing father of the Republic, may enjoy all the discoveries that may simplify his operations and multiply the fruits; that the artisan, the soul of commerce, may find ways to improve his art, the workman his talent, and that you will cut off anyone who might allow the rebirth or continuation of the spirit of superstition that has so long absorbed the human race."[62] A similar request came from the Section du Faubourg Montmartre, which wanted not a "metaphysical education" but "an instruction suited to improve our arts and trades, which will give a strong impulse to our national industry and activity to our factories and commerce and destroy tyranny forever."[63] The ritualistic abhorrence expressed for priestcraft and tyranny should not obscure the more pragmatic content of these messages.

A different note is struck in an address by a Citizen Mittié to the assembly of the Section des Amis de la Patrie, which ordered 400 copies printed and sent to the other 47 sections. Mittié, while favoring the higher levels of the original Condorcet plan, laid particular emphasis on the need for primary schools and especially such schools for the poor. Now that the people were sovereign, and the poor could take part in formation of the laws, it was obviously important that all should receive some schooling; but Mittié gave his attention also to the exceptional poor boy driven by the *penchant irrésistible de son génie*, that is, by a strongly felt talent or aptitude. Before the Revolution, he thought, many such youths had been condemned to live in poverty by manual labor, or to humble themselves before an insolent patron, or to be lost in a life of dissipation. "But today, now that we lay claim to regeneration, the child's own inclination should be the sole rule for his vocation." The father should hand over the boy to *la Patrie*, saying "take him, educate him." Thus the Republic would gain men like Cato, Demosthenes, Aristides, Regulus, "and above all, Brutus." And gambling houses, brothels, and the theater should be avoided.[64]

In the first days of July there were hectic scenes in the Convention,

---

[62] *Adresse des trois sections du Faubourg Saint-Antoine, 4 juillet 1793.* The text is printed in French and German by W. Markov and A. Soboul, eds., *Die Sansculotten von Paris: Dokumente zur Geschichte der Volksbewegung* (Berlin, 1957), p. 92.

[63] Soboul, *Sans-culottes*, p. 498.

[64] *Section des Amis de la Patrie. Discours de Mittié fils, lu à l'Assemblée générale*. . . . BN. Lb[40] 1687.

as delegations from all the sections streamed into its hall to announce their vote (overwhelmingly favorable) on the newly devised democratic constitution. The official speakers of the sections had to be men, but many women were also present. After the Section du Bon Conseil had entered, carrying flags and accompanied by a band, and had announced its acceptance of the constitution, a *citoyenne* added: "Lawmakers, you have produced a republican constitution and we have produced republicans. Get on with your task, and now give us public instruction." The citizens of both sexes of Bon Conseil then withdrew amid cries of "Vive la République" and the applause of the assembly. After the Section des Sans-culottes had said its piece, three women made speeches to present the views of women of their sections. As one of them put it, France was now purged of the vile reptiles of despotism, but the Convention should now "get busy and develop by a national education the Spartan virtues that we have placed in our children's hearts."[65]

Pressure from sans-culottes and *sectionnaires* in the following weeks forced the Convention into drastic actions that it might not otherwise have taken. It decreed a *levée en masse* to repel the foreign invaders and a paramilitary *armée révolutionnaire* to patrol the countryside in search of food. It enacted a General Maximum to hold down wage rates and the prices of various consumer's goods. The Revolutionary Tribunal was enlarged, a voracious Law of Suspects adopted, and Terror proclaimed the Order of the Day. The Girondins and Marie Antoinette went to the guillotine. A republican calendar replaced the Christian one, and the religion of Reason was inaugurated by the Commune at the ex-cathedral of Notre Dame.

It was at this extraordinary moment that the Parisian democracy brought forward yet another plan for a total and comprehensive reconstruction of education.

THE PARIS PLAN OF SEPTEMBER 15, 1793

The new plan, which has never had a name, and may be called simply the Paris plan, represented the confluence of the democratic and popular forces described in the preceding pages. Anonymous, it was soon forgotten. Later liberals remembered Talleyrand and Condorcet, later radicals exhumed Lepeletier and Babeuf, but the plan that had the endorsement of the department, commune, and sections of Paris, the

---

[65] *Archives parlementaires*, 68:381-83. See also pp. 282, 285, 316, 380.

Jacobin club, and the Convention itself has been scarcely remembered even in the historical literature.

During the evening session of September 15, when the Convention had already spent hours of debate on other matters, delegates of "the Department of Paris, the rural districts, the commune, and the sections and popular societies meeting jointly" presented a petition asking that a plan of education drafted by the Department should be enacted.[66] We must first ask whether a plan prepared by the Department really represented the ideas of the rank and file of sans-culottes in the sections or whether the Department had simply imposed its views. The latter alternative seems impossible. As recently as September 5 the sections had streamed into the Convention and in an unusually turbulent scene had forced it to adopt measures of political terror and military defense. It is unlikely that 10 days later the sections would subscribe to a program against their will.

The petition demanded the passage of only three articles of legislation. First that, above the primary schools, there should be three "progressive levels of instruction": one for the knowledge "indispensable to *artistes et ouvriers de tous genres*" (artists, artisans, workmen, and workers of all kinds); another for the knowledge needed for other professions in society; and a third for subjects "whose difficult study is not within the capacity of all men." These corresponded to the secondary schools, institutes, and lycées of Condorcet. The second article called for the adoption of courses of study as shown in an annexed tabulation of which more will shortly be said. The third article called for establishment of the new institutions by the next November 1, and that "consequently the *collèges de plein exercice* (the eight-year colleges) and the faculties of arts, law, medicine and theology shall be suppressed throughout the whole territory of the Republic."

The Convention accepted the petition and adopted the three articles. Lakanal and Grégoire spoke in favor of it for the Commission of Six, as did three members of the Committee of Public Safety. This was the only occasion during the Revolution on which the old colleges and universities were expressly abolished, though it is true, as will be seen, that the action of September 15 was "suspended" on the very next day.

---

[66] *Pétition presentée à la Convention Nationale par le Département de Paris, les districts ruraux, la commune, les sections et les sociétés populaires y reunies. Imprimée par ordre de la Convention Nationale.* BN. Le[38] 455; British Library, Croker R 367; reprinted in *Archives parlementaires* for September 15, 1793, and by Guillaume, *Procès-verbaux . . . Convention*, 2:409-17. The present account draws heavily on Guillaume's discussion on pp. 397-426, supplemented by particulars not available to him in 1890.

Coming so soon after the abolition of the academies in August, and at the beginning of the Terror as a deliberate government policy, it might seem that we have reached a climax of destructiveness in education. But of course the older institutions were in fact collapsing, and even the Talleyrand plan of 1791 had implied their disappearance. When their legal suppression was suspended on September 16 they continued to have a disjointed existence. In the next years they passed through a kind of institutional metamorphosis, in which many of the same men eventually found themselves working under different titles in institutions with different names. In any case the suspension of September 16 meant that the Paris plan of September 15, like so many others, never went into effect. Its interest lies in the thoughts of those who supported it.

For this purpose the address of the spokesman for the petitioners, Dufourny of the Department of Paris, is particularly revealing. He began by observing that not all persons were equal in their "intellectual faculties." As they differed in height and strength, so they differed in intelligence, for which Dufourny suggested a kind of quantitative measure, possibly the first in the history of aptitude testing.

> From Newton to the idiot for whom education can do nothing all the intermediate gradations exist; and if we represent by the number 100 what can be done by the man most favored at the same time by nature, upbringing and circumstances, some would receive from nature no more than enough to produce a 1, 2 or 3, etc. Many perhaps would have enough faculties to produce a 50; but this figure would diminish as faculties grow greater, and very few would have a 90.

He then illustrated by an imaginary shepherd boy in the Lozère, who might have the capacity for a 90. Left in the mountains, he would see nothing but his sheep, a few other boys, and snow; the most he could do with his native intelligence would be to go down into the plain, work for a farmer, excel as his assistant, marry the farmer's daughter, and inherit the property. This was a loss for society. More should have been made of the young man's talents. Therefore education should not be left to the caprice of individuals and families. The nation should take positive steps to seek out and develop the rare potential abilities to be found among its 25 million inhabitants. It should of course also provide for others. There must be schools for all.

> We will invite and assist the poor to come out of their hovels, to come down from their garrets, to participate in these salutary insti-

tutions; and those valuable men who water the land with their sweat and often their tears, those to whom you have given their rights and their dignity and who for four years have been at grips with aristocracy and with poverty . . . , who are the real pillars of society, will become its models by their virtues.[67]

It should be pointed out also that the Paris plan makes no mention of *fêtes nationales*, as if to imply that such political demonstrations were not relevant to the kind of education that the petitioners had in mind.

Before attending to details of this Paris plan let us explore the question of how it originated, and how the various streams in the democratic movement came together in its formation. The Convention, as already explained, had set up a Commission of Six to take over educational planning from the Committee on Public Instruction. It appointed this Commission when it rejected the Sieyès-Daunou-Lakanal plan. The main feature of this rejected plan was that the national system should consist only of primary schools, and that educational institutions above the primary should be provided by free and voluntary private enterprise. Once the question of *éducation commune* was disposed of, the great remaining question was whether national education should have only the one primary level, to which some still adhered, or should be a multilevel system such as Condorcet (and many others) had proposed. Lepeletier had favored the multilevel arrangement for students going beyond his state boarding schools. Robespierre favored it likewise, but he left the Commission of Six on becoming a member of the Committee of Public Safety on July 27.

After Robespierre's departure the Commission of Six was divided, three to three. Those favoring the multilevel system were Grégoire; Lakanal, who had changed his mind since the failure of the Sieyès-Daunou-Lakanal plan; and Léonard Bourdon, who, like Lepeletier, saw no inconsistency between *éducation commune* for all and additional schooling at public expense for a few. Opposed to it, or believing that the state should provide only primary schools, were the Alsatian deputy Rühl, who feared damage to Alsatian regionalism under a nationally uniform system; Coupé de l'Oise, a former curé; and Robespierre's successor on the Commission, whose name is unknown. The Commission was stalemated, unable to fulfill its mandate from the Convention.

Those members of the Commission who preferred the multilevel arrangement turned to the Department of Paris. The Department had long had a low opinion of the colleges and faculties of the University,

---

[67] Guillaume, ibid., 2:410-12.

and was losing patience at the repeated delay after all the discussion and planning since the Talleyrand report, and indeed since the 1760s.[68] The Council of the Department was composed of men of varying degrees of education, more of the practical than of the literary kind. The president of the Council, Dufourny, was an *artiste-ingénieur*, described also as an *ingénieur hydrographe*. Another member was Nicolas Leblanc, the inventor of the new process for making soda, who was also active in the Bureau de Consultation. Still another was François Peyrard, a *géomètre*, a word that at that time might also mean a surveyor. The Department was alarmed that the 10 colleges of the University, along with its higher faculties, might reopen again for the school year 1793-1794 with no real change.

It was the Department that took the initiative, encouraged by the Commission of Six, in developing the plan eventually submitted to the Convention on September 15. It appointed a consultative committee studded with important names—Lagrange, the mathematician; Garat, who lectured on history at the older Lycée and had for a short time been minister of justice; Monge, the scientist and future friend of Napoleon; and Gohier, a lawyer who in 1799 served briefly as a Director of the Republic. This committee produced a plan a few months later.[69] Meanwhile Peyrard, a member of the Department's own committee on public instruction, drew up and published a plan, which called both for compulsory primary education and for *instituts* and a *lycée* in the city, in the sense of these words as used in the Condorcet plan, that is, for intermediate schools and a modernized university.[70] In addition, the Department invited two professors in one of the Paris colleges to submit a plan for the coming school year. What they proposed departed considerably from the pre-Revolutionary course of study; while retaining languages and literature, mathematics and physics, it also included "political and social morality" and "rural, commercial, and industrial economy," to be reinforced by visits to shops and manufactures; but the Department apparently thought their plan insufficiently innovative, for no more was heard of it.[71]

[68] Cf. what the Department had said in November 1791 of "those gothic institutions called colleges piled together in one quarter of the capital . . . those Nations and Faculties . . . those useless processions of the rector, questors, apparitors and other salaried drones," and so forth. See my *School of the French Revolution* (Princeton, 1975), p. 115.

[69] Lacroix, *Département de Paris*, p. 181n. And see below, p. 171.

[70] *Projet d'instruction publique pour le Département de Paris par Peyrard, administrateur du Département et membre de la Commission* [= son comité] *d'Instruction publique*. On Peyrard see Lacroix, *Département de Paris*, pp. 231 and 473.

[71] *Plan d'études, provisoires, par les citoyens Crouzet, principal du collège du Panthéon-français, ci-devant Montaigu, et Mahérault, professeur au même collège. Imprimé par ordre*

The evidence is sporadic, but it shows that the Department also obtained advice from the associations of artists and scientists, especially the Bureau de Consultation des Arts et Métiers. One member of the Department, Leblanc, was a frequent attendant at the governing committee of the Bureau, and the president of the Department council, Dufourny, was by normal occupation a technical man of the kind that the Bureau was designed to serve. The Department also consulted the chemist Fourcroy, who participated regularly in the meetings of the Bureau. Hassenfratz, with his interest in the Bureau and the Lycée des Arts, was also well known in political circles; he had been the spokesman for the commune of Paris during the mass invasion of the Convention on June 1. Hassenfratz, Fourcroy, Dufourny, and Peyrard were members of the Paris Jacobin club. They were all in a position to have a ready exchange of ideas.

These particulars are of interest because they suggest that large parts of the Paris plan, as finally agreed upon by the Department of Paris and the Commission of Six, were really provided by the Bureau de Consultation. If so, then the Paris plan in fact derived from the Condorcet plan of 1792, by way of the labors of the old Committee on Public Instruction before the insurrectionary upheaval of May 31, before the diversion caused by the Sieyès-Daunou-Lakanal proposal, before the arguments over *éducation commune*, and before the Committee had been relegated to the sidelines by appointment of the Commission. In a way, Condorcet was vindicated. Planning for education came around in a circle.

On July 10, about the time when Hassenfratz was presenting the artisans' petition to the Convention, the Bureau de Consultation appointed a committee to do likewise, that is, "to obtain a particular education suited for those destined for the mechanical arts."[72] The committee was composed of Lavoisier, Fourcroy, Hassenfratz, and two others. They seem to have produced a report very rapidly, for the Bureau ordered it to be printed on July 24, with "two copies to be sent to each member of the Convention, and several to each of the forty-eight sections and the constituted authorities of Paris, as well as to the eighty-three departments." Dupont de Nemours printed 2,000

---

du Departement de Paris. BN. Rp 7894. And see Guillaume, *Procès-verbaux . . . Convention*, 2:406-407.

[72] The proceedings of the Bureau de Consultation concerning education in July and August 1793 were printed by Guillaume in the appendix to his second volume, ibid., 2:902-907, but seem to have been discovered by him too late for him to integrate the role of the artisans into his explanation of the origin of the petition of September 15, as given in the same volume on pp. xxv-xxxii and 404-408.

copies on August 5, and another 2,000, together with the draft for a *projet de loi*, or legislative bill, on September 13.

The report prepared by the committee of the bureau was called simply *Reflections on Public Instruction* and was intended to be presented to the Convention.[73] It consisted of some 20 pages of thoughtful analysis followed by elaborate tables setting forth subjects to be studied at four different levels, *écoles primaires*, *écoles des arts*, *instituts*, and *lycées*. It was once believed that it was written by Lavoisier himself, a member of the Bureau's committee, since he was struggling in 1793 to save the Academy of Sciences by combining its interests with those of artisans, inventors, and what a later generation would call technicians. But it is certainly doubtful that Lavoisier or anyone else could have written it between July 10 when the committee was appointed and July 24 when the Bureau accepted it for printing and circulation. It seems likely that the committee of the Bureau took the sensible step of immediately conferring with the Committee on Public Instruction of the Convention, and in particular with the Strasbourg mathematician Arbogast, who was still a member of that Committee, as he had been since its inception in November 1791. During the spring of 1793 Arbogast had worked on a revision of the Condorcet plan, keeping its four levels of education while relieving it of the elitist features of the National Society to which the Convention had vehemently objected.[74] The Committee on Public Instruction approved of this revision on May 28. Then came the popular uprising of May 31 and the confusion caused by the Sieyès-Daunou-Lakanal plan, during which the Arbogast version remained ignored in the Committee's files.

To reconstruct what happened, the committee of the Bureau de Consultation in mid-July made approaches to the Committee on Public Instruction, which took the Arbogast plan from its files and turned it over to the Bureau. The Bureau then made changes of its own and printed the result as its *Reflections on Public Instruction*, which it passed on in turn to the Department of Paris. The Department made a few changes, then secured the adherence of the commune, the sections, the

[73] *Réflexions sur l'instruction publique presentées à la Convention Nationale par le Bureau de Consultation des Arts et Métiers*. Printed at the time, and reprinted in Lavoisier's *Oeuvres*, 6:516-58. On the authorship see Keith Baker and W. A. Smeaton, "The origins and authorship of the educational proposals published in 1793 by the Bureau de Consultation des Arts et Métiers, and generally ascribed to Lavoisier," *Annals of Science* 21 (1965):33-46.

[74] On Arbogast and the activities of the Committee on Public Instruction, see Baker and Smeaton, "Origins and authorship," and Guillaume, *Procès-verbaux . . . Convention*, 1:357, 363, 393, 398-99, 471, and 2:895-901.

popular societies, and the rural districts. All these sent deputations to the Jacobin club on the morning of September 15, to inform the Jacobins and obtain their approval for the great plan of education, which was presented to the Convention at the evening session of that same day. As it turned out, the Bureau de Consultation never presented its own plan to the Convention at all, concluding that the Paris plan covered the same ground and served the same purpose. That is, the Bureau found its own views incorporated in the Paris plan.

This genealogy is sufficiently demonstrated by the great similarity between the tabulations of studies in the three documents: the Arbogast (or Committee on Public Instruction) version of May 28, the *Reflections* or Bureau of Consultation's version of August, and the plan prepared by the Department of Paris and approved by the Convention on September 15.[75] All three use the language of the Condorcet plan—*écoles primaires, écoles secondaires, instituts, lycées*—except that where Arbogast wrote *écoles secondaires* the Bureau wrote *écoles des arts* and the Paris plan wrote *écoles secondaires destinées aux artistes et ouvriers de tous genres*. All three versions define the same four branches of human knowledge, or rather of mental activity in general since imaginative literature and the fine arts figured as one branch. All three introduce *dessin*, that is, "drawing" or "design," as a subject of study, and all three also include *grammaire générale* and the *analyse des sensations et des idées*. These provisions foreshadow the law of 1795, known as the law of 3 Brumaire of the Year IV, which set up the institutions of the Directory, with a National Institute embracing the branches of knowledge and the Central Schools with their "drawing" and "general grammar," which is to say that they also anticipate the Idéologues.

There is a difference among the three in that, from one to the next, we can trace a more explicit concern for the practical needs of the real working classes. All take for granted a primary schooling for everyone and give more attention to a secondary level for boys at about the age of twelve—and explicitly for girls also in the *Reflections* of the Bureau. The desire to offer a vocationally useful schooling can be seen in what is said about mathematics. Arbogast makes only brief mention of arithmetic and geometry for the secondary level. The Bureau adds *arpentage* and *nivellement*, that is, land measurement and surveying. The Paris plan goes into more detail; it combines mathematics and drawing in "descriptive geometry," or the use of three-dimensional geometry for

[75] The tabulations discussed in this and the followings paragraphs are, for Arbogast, Guillaume, ibid., 2:896-901; for the Bureau, *Réflexions sur l'instruction publique*, in Lavoisier's *Oeuvres*, 6:532-35; and for the Paris plan, Guillaume, ibid., 2:414-17.

six listed purposes: drawing for stone masons, drawing for wood-workers, "construction of shadows in drawings," perspective-drawing, surveying and charts, and finally "the graphic description of elementary and basic machines." Or again, under the applied sciences, at the level of the *instituts*, the Arbogast tables are very general and undeveloped. The Bureau de Consultation specifies them under five practical head-ings: the arts of food production, of clothing, of shelter, of healing, and of defense. Each heading has its subheads; the art of clothing divides into the preparation of cloth, the theory of woven goods, and the cutting and joining of fabrics; and the art of healing has no less than eight subheadings, still at the *institut* level: anatomy, surgery, obstetrics, human medicine, veterinary medicine, materia medica, pharmacy, and hygiene. The Paris plan took over all these details from the Bureau with little change.

Two further observations can be made on the Paris plan. One is that the sans-culottes and the Parisian democracy, while concerned with universal elementary schooling, were by no means opposed to higher learning. The tabulations of the Paris plan went into greater detail for the lycées—the universities envisioned for the future—than they did for either the secondary schools or the institutes. In terms of the listed specialties in the lycées, under the four branches of knowledge, it gave most careful attention to the applied sciences, the next most to the pure sciences, the third most to moral and political sciences, and the least to language and literature. The Parisian democracy preferred use-ful and solid subjects to the elegance and good taste of the literary tradition. In general the Paris plan repeats proposals made at the be-ginning of the Revolution and even before it: the 10 Paris colleges were too expensive and should be redistributed throughout the city; the lycée or high-level establishment in Paris should be formed from existing institutions such as the Observatory and the Jardin des Plantes.

The second observation is more of a question. Did the Paris plan imply a two-track system, or separation of boys at about the age of twelve into groups going on into two different kinds of schools, against which democratic and equalitarian thought of the twentieth century was to raise such objection? The secondary schools in the plan were clearly designed for future artisans and workmen, the institutes for those contemplating other professions. The plan called for three "pro-gressive levels of instruction" above the primary, but its authors may have been thinking of a progression in difficulty or elevation of subject matter, not of age or sequence. Age is not mentioned in the plan, except for a statement that a boy must be twelve years old to enter a secondary school, whose course of study is to last two years. No age or length of study is mentioned for the institutes, which are to teach Latin, Greek, a modern language, and mathematics but also applied and practical subjects. It seems significant that drawing is intended for practical purposes in the secondary schools, but for the institutes is listed under the beaux-arts. Was it supposed that a boy would attend a secondary school at the age of twelve and then proceed to an institute two years later? Such is possible, but it is more likely that the authors of the plan had not become aware of a problem, that they intended the secondary schools for the training of working-class boys and the institutes for those going on into public service and the learned professions, considering it reasonable and fair for boys to separate after attending common primary schools. The problem for planners in 1793 was to preserve higher learning and an educated class in time of revolution, while providing more adequate schooling than in the past for the working class by relieving them of such burdens as Latin, and by teaching subjects that would be useful both to the individuals concerned and to society.

Hurriedly adopted by the Convention during the evening of September 15, the Paris plan was attacked the next day by various speakers who demanded its repeal. These speakers were a mixed group, including Coupé de l'Oise who as a former curé may have been doubtful of a state-imposed educational system at all levels; Cambon, a practical man who thought that the skilled trades could be better learned by apprenticeship than in school; and several characters who were emerging as enemies of the new Committee of Public Safety, such as Chabot, Fabre d'Eglantine, and Bourdon de l'Oise (no relation to Léonard Bourdon), actual troublemakers and adventurers whom Robespierre was soon to outwit by entangling them in an alleged foreign conspiracy. The upshot of this discussion was that the Convention refused to repeal its action of the day before, but did suspend it.

Seeking a solution, the Convention enlarged its Commission of Six to be a Commission of Nine, adding to it Gilbert Romme, who had defended the Condorcet plan in the preceding December; Arbogast, who had worked on its revision from March to May; and Guyton de Morveau, now prominent as a chemist, who had written a reforming tract on education 30 years earlier as a young lawyer in Burgundy. The expanded Commission brought forth a plan clearly derived from the petition of September 15 and from Condorcet.[76] And again the outcry was heard against educational bureaucracy, elitism, and professorial oligarchy. "Be careful," said M. E. Petit, "the aristocracy of en-

---

[76] Guillaume, ibid., 2:535-39. The debate went on intermittently for several weeks.

lightenment is the most dangerous; it finds within itself a thousand ways to exist."[77] A. C. Thibaudeau argued for free, private competitive education. "Were the Greeks barbarians because they did not pay professors' salaries?"[78] Fourcroy, who had favored the Paris plan on September 15, now turned against state support above the primary level, except for student scholarships. He himself had given courses of private lectures on chemistry very successfully. He would let students study with whom they chose. For the government to set up institutes and lycées would be to create a new priesthood. "To pay so many teachers, to create so many tenured positions, would be . . . to allow privileged professors to offer dull lectures as they chose."[79]

All that the Convention was able to pass was the Bouquier law of December 19. It was, indeed, the only piece of legislation from 1789 through 1793 of which the intent was the actual creation of new schools. It is with the Bouquier law that the next chapter opens. Meanwhile, to use Guizot's words, let us glance briefly at the ruins over which these laws and plans were soaring.

SOME ACTUALITIES

They were wrecks rather than ruins. The Department of Paris, disappointed that the Convention took no action on the Paris plan of September 15, was still determined that the colleges and faculties of the University of Paris should not reopen on the old basis for the coming academic year. On its own authority, therefore, in October, it ordered the suspension of all teaching in the University of Paris until further notice. The Convention, however, continued to honor the assurances given after confiscation of the college endowments in the preceding March; that is, it maintained the grant of July of 307,552 francs to the Paris colleges, and even raised it to 632,308 for the Year III (September 1794 to September 1795). Thus, while forbidden to teach, the Paris professors continued to draw their salaries, or at least have a claim on them, though in paper money and often in arrears. Holders of scholarships also, except for those of eighteen or older who were in the army and the younger ones withdrawn by their parents during the disorders, continued to have their scholarships paid for by the national government.[80]

[77] Ibid., 2:552.
[78] Ibid., 3:108.
[79] Ibid., 3:97.
[80] Ibid., 2:356-57, 360.

In January 1794 the consultative committee appointed by the Department during the preceding summer issued a provisional plan for the reopening of the Paris colleges. The plan was signed by Berthollet, Lagrange, and Garat and presented a diluted version of the plan of September 15. The 10 colleges would be replaced by seven "institutes" (Condorcet's word), of which five would be in the city—housed in existing colleges and staffed by many of the existing professors—and two in the outlying districts of the Department. Though abortive like its predecessors, this plan contained some interesting features: it would open the institutes to girls as well as boys over twelve years old; it gave less attention to arts and trades than the Paris plan, in some ways anticipating the program of the Central Schools and the views of the *idéologues* (of whom Garat was to be one); and among the six modern languages to be taught the one commonly known as English was listed as Anglo-American. But nothing came of it because meanwhile the Bouquier law of December 19 assumed that education at this level should be left to free private enterprise.[81]

Conditions during the war and the ensuing Terror may be illustrated from what happened at Louis-le-Grand, known since 1792 as Equality College. The number of its students fell from 500 in 1789 to 325 in 1793 to only 50 in 1795. It may be recalled that before the Revolution a great many students at Louis-le-Grand were young men who resided in the college but studied in the higher faculties of law, medicine, and theology. By October 1792 almost a hundred of them had departed as volunteers for the army. From October 1792 until August 1793 about 3,000 other volunteers from all over the country were quartered within the college walls. It proved impossible to separate the students from the soldiers. "Student discipline and studies suffered seriously at this time," in the words of the principal, J. F. Champagne. After the Department forbade instruction, some surreptitious teaching still went on with the diminishing number of younger pupils. Then a part of Equality College, together with the adjoining building of Plessis College, was taken over as a place of confinement for persons awaiting the Revolutionary Tribunal—the famous Plessis prison of the Terror.

In the spring of 1794, as part of the general mobilization, improvised workshops for the manufacture of arms sprang up all over Paris. One of these was at Equality College, where 500 workmen were assembled, and walls, doors, windows, exits, and entrances were knocked down or rearranged. In such turmoil it was just as well that the college

---

[81] Ibid., 4:627-33.

had already been obliged to turn in its coin in return for paper money and that its library of 30,000 books, its geographic globes, and its scientific instruments were likewise confiscated and transported to "cultural depots." In the winter of 1794-1795 the college suffered, as the whole city did, from the more acute shortages of food and fuel and the rising inflation that had to some extent been held in check during the Terror. Under such circumstances most students naturally were kept at home. With the oldest in the army, and those of sixteen and seventeen taking accelerated courses in surgery, medicine, or other subjects useful in the war effort, the famous Louis-le-Grand was reduced to a kind of underground teaching of reading and writing to the few younger boys who remained. The other Paris colleges were simply closed.[82]

There can be no systematic view of what happened to the colleges outside Paris. From sporadic mention in the papers of the Committee on Public Instruction, or in the *Moniteur*, it is known that at least 25 were in operation in 1793 and 1794. For example, in the summer of 1793 the Convention granted 24,000 francs to the College of Sorèze toward payment of its scholarships and 20,000 to the College of Autun for repairs after a fire. The varying fates and troubles of colleges at Poitiers, Angers, Lyon, and Pontlevoy have already been noted. In general, it is not true that education in the colleges ground totally to a halt, and the number remaining active was probably more than 25; but it is also true that they struggled under great difficulties and that the Convention never varied in its intention to abolish and replace them with more modern institutions, which in 1795 proved to be the Central Schools.[83]

The higher institutions outside the universities, except for the academies abolished in 1793, remained in operation throughout these difficult years.[84] Since they had no endowments they suffered nothing from confiscation. Having no connection with the church, and since few of their professors were clerics of any kind, they were unaffected by antireligious outbursts. They offered teaching and conducted research in modern subjects and so could not be accused, like the col-

[82] See the letters of J. F. Champagne in my *School of the French Revolution*, pp. 120-24, 145-54. And see below, pp. 207-08.

[83] Guillaume, *Procès-verbaux . . . Convention*, 2:301, 308, 341; 4:xxxvii-xl. And see above, pp. 108-12, 118-19.

[84] Guillaume, ibid., 4:164-69; J. Fayet, *La Révolution française et la science, 1789-1795* (Paris, 1960); the *Almanach national* for the years in question; on oriental languages, Guillaume, ibid., 2:359; on the origins of the Louvre museum, ibid., 1:311-12 and 3:lxxxviii, xcv, 189, 274-77.

leges and university faculties, of perpetuating superstition or charlatanism. Most of them were also extremely useful to the government in time of war. They nevertheless faced real dangers of dissolution. Some of these dangers were internal, as feuds developed among members who held different political opinions or disputed over proposals for reorganization. Others were external, for all the comprehensive Revolutionary plans provided that the proposed top of the pyramid, or national summit of the arts and sciences, should be formed by merger of bodies already existing. It was for this reason that planners could argue that the highest level would cost no more than had been spent before the Revolution.

Lectures continued as usual at the College of France through the Terror, though to more sparse audiences as young men "flew to the frontiers." Of 19 chairs at the College in 1789, two were abolished during the Revolution—those in canon law and in Hebrew and Syriac—but of the remaining 17, 14 were occupied by the same persons in 1794 as in 1789. The old Royal Garden, or Jardin des Plantes, was reorganized as the Museum of Natural History and became a renowned center for the botanical and zoological sciences. Of its 11 professors in 1789, 10 were still present in 1795, including the botanist Jussieu and the chemists Fourcroy and Brongniart. The staff was enlarged in 1793 by addition of two biologists who became even more famous, Lamarck and Geoffroy de Saint-Hilaire. The former faculties of medicine at Paris, Strasbourg, and Montpellier, relieved of the opprobrium of a university connection, were still more or less active as Schools of Health. The old Observatory was attached to a new Bureau of Longitudes and remained a center of astronomical science despite the anti-Revolutionary sentiments of its director, J. D. Cassini.

The old Royal Library was nationalized as the Bibliothèque Nationale; its holdings were enlarged by the flow of books and manuscripts confiscated from the church and from émigrés; and where in 1789 it had been open to scholars only on Tuesday and Friday mornings, in the Year II (1793-1794), according to the *Almanach National*, it was open from 10 a.m. to 2 p.m. every day except for the *décadi*, the tenth day of the republican calendar, with additional hours during the longer days of summer. The library formerly belonging to the king's brother, the count of Artois, was nationalized as the Bibliothèque de l'Arsénal; and the library of the College of the Quatre-Nations became public property as the Bibliothèque Mazarine. The National Archives were launched by a decree of June 25, 1794, a month before the fall of Robespierre. The Louvre, as a national museum of art, can be dated from a decree of January 16, 1794, when on the initiative of David, speaking for the Committee on Public Instruction, the Convention created a "conservatory of the museum of art" of which Fragonard was a member.

In addition, and operating during the worst years of the Revolution, were eight artillery schools and the old school of military engineering, transferred from Mézières to Metz in February 1794. The schools of Mines and of Roads and Bridges seem to have gone more nearly out of existence at this time, but some of their functions and facilities, along with those of the school of engineering, were soon combined into the new Ecole Polytechnique. Also open, and operating as well as they could during the year of the Terror, were the old Royal Free School of Design, the schools for the blind and for deaf mutes, schools of hydrography in the seaport cities, the school of pharmacy, several veterinary schools, the school of "song and declamation" that became the post-Revolutionary Conservatory of Music, and the school of painting and sculpture, which had formerly been attached to the Academy of that name and when the Academy was abolished was expressly maintained by a decree of September 29, 1793. Since the 1740s the monarchy had supported a program in Arabic and Turkish at the College of Louis-le-Grand; when two professors of these subjects at Equality College raised the issue with the Committee on Public Instruction, in September 1793, the Committee took the action that eventuated two years later in the School of Oriental Languages.

A tabulation drawn up late in 1795 shows the expenditures for the institutions and activities under the jurisdiction of the Executive Commission on Public Instruction. Column 2 of the table in the Appendix reproduces the figures for the Year III, from September 22, 1794 to September 22, 1795.[85] This was the year of the "Thermidorian" Convention, post-Jacobin, post-Robespierrist, and reactionary in the sense of reacting against the Terror, the price controls, and most vehement equalitarian demands. The expenditures of the Year III, however, had almost all been authorized in the Year II or in 1793 or before. The table therefore shows decisions made by the Convention during the radical phase of the Revolution, with the notable exception of the egregious Ecole Normale, of which more will be said, and for which the funds were authorized several months after the death of Robespierre. Given the uncertainties of interpretation, the value of the table lies in suggesting the variety and relative magnitudes of the concerns of the Revolutionary Government, in the Jacobin period, in matters of education and the arts and sciences in general. The table, however,

---

[85] For the tabulation and its sources see the Appendix.

is incomplete, since the military and engineering schools do not appear, not having been under the jurisdiction of the Executive Commission on Public Instruction.

The first comment to be made on Column 2 is that with trifling exceptions all the educational institutions listed in it were inherited from the Old Regime, however much reorganized and adapted to a new era. The exceptions were Bourdon's school, a pet project of some of the Jacobins, and the primary and Central Schools. The small sum spent on primary schools reveals how little the Convention accomplished at this level, and that such elementary schooling as still went on was somewhat randomly supported by local governments and private persons. The small sum for the Central Schools merely shows that they were barely beginning in the Year III. The Ecole Normale was a new creation but intentionally temporary and in any case unsuccessful. The libraries and the museum at the Louvre represented the nationalization and reassembly of books and works of art produced over centuries. More new were the festivals, however much they may be theoretically derived from the royal and ecclesiastical celebrations of earlier times. The interest of the government in them, as in the theater, was in their use as media of adult education for the consolidation of the new republican order.

It is obvious that both elementary and what would later be called secondary schools were severely crippled in the Revolution. Their drastic reform had been demanded for 30 years by the enlightened philosophers, by the old parlements, and by many teachers themselves. The Revolutionary leadership, unable to agree on their instant replacement, let them fall into chaos. Yet by September of 1793 they had not been explicitly abolished. The only institutions of education or learning to be deliberately suppressed seem to have been the academies, the faculties of theology and law, the French Academy at Rome (after the assassination of a French envoy there), the girls' school organized for noble young ladies by Mme de Maintenon at Saint-Cyr in the time of Louis XIV, and the so-called *écoles militaires* or groups of noble cadets in such colleges as Sorèze and Pontlevoy. The Revolutionaries had only contempt for theology; they scorned the law schools, which many of them knew at first hand; and there was no place in 1793 for special education for nobles.

The Revolution was of course destructive and attracted the efforts of various wild men, thieves, ignoramuses, and scorners of higher culture. It is equally true that intellectuals, artists, and men of science took part in it, even in its radical phase. The Convention always opposed vandalism and the defacement of public buildings. At the height of the Terror it decreed that buildings, statues, and inscriptions should be protected, except those that glorified monarchy or feudalism. It paid for salaries and scholarships in the Paris colleges that the Department of Paris had closed, with more going to Equality College than to the nine others because Louis-le-Grand since 1763 had been designed for scholarship students only. At the highest level of the arts and sciences the Convention struggled to preserve what it called the inheritance of the French people. Confiscated palaces and chateaux often fell into dilapidation, and some of their precious contents mysteriously disappeared, but of the 850,828 francs spent for "preservation of national monuments" in the Year III alone, 516,692 went to the Temporary Commission on the Arts and 211,671 to 12 "cultural depots" to which pieces of furniture, art objects, jewelry, and miscellaneous valuables were transported for safekeeping. It is evident too that, even in time of war and economic hardship, the Convention made generous subsidies to the arts and sciences. The more than two million livres for "national awards," mainly for highly educated persons, suggests that the Revolution was a revolution of the intellectuals as well as of the bourgeoisie. Finally, the table reminds us that the metric system (to which decimal currency may be added) originated at this time.

Having surveyed these actualities, we turn again to the plans, laudable intentions, and vast anticipations for which the French Revolution is equally memorable and to a few new creations that do not appear in Column 2 of the table.

CHAPTER 5

DEMOCRATIZATION:
BUILDING THE BETTER WORLD

THE LABORS of the National Convention on matters of education have been compared to those of Penelope at her loom. It may be remembered that Penelope, the wife of Ulysses, during her wandering husband's 10-year absence, was beset by a number of unwanted suitors, to each of whom, in turn, she replied that she would announce her decision when she finished the piece of cloth that she was then weaving. Each night, however, she undid what she had done during the day. She never finished, and no woven fabric was ever produced. Similarly, speakers in the Convention made proposals of plan after plan. Having heard discussion for and against one of these plans, and after postponing, rejecting, ignoring, or simply forgetting, the Convention proceeded to consideration of another, only to repeat the same cycle, and without lasting result. Two problems thus face the historian: first, how to avoid intolerable repetition, and second, how to detect a pattern in the labors of the Convention.

Since December 1792 there had been the Condorcet plan, the Sieyès-Daunou-Lakanal plan, the Lepeletier plan, and the Paris plan of September 15. The Condorcet plan had been put aside, the Sieyès-Daunou-Lakanal plan rejected, the Lepeletier plan enacted temporarily with crippling modifications, and the Paris plan hastily adopted and then suspended the next day. A Commission of Nine was appointed on that same day, September 16, of which Gilbert Romme was the principal spokesman. The Commission offered still another plan but could get no action. In December 1793 a deputy named Bouquier submitted still another proposal, of which the part concerning elementary schooling was enacted into law. The rest of his proposal remained a dead letter. Yet it is not true that the Convention was accomplishing nothing. The metaphor of Penelope's loom is not quite exact. Nor is it impossible to distinguish a pattern.

For a year and a half after the Bouquier law, or until the spring of 1795, we can see a continuing concern with democratization, modified, however, more than in 1793, by other pressing considerations and especially by the needs of the war effort. By an important law of December 1793 the Convention enlarged and centralized the powers of its Committee of Public Safety, which in effect now exercised a revolutionary dictatorship. This ruling Committee suppressed internal rebellion, held the sans-culottes in check, expelled the foreign invaders, and passed to the military offensive, until by 1795 the French were occupying Belgium and the Dutch Netherlands and preparing for the invasion of Italy. The Committee of Public Safety made its influence felt also in education, working through the Committee on Public Instruction, by obtaining legislation in the Convention and by its own executive orders. In a general way, where attempts at democratization in 1793 reflected an upwelling from below, they came in 1794 more by imposition from above. There was a more positive program for building a more democratic society.

The fall of Robespierre in July 1794—followed by reduction in the powers of the Committee of Public Safety, the closing of the Jacobin club, and the end of the Terror—marked no turning point on the military or educational fronts. In education, the change became more evident in the spring of 1795, after two violent uprisings against the Convention, commonly known as those of Germinal and Prairial, or of April 1 and May 20, 1795. On the latter occasion armed invaders streamed into the hall and threatened the deputies. The Convention successfully resisted, but in the following months reacted more strongly against democratization and everything else associated with the radicalism of the preceding three years. The last months of the Convention saw the enactment of several pieces of legislation, of which the most comprehensive was the law of 3 Brumaire of the Year IV, known more briefly as the Daunou law. After all the doing and undoing, weaving and unraveling, the Daunou law revived important aspects of the Condorcet plan, notably its multilevel provision for schools in a national system, but without Condorcet's overriding concern for equality. So far as democratization remained alive under the Directory it was in an attenuated sense, meaning hardly more than a republican dislike for the ranks and privileges of the Old Regime.

The present chapter traces developments from December 1793 to about June 1795. The work of the final months of the Convention offers a more proper opening for the next.

THE BOUQUIER LAW

Gabriel Bouquier was an obscure deputy from the Dordogne, who, when added to the Committee on Public Instruction in October 1793, had apparently never spoken in the Convention except when he cast his vote for the death of Louis XVI. A literary man, he became more widely known in 1794 for writing the verses for a musical spectacle that had 24 performances in Paris, called a *sans-culotterie dramatique*, celebrating the uprising of August 10, 1792. He also became one of the most active of the Committee in the preservation of paintings and art objects. But so far as can be known, he had taken no interest, at the time of entering the Committee, in the educational efforts of the preceding year.

Bouquier nevertheless gave his name to what has been called "the first French school law."[1] He came forward with a plan for which he claimed the simple virtues of "liberty, equality and brevity." It rejected all the language hitherto used in the educational debates—*primaire, secondaire, instituts, lycées*. It called for no central administration. It proposed simply a "first stage" and a "last stage" of public instruction. The first stage should provide elementary schooling for all boys and girls from the age of six, with teachers to be paid from public funds in proportion to the number of their pupils. The last stage involved no schools at all but consisted in "the meeting of citizens in popular societies, theaters, civic games, military evolutions, and national and local festivals." That is, for the adolescent ages the concern of the Republic should be in civic formation to be acquired in company with adults. The only schools for these ages would be private enterprises that parents might select as they wished, and for which they would pay, with the state providing funds to enable a certain number of poor but talented youths to attend them. At a higher level the state would carry the costs and maintain salaried professors for numerous institu-

---

[1] J. L. Crémieux-Brilhac, ed., *L'Education Nationale* (Paris, 1965), p. 17. For the text and other details on the Bouquier plan and ensuing Bouquier law see J. Guillaume, *Procès-verbaux du Comité d'Instruction publique de la Convention Nationale*, 6 vols. (Paris, 1891-1907), 3:xxiv-xlviii, 56-62, 191-96; M. Gontard, *L'Enseignement primaire en France de la Révolution à la loi Guizot (1789-1833)* (Paris, 1959), pp. 116-20. For inconclusive legislation preceding the Bouquier law see Guillaume, ibid., 2:688,851.

tions teaching "sciences useful to society." These included medical schools and hospitals; schools of military engineering, artillery, and land mines; road and bridge building; and astronomy and hydrography as useful to navigation. The less useful or pure arts and sciences, like adolescent schooling, should be left to private initiative. The state would not pay for them, but it would make available to interested persons, adolescent or adult, in every town of importance (from confiscated property more or less under the control of the Committee on Public Instruction) a library, a museum, a cabinet of natural history, a cabinet of instruments of experimental physics, and a botanical garden to be attached to each hospital.

Bouquier thus reverted in effect to the Sieyès-Daunou-Lakanal plan, and even to the Talleyrand plan, which also had called for elementary and advanced education at public expense while leaving the intermediate level to be paid for by private families and local governments except for a few national scholarships. Such, indeed, was the pattern of French education as late as the early decades of the twentieth century. Bouquier's plan was distinctive, however, in two ways. With his concentration at the highest level on useful subjects, which meant subjects useful in the military emergency, he said nothing of such institutions of pure learning as the College of France or of possible successors to the former academies. At the elementary or "first stage" he insisted that education, while financed by the state, should be "free" in the French sense of *enseignement libre*; that is, any person should be free to open a school (and in this case derive his or her income from public funds) with a minimum of control or supervision.

This was a striking provision in the context of December 1793. These were the weeks of most radical antireligious excitement and deliberate Dechristianization. The cult of Reason at Notre Dame de Paris had taken place only a short time before. There were loud demands on all sides that no priest, religious sister, or anyone connected with the clergy should be allowed to teach. The Committee on Public Instruction was divided. Bouquier now calmly proposed to ignore the whole issue. Any *citoyen* or *citoyenne*, he said, should be free to open a school simply by announcement of intent to the municipality and on obtaining a certificate of good citizenship and good conduct. He indeed added that anyone teaching "precepts and maxims contrary to republican law and morality" would be denounced and punished, and that elementary teachers must use books (which did not yet exist) approved and adopted by the national government. Nevertheless, the avoidance of all mention of clerical status as an impediment to teaching showed a tolerance unusual at the moment.

The Convention adopted only the first three articles of the Bouquier plan, which is to say those articles that pertained to elementary schools and teachers. The recurring problem of a multilevel versus single-level system was postponed or evaded, as was any action on higher technical establishments. The "first French school law" provided only for the free and universal education of younger children. By an amendment, the Convention added the feature of compulsion; all parents were required to send their children to some school, under serious financial penalties for failure to comply. By another amendment, and observing that in thinly inhabited or remote rural areas a teacher could not earn a living if paid in proportion to the number of pupils, the Convention specified a minimum salary of 500 francs a year.

The Bouquier law was enacted easily and rapidly, without opposition in the Convention, and was warmly praised in the Jacobin club. Both Danton and Hébert expressed approval, as did Félix Lepeletier, Dufourny, and Hassenfratz, whose active interest in these matters we have seen in the last chapter. It has always been a question how an unknown deputy after a year of fruitless debate so readily obtained the passage of an actual law. One explanation is that the law represented a minimum on which members of the Convention could agree at the climax of the Revolution: instruction for all in reading, writing, arithmetic, civic training, and common morals, and participation by all in the adult education of political activity and national festivals. It is also possible that the Committee of Public Safety intervened. The Committee, and especially Robespierre, were trying at this very time to restrain the movement of Dechristianization. They knew that extreme antireligious outbursts divided the country and discredited the Revolution. It could be foreseen also that such outbursts would severely limit the number of available teachers. It may be supposed, therefore, unfortunately without direct evidence, that Robespierre or some other member of the Committee of Public Safety approached Bouquier, as a little known and noncontroversial member of the Convention, and persuaded him to submit the plan that has been described. We may even imagine that the Committee dictated the terms of the plan, recalling that the Committee of Public Safety had ordered the establishment of "a primary school in every place of 600 inhabitants" some six months before. (See p. 134 above.) In any case, three days before final enactment of his law Bouquier was elected to the presidency of the Paris Jacobin Club, an honor that rotated every two weeks. He clearly had friends in high places.

Serious efforts were made to put the Bouquier law into effect, but they ran into unsurmountable difficulties.[2] Implementation was decentralized; it depended on the action taken in the 557 districts and over 30,000 communes or municipalities. Each of these had to set up a committee to receive the applications of prospective teachers, issue the required certificates of reliable citizenship, make the appointments, find schoolrooms, and arrange for the salaries. There was a shortage of persons to serve on these committees and an even worse shortage of applicants. Some who had been teachers before the Revolution refused to apply, or were afraid to teach under the new conditions, or were rejected by the local authorities, which reflected varying opinions throughout the country. Some intensely patriotic and republican local committees imposed stricter standards for the certificates of citizenship than the Bouquier law envisaged. Some, though the law allowed it, would accept no actual or former priest or religious sister. Young men sufficiently literate to teach school were scarce because they were in the army. Many local committees simply reappointed under the new law the teachers they already had. In other cases such persons simply continued to conduct their schools without bothering to apply. Much or perhaps most of the elementary teaching that still went on thus added nothing to what had existed before. There was universal complaint about the shortage of elementary schoolbooks, especially of books suited for the new Revolutionary generation, such as the Bouquier law called for, but which had not yet been written. In addition, and at opposite ends of the social scale, some poor families objected to sending their children to school at all, and in other families, where education was valued, parents disliked the politicization and propaganda in schools authorized by local zealots.

Any quantitative statement is therefore misleading. In Floréal of the Year II the government sent a circular to the 557 districts concerning the application of the Bouquier law. During the summer of 1794 some 474 replies came in. Of these, 400 reported that they did in fact have schools, a "school" meaning a one-room school with one teacher. In these 400 districts 23,125 schools were to be expected, but only 6,831 existed. Doubtless there were "unofficial" schools that escaped the notice of the local authorities. Geographical distribution was very unequal. About 50 districts reported that their number was about complete. The others ranged down from "a few" to "none." In the district of Grenoble, which would require about 400 teachers, only four were

2 On application of the Bouquier law, with data on numbers of schools, and so forth, see Guillaume, ibid., 4:xl-xlix and 891-910; Gontard, *Enseignement primaire*, pp. 122-34.

reported. Information gathered in the following November showed much the same results. Grenoble still had only four. Montpellier reported total compliance. Paris had about 250 teachers, of whom 100 were men and 150 women. The section Panthéon-français, which we have seen taking the lead in demands for education in 1793, now had six men and five women teachers and was among the best supplied of the Paris sections.

In May 1795 the situation was still discouraging, according to two reports to the Committee of Public Safety sent in by members of the Convention "on mission" in the departments.[3] Jard-Panvillier reviewed the difficulties as he observed them at Beauvais: it was impossible to find enough teachers, the elementary schoolbooks ordered by the Convention were not yet available, and people in small villages that had formerly had their own schoolmaster, and where no school was yet established under the new law, would not "send their children of young ages over considerable distances by bad roads." C. F. Dupuis reported similar problems from Besançon. It was hard to find proper *jurys d'instruction*, that is, local school committees, and he added: "I have been sorry to see that almost everywhere people are busier in commenting on the laws, finding fault with them or proposing to reform them than in executing them." In short, revolution had not yet yielded to stabilization, nor spontaneity to bureaucracy.

Application of the Bouquier law was made more difficult in some parts of France by supplementary legislation enacted in January 1794, requiring the teaching of French in the peripheral provinces where French was not used in popular speech. The problem of the national language was of sufficient importance to deserve treatment by itself.

A National Language

French in the eighteenth century was an international language, commonly spoken in the salons, courts, chancelleries, and learned academies of Europe, and books and periodicals written in French reached even wider social and international circles. It was not, however, the language of all Frenchmen. The Republic inherited the boundaries of the monarchy, which over the centuries had brought the regions of various French dialects under its control and had annexed areas where the language was not French at all. These included the Breton spoken

[3] A. Aulard, ed., *Recueil des actes du Comité de salut public*, 28 vols. (Paris, 1889-1955), 23:86, 116.

in Brittany, Flemish in the extreme north, German in Alsace and parts of Lorraine, Italian in the extreme southeast and in Corsica, and Basque and Catalan along the Pyrenees border. The various *patois* consisted of the northern dialects of the *langue d'oïl*, from which standard French had developed, and the southern dialects of the *langue d'oc*, which were less intelligible in the north, being closer to the other Romance languages of the Mediterranean basin. In all these areas educated persons employed standard French, without which neither the National Convention nor the government of the Old Regime would have been possible. Some of these persons still used the local speech in the privacy of the home or in dealing with tradesmen or servants. Standard French was a kind of lingua franca of the educated, within France itself as in Europe. It was to some extent a badge of class, like a knowledge of reading and writing. In many parts of the country it was unknown or at least unfamiliar to the mass of the population.

The Revolution as a whole, by activating and politicizing large numbers of people, was itself an education in the national language. The "last stage" of Bouquier's plan, though not made part of the Bouquier law, nevertheless existed in fact. The popular societies and the festivals of this "last stage" brought the educated and the uneducated together. In the popular societies and local clubs the uneducated could take part in discussions. In the festivals they listened to the speeches and orations that marked such occasions. The Revolutionary press provided interesting reading matter; the language of most of it was irreproachable, but even the studied vulgarisms of Hébert's *Père Duchesne* were recognizably French; and those who could not read such journals could hear them read aloud in clubs and taverns. In addition, participation in local government went fairly far down in the social scale, and officials of the smallest communes had to understand the new laws and administrative orders emanating from Paris.

There was also the army.[4] Almost a million men were in military service in 1794. It was the largest army yet seen in Europe. Men from all parts of the country were brought together. The needs of command and of comradeship promoted uniformity of speech. This national army even developed its own press. Soldiers' newspapers appeared in the individual armies, the *Armée du Nord*, the *Armée des Côtes de Cherbourg*, and others. In 1794, following the general pattern of central-

---

[4] J. P. Bertaud, *La Révolution armée: les soldats-citoyens et la Révolution française* (Paris, 1979); M. Martin, *Les origines de la presse militaire à la fin de l'Ancien Régime et sous la Révolution* (Vincennes [service de l'armée], 1975); A. Soboul, *L'armée nationale sous la Révolution* (Paris, 1945).

izing control, the Committee of Public Safety tried to replace these locally edited journals with others written in Paris. In Ventôse of the Year II (March 1794) the government was subsidizing seven Parisian papers (including the *Père Duchesne*) of which 30,000 copies a day were sent to the armies. A little later Carnot, of the Committee of Public Safety, supervised the editing of the *Soirée du Camp*, an official publication designed to keep the armed forces informed and well disposed to the Revolutionary Government, and of which about 10,000 copies were circulated. In the army of the Year II, where the barrier between officers and enlisted men was highly permeable, and the educated and uneducated shared a common purpose, it was thought that the troops had to understand what they were doing and be motivated by their own feelings rather than by automatic obedience. It is probable that the army, over the whole period of the wars from 1792 to 1814, through providing travel to young men in France and foreign countries and through its lessons in camp hygiene, care of weapons, group living, and the general raising of political consciousness, had more effect on popular education than all the laws of the Revolution and Empire.

Since early in the Revolution efforts had been made to translate the decrees of the Revolutionary assemblies into languages understandable by the common people. A man named Dugas ran a whole establishment specializing in the *langue d'oc*, and by the end of 1792 his translations penetrated much of southern France. The difficulties were great, for the *patois* were varied, some had no accepted written form, and some had no words to convey ideas of the "constitution" or "citizenship" or the "rights of man." The year 1794 saw an especial drive to create a truly national language. It was unsuccessful. As late as 1864 40 percent or more of the people of the southern third of France, and of Brittany and Alsace, were judged unable to speak French. The Ferry school laws of the 1880s then spread the national language more widely. Here again the Revolution anticipated what it could not achieve.

It is the aims of the linguistic nationalizers of 1794 that are of interest, since their significance goes beyond their immediate circumstances.[5] These aims can be seen in a report by Barère, speaking for the Committee of Public Safety on January 27, in another report by

---

[5] The best account is still in F. Brunot, *Histoire de la langue française*, 13 vols. (Paris, 1905-1979), 10 (Pt. 1):173-266. See also M. de Certeau, D. Julia, and R. Ravel, *Une politique de la langue: La Révolution française et les patois: L'Enquête de Grégoire* (Paris, 1975), which prints the text of the reports by Barère and Grégoire as well as the inquiry of 1790 by Grégoire and replies to it. Also D. Julia, *Les trois couleurs du tableau noir: la Révolution* (Paris, 1981), pp. 215-26.

the Abbé Grégoire, speaking for the Committee on Public Instruction on June 4, and in the demands of a few ultra-democrats, the "last of the Mountain," made in November in the Convention and in the Paris Jacobin club a few days before it was closed. The hope of creating a national language was an aspect of democratization, and so reached its climax in 1794.[6]

In the winter of 1793-1794 Brittany was disturbed by the Vendéan rebellion against Paris; Alsace was in turmoil, being located in the war zone, and with over 20,000 uprooted Alsatians fleeing across the Rhine into Germany; and Corsica was occupied by the British. There were partisans of the Revolution in all these regions, especially in the towns among those who could speak French; but undoubtedly the mass of the population found it hard to comprehend what was happening. Barère and the Committee of Public Safety therefore addressed themselves to the problems of the more strictly foreign languages, not the *patois*, seeing in these languages a medium in which disaffected priests, aristocrats, royalists, foreign spies, and other enemies of the Revolutionary Government could easily operate. Barère's eloquent but somewhat confused speech was designed to combat counterrevolution in general, as expressed both by foreign influence and by class attitudes within France itself.

A knowledge of proper French before the Revolution, he said, with some exaggeration, had been the hallmark of "certain classes of society," of the so-called "good company" in which "one had to spew out the language in a special way in order to appear well bred."[7] These distinctions were now disappearing. "Free men are all alike, and the vigorous accent of liberty and equality is the same." It was also true that despots flourished by dividing their peoples, and a monarchy was a tower of Babel. "In a democracy, on the contrary, the oversight over government is entrusted to each citizen; to oversee it one must know it, and most of all one must know the language." Four regions presented an especial difficulty, those where the *idiome* was Breton, German, Italian, or Basque, though Barère admitted that most Basques

[6] A different view is taken by Professor Patrice Higonnet (of Harvard University) in "The politics of linguistic terrorism and grammatical hegemony during the French Revolution," *Social History* 5 (1980):41-69. It is here argued that the Revolutionary leadership of 1794, being bourgeois, and hence unwilling to bring about real economic equality by laws against property, chose to enforce equality of language as a substitute, only to deceive the people again by attaching importance to correct grammar and so reinstating class differences.

[7] The text of Barère's speech, and of the ensuing law of 8 Pluviôse of the Year II and later amendments, is printed in Guillaume, *Procès-verbaux*, 3:348-59.

were good patriots. People knowing only these languages were easily deluded by fanatical priests and stubborn aristocrats. In Breton, he said, the same word was used for both religion and law, and the Bretons imagined that every change in the laws meant a change in their religion. Where these *idiomes* were the common speech "public education cannot be established and national regeneration is impossible." "The language must be popularized, and this aristocracy of language must be destroyed, for it seems to produce a civilized nation in the midst of a barbarous one." Barère therefore proposed that in every rural commune in certain named departments, where Breton, German, Italian, and Basque were spoken, a teacher of French should be installed to give lessons in the elementary schools being organized under the Bouquier law, to deliver lectures to adults on the *décadi*, and to explain the laws, especially the laws concerning agriculture and civic rights. The Convention enacted this proposal, adding Flemish and Catalan to the four others. It proved so difficult to find suitable French teachers, especially for the villages that most needed them, that the law had little effect.

The Abbé Grégoire attacked the *patois* as well as the non-French *idiomes*.[8] He was a liberal-minded priest who had accepted the Civil Constitution of the Clergy and now sat in the Convention while being also the constitutional bishop of Blois. A democrat who had urged universal suffrage as early as 1789, he was also a humanitarian and what would now be called an assimilationist. He had strongly favored the granting of equal rights to Jews and had worked for the abolition of black slavery in the colonies; he later wrote a book (disliked by Thomas Jefferson) to show that blacks had potentially the same abilities as whites. He believed that in a better world all human beings would be more alike. At least within a single country they should be able to communicate in a common language without regional or class barriers. He had long reflected on linguistic divisions within France, and in 1790 had conducted a private survey, sending a circular to priests and others of his acquaintance throughout the country, by which he gathered detailed information on the popular speech of many localities. At the time of the passage of Barère's law he had urged the extension of its terms to other departments where a French *patois* was spoken.

On June 4, having gained the support of the Committee on Public Instruction, of which he was a member, he presented a report to the Convention "on the need and methods for extinguishing *patois* [plural]

[8] Ibid., 4:487 and 494-98.

and universalizing the use of the French language." The report was full of the curious and mistaken theories of an amateur ethnologist. Its message, however, was clear. Only in 15 of the 80-odd departments, said Grégoire, was French the language of the common people. There were 30 different *patois*, mutually unintelligible; indeed, in some places the words for the same vinestocks, grains, and farm implements varied from village to village. The *patois* inhibited trade. They also perpetuated superstition. Modern popular manuals should be prepared to enlighten the people. For example, a farmer who was afraid to take up his scythe before consulting an almanac needed a short manual on meteorology. Such manuals would have to be written in a common language. In the new France everyone was to qualify for public office; they could not hold office unless they knew French. Otherwise there would always be two classes, the governing and the governed. Nor need there be in the future, as in the past, a difference between noble and ordinary styles of writing and speaking. If applied to social status, the consequences of such differences "prove the importance of my project in a democracy." He hoped also that pronunciation and grammar might be standardized, and he wanted to teach correct grammar to everybody. As for the *patois*, they might survive for their historic interest and folkloric value.

The Convention simply returned Grégoire's proposal to the Committee for further study and ordered an abridgment of his speech to be printed and sent to all departments, districts, communes, and popular societies throughout the Republic.

In November 1794, four months after Thermidor, the Committee on Public Instruction brought another bill to the floor of the Convention, proposing various modifications in detail of the now year-old Bouquier law.[9] The question of a national language came up along with others still raised by the most insistent democrats of the collapsing Mountain. At the Jacobin club, at one of its last sessions, it was again said that *éducation cummune* was necessary because some people wanted "to raise themselves above others" and that "the object of education is to make men completely democratic."[10] In the Convention the deputy Duhem, a Montagnard who now regretted his part in the overthrow of Robespierre, feared that if private schools were allowed the public schools would be deserted or would turn into charity schools; this matter, he said, was "more important than is thought for the

[9] Ibid., 5:232-33, 236.
[10] A. Aulard, ed., *La Société des Jacobins*, 6 vols. (Paris, 1889-1897), 6:608-12.

establishment of democracy."[11] It was Duhem also who demanded that the language of instruction should be French alone.

The Committee, with Lakanal as its spokesman, in this bill of November 1794, proposed that in regions having a "particular idiom" instruction should be both in the idiom and in French, that is bilingual, "in such a way that French should become familiar to all citizens of the Republic." Duhem and a few others objected. For Duhem, French was the *langue mère*, the mother tongue, even of Bretons and Alsatians, because the Republic was as much a mother as was a female parent. The point was not absurd; the essence of the new order was to define the individual by membership in a political community, not by membership in a family or kinship group. Children, said Duhem, should be forced to hear and speak only French in the elementary schools. They would thus learn to use their true mother tongue. "If on the other hand you teach in both languages you will naturally dignify the *idiome* or the barbarous *patois*; you will accustom citizens to regard French as a learned language and to take pride in preserving the language of their parents. But if children are forcibly instructed in French, they will end up by gradually habituating their parents to it also."

To which Lakanal replied:

It is impossible in the present order of things to teach exclusively in French. The teacher must first make himself understood by his pupils, who in these regions, when they arrive at school at the age of six or seven, have never spoken anything but their idiom. Children must also make themselves understood by other citizens; otherwise you will turn them into little isolated and unhappy beings. . . . The Committee, in leaving idioms in the teaching process, wishes only to use them as a vehicle for the better understanding of French.[12]

Others spoke on both sides of the question until an amendment proposed by Gilbert Romme was adopted: "Teaching will be in French. The idiom of the region can be used only as an auxiliary means."

The national language thus seemed to win out over the "idioms" and the *patois*. Whatever "auxiliary" might mean, it implied that elementary teachers must be bilingual. Such a provision went beyond the Barère law of the preceding January, which had required only the addition of a French teacher to regular teachers in the peripheral departments. The Romme amendment, though offered as a compromise and

[11] Guillaume, *Procès-verbaux*, 5:244.
[12] Ibid., 5:232-33.

really only restating the Committee's proposal, made the universalizing of elementary education not only more difficult but impossible. With teachers in short supply for so many other reasons, to require them to teach in French, or even bilingually, in the 30,000 communes of France was altogether utopian. When the Daunou law of October 1795 replaced the Bouquier law it said nothing about the language of instruction.

NATIONAL FESTIVALS AND A NEW CIVIC ENVIRONMENT

It is ironic that those parts of the Bouquier plan that were not enacted were the most fully realized. The law that bears his name concerned only the elementary schools but did little to promote them. The "last stage" of public instruction as outlined in his plan, though not adopted as such, already existed in fact as a form of education for young persons and adults. This stage, to repeat, consisted in "the meeting of citizens in popular societies, theaters, civic games, military evolutions, and national and local festivals." The busy activity of the popular societies began to slow down in 1794 under pressures from the Committee of Public Safety and disappeared under the post-Thermidorian governments. The same was true of theatrical productions with strong Revolutionary content. National and local festivals remained fitfully alive for several years. Finally, where Bouquier's plan called for state-supported higher instruction in useful subjects, the Convention in 1794 organized a number of projects for accelerated practical training, the *cours révolutionnaires*, to which both the present Ecole Polytechnique and Ecole Normale Supérieure look back for their origins.

Of all activities of the French Revolution the hardest for a modern observer to enter into with sympathetic understanding are the measures taken for the civic indoctrination of the population as a whole.[13] We are inclined to see in them, not so much an acute form of the

[13] James Leith, *Media and Revolution: Moulding a New Citizenry in France during the Terror* (Toronto, 1968), originating as a series of radio talks for the Canadian Broadcasting Corporation, is an excellent brief treatment with an extensive bibliography. Leith has also published *The Idea of Art as Propaganda in France, 1750-99* (Toronto, 1965). See also the whole second volume of the *Proceedings of the Consortium on Revolutionary Europe, 1980*, ed. Donald D. Horward (Athens, Ga., 1980), containing papers on painting, sculpture, music, and architecture during the Revolution. Also M. Ozouf, *La fête révolutionnaire, 1789-94* (Paris, 1976); Julia, *Trois couleurs*, pp. 332-57; D. L. Dowd, *Pageant-Master of the Republic: Jacques-Louis David and the French Revolution* (Lincoln, Neb., 1948); and A. Mathiez, *La théophilanthropie et le culte décadaire, 1796-1801* (Paris, 1904).

patriotic celebrations once more common in democratic societies, as the signs of a compulsive ideology and foretaste of the mass manipulation used more recently by totalitarian regimes. Neither the perpetual moralizing nor the earnest deism of the Revolutionary festivals appeals to the modern taste. Oratory has become a lost art. Heroes are no longer exalted. Recitation of topical verses at public gatherings seems merely quaint. The notion that the French people could be reshaped by such methods seems merely naive.

Naive or not, it was a philosophy of environmentalism that underlay the program of adult education as it did the planning for the schools. The idea was to create a world of sights and sounds by which grown men and women would be remade for the Revolution. The very names of things were changed. The historic provinces gave way to departments named after rivers or other natural objects—for more compelling reasons, it must be said, than mere nomenclature or public relations. At the height of the Revolution the streets, squares, and buildings in Paris (as elsewhere) were renamed: the Place Louis XV became the Place de la Révolution, the church of Sainte-Geneviève the Panthéon, the Palais-Royal the Palais-Egalité. Some of this was hardly avoidable in the circumstances, and was found in less violent revolutions, as when King's College became Columbia College in New York. And if we think it odd that the former church of Sainte-Geneviève was used to commemorate great men, including Rousseau and Voltaire, we should recall that this was a time when statues of statesmen, generals, and admirals were put up in Westminster Abbey, and Dr. Johnson was buried there.

In Floréal of the Year II (May 1794) the Committee of Public Safety issued a series of decrees to bring the Revolutionary efforts of artists under central planning. These climactic months of the Revolution saw also a climax in the arts. For example, where only a hundred Revolutionary songs had been composed in 1789, the number reached 596 in 1793 and rose to 700 in 1794, after which it abruptly declined.[14] The decrees of Floréal invited painters, sculptors, poets, musicians, and architects to submit their works to a public competition, in which government committees would decide on awards, grant subsidies, or in the case of architecture determine which proposed structures should be built. There was a lively response, but as with the schoolbooks for which a similar contest was announced, the results were inhibited or

[14] J. Leith, "Music as an ideological weapon in the French Revolution," *Annual Report of the Canadian Historical Association, 1966* (Ottawa, 1967), pp. 139-40; C. L. Donakowski, *A Muse for the Masses: Ritual and Music in the Age of the Democratic Revolution* (Chicago, 1977), pp. 33-75.

nullified by the rapid political changes that followed the death of Robespierre. Of more lasting effect were the large sums devoted to schools of the arts, especially music, which was valued for its rousing effects both in public gatherings and in the armies.

The works proposed in architecture and urban design are of especial interest, since their purpose was most obviously to create the new environment in which a regenerated citizenry was to live. There were plans for assembly halls, courthouses, theaters, and temples of civil religion. That there were no plans to house schools or institutions of higher learning seems strange, until we remember that the Convention had not yet decided whether such establishments above the elementary level should be public or private. The plans called for many fountains and gardens and great open spaces for mass meetings, processions, athletic contests, and military displays. Everywhere there should be statues of famous men of the past and allegorical figures depicting liberty, equality, law, and virtue. Mostly the buildings would be presented in the classical repertory of colonnades and pediments, domes and arches, friezes and urns. A few bold spirits dreamed of more futuristic buildings designed as pure unadorned oblongs, pyramids, and spheres. Some of these stirrings in the arts had been evident before 1789, and reflected the Enlightenment as much as the Revolution. In any case, the purpose was to turn the mind away from the Christian tradition as embodied in the Gothic (still a term of disparagement) and to obliterate the royal and aristocratic frivolities of the rococo.[15]

As architecture would transform space, so the republican calendar would transform the perception of time. People would no longer live in the cycle of the Christian year, with its recurring Sundays, saints' days, fast days, Christmas, Lent, and Easter. Nor would they be confused by barbarously irregular months indivisible into seven-day-weeks. The new calendar set up 12 consecutive 30-day months each divided into a 10-day "week" or *décade*, of which each day was rationally numbered, *primidi, duodi, tridi*, and so on, to *décadi*, the day of rest from work. (It was of course necessary to add five days at the end of the year, or six in leap year, first called the *sans-culottides*, but after 1794, more blandly, the *jours complémentaires*.) Adopted in October 1793, the calendar was made mandatory only for public officials. It was also used in the press. From documents of the time it is evident that public officials and other firm partisans of the Republic did in fact become very proficient in its use. On the other hand, it must have long per-

[15] Leith, "Space and Revolution: Architectural Planning in Paris during the Terror," in *Consortium*, pp. 28-42, with illustrations.

plexed the mass of the population, as the metric system did, and anyone who could remember which day in the new calendar was actually
a Sunday, and attended church on that day, might be suspected of less
than adequate attachment to the new order. The *décadi* became the
day of public avowal and celebration of the Republic.

The best remembered of the festivals of the French Revolution,
sometimes known in English as the "worship" of the Supreme Being,
occurred on the *décadi* of 20 Prairial of the Year II, or June 8, 1794.
Robespierre took the lead on this occasion, but the event expressed
far more than Robespierre's ideas alone. Its immediate origin lay in
the deliberations of the Committee on Public Instruction.[16]

The Committee, since its inception, had made national festivals one
of its chief concerns. The coupling of adult education with schools, or
of festivals with instruction for the young, had characterized most of
the Revolutionary educational plans, including Talleyrand's, and the
relative neglect of such festivals in the Condorcet plan had been one
of the main grounds of complaint against it. Rousseau had stressed
the need for patriotic festivals in his advice to the Poles 20 years before. Festivals had in fact sprung up spontaneously throughout France
since the *fête de la fédération* of 1790 celebrating the first anniversary
of the fall of the Bastille. The most gigantic of such demonstrations
had occurred in Paris in August 1793, the Festival of Unity and In-
divisibility, marking the popular acceptance of the constitution of the
Year I. It was not a new topic when the Committee on Public Instruction, a few days after passage of the Bouquier law, instructed one of
its members, J. B. Mathieu, to prepare legislation on what it now
called *fêtes décadaires*.

Mathieu soon produced a detailed draft. There should be five national festivals, each in observance of an important Revolutionary date,
and local celebrations everywhere in France on each of the 36 *décadis*
of the year. Local invention would be supplemented by central planning and assistance. For example, the government would supply villages where no one "might have the confidence to mount the tribune
to instruct his fellow citizens" with a set of "philosophical and patriotic
instructions or speeches" that could be read aloud. A national contest
would be opened for the composition of hymns and chants that, when
approved, would be the same throughout the Republic. One hymn
would celebrate "the Supreme Being, nature, and the public and private virtues dear to republicans." An article of the declaration of rights
of 1793, *that any individual usurping the sovereignty shall be instantly*

<hr>

[16] Guillaume, *Procès-verbaux*, 3:lxxviii, 500, 505, 512.

put to death by free men, was to be "turned into verse by republican poets and chanted in chorus, every *décadi*, at every point in France at the same hour." The hour would be announced by the roll of drums, and at frontier places by the firing of cannon.[17]

The Committee adopted Mathieu's draft, ordered it printed and circulated, and instructed Mathieu to consult with the Committee of Public Safety on its implementation. The governing committee then assumed the initiative and charged Robespierre with the task of preparing a great public announcement. Robespierre worked on this congenial project for a month. He wished to expound republican morality, which in everyday matters of sex, the family, work, and honesty was hardly different from that of the Catholic church, and at the same time to soften the impact of Dechristianization by countering the atheism that he regarded as one of the more shameful luxuries of aristocrats. Hoping to unify the country, he would preach a deism that was common to his generation, as when Jefferson put American independence under the laws of Nature and of Nature's God. The result was Robespierre's famous speech in the Convention on 18 Floréal of the Year II. It mixed arguments for the freedom of private religious belief with a public deistic cult in which all could share, and the need for a public education that should be (with echoes of Lepeletier) "common and equal for all the French." The Convention thereupon enacted its decree of the same date, of which the first article read: "The French people recognize the existence of the Supreme Being and the immortality of the soul." The last article called for a special festival of the Supreme Being on the coming 20 Prairial. The rest of the decree reproduced parts of Mathieu's plan, that is, provision for the five national holidays and for 36 decadary observances. Each of these decadary festivals had a name, and the names of 21 of Robespierre's 36 were exactly the same as in Mathieu's draft. The 21 included Liberty, Equality, Love of Country, Truth, Heroism, Conjugal Faith, Maternal Tenderness, Old Age, Agriculture, and Industry. Others were almost the same in the two versions: where Mathieu said Humanity Robespierre said Human Race, and where Mathieu said simply Nature Robespierre said the Supreme Being and Nature, but the words Supreme Being figured in Mathieu's draft also. Curiously enough, Mathieu's festival of Electricity was omitted by Robespierre, who had become famous 10 years earlier for defending the lightning rod.[18]

[17] Mathieu's draft is in ibid., 3:508-12. The italics above (article 27 of the declaration of rights of the constitution of 1793) are in the original as reprinted by Guillaume.

[18] Passages from Robespierre's speech and the whole decree of 18 Floréal are in ibid., 4:339-46.

The sun shone on 20 Prairial for a perfect day in June. Careful preparations had been made under the supervision of the painter David, who was now a member of the Revolutionary Government and virtual dictator in the arts. Throughout the morning tens of thousands of citizens gathered in the Tuileries garden. At the eastern end of the garden a large dais or amphitheater had been erected, with the Tuileries palace in the background. Around this dais were posted various signs conveying sentiments appropriate to the occasion, such as that "to honor the Deity and punish kings are the same." A men's chorus stood at the right on the dais, a women's chorus on the left. After deputies from the Paris sections had entered the palace to announce the assembling of the people, the entire membership of the Convention, accompanied by a large body of musicians, issued forth and took their seats. "After a grand symphony" Robespierre, as president of the Convention for the usual two-week period, delivered his first address of the day, a kind of politico-religious sermon in praise of the Supreme Being. The women's chorus then chanted a hymn, *Père de l'univers*, with the men's chorus and the whole body of spectators responding in couplets. Robespierre, accompanied by delegates from the Paris sections, then descended and put a torch to the figure of Atheism, whose expiring flames revealed a seated figure of Wisdom. After a second address by Robespierre, the whole vast assemblage marched to the Champ de Mars, where a simulacrum of a Mountain had been built. "Square battalions of adolescents" formed a circle around its base. Youths and old men ascended its slope on the right while women and younger children did so on the left. The Convention occupied the summit. Another hymn was sung, with the crowds joining in the refrain. The male voices on the Mountain then roared out some newly written words to the tune of the Marseillaise and swore an oath for the destruction of tyrants. Salvos of artillery followed, and all present, men and women, "mingled their sentiments in a general embrace and concluded this fine day by raising to heaven the *cri de la patrie: Vive la République française!*"[19]

It should be added that similar if less elaborate festivals took place all over France. Within a few weeks the Committee on Public Instruction received at least a hundred messages from places as far apart as Saint-Malo and Avignon, reporting on the event there, and often en-

---

[19] Ibid., 4:583-90, prints three eyewitness accounts written shortly after 20 Prairial. David's great plan for the festival, along with other preparatory measures, are to be found on pp. 347-66; they of course tell less of what actually happened. There is also an account in the *Moniteur* for 25 Prairial.

closing odes, hymns, chants, strophes, stanzas, or prayers composed locally in honor of the Supreme Being.[20]

The ceremony of 20 Prairial in Paris reveals features that the planners hoped would characterize all the *fêtes nationales* and the *culte décadaire*. One was public participation, as obtained especially through mass singing and mass responses. Another was the bringing together of both sexes and all ages, with those of school age mixing with persons old enough to be their grandparents. The symbolism of the Republic is evident, though the Mountain was replaced by less aggressive emblems after 1794. The *fêtes* were highly didactic, setting up written maxims and precepts to tell spectators what to think. They were also loquacious with many official speeches, though how such large audiences could hear a speaker in the absence of a public address system is hard to understand. There was no personality cult, no attempt to glorify a leader by name; and indeed Robespierre's prominence on this occasion was used by his enemies to denounce him as a would-be dictator. One has the impression that even if blown-up photographs of a great leader had been possible they would not have been used; and it is significant that when Bonaparte seized power five years later he made no attempt to adapt the festivals to his purposes. The festivals remained expressions of a desire to be free.

This insistence on liberty as sung and shouted from thousands of throats impressed two eyewitnesses to the events of 20 Prairial who were by no means friendly to Robespierre. One was Sylvain Maréchal, a radical who vaunted his atheism; the other was Boissy d'Anglas, a moderate member of the Convention whose importance would come after Thermidor. Both thought the committing of Atheism to the flames rather ridiculous, but both felt and shared in the gigantic surge of emotion that swept the Tuileries garden and the Champ de Mars on that day.[21]

Nothing as intense as the Festival of the Supreme Being happened thereafter. The memory of it was poisoned by its coincidence in date with the worst of the Terror. Of the 2,639 persons guillotined in Paris during the Revolution well over half were put to death in the two months of June and July of 1794. Robespierre himself, attacked by his own colleagues, went to the guillotine on July 28. Not many could share the fervor of his deistic religion. The heat of patriotic excitement abated as the foreign armies were driven from France. Nothing was done to carry out the details of the law of 18 Floréal. The great na-

---

[20] Guillaume, *Procès-verbaux*, index volume 1:407-10.
[21] Guillaume, ibid., 4:586, 590.

tional holidays continued to be celebrated, but local observance of the *décadi* became feeble and sporadic, often consisting in no more than a thinly attended public meeting in which local administrators made speeches to an audience of school children, government employees, and a few still fiery patriots. In the neodemocratic atmosphere of 1798 the Directory attempted to enforce the republican calendar and strengthen the decadary cult, making them even more mandatory than in 1794, but without positive or lasting result. When the decadary celebrations were abolished in 1800, and the republican calendar was suppressed in 1806, both had languished so long that their disappearance was not regretted except by a few stalwarts for whom the great Revolution had already become a legend.

It is therefore doubtful what the vast program of adult education really accomplished. The most sympathetic historians make no specific claims for it. Albert Mathiez, conceding the failure of its announced purposes, yet believed that it had blunted the resurgence of the Catholic church. A more recent writer, Mona Ozouf, attempts a more sweeping conclusion. "Rights, liberty, country," she says, "which the Revolutionary festival bound together at the dawn of the modern laic and liberal world, were not soon unbound. The transfer of sacredness to political and social values had become an accomplished fact, defining a new legitimacy and a henceforward untouchable patrimony."[22] One may agree that this is what happened and yet think that it was a consequence, not so much of the festivals and the civil cult or of any official program, as of the experience of the whole Revolution for the French people, the principles announced by the Revolution, and the war by which they were defended against armed intervention. Yet some residue remained. Throughout the next century a few idealists always remembered the *fêtes nationales*.

THE ACCELERATED "REVOLUTIONARY COURSES"

The Revolutionary Government in 1794 was primarily concerned with mobilization, being in a desperate war with the armies and navies of Great Britain, the Netherlands, Austria, Prussia, Spain, and the north-Italian kingdom of Piedmont. Questions of education were subordinated to military requirements. Increasingly the Committee on Public Instruction cleared its decisions with the Committee of Public Safety, and most educational projects of the Year II reflected the views of the

[22] Ozouf, *Fête*, p. 340.

two committees together. On April 1 the Committee of Public Safety reorganized the whole executive apparatus of the government by replacing the existing ministries (as set up in 1790) with 12 executive commissions, most of which were to deal with some phase of the war effort. One of these was an Executive Commission on Public Works, which among its other activities soon developed a School of Public Works, later called the Polytechnic. Another was an Executive Commission on Public Instruction. The executive commissions were responsible to the committees of the Convention. Since the constitution adopted in 1793 remained suspended, the idea of a separation of powers was abandoned. In principle, the National Convention represented the sovereignty of the people and acted through its committees, including the Committee of Public Safety, which it reelected each month, while the committees worked through the executive commissions that were their administrative arms. In practice, the Committee of Public Safety dominated the Convention and the other committees and coordinated almost everything else, until after the repudiation of Robespierre by the Convention and his death at the end of July 1794.

Still open at the beginning of that year were questions connected with the "last stage" of Bouquier's plan. The Convention, although it adopted the first stage, had neither accepted nor rejected the last stage but only postponed its consideration of it. According to Bouquier's last stage, it may be recalled, the only public or state-supported schools above the primary level would be those for the useful sciences. In March 1794 the Committee on Public Instruction deputed two of its most eminent members, the chemists Fourcroy and Guyton de Morveau, to confer with the Committee of Public Safety on implementation of the last stage. A few weeks later the matter came up in the Convention. Bouquier, with the support of the two committees, delivered another violent attack on the colleges of the Old Regime, calling them "caverns of unreason" and "pedagogical aristocracies," and he renewed his argument that no public secondary level was necessary to replace them. It was enough, he insisted, if the Republic should sponsor national festivals and a decadary cult and maintain certain more advanced practical schools.[23]

By no means did everyone in the Convention agree. It was an even worse time than usual for any calm discussion, since it was in these very weeks that both "ultras" and "citras," Hébertists and Dantonists, including several members of the Convention itself, went to the guillotine. Opposition to Bouquier's ideas was expressed by the "moder-

---

[23] Guillaume, *Procès-verbaux*, 3:571-75.

ate" Boissy d'Anglas, who declared that the Republic must preserve the "vast heritage" of culture left by the Old Regime. He boldly used the very words that Bouquier and others avoided. There must be *écoles secondaires* with *instruction gratuite* to produce the educated class of French society. "The national institute that you will create," he said, "whether you called it an *Academy* or a *Lycée*, or even if you called it a *University*, rehabilitating a word that has become almost odious, will offer in its details all branches of public teaching, and as a whole it will provide for the highest level of human knowledge." Boissy refrained or was prevented from expressing these views on the floor of the Convention, which however authorized their publication in two brochures.[24] At the moment such ideas were out of favor. The Jacobin Montagnards, who were busily centralizing so much else, did not apply their doctrines of centralization to the schools. The future form of education in France, a great pyramid or hierarchy of public institutions, anticipated by Rolland d'Erceville, Talleyrand, and Condorcet, was most clearly anticipated at the height of the Revolution not by the Jacobins but by a man who was unquestionably a bourgeois, soon to be a Thermidorian, then a senator under Napoleon, and still later a liberal peer under the Restoration. That many in the Convention were impressed by Boissy's arguments, or that the ruling Committee set a low priority on the matter, is shown by the fact that the Convention again refused to adopt Bouquier's last stage. It simply adjourned the discussion.

Instead, throughout the year 1794, the government organized a number of short-lived and purely practical teaching arrangements, the *cours révolutionnaires*.[25] The word *révolutionnaire* at this time had taken on the special meaning of innovative, fast moving, and designed to get quick results. The "revolutionary courses," each lasting only a few weeks, gave a speeded up instruction in each case to several hundred young men in skills for which there was an urgent need. Of especial importance in launching several of the revolutionary courses was one

---

[24] *Quelques idées sur les arts, la nécessité de les encourager, sur les institutions qui en peuvent assurer le perfectionnement* . . . and *Courtes observations sur le projet de décret sur le dernier degré d'instruction, adressées à la Convention Nationale*, both reprinted (with omissions) in ibid., 3:638-56 and 182-87. For the quotation see 3:651.

[25] On the *cours révolutionnaires* see Guillaume, *Procès-verbaux*, 4:xxi-xxxvi; Julia, *Trois couleurs*, pp. 292-304; G. Bouchard, *Prieur de la Côte-d'Or* (Paris, 1946), pp. 257-85. C. A. Prieur, called Prieur-Duvernois before the Revolution and Prieur de la Côte-d'Or during the Convention to distinguish him from another Prieur, although an active member of the Robespierrist Committee of Public Safety, was uninvolved in the Terror and so survived the events of Thermidor; he continued to play a role in educational planning.

member of the Committee of Public Safety, Prieur de la Côte-d'Or, a thirty-year-old graduate of the old royal engineering school at Mézières, who was now in charge of military supply.

The first of these courses, launched in February, was designed to expand the production of munitions for the army.[26] It was purely practical, but one of the practical needs felt in 1794 was to engage the whole population in the war. It was democratic in trying to involve everybody. Every one of the 557 districts in France was to choose, from a list provided by the popular societies, two men between twenty-five and thirty years old, "one of whom must know how to read and write" (naturally in the national language!), and all of whom must be "robust, intelligent and accustomed to work."[27] Each section of Paris would do the same. Almost all the districts and sections complied. Travel expenses were provided, and over a thousand men congregated in Paris, where they were lodged by the municipality and paid three livres a day for 30 days. For teachers the Committee of Public Safety gave them nine notable men of science, including Fourcroy, Guyton, Hassenfratz, Dufourny, and Monge.

The course consisted of three parts, one devoted to the production of saltpeter, another to the manufacture of gunpowder, and a third to the forging and boring of cannon. The men heard explanatory lectures by the scientists, received engraved plates illustrating the relevant machines and procedures, and did practical work in the shops. They were kept at a high pitch of patriotic fervor by visits to the Paris Jacobin club, the attentions of the Convention, and a grand festival "of saltpeter, gunpowder and cannon founding" that served as a kind of commencement. On March 20 the Committee of Public Safety assigned them to various roles, sending some to centers of armament manufacture throughout the country and others back to their home districts to spread a knowledge of what they had learned.

This revolutionary method was judged so successful that plans were soon made for its application in other fields. The main idea was to multiply knowledge rapidly by bringing young men from all parts of France, giving them some speedy lessons, and sending them back to give a similar course to additional persons in their home districts. In May the Committee on Public Instruction drafted a plan to produce

---

[26] C. Richard, *Le Comité de Salut Public et les fabrications de guerre* (Paris, 1921), pp. 469-86.

[27] This order by the Committee of Public Safety, not in Guillaume, may be found in the *Moniteur* for 2 Ventôse of the Year II; see also the contemporary description of the school in the *Moniteur* of 11 Ventôse.

teachers in this way for elementary schools under the Bouquier law.[28] We find here the Committee's first use of "normal" in this connection (it had originated in Austria a few years before), meaning the normalizing or standardizing of the training of teachers. By this plan each district in the Republic would send four young men to Paris, where they would remain for two months, be lodged and paid four livres a day, and after finishing the course would return each to his home district or canton and there give a similar course, for women as well as men, to persons wishing to register as teachers under the Bouquier law. Had the plan gone into effect tens of thousands of teachers might have been produced, though it is a question whether they could have learned much from such abbreviated instruction. In any case nothing was done until the following November, by which time circumstances had changed, and the Ecole Normale proved to be entirely different from what had at first been intended.

Following the same model was the School of Mars, which brought together 3,500 young men on a stony and still unoccupied field north of the Bois de Boulogne from July to October.[29] Barère's speech explaining the school to the Convention, as proposed by the Committee of Public Safety, is of interest both for its realistic facing of facts and its statement of ideal purpose. For four years, he said, the Revolutionary assemblies had repeatedly discussed national education. "What have they accomplished? What have they established? As yet, nothing." There was a "void" that was becoming disastrous and that the Republic must hasten to fill. A school was needed for youths too young for the army and too old for primary instruction. Though it would prepare for both military and civilian occupations, it would be conducted on military lines. It would be very different from the old écoles militaires of the monarchy. "To enter a royal military school you had to be descended from some feudal brigand, some privileged rascal, some ridiculous marquis, modern baron or court lackey. Those called to the School of Mars will have to belong to a republican family, to parents of little fortune, useful inhabitants of the countryside, artisans without property, or volunteers wounded in defending our independence."

The school turned out very much as projected. Boys of an age between sixteeen and seventeen-and-a-half, chosen for their patriotic ardor, came to the Plaine des Sablons from all the districts of France.

[28] Guillaume, *Procès-verbaux*, 4:451 n. 4, and 461-62.

[29] A. Chuquet, *L'Ecole de Mars (1794)* (Paris, 1899); Barère's report for the Committee of Public Safety, 13 Prairial (June 1, 1794), in Guillaume, *Procès-verbaux*, 4:521-30; Guyton de Morveau's final report, 2 Brumaire of the Year III (October 23, 1794) in *Moniteur* for 4 Brumaire.

They lived in tents, received uniforms and weapons, and had the use of their own military band supplied by the institute of music. Almost all were from poor families. A few were illiterate, as we know from the report of a health officer at the school, who claimed that in an experiment with six of the pupils he had taught them to read and write in 25 lessons. Mainly they learned military discipline, the operations of infantry, cavalry and artillery, the arts of fortification, army administration, hygiene, and elementary medicine. The school ended as often happened with a festival, the Fête des Victoires on 30 Vendémiaire of the Year III, on the Champ de Mars, where the 3,500 young men in their various companies carried out military evolutions, engaged in mock combat, and went through the procedures for attacking and defending a fort. They then returned to their homes to spread their knowledge and enthusiasm and to await their future, which, depending on their age and abilities as judged by the managers of the school, might be conscription into the army at age eighteen, or assignment as aides to headquarters in the field, or if they had enough understanding of mathematics a chance to take entrance examinations for the newly founded School of Public Works.

This school, the future Ecole Polytechnique, had its origins in the military crisis of 1793, when as the Austrian armies pressed into France the two old royal schools of engineering were collapsing.[30] Both these schools, for military engineering at Mézières near the Belgian border and for civil engineering or "Roads and Bridges" in Paris, as royal establishments serving the favored elements of the Old Regime, were crippled by emigration and other forms of antagonism to the new order. Drawing on unofficial plans made in 1793, the Committee of Public Safety on March 11, 1794, created an Executive Commission of Public Works and at the same time authorized a Central School of Public Works to be administered by the Commission. The idea at first was to consolidate and replace the two older schools, though in fact they were allowed to continue, since even if ineffective they contributed to the war effort. The mission of the School of Public Works, from the beginning, was to produce men with some knowledge of engineering, both for military purposes as in the building and maintenance of fortifications at the frontiers and for such civilian needs as

[30] Guillaume, *Procès-verbaux*, 4:1006-10; 5:79-81, 627-52; 6:299-311; Julia, *Trois couleurs*, pp. 297-305; J. Fayet, *La Révolution française et la science* (Paris, 1960), pp. 272-84; A. Fourcy, *Histoire de l'Ecole Polytechnique* (Paris, 1828), pp. 1-75; T. Shinn, *L'Ecole Polytechnique, 1794-1914* (Paris, 1980), not very helpful on the first years of the school, on which more is to be found in M. Crosland, *The Society of Arcueil: A view of French Science in the time of Napoleon I* (London, 1967), pp. 192-208.

public buildings, harbor works, and "interior circulation" through improvement of roads and canals. As a provisional establishment, with hastily assembled teachers and temporary quarters, it had about 200 students by June 1794. It was more formally organized by a report of Fourcroy and decree of the Convention of September 28, 1794. Reorganized again, it was renamed the Ecole Polytechnique in August 1795, and as such it has lasted until our own time.

For the year and more that it went under its original name the Central School of Public Works represented a transition from the idea of an accelerated revolutionary course to that of a permanent institution. Students were supposed to be from sixteen to twenty years old on admission, but in fact many who assembled in December 1794 were older or younger. It was provided also that some young men, though old enough for the army, might be physically unqualified for it and yet be useful to the country by their intellectual faculties—and that "wise legislators should put each citizen in his place, using the dispositions of nature for the greater public advantage."[31] As in the other revolutionary courses the successful candidates were brought from all parts of France, provided with travel money, and in this case given a salary of 1,200 francs from which they paid for their board and room. The aim was to turn out a finished product as soon as possible. On the other hand, it was not intended that students on completing their studies should simply go home. From the beginning, it was foreseen that the School might develop into a permanent establishment. Its course of study was set in September 1794 at three years. To speed up the production of engineers, however, the first three months, in Fourcroy's words, would consist of "revolutionary instruction of whose advantages the Convention is well aware." According to their performance in this brief and intensive period, the students were sorted into three classes so that all three annual classes should at first begin simultaneously. A top or "third year class," composed of the students who seemed most advanced after the initial three months, remained at the school for only a year and were then available for assignment to practical duties. The middle group, as planned, remained two years, and those who were the least prepared stayed for the full three.

Most of all, the School of Public Works set up entrance requirements. Where the school for saltpeter, powder, and cannon was for artisans, only half of whom had to be literate, and where the School of Mars had been meant for youths of poor families, the School of Public Works admitted its students by competitive examination. The

[31] Fourcroy's report of September 24, 1794, in Guillaume, *Procès-verbaux*, 4:1008.

idea of equal recruitment from all departments was given up. The examination, administered by the Commission on Public Works and offered locally in 22 places in France, consisted partly in oral tests of political reliability or republican principles and partly in oral and written tests on arithmetic, algebra, geometry, and trigonometry. Some heated patriots demanded that the political tests should take precedence over the intellectual. Their advice was rejected. It was a question, also, of what a sixteen-year-old could be expected to know of mathematics, considering the disruption of the colleges in the preceding four years. The Commission therefore, in its instructions to examiners, urged them to look for signs of intelligence rather than of acquired knowledge—they should note "the intelligence of the candidates, and especially their disposition to learn new things, taking account both of their age and the time spent in prior study, and of the degree of vivacity and precision in their replies to the questions proposed to them."[32] Fourcroy, however, stressed prior studies. "We want those," he said, "who are already the best prepared, so that the Republic may sooner enjoy the exercise of their talents. It is evident that the only way to detect these talents is by passage of an examination, which gives a precise measure of each person's intelligence and aptitude."[33] These words, spoken exactly two months after the death of Robespierre, have been taken as signs of a bourgeois reaction against the democracy of the Year II, and of a process by which elite groups used schooling to confirm their position. In fact, the plan of the Committee of Public Safety, expressed in Barère's speech of the preceding March 11, had also specified competitive examination as the mode of entry to the School of Public Works. Examinations had also been required for entrance to the engineering and technical schools of the Old Regime. The actual need for qualified personnel may be as strong a force, and as realistic an explanation, as ideology or class preference.

There is a list of the 384 students admitted to the School of Public Works in the entering group of 1794.[34] Compiled 30 years later, it provides also a few words on subsequent careers. Of the 384, only 161 went on into occupations for which the school was designed: 97 into civil engineering (*Ponts et Chaussées, ingénieurs géographes*, and *mines*), 41 into military engineering (*génie*), and 23 into the artillery. A half-dozen or so in each case wound up as private landowners, manufacturers, ecclesiastics, prefects under Napoleon, or professors in the

[32] Quoted by Fourcy, *Histoire*, p. 33.
[33] Guillaume, *Procès-verbaux*, 4:1008.
[34] Fourcy, *Histoire*, pp. 391-98.

Napoleonic system of public instruction, the latter category including the physicist J. B. Biot, long a luminary of the College of France. No less than 87 became members of Napoleon's Legion of Honor. Almost all the men entering these professions remained in the school for two, three, or in a few cases four years. The same list, however, designates 207 of the entrants of 1794 as *retirés*, that is, withdrawn from the school without proceeding to any other government school or service. Over half of these 207 withdrew in 1796 and 1797, that is, after an extended period of study. It is not possible to distinguish in this category of *retirés* between those who left because they were unable to do the work and those who simply decided to embark on a different career.

It is clear that the School of Public Works, as launched in the revolutionary year 1794, produced a good many useful graduates. It is also clear that, with one half the entrants of 1794 "withdrawing," it involved considerable waste. The founders of the School formed a mixed judgment of its first year.[35] The hasty recruitment, even with examinations that were unavoidably improvised and politicized, brought in many young men who were weak in mathematics. The winter of 1794-1795 saw such a collapse of the paper money and such shortages of food and fuel that many students were unable to subsist in Paris and went home. As young men and patriots the students also became active in politics, so much so that the government organized them into a unit of the National Guard. As such, they were expected to help in protecting the Convention against the insurrections of Germinal and Prairial in the spring of 1795. Some, however, suffering from the same scarcities as the populace, showed sympathy with the insurgents and were suspected of regretting the end of the Terror. There was talk in official circles of abolishing the School. Prieur and Fourcroy managed to save it, in the reorganization of July 1795, which is noted in the next chapter.

Last among the revolutionary courses of 1794 were the Schools of Health.[36] The disappearance of the Paris Faculty of Medicine as an

[35] See Prieur de la Côte-d'Or's report of June 1795 in Guillaume, *Procès-verbaux*, 6:299-311.

[36] Ibid., 4:969, 978-80, 1009; 5:281-83, 291, 372-75; 6:721, 724; T. Gelfand, *Professionalizing Modern Medicine: Paris Surgeons and Medical Science and Institutions in the Eighteenth Century* (Westport, Conn., 1980), pp. 167-75; P. Huard, *Science, médecine, pharmacie de la Révolution à l'Empire, 1785-1815* (Paris, 1970); E. H. Ackerknecht, *Medicine at the Paris Hospital, 1795-1848* (Baltimore, 1967), pp. 31-37. "The new school and the new medicine were children of the Revolution, originating in the tumult, cold and hunger of the year III (1794)" (Ackerknecht, *Medicine*, p. xii).

organized body removed an obstacle to changes that had been considered since before the Revolution. With an army numbering a million, and often engaged in combat, the need for medical and surgical personnel went beyond what any European country had ever experienced. On August 24 the Committee of Public Safety ordered action, which after several months of planning took the form of law on December 14. By this time 900 army health officers had already died in the war. Since the word "medicine" was a reminder of the old Faculty, with its defensive attitudes and its exclusion of surgeons, the new institution must have another name. Fourcroy, reporting in the Convention for the Committees of Public Safety and Public Instruction, called for a Central School of Health in Paris on the model of the revolutionary courses. Recruitment of students should be as for the School of Public Works, except for differences in the sciences on which candidates would be examined. These would include physics, chemistry, botany, and anatomy. Students should be between seventeen and twenty-six years old on entrance. One should be selected in each of the 557 districts, receive travel funds, and be paid the same salary as those in Public Works. To obtain enough qualified students the requirement of geographical distribution was almost immediately relaxed, and the age limits were expanded to reach from sixteen to thirty. Three Schools of Health were in fact set up, at Paris, Montpellier, and Strasbourg, the principal centers of advanced medical study before the Revolution. Though their faculties were dissolved various individual professors, reinforced by professors from the old College of Surgery, provided a link from the old to the new medical regime. Surgery and medicine were at last combined into a single profession. The course lasted three years, but, as in the School of Public Works, the first entering group was divided into three classes—beginners, intermediate, and advanced—so that the advanced students might be sent out at the earliest possible moment. Or as the organizing law put it: "Those who, at whatever period in their studies, have acquired the knowledge necessary for the practice of their art in the hospitals and armies will be employed in this service by the Commission of Health, according to information furnished by the assembled professors in each School."[37]

The Paris School of Health, by far the most important of the three, was installed in the modern building built for the College of Surgery in 1775. As in the pre-Revolutionary College of Surgery, and in con-

[37] Guillaume, *Procès-verbaux*, 5:283. This is the law of 14 Frimaire of the Year III. Fourcroy's speech of 7 Frimaire proposing the measure is abridged in 4:979-80, and may be found in full in *Moniteur, réimpression*, 22:663-66.

trast to the old Faculty of Medicine with its medieval traditions, professors at the School of Health were salaried by the state, appointed for life, and expected to give their full time to teaching. One of those appointed in 1794 was Philippe Pinel, a physician of wide interests, though remembered in later times for his work with the insane. Some of the students were young, but others in view of the age limits had begun medical or surgical studies before the Revolution, or had already served a kind of medical apprenticeship in the armies. Like their fellows in the School of Public Works, they found living in Paris in the winter of 1795 very difficult and became involved in political agitations for which they were sometimes denounced. Their studies were meant to be practical. They learned about drugs and medicinal plants, were trained in clinical observation in the hospitals, and took part in amputations and other surgical procedures. They also were subjected to frequent examinations in their courses, but no medical degree or title was awarded. In the continuing Revolutionary reaction against privilege and corporatism there was no public control over entrance into medical practice until 1803. But by 1798 about 150 students had completed their studies at the Paris School of Health and were serving in the armies and in civilian hospitals. They were assisted by various categories of health officers of lesser attainments.

Not a school, but meant to be an educational institution, was the Conservatory of Arts and Trades, initiated by a decree of October 10, 1794. It was intended to house various collections of models and machines, including those belonging to the former Academy of Sciences and to the Bureau de Consultation, along with some of their books and papers. Interested artisans, mechanics, and "manufacturers" would be able to come to the Conservatory to see how the latest inventions were built and how they worked, for which purpose a staff of demonstrators would be on hand. No suitable location was found, however, until 1798, when the Conservatory opened in the old Priory of Saint-Martin-des-Champs, where Léonard Bourdon's school had once been. The establishment grew into the present Conservatoire des Arts et Métiers in Paris.

For a glimpse of the kind of education that young men could receive in 1794 and 1795 we can turn to a report by J. F. Champagne, the principal of Equality College, known before the Revolution as Louis-le-Grand.[38] The Executive Commission on Public Instruction had asked for information on scholarships in the 10 pre-Revolutionary colleges. Champagne replied, in October 1795, that there had been 800 such

---

[38] See my *School of the French Revolution* (Princeton, 1975), pp. 157-65.

scholarships. But in 1791 the Department of Paris had forbidden new appointments to the scholarships, so with older scholars completing their studies, and no younger ones coming in, the figure of 800 had declined to 500, and the average age was higher than in the past. By decree of the Convention the 500 remaining scholars had a continuing right to support at the national expense. Who and where were the 500? About 250 were in the army, with a right to return to their education at the end of their military service. Champagne thought that about 80 had in effect abandoned their scholarships, and about 80 of the youngest, from fifteen through seventeen in age, were simply awaiting the resumption of normal instruction. This left about a hundred.

"One hundred," he said, "are engaged in the study of medicine or mathematics, or occupy various administrative posts. These are from sixteen to twenty-three years old." Most of these hundred scholars were residing in Equality College, which had more scholarships than the others and was the only one of the pre-Revolutionary Paris colleges still open. Those studying mathematics undoubtedly went out from the college for studies at the School of Public Works. Those studying medicine went out to the School of Health. Given their ages, they had held their scholarships since before the Revolution. Here again was a thread of continuity from the Old Regime to the new.

THE ECOLE NORMALE: DEMOCRACY CONFUSED AND CONFOUNDED

Among the revolutionary courses as originally projected was the Ecole Normale, for which the first plans were made in June 1794 at the height of the Revolutionary or Jacobin dictatorship. The purpose at this time was to produce a universal literacy, to provide all the children of France with an elementary knowledge of reading, writing, and arithmetic, along with natural morality and republican patriotism. Toward this end about a thousand men would come to Paris, receive instruction on the teaching of these subjects to young children, and return home to teach teachers how to teach, so that a network of hundreds of local normal schools would be rapidly developed. The Ecole Normale that existed in Paris from February to May 1795 was an altogether different establishment. It attempted to publicize the latest findings of modern science and the highest flights of literary endeavor. Far from aiming at being helpful to schoolteachers, it became involved in the preparation of "professors" for the Central Schools that were then beginning to be organized. It was a peculiarity of these schools (for which see the next chapter) that they represented a confused mixture of what would later be called secondary and higher education. It must always be remembered that the word *secondaire* as used in France at this time (it was as yet used nowhere else) had not yet settled into its nineteenth- and twentieth-century meaning. In any case the Ecole Normale of 1795 was aimed at the production of an educated minority.

The Ecole Normale thus offers a paradigm of the weakening impulse for democratization. Post-Thermidorian, "reactionary," representing a transition from "democratic" to "bourgeois" and "elitist" values, it revealed also a kind of incursion by the intellectuals, or by those intellectuals—neo-*philosophes* and *idéologues*—who believed that, with the violent phase of the Revolution now behind them, the spirit of the Enlightenment, or spirit of the true Revolution—progressive, scientific, anticlerical, liberal—could be made to prevail.

The man who more than any other converted or perverted the Ecole Normale from its original purpose was D. J. Garat, who in October 1794 became head of the Executive Commission on Public Instruction. This commission when set up in the preceding April had been headed by three friends of Robespierre, who were replaced shortly after Robespierre's fall. It was now the fashion to refer to the Robespierrist Committee of Public Safety as the "triumvirs" or the "decemvirs," to see their late regime as one of anarchy and tyranny, and to claim (what was palpably false) that they had intended to destroy the arts and sciences and all learning and education. The Thermidorians said things as bad about their predecessors as the most overwrought Jacobins had said about the monarchy of Louis XVI. Many Thermidorians had in fact supported the revolutionary dictatorship until nearly the end. They had all the more reason to protect themselves by exaggerated denunciation from the mounting revulsion against all that had happened during the Terror.

The Executive Commission on Public Instruction is of all the more interest because it was carried over as the educational section of the ministry of the interior under the Directory, and so on into the Napoleonic years. It was in a way the first French ministry of education. As reorganized on October 3, 1794, it consisted of three sections, a first section for educational institutions, a second section for *sciences et arts*, and a third for *morale publique*. Garat headed all three, but was also the head of the first section. Chief of the second section was P. L. Ginguené, who like Garat was of the group known as *idéologues*. The third section was directed by a less known and more transitory figure, Clément de Ris, whose own sons attended one of the best "private" schools in France, Pontlevoy, described on page to come above. The bureaus under the section chiefs were staffed by men of significant attainments, including the mathematicians Sylvestre Lacroix and A. M. Legendre; La Chabaussière, author of a widely used republican catechism; the naturalist Millin; Lebreton, another *idéologue*; and two professors in the pre-Revolutionary Paris colleges, Dumouchel, the last rector of the old University, and Mahérault, who with his colleague Crouzet had written the plan by which the Department of Paris had hoped to reopen the Paris colleges at the end of 1793.[39]

All these men were warm supporters of the Revolution. Garat was well to the left. A professor of sorts, he had lectured on ancient history at the Lycée since 1786, and continued to do so during the Revolution; he had boasted of his democratic opinions and could still use the word in a favorable sense in the fall of 1794. As minister of justice in 1792 he was thought to have been too willing to excuse the September massacres, and as minister of the interior in 1793 he was suspected of complicity in the insurrection of May 31. A few years later he pressed for the revolutionizing of Italy, and at the time of the Fructidor coup d'état he published a journal, *Le Conservateur*, which was in fact "radical," aiming to conserve the Republic against royalist "cutthroats" and "brigands." When Bonaparte went to Egypt in 1798 he delivered a series of lectures at the Lycée on the "history of the pharaohs," arguing that "revolutions that will change the whole earth are beginning now in Egypt for Asia, for Africa and for Europe."[40] If Garat transformed the Ecole Normale from a teacher's college into an institution of high culture it was not because he was a reactionary. It was perhaps because of a vagueness in what he meant by democracy.

Shortly after his appointment to the Executive Commission Garat began to exert a strong influence on Lakanal, a member of the Convention and of its Committee on Public Instruction, to which Garat and his Commission were technically subordinate. Garat wrote a speech that he prevailed upon Lakanal to deliver in the Convention as if it were his own. Called a "report on the establishment of normal schools [plural]," it was delivered on October 24 and was immediately printed. After reviewing the horrors of the recent past, and with references to d'Alembert, Diderot, Rousseau, Bacon, and Locke, the speaker (that

---

[39] On the Executive Commission see Guillaume, *Procès-verbaux*, 4:xi-xvii, 210-36, 877-97; 5:xiii-xv, and passim through the index. There are informative articles on Garat and on many of the others in Michaud, *Biographie universelle*, which however generally ignore their subjects' work on the Executive Commission. On La Chabaussière see chap. 6 n. 23, below.

[40] Michaud, *Biographie universelle*, ed. p. 538.

is, Garat) went on to say that the normal schools (still in the plural) would produce "a very large number of teachers able to execute a plan for the regeneration of the human understanding in a Republic of twenty-five millions all made equal by democracy." The schools would teach the art of teaching. "For the first time on earth, nature, truth, reason and philosophy will also have their seminary," that is, a place such as the seminaries in which the Church had taught young men how to be priests. A "learned and philosophical youth" would open normal schools everywhere. A pure and abundant stream would flow throughout France. "In the Alps and the Pyrenees the art of teaching will be the same as in Paris." "Human reason will produce everywhere the same results."[41]

It is clear that at this point Garat was still thinking of a nationwide system of teacher training for popular education. Whether the great minds of France were the best suited to tell teachers how to convey the "3 Rs" to six- and nine-year-olds seems not to have been for him a problem.

A few weeks later the question arose again, as so often in the past, of what should be done about the higher levels of instruction, "higher" now meaning everything above the primary schools. The first section of the Executive Commission drew up an *Aperçu*, or sketch, which though unsigned expressed the views of Garat and his co-workers.[42] The Aperçu revived elements of the abortive Condorcet plan of two years before. After noting that universal and free primary schools already existed, or were coming into being under the Bouquier law, it addressed itself to the higher levels. Of these it proposed only two, or possibly three. Above the primary schools there would be 44 *instituts*, one for every two departments, and above the *instituts* 11 *lycées*, of which two would be in Paris. The authors of the Aperçu went on to say that they omitted the proposed Ecole Normale from their calculations because they considered it a temporary revolutionary establishment. If, however, they continued, the Ecole Normale should become permanent, then it would constitute the fourth and highest level of instruction. The point was confirmed by the salaries suggested for the several levels—1,200 for an elementary teacher (or 1,000 if female), 4,000 for professors in the *instituts*, 6,000 for those in *lycées*, and an astonishing 12,000 for those in the Ecole Normale if it should become permanent.

The Aperçu reflects the confusions of a transitional document. It

---

[41] Guillaume, *Procès-verbaux*, 5:xix-xx, 157-58.
[42] Ibid., 5:259-65.

made provision for universal elementary education at public expense; of an estimated total annual outlay of over 60 million francs, 54 million were to go for the primary schools. In the *instituts* the professors would be paid by the state; that is, there should be no fees; and each *institut* would have scholarships to pay the board and room for 100 students. Each *lycée*, at what might be called the higher rather than the secondary level, would have places for 25 students who received a stipend from the state, called a salary and amounting to 1,200 francs, as in the School of Public Works and the Schools of Health that were originating at this same time. In these matters this Thermidorian document was as democratic as the Condorcet plan. Unlike Condorcet, however, the new planners left a gap between the primary schools and the *instituts*. They took care to coordinate their *instituts* with the more advanced *lycées*, for the same subjects would be taught at both these levels; but there was no evident relation between the *instituts* and the lower schools devoted to reading, writing, and computation. Finally, the Ecole Normale, should it become permanent, would be a very high-level institution indeed, the summit of the pyramid, far above the tiresome business of training thousands of elementary schoolteachers.

These ideas were formally presented to the Convention by Lakanal on December 16.[43] His speech showed the same transitional features as the Aperçu with all definitions and purposes now even more confused. What the Aperçu and Condorcet had called *instituts* were now called "central schools." Each central school would have 14 professors of 14 prescribed subjects, ranging from mathematics, Latin, and physics to hygiene, obstetrics, and "analysis of sensations and ideas," the telltale sign of Garat and the *idéologues*. The schools were called "central" because each would be in the center of a surrounding host of primary schools, each in an area of 300,000 inhabitants, and each serving as a center of regional enlightenment. What the Aperçu and Condorcet had called *lycées* were now dropped altogether. The central schools would do the work both of *instituts* and *lycées*; that is, no distinction between secondary and higher education was made. Condorcet's *écoles secondaires*, said Lakanal, were unnecessary and even aristocratic. The central schools would draw pupils directly from the primary system. The primary schools, for children up to the age of eleven, would on the one hand teach what everybody needed to know (reading, writing, arithmetic, etc.) and, on the other, give introductory notions of all subjects taught in the central schools. They would be the "vestibule" to the whole system, that is, a one-track plan was envis-

[43] Ibid., 5:298-309.

aged, with the primary schools preceding the higher levels, not set apart from them as later happened. Children (if boys) who had sufficient "genius" would proceed to the central schools at about the age of twelve and would be financially assisted by the state for this purpose. In short, Lakanal's proposal of December 1794 expressed almost the last thoughts of the Convention on democratic and universal education and the first intimations of what was finally adopted, first in a law of 3 Ventose of the Year III (February 21, 1795) that created the Central Schools, and then in the comprehensive law of 3 Brumaire of the Year IV, or Daunou law (October 25, 1795) that codified the final labors of the Convention on education.

The Ecole Normale opened with considerable fanfare in the amphitheater of the Museum of Natural History on 1 Pluviôse of the Year III, or January 20, 1795.[44] The weather outside was at eleven degrees below zero Centigrade. Inside, in addition to the professors and students, was an assemblage of ladies and other invited guests, and two members of the Convention to add official dignity to the proceedings, Lakanal himself and an aged colleague, seated in chairs above those of the professors and wearing the dress uniform of members of the Convention *en mission*, complete with tricolor sashes and swords. They continued to preside in this costume throughout the life of the School.

The School was plagued from the beginning by cross-purposes and misunderstandings. Its course of study was set for four months. Some hoped that it would become permanent, with successive cohorts of students entering later. Others saw it as an establishment to last for the four months only. Its opening had been delayed for a month by the problem of finding a large enough hall. (The Ecole was in reality a vast one-room schoolhouse.) The first plan had been to put it in the church of the Sorbonne, where over 100,000 francs were spent on alterations before the idea was given up. It had then been proposed to house it in the hall of the Jacobin club, vacated by the Jacobins only a few weeks before; this idea, too, was abandoned. The amphitheater of the Museum was a large lecture hall in a fine modern building, begun just before the Revolution and now barely finished. Its only

---

[44] For the Ecole Normale, apart from the documents published by Guillaume, see the work of his contemporary, Paul Dupuy, *L'Ecole Normale de l'An III* (Paris, 1884), reproduced in *Le Centenaire de l'Ecole Normale, 1795-1895* (Paris, 1895), pp. 21-209, where it is more easily consulted since the edition of 1884 has become rare. Later accounts, as in J. Fayet, *La Révolution et la science*, pp. 329-54, hardly go beyond Dupuy's thoroughly researched study. The following pages are likewise drawn mainly from Dupuy.

deficiency was that it had only 750 seats and so could accommodate hardly more than half the 1,400 students.

Garat had prepared the list of its professors, in which he included himself. The Ecole Normale, he said, must be "the foremost school in the world."[45] Its teachers must be the most distinguished practitioners in their several fields, men who would display the glories of French culture. Each of these giants was also expected, at the close of his course, to write a textbook on the elements of his subject, but in the general uncertainty the "elements" sometimes referred to the needs of the primary schools and sometimes to those of the Central Schools soon to be established, thus further blurring the notion of what any particular school was supposed to be. Twelve subjects were taught by 12 professors, two of whom had an assistant, so the total was 14. Half of them (and all but one of those concerned with the sciences) had been members of the Royal Academy of Sciences abolished in 1793. The exception was Thouin, who was supposed to teach Agriculture; he had long worked at the old Jardin du Roi on the scientific classification of plants and became one of the first members of the National Institute later in 1795. The names of professors and their subjects are given in the accompanying table.[46]

These select teachers faced a motley mass of students, recruited in a roughly democratic way. No qualifications were specified for admission, except that they should be men at least twenty-five years old, since exemption from military service was not granted for this purpose. The school was thus a project in adult education. Each of the 500-odd districts of the Republic chose a number of persons to be sent to Paris in proportion to population and by methods that were determined locally in each district. The contrast to the care taken by the central government in organizing the schools of engineering and medicine is evident.

Something is known of 250 of the 1,400 students.[47] About a third of them, or 75, were already primary schoolteachers. About 60 were *professeurs de collège* in the pre-Revolutionary sense, whether teaching in colleges that were still open or out of work because their colleges were closed. These included several from the colleges of Paris, notably Mahérault and Crouzet already mentioned in preceding pages. About

[45] Garat to Lakanal, 15 Nivôse of the Year III (January 4, 1795), Guillaume, *Procès-verbaux*, 5:684. On the process leading to the choice of professors see ibid., 5:159-60 and Dupuy in *Centenaire*, pp. 72-83.

[46] See the prospectus, regulations, and schedule for the school published on 24 Nivôse of the Year III, reproduced by Dupuy in *Centenaire*, pp. 100-104.

[47] Ibid., pp. 116-35.

Schedule at the Ecole Normale

Day of the *décade*	Subject	Professor
First and sixth	Mathematics	Lagrange* and Laplace.* Both had been eminent in mathematics and astronomy for many years.
	Physics	Haüy.* Founder of crystallography.
	Descriptive Geometry	Monge.* Notable geometer; soon active in Ecole Polytechnique.
Second and seventh	Natural History	Daubenton.* Age 79. Member of the College of France and Museum of Natural History.
	Chemistry	Berthollet.* Had worked with Lavoisier.
	Agriculture	Thouin. Had worked with Buffon at Jardin des Plantes.
Third and eighth	Geography	Buache* and Mentelle. Buache had been Royal Geographer before 1789.
	History	Volney. Philosophical author of *Travels in Syria* and *Ruins of Empires*.
	Moral Philosophy	Bernardin de Saint-Pierre. Author of then-famous tender love story, *Paul and Virginia*.
Fourth and ninth	Grammar	Sicard. Famous as teacher of deaf mutes and for his theory of language.
	Analysis of the Understanding	Garat. Had lectured at the Lycée on history since 1786.
	Literature	La Harpe. Had also lectured at the Lycée since 1786, and was still doing so in 1795.

Note. The Fifth day, the *quintidi*, was reserved for conferences in which all the professors, assembled in the presence of the students, and with eminent *savants, artistes,* and *gens de lettres* invited to attend, would consider "elementary books for the use of pupils in the primary schools of the Republic." No such books ever eventuated.

*Member of the former Royal Academy of Sciences. Alexandre Vandermonde, also a member of the former Academy, was added on February 7 as professor of political economy.

50 were administrators and employees of the local governments that sent them. Since there was no formal exclusion of the clergy, about 30 were priests, for the most part probably also to be included among the 60 professors. That nobles could also be admitted is shown by the freakish case of Admiral Bougainville, aged sixty-six, who had served with Montcalm at Quebec 40 years before and then gone on to become famous as an explorer of the Pacific. He kept up his interest in the sciences after retirement from the navy and was soon active in the Institute and in the Bureau of Longitudes.

It was the freedom of the districts to choose the students that led to such haphazard results. In some places the district administrators consulted with their subordinate villages and communes, many of which were eager to develop primary schools and so to select and send young men who would return and advance the program of normal schools as originally planned. It was from these districts that the primary school teachers mostly came. In other districts the administrators invited applications and formed lists of candidates; most of the priests and professors came from these districts. In still other districts the administrators simply made the choice themselves; they chose the preponderance of the government employees.

It is not known how accurate a sample of the 1,400 students this known group of 250 was. It can be said, however, that the students at the Ecole Normale were a heterogeneous assemblage. Some were genuinely eager to improve themselves as teachers of young children. Some, who had taught in colleges, hoped for employment at the higher levels that the Convention was expected soon to inaugurate. Some were devoted to the sciences. And undoubtedly some looked on the whole experience as a chance for a visit to Paris.

Class hours at the Ecole Normale ran only from eleven in the morning to a quarter-past one in the afternoon, on eight of the 10 days of the *décade*. Each subject was offered only twice during the *décade*, a first occasion on which the professor gave a lecture, and a second, five days later, on which students asked questions and received replies. It was hoped that this second occasion would also produce lively discussions and that the professor might even learn from the students, whose ideas might be of use in preparation of an elementary textbook on the subject. The table suggests how overloaded the plan of study was and how far over the heads of their audience most of the professors were. It will be seen that three subjects, expounded by three professors, were scheduled for each meeting of two and a quarter hours. The predictable consequences were that professors complained of having too little time to develop their ideas and that some talked too long and so shut out others. The problem was the more serious because the professors were urged to speak in apparently impromptu fashion, without reading from a prepared text.

Stenographers (then a new word) took down verbatim what was said both in the lectures and in the question and discussion groups. The purpose was not only to preserve the message of this "foremost school in the world" but also to furnish the students with an immediate record, which they could study before the question and discussion period five days later. This excellent pedagogical idea was difficult to realize. The stenographer hurriedly transcribed his sometimes illegible jottings, rushed the result to the printer, who had to submit proofs for correction to the professor, who sometimes rewrote the language and was sometimes slow in returning the proofs to the printer, who then had to run off and deliver 2,000 copies (for the students and various important persons) all within less than five days. It is not surprising that the system broke down. Nor was it realistic to expect that even an assiduous student could digest such material on 12 disparate subjects every 10 days.

Nor did the courses turn out according to the prospectuses that professors had to submit at the beginning. The mathematicians and some of the scientists complained of pressure of time. Bernardin de Saint-Pierre, the moral philosopher, failed to appear until the final month, although he collected his salary. Sicard went off into proposals for spelling reform and exhibiting the deaf mutes to whom he had taught sign language as a means of illustrating certain fundamentals of communication. La Harpe read at length from the orations of Cicero, with comments, as a way of lashing out at triumvirs, tyrants, vandals, and sans-culottes. Garat, who had hoped that his analysis of human understanding would underlie the philosophy of the school, was unable to finish. He was attacked by La Harpe for atheism and increasingly in the Convention for his Jacobin past; he gave up his functions on the Executive Commission in May, at about the time when the Ecole Normale came to an end. Only Daubenton, Haüy, and Buache and Mentelle actually covered the ground in four months that they had committed themselves to at the outset.

The students, like those in the Schools of Public Works and of Health, had to suffer the miseries of the cold and hungry winter of 1795. There was much absenteeism, understandable since only half could find seats in the hall. Some went to lectures at the Lycée des Arts instead. Many complained that the School did not offer what they had expected, and those really wanting to be primary teachers were doubtless the most disappointed; but others found the experience stimulating, and probably among these were the ones, about 80 in number, who are known to have become teachers in the Central Schools. Those who depended on stipends from the government, as the inflation of paper money became catastrophic, found it hard or impossible to pay for food and lodging in Paris. By the third month of the School many students were going home.

The School was denounced as a fiasco both in the Convention and in the press. The Committee on Finance of the Convention objected to its inordinate cost, which in fact reached 3,500,000 francs.[48] Some on the Right feared it as a hive of Jacobinism, which was untrue. The most serious assault came from democrats on the Left. A crushing satire, *The Tower of Babel at the Jardin des Plantes*, was published by an anonymous writer who was obviously a person of equalitarian sympathies. In the Convention the most effective attack came from Gilbert Romme. A former member of the Committee on Public Instruction, Romme had defended the Condorcet plan in 1792 and had tried to save something of the Paris plan of September 1793. "I think," he said on April 16, 1795,

> that the aim of the Ecole Normale has completely miscarried. . . . One of its greatest faults is that the professors have assumed an already advanced knowledge in their students. . . . It has been supposed that young persons could keep their attention in one session on several different subjects passing rapidly before their eyes. The professors themselves would be incapable of such attention. . . . Since I see nothing in the present institution but organized charlatanism, I demand its suppression.[49]

The professors at the School nevertheless hoped to perpetuate it, and collectively submitted a paper to the Committee on Public Instruction, arguing that the School should be maintained, not as an institution for elementary teachers (which they had never really intended) but as a training center for professors in the Central Schools whose creation the Convention had ordered a few weeks before. Lakanal and Garat pressed for the same solution. The Central Schools, said Lakanal, would give life to the Ecole Normale, which would thereby become "the metropolis of human knowledge in France." In the end,

---

[48] Ibid., p. 206. Ginguené, Garat's successor as head of the Executive Commission, reported in October 1795 an expenditure of 1,884,648 francs for the Year III (to which he added 29,153 for the Year IV), as shown in the Appendix to the present book. Dupuy's estimate is higher because not confined to funds channeled through the Executive Commission.

[49] Guillaume, *Procès-verbaux*, 6:96.

after more debates and committee meetings, the Ecole Normale was closed, not to reopen, on 30 Floréal of the Year III, or May 19, 1795.[50]

The very next day came the insurrection of the first of Prairial. Angry men and women swarmed into the hall of the Convention with cries of "bread and the constitution of 1793!" They wanted not only more to eat but to put an end to the existing government by bringing the suspended democratic constitution, adopted almost two years before, into effect. Someone fired a pistol that killed one of the deputies, whose head was cut off and put on a pike. This grisly object was brandished in the face of the presiding officer, Boissy d'Anglas, who maintained the dignity of the Convention by gravely nodding to it. Saved by a few soldiers and people from the less radical sections of Paris, the Convention reacted with strong measures of repression. Several of its own members were arrested on charges of complicity in the uprising. One of these was Romme, who apparently had had no involvement in the affair but urged clemency toward the invaders of the hall. He and some others were condemned to death. Before the sentence could be executed they killed themselves with a single dagger passed from hand to hand.

The suicide of Gilbert Romme, the collaborator of Condorcet and veteran of the Committee on Public Instruction, stands as a lugubrious sign of the end of the road, so far as serious efforts at democratization of education during the French Revolution are concerned.

As for the Ecole Normale, it produced no elementary textbooks, nor did its students return to open local normal schools in their home districts. It contributed nothing to primary education and little if anything to the coming Central Schools, which drew nine-tenths of their teaching personnel from other sources. It was something like the Lycée of 1786 in which both Garat and La Harpe had begun their lecturing careers, that is, a public forum in which scientific and literary men could address a voluntary gathering of interested adults. There was no connection between it and the Ecole Normale set up by Napoleon in 1808, when, in the usual Napoleonic attempt to draw on both Revolutionary and pre-Revolutionary precedents, the *agrégation* of 1766 was also revived.

Thanks to the stenographers, the lectures and proceedings of the Ecole Normale were published in seven volumes in 1796, and again in 10 volumes in 1800 and 1808. The retrospective fame of the School

---

[50] Dupuy, *Centenaire*, p. 185.

came to rest on these volumes.[51] The School was remembered as Garat and Lakanal hoped that it would be, as a great showcase of French culture, especially in the natural sciences, during a critical moment in the period of half a century when France was in fact the leading scientific center of Europe. The professors at the Ecole Normale, except for Bernardin de Saint-Pierre and La Harpe, were concerned above all else with the progress of knowledge. Their platform at the Museum was a kind of early version of the National Institute established in the fall of the same year. Every one of the professors at the Ecole Normale except La Harpe, and even including Bernardin de Saint-Pierre, became a member of the Institute at its formation. We enter here on the theme of the next chapter.

[51] *Séances des écoles normales [sic], receuillies par des sténographes, et revues par les professeurs,* 7 vols. (Paris, 1796). There is a relatively recent account of the content of these lectures, based on these volumes, in Sergio Moravia, *Il tramonto dell'Illuminismo* (Bari, 1968), pp. 380-405.

CHAPTER 6

MODERNIZATION:
THE PATHS OF
PROGRESS

OF THE FOUR oversized words used as chapter titles to give structure to the present book, "modernization" is the most uncertain in meaning. It may be said to occur when a society makes a conscious and successful use of knowledge, especially new knowledge, to increase its powers and well-being. It depends therefore on the state of knowledge, its availability, its dissemination through the society, and the development of institutions for the application of knowledge to practical purposes. These in turn imply organization, to guide and coordinate the labors of many people. Modernization thus overlaps with all that is covered by the three other words—nationalization, by which a large functioning community comes into being; politicization, by which rival leaders assemble followers and publicize collective goals; and democratization, by which, at a minimum, most persons feel that they willingly belong to a larger community, that they have rights that can be depended on, and that their own abilities count for something in the attainment of desirable goals. All four words refer to a process, not a condition. It is not that France during its Revolution or for long afterwards was quite nationally unified, politically effective, democratic, or modern, but only that the trend was in these directions. Since the eighteenth century the common word for this trend has been "progress."

Our focus in the present chapter is on the final months of the National Convention and the four years of the Directory, or from mid-1795 to late 1799. France before the Revolution, relative to the world of that day, was already one of the most modern countries. Others have modernized without revolution. Yet in France, as the violent phase of 1792-1794 and the crisis of the war receded, giving way to a "bourgeois" Republic, new signs of modernity made themselves evident in many ways—mechanization of the cotton industry in northern France on the British model, the first industrial exhibition in Paris in 1798, the building of the semaphore telegraph from Paris to other cities, the use of balloons for military purposes, the beginnings of vaccination under government auspices, and even the invention of the lead pencil—eventually so helpful to both private citizens and bureaucrats.

IDÉOLOGUES AND INTELLECTUALS

It is a striking feature of the French Revolution that no one occupied the limelight for more than a short time, at most only two or three years. The Revolution was a stage with a constantly shifting *dramatis personae*, in which men mainly of the middle class constantly came and went. Robespierre himself would hardly be remembered except for the last two years of his life. In matters of education there was a general shift by the summer of 1795. Of those whose names have figured in the preceding pages only four continued to play a role—Fourcroy, Lakanal, Prieur of the Côte-d'Or, and Garat. Condorcet and Romme were dead; Bouquier, Léonard Bourdon, and Dufourny returned to obscurity; Félix Lepeletier withdrew into the shadows of the Babeuf conspiracy; Barère narrowly escaped deportation; Arbogast went back to teaching at Strasbourg and Hassenfratz became a professor at the Polytechnique; and the Abbé Grégoire turned his attention to rebuilding the constitutional church. Others whose role had been minor now became prominent. Among these were Daunou, who along with Sieyès had lain low since the Sieyès-Daunou-Lakanal plan of June 1793, and Boissy d'Anglas, who had defended the public support of higher studies against partisans of the Bouquier plan in 1794. And among the new faces in the educational controversies were several of the group known as *idéologues*, or more specifically, Daunou, Ginguené, Destutt de Tracy, and Cabanis.[1] Garat also was one of the chief *idéologues*.

Idéologie was a word coined in 1796 by Destutt de Tracy to describe his theory of knowledge. It did not mean the "ideology" of later times. It was essentially an epistemology, holding that all reliable knowledge derived ultimately from sense perception, so that all valid knowledge

[1] On the *Idéologues* see Emmet Kennedy, *Destutt de Tracy and the Origins of "Ideology"* (Philadelphia, 1978); M. Regaldo, *Un Milieu intellectuel: La Décade philosophique*, 5 vols. (Lille and Paris, 1976); S. Moravia, *Il tramonto dell'illuminismo: filosofia e politica nella società francese, 1770-1810* (Bari, 1968), pp. 315-444; T. E. Kaiser, "Enlightenment and Public Education during the French Revolution: The Views of the Idéologues," *Studies in 18th Century Culture* 10 (1980):95-111.

must rest on "the analysis of sensations and ideas," accompanied by the study of "general grammar," or the relation among words as found universally in all languages, and so indicative of the operation of the human mind. "Ideology" was offered as a basis for the unity of all knowledge, from the highest science to the most commonplace observation. It was also a polemical philosophy, maintaining that ideas for which no basis in sense perception could be found—such as the ideas of God, the soul, revelation, heaven, immortality, and innate ideas— were errors of the past from which human beings should be liberated. It was most strenuously rejected by those who found meaning in religion.

There were a number of poles of attraction around which the Idéologues took form as a group. One was at the salon of Mme Helvétius, the aging widow of the philosopher, who lived at Auteuil on the outskirts of Paris. When her salon revived after the Terror, one of its first activities was to bring out an edition of Helvétius' writings in 14 volumes. Her house was a gathering place for Garat, the moving spirit of the Ecole Normale and head of the Executive Commission on Public Instruction until May 1795, and for Ginguené, first Garat's aide, then his successor at the Executive Commission and chief of the bureau concerned with public instruction within the ministry of the interior until 1797. Garat and Ginguené mingled with Cabanis, Daunou, Destutt de Tracy, and others in the salon at Auteuil. A less organized connection was provided by another and much younger widow, Sophie Condorcet, who assisted Daunou in the publication of Condorcet's writings, translated Adam Smith's *Theory of the Moral Sentiments*, was romantically involved with Garat, and had a sister who was married to Cabanis. Another pole of attraction was the *Décade philosophique*, a journal of commentary and opinion founded in 1794, which appeared every 10 days until 1807. Its main editor was Ginguené, assisted by J. B. Say, a young man who was to become famous as a founder of free-market economics. Destutt de Tracy, Garat, Cabanis, and the grammarian Domergue were among the many contributors to the *Décade*. Still another pole was the National Institute, which held its first meeting in December 1795. Its original members included Garat, Ginguené, Destutt de Tracy, Cabanis, and Domergue, and it was at a session of the Institute in 1796 that Destutt de Tracy first used the word "ideology."[2] Except possibly for Cabanis, a medical

[2] Kennedy, *Destutt de Tracy*, p. 46. *Idéologie* was first used as a word in a book title in 1801 in a short work by Tracy designed for the schools, *Projet d'éléments d'idéologie à l'usage des écoles centrales de la République française* (Paris, An IX). The noun *idéologue*, however, originated when Napoleon used it as a term of disparagement.

doctor and founder of "physiological" Ideology, none of the really scientific men of this first group at the Institute—Lagrange, Laplace, Lalande, Monge, Guyton, Fourcroy, Haüy, Lamarck, Daubenton, Lacépède—was an Idéologue. Nor were the more purely literary spirits—Bernardin de Saint-Pierre, Louis-Sébastien Mercier, and Marie-Joseph Chénier. In the remarkable intellectual galaxy of these years between the Terror and Napoleon the Idéologues were only a part, but they were the part whose views had the greatest effect on the educational system.

Typical, too, was Germaine Necker, Mme de Staël. She was close to the Idéologues but not one of them. Nor as a woman could she be elected to the National Institute, or even write for the *Décade philosophique*. But she had an extensive intellectual acquaintance, which included Ginguené and Daunou along with Talleyrand and the young Benjamin Constant. In 1800 she published her book, *On literature in its relationship to social institutions*. By "literature" she meant emphatically to include writings on political and philosophical subjects. It was not her purpose to deal with education, but she remarked in her preface that "equality, the inherent principle of any philosophical constitution, can only subsist if you classify differences in education even more strictly than feudalism used to do in making its arbitrary distinctions." She thought it essential for some to be better educated than others. Since in a proper society no one could rule by force, it was necessary to rule by reason, and this meant by persons trained in language and literature, able to communicate, to persuade, to propose, to argue, to clarify difficult problems, to enlist support and appeal to the feelings of others. Educated leadership was "especially necessary in a state founded on a democratic basis."[3]

She expressed here an attitude that prevailed in governing circles among the Thermidorians and during the Directory. Remembering with horror the Terror, during which several of them had been imprisoned (and friends had died); fearful of a renewal of popular violence; feeling an equal dislike for the monarchy, the nobility, and the church of the Old Regime; these people, most of them originating in the pre-Revolutionary bourgeoisie (though a few were noble, like Destutt de Tracy, and like Talleyrand, who returned from America in 1796), were eager or at least willing to accept the Republic, if only the Republic incorporated the gains made in the early years of the Revolution. It should be a Republic equipped with a free press, public dis-

[3] Mme de Staël, *De la littérature considérée dans ses rapports avec les institutions sociales*, 2nd ed. (Paris, 1801), 1:53.

cussion, legislative chambers, and open elections, so arranged by a system of electoral colleges that while most adult men had a vote only substantial and educated persons would be elected. Committed to private property, intelligent leadership, economic freedom, education, economic development, and equality in the sense of opportunity for the talented, the "Directorials" were predecessors to nineteenth-century liberals.

The Half-Revival of Condorcet

Condorcet's famous book, *A Sketch of the Progress of the Human Mind*, written while he was in hiding from the guillotine in 1793 and 1794, was first published early in 1795. The Committee on Public Instruction, on April 2, ordered 3,000 copies of it distributed, most of them to students and professors at the Ecole Normale. As Daunou said in the Convention: "Here is a book for students, offered to your republican schools by an ill-fated philosopher. The improvement of the social state is indicated in it as the most worthy aim for the activity of the human mind, and your students, by studying the history of the arts and sciences, will learn to cherish liberty and to detest and overcome all tyrannies."[4] Or as Ginguené wrote in the *Décade philosophique*, reviewing Condorcet's book, in a rhetorical question demanding a resounding negative answer: "Would it be absurd today to suppose that the improvement of the human race should be thought susceptible to indefinite progress?"[5]

Condorcet—along with Condillac, the French Locke, with his sensationalist psychology and philosophy—became a kind of guru to the Idéologues. He had been a proto-Idéologue himself; the first words of the *Progress of the Human Mind* announced that correct ideas arose from sensation, and the succeeding chapters of the book formed an intellectual history, in which human beings groped their way to knowledge through primitive times, classical antiquity, the dark ages, the revival of learning, and the Enlightenment, to the American Revolution, the "first philosophical revolution," and to the climax of the

[4] J. Guillaume, *Procès-verbaux du Comité d'Instruction publique de la Convention Nationale*, 6 vols. (Paris, 1891-1907), 6:11. The proper title of Condorcet's book is *Esquisse d'un tableau des progrès de l'esprit humain*; it was immediately translated and published in England in 1795, and in the United States in 1796. For the germination and content of the book see Keith Baker, *Condorcet: From Natural Philosophy to Social Mathematics* (Chicago, 1975).

[5] *Décade philosophique*, 20 Prairial of the Year III, p. 486.

French Revolution, signifying the triumph of reason, with its future goal of true and genuine equality.

Condorcet, however, was only half-revived by his admirers of 1795. What was revived was Condorcet the *philosophe*, not Condorcet the democrat. It was his faith in science, not his faith in equality. The elitism of which he was accused in 1792 was not complained of in 1795. It was thought that progress depended more on the few than on the many. It seemed more important that the directing elements in society should be enlightened than that everybody should have some number of years in school.

Condorcet's multilevel plan for educational institutions, a pyramid of *écoles primaires, écoles secondaires, instituts*, and *lycées* culminating in a *Société Nationale*, was revived and implemented in principle. The pyramidal idea had never really died; dating from before the Revolution, it had appeared in the Talleyrand plan, Lepeletier and Robespierre had favored it, the Paris plan of September 1793 had embraced it, the Executive Commission had adopted it in 1794, and the Ecole Normale had been imagined as a summit to a whole system. Although nothing had been done about it by the Revolutionary Government at the time of the Bouquier law, it was not rejected but only postponed while the Jacobins put their emphasis on elementary schools. Now when the multilevel pyramidal structure actually went into effect, late in 1795, it was subject to curious deformations. There came indeed to be a pyramid of schools, with a National Institute at the top. But it was a shaky pyramid, and some very important establishments remained outside it. A bifurcated system developed, which became permanent in France, with one part eventually called the *université* and the other the *grandes écoles*.

The notion of one total plan, all-embracing and rational, with all parts coordinated and interlocking and replacing the chaos of inherited institutions, had to yield before the demands of reality and the pressure of events. The planners of 1795 did not write on a clean slate. Primary schools, though none too successful, did in fact exist under the Bouquier law. The Convention had already decreed, in February 1795, that the old colleges should be replaced by Central Schools, and steps were already being taken to open them in the following autumn. The ad hoc arrangements of the Year II, the revolutionary courses, had in some cases already taken root as viable establishments, especially the Schools of Public Works and of Health. Higher institutions from before the Revolution still stood, notably the old Royal College, now the College of France; the old Royal Garden, now the Museum of Natural History; the old Royal Library, now the Bibliothèque Nationale; and the old Royal Observatory, now the Bureau of Longitudes. It had once been supposed that these would be merged into one Olympian mountain of knowledge, but this never happened.

In one respect the planners of 1795 were in the same position as their predecessors. They agreed that education was a political question. Planning for education and for the new constitution must go together. Not only must the young be trained to live under a republican regime, but the constitution itself was to be an eductional force, teaching how to live in an orderly and predictable world. After the insurrection of Germinal, in April, the Convention appointed a Commission of Eleven to prepare a new constitution, since there was now no thought that the suspended popular constitution of 1793 should ever go into operation. In June the Committee on Public Instruction began to work jointly with the Commission of Eleven on educational problems. In these discussions the Committee on Public Instruction was represented mainly by Fourcroy and Lakanal, the Commission of Eleven by Boissy d'Anglas and Daunou. Fourcroy still retained some of his democratic and Jacobin sympathies. Boissy, who had had to face the severed head of a colleague on the floor of the Convention on May 20, was no friend of the populace.

Boissy, for the Eleven, on June 23, submitted to the Convention an elaborate draft for the constitution to which a plan for education was attached.[6] Extremely grudging with public support, it cut by half the number of Central Schools agreed upon in February and left the financing of primary schools to the option of local governments, with the national government providing no more than lodging and a schoolroom for a schoolmaster, for boys only. The plan allowed and even encouraged *enseignement libre*, or freedom for private persons to open schools as they wished. It considered at more length the institutions of interest to the intellectual elite: high-level special schools, a National Institute, and a program of rewards and honors for outstanding students, professors, artists, scholars, and writers.

Fourcroy objected strongly to these proposals in the privacy of the Committee on Public Instruction, as shown by some notes that he turned over to Lakanal.[7] He feared for the "popular cause." He thought it wrong to reject principles already agreed on, that primary schoolteachers should be salaried by the state, and that there should be a Central School in every department. He favored *instruction gratuite* in

[6] Guillaume, *Procès-verbaux*, 6:333-42. See also pp. xxi-xxviii, 52-54, 132, 244, 278, 305.

[7] Ibid., 6:504, 511-12, 644.

both primary and Central Schools. "If education is free or paid for by the state, more will be paid by the rich than by the poor." Paid for by all, schooling would cost very little to each person; paid for by fees, it would be costly for everyone having children in school, and too costly for the poor. And he asked a question seldom raised in these discussions: "You have taken away the property of the colleges; what are you doing for instruction if you don't pay the professors?" But Fourcroy was unable to persuade a majority of his colleagues on the Committee on Public Instruction, which went along with at least the financial aspects of the plan of the Commission of Eleven. It must be observed that, quite apart from a declining concern for democracy, the public finances were in chaos. The paper money, not repudiated until a year later, had lost almost all its value; in July 1975 a livre in paper had fallen to one-thirtieth of its value in metal. The fact that the Convention decreed, at this very time, that French money should henceforth be denominated in francs and centimes of course made no difference.

Fourcroy was concerned also with the future of the technical schools, and especially of the School of Public Works in whose formation he had been active the year before. He and Prieur of the Cote-d'Or saved it from the sad fate of the Ecole Normale. It was agreed that the whole program for education should be presented to the Convention in two parts. The part for the technical and military schools was presented by Fourcroy, in a long speech on 30 Vendémiaire (October 22). The other, or pyramidal part, for the educational mainstream from primary schools up to the Institute, was presented by Daunou and enacted on 3 Brumaire (October 25).

The law of 30 Vendémiaire regularized the School of Public Works, renamed the Ecole Polytechnique a few weeks earlier, and clarified its relation to the other technical schools, which were in effect modified survivals from the Old Regime.[8] It was now finally decided that the Polytechnique, instead of replacing the others as a grand new single establishment, would be simply preparatory for them. For all these schools strict entrance requirements were prescribed; there should be serious competitive examinations; students as well as professors were to be salaried by the state; and the number of students should be limited to the number of places available each year in the relevant government service. The term of study at the Polytechnique was set at

[8] The text of the law is in ibid., 6:774-83; Fourcroy's speech introducing it is on pp. 839-50. See also the important speeches by Prieur, ibid., 6:299-311, and by Fourcroy, 6:601-604. For a good summary on the *Polytechnique* and the schools of public service in 1795 see also D. Julia, *Les trois couleurs du tableau noir: La Révolution* (Paris, 1981), pp. 297-305.

three years. But after the first year the student might, by passing further examinations, transfer to the School of Geographers, after two years to the Artillery School or the School of Mines, and after three years to the School of Military Engineers or the School of Roads and Bridges. These schools as a group were henceforth called schools of public service, or *écoles d'application*, that is, of applied sciences. The Polytechnique, taking in boys as young as sixteen, gave them instruction in basic mathematics and physical science and for several years had a monopoly on admission to these higher schools, which could be entered only by young men from the Polytechnique.

Several observations can be made. First, the concern of the government in technical and engineering subjects was primarily, though not exclusively, for the education of its own personnel. This was perhaps not unusual at a certain stage of modernization; West Point, founded in 1802, was the first engineering school in the United States and remained the only one for 20 years. Second, the government was far more exacting in the education of its own personnel than it was for schools for the public at large. The insistence on competition and examination for admission to these schools, and for further examination during the course of study, as laid down in the law of 30 Vendémiaire, contrasts sharply with the easygoing rules for the Central Schools as set forth in the law of 3 Brumaire three days later. Finally, what was left of democratic sentiment was turning into something more like meritocracy. Prieur, who had served in the Robespierrist Committee of Public Safety, and Fourcroy, who had been an outspoken Montagnard in 1794, both insisted that admission to these schools, while depending on high qualifications, must not be limited to families able to pay the cost. Their concern was not so much with social mobility as with performance, or with service to the state, by which they meant service to the public. Prieur explained why all students in these schools should have all their living expenses as well as tuition paid for by the government. For young men of means, he said, it would enable the school to enforce discipline and serious study. But it was also necessary for the recruitment of talent; if enough talented persons were to be found, the pool of candidates must not be restricted.[9] Or as Fourcroy put it, it was necessary to extract a sufficient number from the educational system by "severe examination."[10]

[9] Guillaume, *Procès-verbaux*, 6:307-309.

[10] Ibid., 6:840. There is a useful contemporary description of schools of all levels, written in 1798 by a Danish visitor, and giving details on their physical quarters, teachers, and programs of study, reprinted by M. Crosland, ed., *Science in the Revolutionary Era, described by Thomas Bugge, Danish Astronomer Royal and Member of the International*

The part of Condorcet's dream that expected progress from the applied sciences was carried forward in the law of 30 Vendémiaire. The remainder, with glaring excisions, was institutionalized in the law of 3 Brumaire, which remained the basic law on education until transformed under Bonaparte seven years later.

THE LAW OF 3 BRUMAIRE OF THE YEAR IV

This law, known also to historians as the Daunou law, was the only piece of legislation enacted during the Revolution that applied to all levels of education, since the Bouquier law had dealt only with primary schools. It arose from the same discussions as those that produced the constitution of the Year III, which was adopted in August 1795 and was in effect from October 1795 until the Bonapartist coup d'état of Brumaire in November 1799.

The new constitution reflected the fear of a concentrated executive power, and of democratic demands, inspired by the Revolutionary Government of 1793-1794.[11] By it, there existed two elected legislative chambers, the Five Hundred and the *Anciens* or "elder" house; an Executive Directory of five persons, one of whom was replaceable each year by a successor chosen by the two chambers; and a number of ministries, one of them a ministry of the interior, whose sphere of interest included in its Fifth Division the supervision over public instruction. Under Ginguené—who was assisted by Dumouchel, a former professor and rector of the pre-Revolutionary University of Paris—the personnel, files, and functions of the Executive Commission on Public Instruction were incorporated into the ministry of the interior as the Fifth division. The constitution also provided for a restricted form of universal male suffrage, granting a vote to all men except household servants, with rigorous sifting through electoral colleges, and providing further that beginning in the Year XII (1803-1804, by which time of course the constitution had been superseded) no young man could become a voting citizen unless he knew how to read and write.

Title X of the constitution was addressed to education. One article assured *liberté de l'enseignement*, that is, the right of private schools to

---

Commission of the Metric System (1798-99) (Cambridge, Mass., and London, 1969). Bugge's book was first translated and published in London in 1801. Crosland includes shorter excerpts from other contemporary visitors.

[11] The constitution is conveniently printed with comments by J. Godechot, *Les constitutions de la France depuis 1789* (Paris, 1970), pp. 93-141.

exist. Another provided for *écoles primaires*, or public elementary schools, purposely confined to the teaching of reading, writing, arithmetic, and morality, that is, excluding the elements of higher studies that some had favored in the past. A more indefinite article authorized schools above the primary. The existence of a "national institute charged with collecting discoveries and improving the arts and sciences" was also written into the constitution. So were "national festivals to promote fraternity among citizens and attach them to the constitution, the country, and the laws."

The educational law of 3 Brumaire contained six titles.[12] Title I provided for primary schools, "one or more in each canton," to be administered locally by the departments, but with parents paying fees, from which a quarter of the pupils might be exempted at the judgment of local governments for reasons of need, and with the state providing no salaries but only a schoolroom and lodging for the teachers. Only by a tardy amendment were primary schools for girls included. No number of years of attendance was specified. The whole arrangement marked a sharp falling-off not only from the aspirations of Jacobin democrats and the Bouquier law but also from the Talleyrand plan of 1791 and the first Revolutionary constitution of 1789-1791, which had called for universal free instruction at the elementary level. It is clear also that these decisionmakers of 1795, in requiring that male citizens beginning in 1804 should know how to read and write and yet providing neither free nor compulsory primary education, were not eager to enlarge the electorate. The notion persisted that primary schools should lead on for some pupils to the higher levels, or that they should be a "vestibule" to more advanced studies, as Lakanal had said in December 1794; but since the primary schools were confined to the rudiments, they gave too little relevant preparation. To make matters in this respect worse, the *écoles secondaires* proposed by Condorcet, which he had viewed as advanced primary establishments, were entirely omitted from the law of 3 Brumaire.

Next above the primary schools, and provided in Title II, were the Central Schools, of which one was to be in each department as its "center" of educational and learned activities. The Central Schools became the most distinctive feature of the educational system during the Directory and are treated at length in the following pages. The lack of any articulation with the primary schools became one of the most

[12] For the text of the law and Daunou's speech introducing it see Guillaume, *Procès-verbaux*, 6:786-800 and 869-73; for earlier versions and discussions, 5:284n, 298-309, 541-44; 6:330-42, 580-82. The law is also printed in the *Moniteur, réimpression*, 26:323-26, with Daunou's speech on pp. 255-61.

widely acknowledged weaknesses afflicting the Central Schools. Such was the lingering discredit of the Ecole Normale that the law of 3 Brumaire made no mention of teacher training; it was tacitly supposed that teachers would learn what they needed to know in the Central Schools.

Nor did the law make any provision for what Condorcet had called *lycées*, which he had seen as replacing the old universities, with 10 of them distributed in important cities throughout the country. Instead, above the Central Schools, it called for 10 "special schools," with no expressed concern for geographical decentralization. Ten kinds of these advanced special schools were envisaged for subjects as follows:

> Astronomy
> Geometry and Mechanics
> Natural History
> Medicine
> Veterinary Art
> Rural Economy
> Antiquities
> Political Sciences
> Painting, Sculpture, and Architecture
> Music

None of these higher special schools came into being, except for the schools of medicine that were already in operation. The existing schools for the blind and deaf were also classified as special schools. Explicitly excluded were the schools of engineering, artillery, and "other public services," whether existing or to be established, as provided in the law of 30 Vendémiaire. The law of 3 Brumaire made no mention at all of the College of France, Museum of Natural History, or Bureau of Longitudes, which remained separate centers of advanced study.

Title IV concerned the National Institute; Title V subsidies, rewards, and public honors; and Title VI the national festivals. This last title prescribed several national and local celebrations but made no mention of the decadary cult that had already fallen out of favor. Title V provided that certain citizens should be chosen by the Institute each year to travel at home or abroad at national expense to make scientific and scholarly observations. It authorized the continuation of the French school of art at Rome, for students who would remain up to five years with all costs paid by the Republic—as by the academy of painting before the Revolution. It likewise decreed that in each of the Central and special schools there should be 20 students whose living costs should be paid for by the nation; but this provision was only sporadically carried out.

The National Institute, already authorized by the constitution of the Year III, was the most lasting creation of the law of 3 Brumaire. It is enlightening to compare it with Condorcet's plan of 1792 for a National Society of the Arts and Sciences, as described on pp. 126-27 above. One notes that the Institute, unlike Condorcet's National Society, had (until 1801) no foreign members, whether because of three years of war or a growing self-satisfaction with the glories of French culture cannot be said. The Institute also had no powers over teaching or over appointments of teachers in the special or Central Schools, such as Condorcet had proposed for his National Society. Boissy d'Anglas had wanted a teaching Institute, but Daunou and Fourcroy, remembering the outcry in 1792 and 1793 against bureaucracy and privilege, succeeded in keeping the teaching establishments independent from the Institute. In the long run the Institute became a primarily honorific body, whose members were chosen at a mature age for attainments in work already done elsewhere.[13]

The National Institute, like Condorcet's plan, included a "class" for "moral and political sciences" and thus carried on one of the significant innovations of the Revolution. But it had only three "classes" instead of Condorcet's four, for it omitted what had been the largest of Condorcet's classes, the one devoted to the applied sciences. As organized in 1795 the three classes of the Institute were each composed of several sections, with each section consisting of six members residing in Paris and six in the remaining parts of France, as follows:

FIRST CLASS: PHYSICAL AND MATHEMATICAL SCIENCES
Mathematics
Mechanical Arts
Astronomy
Experimental Physics
Chemistry
Natural History and Mineralogy
Botany and *physique végétale*
Anatomy and Zoology
Medicine and Surgery
Rural Economy and Veterinary Arts

SECOND CLASS: MORAL AND POLITICAL SCIENCES
Analysis of Sensations and Ideas
Morale
Social Science and Legislation

[13] Roger Hahn, *The Anatomy of a Scientific Institution: The Paris Academy of Sciences, 1666-1803* (Berkeley, 1971), p. 300.

Political Economy

History

Geography

THIRD CLASS: LITERATURE AND FINE ARTS

Grammar

Ancient Languages

Poetry

Antiquities and Monuments

Painting

Sculpture

Architecture

Music and Declamation

Of the 60 original Paris members of the First Class, two-thirds had been members of the old Royal Academy of Sciences, including 17 of the 18 in mathematics, astronomy, and experimental physics. Handfuls of the other two classes had belonged to the old Academy of Inscriptions. The new thinking generated by the Revolution was best seen in the Class of Moral and Political Sciences, first devised by Condorcet, and so "progressive" in its implications that Bonaparte broke it up in 1803, and it was not reconstituted until 1832. Within this class, the section for the analysis of sensations and ideas became the home of the Idéologues. Its six Paris members included Garat, Ginguené, and Cabanis, plus the lesser Idéologues Volney and Lebreton; Destutt de Tracy, who lived at Auteuil outside the city limits, became an associate member "from the departments." Other sections of the Second Class soon received various personages who had figured in the educational debates since early in the Revolution—Talleyrand, Sieyès, Lakanal, Daunou, and Grégoire, as well as J. F. Champagne of Equality College.[14]

If pure science, philosophy, and the arts thus seemed well taken care of at the Institute, the same was less clearly true for the applied sciences. Since 1791 two organizations had arisen, the Bureau de Consultation and the Lycée des Arts, in which scientific men had met with artisans, mechanics, small manufacturers, and unsophisticated inventors. Both had received subsidies from the government to help carry on their work. The Lycée had held classes open to the public, and in December 1795 it petitioned the newly installed minister of the interior for a continuation of financial aid. It proposed to offer 23 courses

[14] A. Potiquet, *L'Institut National de France: ses diverses organisations, ses membres, ses associés et ses correspondants* (Paris, 1871), pp. 2-62. See also M. S. Staum, "The Class of Moral and Political Sciences, 1795-1803," *French Historical Studies* 11 (1980):371-97.

for the winter term of 1795-1796, including such practical subjects as simple mathematics, bookkeeping, surveying, perspective drawing, stenography, navigation, engraving, French grammar, and the English and German languages. (There were to be courses also in Latin, belles-lettres, and political economy.) The petition asked likewise for continued subsidy for the *Journal du Lycée des Arts*, in which new inventions and discoveries were reported. The minister rejected the petition on the ground that all useful functions of the Lycée would be performed by the Institute and the Central and special schools.[15] The Lycée nevertheless managed to carry on for a while, offering free instruction for 200 *artistes indigents* in 1796-1797. Its building burned down in 1798, but it continued to exist and was mildly favored by the government during the Napoleonic years. The Bureau de Consultation, which unlike the Lycée was a creation of the government, established in 1791, was abolished in 1796, with its functions of encouraging and publicizing inventions transferred to the Institute.

The Institute, however, was a high-level establishment. Its First Class was more concerned with the more abstruse reaches of science than with popular technical education, or with any kind of teaching at all. It lacked the class in applied science that Condorcet had envisaged and for which the small section in mechanical arts was hardly an adequate substitute. The applied sciences and practical arts had been intentionally set aside, outside the pyramid of which the Institute was the apex, and concentrated in the Polytechnique and the technical schools to which it was the gateway, and which were exclusive in their insistence on exceptional talents in mathematics and physics. Not much remained for ordinary working-class youth except the Conservatory of Arts and Trades, which in any case was not a school and which, though launched in 1794, did not open until 1798 and never achieved the distinction of the more purely scientific institutions. There were many who thought that skilled technical work was best learned by apprenticeship, and possibly, especially for the eighteenth century, this view was not mistaken. What effect the combination of excellence in high science with less organized lower level technical training may have had on modernization is a question that has been much debated but never finally answered.

As Dominique Julia has observed, the spirit of Diderot's *Encyclopédie* was embodied in these establishments of 1795, but without Diderot's enthusiasm for the everyday operations of trained workers in their

<hr>

15 Archives Nationales, F[17] 1143. On the Lycée des Arts and Bureau de Consultation see above, pp. 151-54.

workshops. His additional remark, that the empire of the engineer was beginning while the reign of the man of letters was ending, seems more open to question.[16] Certainly French engineering excelled at this time, but the influence of literary people, especially in Mme de Staël's extended sense of the word literature, continued for a long time to prevail. Intellectuals, writers, *philosophes*, and *idéologues* continued to have their say. Indeed, a kind of takeover of the Revolution by the intellectuals had occurred.

THE PUBLIC AND THE PRIVATE SECTORS

By setting up an actual system of education under the authority of the state, the law of 3 Brumaire not only founded a national system of public instruction but also crystallized the modern distinction between public and private schools. The sense in which the pre-Revolutionary system was public was explained in the first chapter of this book. Now, with the arrangements of 1795 (the constitution plus the laws of 30 Vendémiaire and 3 Brumaire) there came to be two obviously distinct kinds of educational institutions: one, a private sector, existing under the constitutional guarantee of *liberté d'enseignement*; the other a public system created by the state, which defined its objectives, marked out its various levels, ordered the recruitment of teachers, and in general gave encouragement and support, except for finances, since only the highest levels of science and a few professional schools were paid for from the national treasury. The two sectors persisted for a long time; the difference was scarcely concealed by the Napoleonic "monopoly"; and as late as the 1870s, at the important secondary level, there were about the same number of students in the private as in the public system, about 80,000 in each case. The public system, on which so much thought, planning, and oratory were expended during the Revolution, and which being official has tended to preoccupy historians, was for a long time in competition with private enterprise, including the enterprise of the Catholic Church, which the Revolution turned from a "public" into a "private" body. By no means all private schools, however, were operated by the clergy; as late as 1854 two-thirds of private secondary schools were conducted by laypersons, with the church gaining ground only after that time.[17]

At the elementary level, the public and private sectors suffered from

[16] Julia, *Trois couleurs*, p. 309.

[17] The figures for the 1870s and for 1854 are from A. Prost, *L'Enseignement en France, 1800-1967* (Paris, 1968), p. 45.

disadvantages that they had in common.[18] One was the difficulty in finding teachers. Another was a weakness in effective demand. Especially in the poorest and least developed regions the most depressed families saw no value in sending their children to a school of any kind. Among educated notables, the administrators of departments and municipalities who were responsible for the public schools, there were many who shared the old fears of La Chalotais, that to teach everyone to read and write would drain laborers from their fields. Both the clergy and the secular liberals rejected this view, each group hoping to improve and raise up the populace according to its lights, but neither could altogether overcome the popular skepticism and middle-class indifference that existed.

The *écoles primaires*, or state elementary schools, faced difficulties as great as under the Bouquier law, or indeed greater. From an official survey made in 1798, which yielded random but probably representative results, it can be said that in 892 of the communes of France (which numbered over 30,000), there were 1,220 elementary schools, of which only 37 percent were public and 63 percent were private.[19] In Paris in June 1798 there were 50 public primary schools but some 2,000 private elementary schools that must have been small but probably had more pupils.[20] One difficulty was that for the state schools parents had to pay fees, whereas many of the private schools were free. There was no sharp distinction in this respect, however, for some local governments contrived to pay their schoolmaster or schoolmistress a salary, and private teachers could offer free instruction only so far as they were priests or former religious sisters supported by charitable donations.

The scene was further confused by the existence of two Catholic churches in France, the constitutional church whose clergy accepted

---

[18] For the private schools, both elementary and "secondary," see L. Grimaud, *Histoire de la liberté d'enseignement en France*, 6 vols. (Paris, 1944-1947), 2:269-381. For the elementary schools there is the recent work of E. Kennedy and M. L. Netter, "Les écoles primaires sous le Directoire," *Annales historiques de la Révolution française* [henceforth *AHRF*] (January-March 1981), pp. 3-38; E. Kennedy, "The French Revolutionary catechisms: Ruptures and continuities with classical, Christian and Enlightenment moralities." *Studies on Voltaire and the Eighteenth Century* 199 (1981):353-62; J. Morange and J. F. Chassaign, *Le mouvement de réforme de l'enseignement en France* (Paris, 1974), of which the whole second part, by Chassaign, pp. 97-184, is on the schoolbooks and republican catechisms used in the *écoles primaires*; and M. Gontard, *L'enseignement primaire en France de la Révolution à la loi Guizot* (Paris, 1959), of which pp. 156-88 are on the years of the Directory.

[19] Kennedy and Netter, "Les écoles primaires," p. 10.

[20] M. Reinhard, *Nouvelle histoire de Paris: La Révolution* (Paris, 1971), p. 395.

the Republic, though they were no longer salaried by it, and the refractory, orthodox or Roman church, whose clergy were generally opposed to almost everything that had happened since 1789. Since church
and state were in principle separated under the Constitution of 1795,
the government interfered very little with the educational efforts of
either group until late in 1797.

Both sets of clergy concentrated on opening or reopening elementary schools. The orthodox, or refractories, consisting of unorganized
individual priests and sisters whose religious orders had been dissolved, looked to the émigré bishops for guidance. These bishops,
from exile in England or Germany, sent instructions to their former
dioceses urging that children be instilled with a horror for the Revolution. They formed a counter-revolutionary force in the full sense of
the word. The constitutional clergy had resident bishops in each diocese as reorganized in 1791, among whom the most important was
the Abbé Grégoire, bishop of Blois, that is, of the department of Loir-
et-Cher. These bishops issued occasional encyclicals and in 1797 came
together in a National Council, which published a *Synodical letter to
fathers, mothers and all persons charged with the instruction of youth.*[21]
The constitutional bishops envisaged a whole system of elementary
schools, one for boys and one for girls in each parish, to exist side by
side with the official primary schools in each commune. While accepting the Republic and the general principles of the Revolution they
denounced its irreligion and anarchy, and insisted that children could
be brought up both as good patriots and as good Christians. The two
sets of clergy disputed vehemently with each other and competed for
each other's pupils, some of the constitutionals even demanding that
the refractories be repressed by the government. To the refractories,
the constitutionals were schismatics who would in due course be ob-
literated.

It would seem that both the Republic and the constitutional church
might have been the stronger had they been able to compromise against
a common foe. And for a while it seemed that compromise might be
possible. In a recent study, arising from a detailed analysis of replies
to the survey of 1798 already mentioned, the authors conclude that a
"hybrid system" of elementary schools was developing after 1795.[22]

---

[21] Grimaud, *Histoire*, 2:296-305. *Collection des pièces imprimées par ordre du Concile
National de France* (Paris, 1797 [An VI]), including the *Lettres synodiques*. BN. Ld⁴
4061.

[22] Kennedy and Netter, "Les écoles primaires," pp. 12-19, where they argue this re-
visionist thesis against Grimaud and others who have emphasized the difference and
hostility between public and private elementary schools.

The state schools were in principle religiously neutral, but some of their teachers, whether from conviction or under pressure from parents and local curés, in fact introduced Bible readings or other religious materials. Some teachers in the Christian schools used some of the republican books, even the republic catechisms, approved by the government in 1796, when the contest for the writing of school texts announced in 1794 finally came to a close. There were other signs of "hybridization," as when teachers in state schools gave their pupils a holiday on Sunday, and those in religious schools did the same on the *décadi*.

Both kinds of schools stressed moral instruction in addition to elementary literacy and computation, and their views on ordinary duties and behavior were not very different. There was not much in Lachabeaussière's widely used *Catéchisme républicain* to which a serious Christian could object, except for its omissions. The four principal virtues, said Lachabeaussière (in the classical tradition), were justice, prudence, temperance, and courage. The four principal vices were wrath, pride, greed, and envy, to which he added idleness since it was the source of all others. The ideal family was much the same for both parties. The Revolution authorized divorce, but the republican morality books said nothing about it. It is now known from demographic studies that contraception and family planning became more common during the Revolution, but this fact could never be suspected from a reading of the Revolutionary moralists. As for religion, the republican catechisms showed a deistic respectfulness toward God, though with a dose of agnosticism.[23]

[23] [Poisson de] Lachabeaussière, *Catéchisme républicain, philosophique et moral* (Paris, An II), reprinted as *Catéchisme français, ou Principes de la morale républicaine à l'usage des écoles primaires* (Paris, An III). This work was awarded first prize by the government for schoolbooks in its category in the Year IV and was many times reprinted until the Year VIII, again during the revolution of 1848, and at least three times from 1879 to 1882 in connection with the Ferry laws. It was translated into Dutch in 1796 and into Italian at about that same time, in connection with the formation of the Batavian and Cisalpine republics. Its catechetical questions and answers are arranged in 52 rimed quatrains, a few examples of which follow:

I.

Qui êtes vous?

Homme libre et pensant, républicain par choix,
Né pour aimer mon frère et servir ma patrie,
Vivre de mon travail ou de mon industrie,
Abhorrer l'esclavage et me soumettre aux lois.

It was both ideology and politics that made compromise impossible. Some teachers in the state schools, and some in both the national and local governments, simply believed that revealed or organized religion was a fraud perpetrated by priests. They held that natural religion and natural morality were enough. They would accept Helvétius' maxim— "no priests or no true morality." Teachers in the religious schools, on the other hand, and the bishops of both the constitutional and the refractory church, attacked "philosophism" and the misuse of reason. They said that moral character could not be formed by rational argument and demonstration, that the child's emotions must be trained by religious instruction, and that no sound morality would long outlast the disappearance of religious belief. The two sides exchanged epithets, denouncing each other as fanatics on the one hand or atheists on the other.

Politically, the government of the Directory did not or could not live up to its constitutional principles. As enthusiasm for the Revolution ebbed and a restoration of the Old Regime began to seem possible, the most committed Revolutionaries, including *idéologues* and the ambitious General Bonaparte, then winning victories in Italy, ex-

---

II.
Qu'est-ce que Dieu?

Je ne sais ce qu'il est, mais je vois son ouvrage:
Tout à mes yeux surpris annonce sa grandeur:
Je me crois trop borné pour m'en faire l'image,
Il échappe à mon sens, mais il parle à mon coeur.

III.
Qu'est-ce que l'âme?

Je n'en sais rien; je sais que je sens, que je pense,
Que je veux, que j'agis, que je me ressouviens;
Qu'il est un être en moi qui hors de moi s'élance;
Mais j'ignore où je vais, et je ne sais d'où je viens.

[Who are you? A free and thinking man, by choice a republican, born to love my brother and serve my country, to live by my labor or industry, to abhor slavery and submit to the laws. What is God? I know not what he is, but I see his work: Everything announces his greatness to my astonished eyes: I think myself too limited to form an image of him; he escapes my senses but speaks to my heart. What is the soul? I know nothing of it; I know that I feel, that I think; that I will, that I act, that I have the power of memory, that there is in me a being that leaps beyond myself; but I know not whither I am going, nor whence I come.]

Lachabeaussière was by profession a writer of comedies and wrote reviews of the theater for the *Décade philosophique*.

ecuted the coup d'état of Fructidor in September of 1797. A more ardently republican and neodemocratic phase followed in 1798, in which all religious schools were suspected of undermining the post-Revolutionary order, as indeed some of them were actually doing. Laws were passed to protect the public schools by restraining the private ones. Schools were ordered to observe the republican calendar. Some were closed, only to reappear under another name, somewhat as happened with the newspaper press. It was enacted that no one could in the future obtain employment from the state, or enter the Polytechnique and similar institutions, unless he had attended a public school. (The Parlement of Paris had once attempted this same tactic against the Jesuits.) Local governments were ordered to send inspectors on surprise visits to private schools to find out whether they were instilling fanaticism and hatred for the Republic, or were using authorized books, or were duly teaching the constitution and the rights of man. In some schools, the inspectors reported with shocked indignation that they saw crucifixes and pictures of saints hanging on the walls. As one republican journal remarked, warning against the girls' schools, if the magistrates opened their eyes they would find "nestfuls of ex-religious sisters engaged in turning out little bigots."[24]

At the elementary level the public system could not successfully compete, partly because of the fees it charged and partly because many families objected to the nonreligious, or sometimes antireligious, and in most cases highly politicized atmosphere of the *écoles primaires*. A few years later Napoleon in effect gave up the struggle, surrendering elementary teaching to the Brothers of the Christian Schools who had done much of it before the Revolution. The growth of a public primary system had to await the 1820s and the Guizot law of 1833.

It is not possible to say much about private schools at the next higher level, corresponding to the Central Schools in the public sector.[25] The clergy were less concerned with adolescent education than with the teaching of younger children. The *Synodic Letter* issued in 1797 by the council of constitutional bishops made no mention of the subject. Probably the proportion of lay schools was higher here than

[24] Grimaud, *Histoire*, 2:275. For contemporary reports on the inspection and control of private schools in Paris see also A. Aulard, *Paris pendant la réaction thermidorienne et sous le Directoire*, 5 vols. (Paris, 1898-1902), 4:571 and 5:97, 115, 168, 389, 424, 522.

[25] See in addition to Grimaud, G. Vauthier, "L'enseignement secondaire libre à Paris sous le Directoire," *AHRF* (1929), pp. 467-75, and D. Julia and W. Frijhoff, "Les grands pensionnats de l'Ancien Régime à la Restauration," *AHRF* (1981), pp. 153-98, which gives statistics on the schools that had been *écoles militaires* before the Revolution and continued mostly as private schools thereafter.

at the elementary level, but lay schools often offered the mild form of religious instruction that even parents alienated from the church usually desired. No estimate of the number of private "secondary" schools is available, but we know that there were about 350 colleges before the Revolution and that some of these emerged as Central Schools in 1795; but there were only about 80 Central Schools within the pre-Revolutionary borders of France, so that some of the old colleges can be assumed to have reemerged as private institutions. In Paris, where there came to be three Central Schools, there were 20 private schools during the Directory and 31 in 1803. In Paris and elsewhere some private schools were day schools and some were *pensions*, that is, partly schools and partly boarding houses where students might live while attending classes in the public Central Schools. Some private schools taught modern languages and other practical subjects that the Central Schools ignored. Some had the graded annual classes and strict plans of study that had characterized the pre-Revolutionary colleges, and which the Central Schools deliberately rejected. Some were middle-class establishments like those before the Revolution at Lille, as seen on page 28 above. Others were more fashionable, like the *pension* Savoure, where Napoleon placed his twelve-year-old brother Jerome in 1796. We have seen (pp. 110-12) what happened to the famous schools at Pontlevoy and Sorèze during and after the Revolution. These two, and others of the former royal *écoles militaires*, were transformed by the Revolution from schools appealing mainly to the nobility into upper class boarding schools on the nineteenth-century pattern, open to the elites and notables of the new era, whether of old-noble or new-bourgeois status and style of life.

At the highest level, except for a few privately organized law schools, and the two Lycées, and informal gatherings at which lectures could be heard, there were no private teaching establishments, all institutionalized higher instruction being provided and superintended by the state. Some of the private establishments filled small but significant niches. For example, a German traveler in 1796 found that lectures at the Lycée republicain were attended by women, who assiduously took notes "with the ardor of a student at Jena."[26]

THE CENTRAL SCHOOLS: PROGRESSIVE EDUCATION

The Central Schools, growing out of the ideas of Garat, Lakanal, and the Commission on Public Instruction late in 1794, were authorized

[26] Adolphe Schmidt, *Paris pendant la Révolution*, 4 vols. (Paris, 1880-1894), 4:184.

by a law of 3 Ventose of the Year III, or February 21, 1795. (See above, p. 213.) They were established gradually, one in each department, until by 1799 about a hundred of them were legally in existence. At this time the French Republic consisted of 103 departments, of which eight were in the Belgium-Luxembourg area and four on the German Left Bank of the Rhine; these departments in principle enjoyed exactly the same public facilities as those within pre-Revolutionary France. In 1799 the minister of the interior sent out a questionnaire to which 78 departments in France and all those in Belgium replied. The replies show an enormous variation from place to place. In some departments, a Central School was well established as a going concern, in others only a fraction of the prescribed plan of studies was implemented, and in a few no Central School existed except on paper.[27]

Expressly intended to replace the old colleges, the new schools incorporated modern ideas of education, not only in an eighteenth- but also in a twentieth-century sense. They had virtually no admission requirements, no graded classes, and no set term of years of study. They gave no degree or certificate. No study was prerequisite to any other. Instruction was by "courses" rather than "classes," that is, each teacher taught only his own subject; and lecturing, supplemented by questions and discussion, was favored over drill and recitation. All courses were electives for the students, and examinations were optional for the professors. There was no religious instruction, and teachers and students of any religion or no religion were welcome. The planners meant to favor science and mathematics and a modern approach to other subjects, so that the student of grammar, for example, was not to learn

---

[27] For quantitative details see my article, "The Central Schools of the First French Republic: A Statistical Survey," in *The Making of Frenchmen: Current Directions in the History of Education in France, 1679-1979*, ed. D. N. Baker and P. J. Harrigan; a special issue of *Historical Reflections* (Waterloo, Ont., Canada, Summer-Fall 1980), pp. 223-47. Knowledge of the Central Schools has been greatly advanced by the special number of *Annales historiques de la Révolution française* (January-March 1981), mentioned in note 18 above for its article on primary schools, and in note 25 for the one on certain private schools or *grands pensionnats*. The other four articles all deal with the Central Schools: M. M. Compère, "Les professeurs de la République"; C. Desirat and T. Horde, "La fabrique des élites: théories et pratiques de la grammaire générale dans les écoles centrales"; M. Guy, "L'enseignement de l'histoire dans les écoles centrales"; and my "Le Prytanée français et les écoles de Paris (1798-1802)." These four articles draw heavily on the questionnaire of 1799 mentioned above (*enquête du 20 floréal An VII*) but also on other sources. For the questionnaire see also note 79 below. Many monographs have been written over almost a century on individual Central Schools; see the list given by M. Guy, on pp. 120-22 of this issue of the *AHRF*, which is intended to be used as a supplement to the list in A. Troux, *L'école centrale du Doubs à Besançon (An IV-An XII)* (Paris, 1926), pp. xv-xxi.

arbitrary rules but to understand the reasons underlying them, and history was made relevant to the present by showing progress toward the Enlightenment and the Revolution. The faculty of each school was self-governing; there was no principal or head. The schools were day schools, without boarding facilities. They were "comprehensive" in stressing both cultural and vocational aims, and in teaching the sons of both professional elites and artisan and shopkeeping families. Students were made to participate in the community by visits to workshops and taking part in national festivals. The schools were likewise open to the community in that each had a library open to the public, and adults were welcomed in the classrooms to hear lectures or observe scientific demonstrations, so that instruction of the young was blended with continuing education.

The liberality of these arrangements was prescribed by a fixed national scheme.[28] The central government simply mandated a model that local governments were expected to follow. All the Central Schools were meant to be alike. Each department had one, regardless of population. Each department had administrative supervision over its school, exercised through a local board of public instruction. The departmental authorities, however, had little freedom, since they had to find and employ teachers whose number and salaries were set by the national government and to provide and maintain physical quarters for the school, while hoping that the central government would make nationalized properties (usually the former college) available for the purpose. Each school, with nine professors and a librarian, whose salary by law equalled that of a departmental administrator (about 2,000 francs), represented a cost, when miscellaneous charges were added, of about 25,000 or 30,000 francs a year. Each department was expected to raise this sum by a kind of surtax added to the national real estate tax. The law of 3 Brumaire provided also that the professors in each Central School, in addition to their salaries, should divide among themselves the proceeds of a fee of not over 25 francs a year to be paid by the students. A quarter of the students might be excused from the fee by the departmental authorities. In any case, the sum of 25 francs was so trifling (in comparison to the expense) that all students in effect enjoyed *instruction gratuite* at the cost of fellow citizens in the department. It will be recalled that the law of 3 Brumaire made no provision for salaries for primary schools at all. The interest of the State was in the production of an educated minority, though not a minority of birth

[28] The law of 3 Brumaire of the Year IV; see note 12 above.

or fortune, since a good many boys of modest condition did in fact attend the Central Schools.

It seems to have been thought that a central plan could be carried out without much central authority, or that national uniformity could be achieved by voluntary local action. Neither the minister of the interior nor his aides in the Fifth Division were able to do very much. Their abundant correspondence with the Central Schools consists of exhortations, warnings, advice, unenforceable instructions, requests for reports, and enquiries and surveys from which statistics could be assembled. This embryo of a later ministry of public instruction had no control over the qualification or placement of teachers, no budgetary freedom, no traveling inspectors. It could only attempt to carry out the details of the law of 3 Brumaire. Here again, the supposed tradition of Revolutionary centralization must be understood in a qualified sense. There was centralization of planning but as yet little centralization of power.

Specifically, the law called for nine professors to teach nine subjects in each school, together with a library and a librarian, and with a botanical garden and cabinet of scientific equipment. The only requirement for admission to any of the courses was age, and the planners grouped the courses with names as follows, thus indicating a sequence in which they hoped the subjects would be studied:

MINIMUM AGE TWELVE
Drawing
Ancient Languages
Natural History

MINIMUM AGE FOURTEEN
Mathematics
Physics and Chemistry

MINIMUM AGE SIXTEEN
General Grammar
Belles-Lettres
History
Legislation

The law gave no further details, but from the reports sent in to the ministry in 1799 we can tell what happened in practice.

The age limits were universally disregarded, and the ages of students, not counting adult auditors, might run from eleven to over twenty in almost any course. The professors in each school arranged their own class hours and the length of their courses. Almost all professors held only one class, which they met for an hour and a half or two hours either every day or every second day of the *décade*. Each could limit his course to one year or extend it to two or even three years as he chose. The Physics-Chemistry course lasted for one year in 24 schools, for two years in 28, and for three years in two, while the frequency of classes ran from three to eight meetings per *décade*.[29] In most places the course in History lasted for two years, in some for three, and the professor at Nancy planned to traverse the whole of ancient and modern times in nine years, meeting his class for three hours six times a *décade*.[30] Conflicts of schedule were in any case not very serious, since in a given year some students took only one course, some took two, and only a small minority took as many as three. The Central School at Besançon had a plan by which a student could cover all nine courses in nine years, but it reported that no student had ever expressed the intention of doing so.[31] Perhaps the widest departure from the norm was at Lyon, where the school put General Grammar and History at the first or lowest level, Drawing and Belles-Lettres at the second, and Physics-Chemistry and Natural History at the third. Lyon, which had suffered heavily during the Terror, was not inclined to take orders from Paris; it did not even reply to the questionnaire of 1799.[32]

It was a principal duty of the departmental administrators and local boards to recruit the teachers, and they did so with surprising success considering that they received no assistance from national headquarters. In Paris, which had three Central Schools because of its large population, some of the teachers were eminent men, or later became so; they included the paleontologist George Cuvier in Natural History, Sylvestre Lacroix in Mathematics, M. J. Brisson in Physics and Chemistry, F. U. Domergue (the Idéologue) in General Grammar, P.C.L. Guéroult (formerly of the University of Paris, later the first head of the Ecole Normale established in 1808) in Ancient Languages, and J.P.L. Fontanes (later head of the Napoleonic university) in Belles-

---

[29] Archives Nationales, F^{17} 1341^A no. 144.

[30] M. Guy, "L'enseignement de l'histoire," p. 105.

[31] Archives Nationales, F^{17} 1339, doss. 11, no. 117.

[32] And hence, for the point in the preceding sentence, see S. Charléty, *Histoire de l'enseignement secondaire dans le Rhône de 1789 à 1900* (Paris, 1901), p. 37. There were many plans that closely followed the law of 3 Brumaire, for example, one announced by the professors at Versailles, setting forth the aims, content, and hours of their courses in a brochure of 24 pages: *Aux pères et mères de famille habitant le département de Seine-et-Oise* (Versailles, n.d., but probably the summer of 1795 or 1796). Doubtless at the Bibliothèque Nationale, but the copy used is at the British Library, Croker, F 499-20.

Lettres.[33] All these except Guéroult were members of the National Institute. Positions in the Paris Central Schools were also offered in 1795 to three sexagenarians of the pre-Revolutionary intelligentsia, Morellet, Marmontel, and Suard, but they all declined, doubtless without loss to the students.[34] Outside Paris most of the teachers were recruited locally, though some came from Paris, and the most successful of the Central Schools became, as the planners intended, the centers of intellectual life of their respective departments. The kind of men who had formerly frequented the provincial academies now found a new focus for their interests, where they could either teach or attend lectures as auditors.[35]

A study has been made of 629 professors in the Central Schools on the basis of their replies to the questionnaire of 1799. It shows that the professor of Drawing was usually a painter, and the professor of Legislation a lawyer, sometimes also a member of the departmental administration. Medical doctors were prominent among professors of Natural History. Those teaching the other subjects had most commonly been teachers by previous occupation, either full or part time: as many as 90 percent of those in Ancient Languages, and 80 percent in Mathematics and Physics-Chemistry, a reminder that mathematics and science had not been as neglected before the Revolution as has often been claimed. Seven out of 10 of the former teachers had taught in the old colleges, the others mostly in "private" schools. Veterans of the *congrégations séculières* abolished in 1792 were well represented, with 42 identified as Doctrinaires, and 41 as Oratorians. About 78 of the professors had been enrolled in the Ecole Normale of 1795. About a third, not counting those of Drawing, were or had been priests. Recalling that many clerics in the pre-Revolutionary colleges had been more teachers than ecclesiastics in their frame of mind, and observing that actual priests, ex-priests, and lesser clergy in the Central Schools were of the kind most receptive to new ideas, the author of this study, M. M. Compère, is prompted to ask whether the Central Schools marked so abrupt a change from the Old Regime, or so sudden a step in secularization, as has been supposed.[36] It is clear, however, that modernizing tendencies present before 1789 had prevailed. Teaching, even for men with a clerical background, was becoming a recognized profession dissociated from the church.

[33] Professors in the Central Schools were considered so important that their names were given, with addresses where possible, in the *Almanach national* every year.

[34] Archives Nationales, F[17] 1344[27].

[35] Compère, "Les professeurs," as in note 27 above.

[36] See Compère's tabulations, ibid., pp. 43 and 54.

Students in the Central Schools came from families well disposed toward the Revolution, and mostly living in the towns in which the schools were located, since there were no boarders. Some schools, however, had pupils who lived in nearby private *pensionnats* or boarding establishments. This was especially true in Paris, where two of the three Central Schools, called the Panthéon and the Quatre-Nations, like their predecessors the 10 colleges of the University of Paris, attracted most of their students from other parts of France. Some of them lived at the Prytanée français, the new name in 1798 for Equality College (formerly Louis-le-Grand), in which the scholarships inherited from the Old Regime were now concentrated. For 885 of the 979 students registered in the three Paris schools in the fall of 1799 we can know something of their social status.[37] About 30 percent were the sons of well-to-do property-owning families; another 30 percent of artisans, shopkeepers, and even ordinary workers; 25 percent of government officials and lesser employees; and 12 percent of lawyers and other members of liberal professions. For the schools outside Paris information is sparse and sporadic. At Besançon in 1802 the prize winners included the sons of a hairdresser, a locksmith, a carpenter, a *concierge*, and someone called an *employé à l'histoire*. At Carcassonne there were sons of "a poor country doctor," a shoemaker, two widowed mothers, an ex-soldier with three children, and a minor employee of the departmental administration. At Aix-en-Provence one father was listed as a noble, another as an attorney at the former parlement of Provence, others simply as a tailor, a jeweler, a gardener, a printer, and a notary. While having few of the very rich who might prefer private schools, and even fewer of the very poor who had no schooling at all, the Central Schools represented a broad spectrum across the bourgeois and working classes.[38]

The questionnaire of 1799 did not ask for the number of students in each school, but it did ask each professor for the number in his own class. From their replies, with emendations, one obtains a total of 17,626 course enrollments within the pre-Revolutionary French borders, and since we know from many monographic sources that each student on the average took somewhat less than two courses, we can infer with

[37] See my tabulation, "Le Prytanée français," ibid., p. 138.

[38] Troux, *Besançon* (n. 27 above), pp. 104-105; A. Poux, *Plan d'études et programmes de l'Ecole Centrale de l'Aude (Carcassonne)* (Carcassonne, n.d., but about 1910); C. Bloch, "L'instruction publique dans l'Aude pendant la Révolution," *Revue internationale de l'enseignement* 27 (1894):216-17; and F. Nicollet, *Histoire de l'enseignement secondaire en Provence. L'école centrale du département des Bouches-du-Rhône, 1798-1802* (Aix-en-Provence, 1913).

some certainty that in 1799 there were about 10,000 students in the Central Schools as a whole, within the pre-Revolutionary borders. There were probably a few more when the Central Schools were suppressed in 1802.[39]

Since there had been about 50,000 in the old colleges it is clear that the Central Schools were not successfully replacing them, and that they suffered from a resurgence of schools, now called "private," whose existence was guaranteed by the constitution. When Sorèze became a private school it attracted more students than the Central School of the Tarn at Albi. The Central School at Angers (Maine-et-Loire), with somewhat less than 200 students, suffered from having three private schools in the city, which together had nearly 400, over half of whom were boarders. At Lille the Central School had about 200 students, but it competed with 34 private schools in the department of the Nord. One of the largest and most successful of the Central Schools was at Strasbourg, but it was patronized mainly by the French-speaking and official element in the population, so that the old German *gymnase protestant*, a "public" school in the pre-Revolutionary sense, becoming "private" in 1795, easily rivaled or exceeded it in numbers. It is probable that in all France there were fewer than 20 Central Schools with as many as 200 pupils, whereas there had been 80 colleges with at least this many before the Revolution.[40]

Free to study whatever they wanted to, the students distributed themselves among the courses very unequally. The 17,626 enrollments were made up as follows:

Drawing	6,038
Ancient Languages	2,154
Natural History	1,664
Mathematics	3,440
Physics and Chemistry	1,156
General Grammar	1,179
Belles-Lettres	707
History	826
Legislation	462

[39] See my "Central Schools of the First French Republic," in Baker and Harrigan's *The Making of Frenchmen*, p. 227; and note 11 of chap. 1 above.

[40] J. Fabre de Massaguel, *L'école de Sorèze de 1758 au 19 fructidor An IV* (Paris, 1958), p. 188; B. Bois, *La vie scolaire en Anjou pendant la Révolution, 1789-1799* (Paris, 1929), p. 476; P. L. Marchand, "L'enseignement secondaire dans le département du Nord au lendemain de la Révolution et la loi de Floréal An X," *AHRF* (1974), pp. 235-60; R. Reuss, *Histoire du Gymnase protestant de Strasbourg pendant la Révolution* (Paris, 1891), pp. 161, 186.

The extreme preponderance of Drawing is apparent. Mathematics (at its various levels) was a favorite subject, but the low figure for Physics and Chemistry suggests that the plan for emphasizing modern subjects was not very effectively carried out, especially when we remember that there had been perhaps as many as 5,000 students studying physics in a given year in the colleges of the Old Regime. Sylvestre Lacroix, who taught mathematics at the Central School of the Quatre-Nations in Paris, and was later of the College of France, and who in 1804 published a retrospective defense of the Central Schools, nevertheless thought that an exceptional student could go further in mathematics in a good college before the Revolution, as indeed he himself had done.[41]

The freedom in election of courses, by which a student could attend only one, or two, or three as he or his parents preferred, together with the fact that few students remained in the school for more than two consecutive years, meant that the schools lacked institutional coherence and identity, and the students were deprived of any sense of annual progression. A list exists of the names of 102 pupils, with the courses in which they were enrolled in the Year VII (1798-1799) at the Central School of the Haute-Marne at Chaumont.[42] Twenty of these students took only one course, 67 took two, and 15 took three. Eighty-six of them were studying Drawing, among whom eight studied nothing else, 63 took one other course in addition to Drawing, and 15 took two other courses, the additional courses being chiefly Ancient Languages, Mathematics, and General Grammar, which, however, was divided at Chaumont into a class of 27 in elementary grammar and only 11 in General Grammar in the sense meant by the law of 3 Brumaire. It is clear that most of these students at Chaumont

---

[41] For the figures, with a critique of their accuracy, see my article, "Central Schools of the First French Republic," cited above in note 39. L. Pearce Williams, in "Science, Education and the French Revolution," *Isis*, 44 (1953):311-30, concluded from a study of the questionnaire of 1799 that the Central Schools had only a few students studying mathematics and physics beyond an elementary level, and that their reputation for preparing students for the entrance examinations to the Polytechnique has been much exaggerated. For what is said above about Lacroix see his *Essai sur l'enseignement en général et sur celui des mathématiques en particulier* (Paris, 1805; new ed., Paris, 1816), p. 66. Lacroix was a great writer of textbooks, which were translated into English, but he was sufficiently eminent as a mathematician to be included in C. C. Gillispie, ed., *Dictionary of Scientific Biography*, vol. 7 (1973). He was also an early biographer of Condorcet; see R. Taton, "Condorcet et S. F. Lacroix," *Revue d'histoire des sciences*, 12 (1959):127-38 and 243-62.

[42] *Examen général et public des élèves de l'Ecole Centrale de la Haute-Marne, An VII de la République* (Chaumont, An VII). Archives Nationales, F^{17} 1344^3 no. 9. This brochure, in 51 pages, also gives details of the content of the examinations and hence presumably of the courses.

were seeking elementary instruction. Only four of the 102 were in the Physics-Chemistry course, and hardly more in any of the others except those mentioned above.

Nor could many of the students, most of them living at home and attending one or two courses for a few hours during the *décade*, have much sense of attachment to the school or continuity in their schooling. At Aix-en-Provence, out of 14 boys entering in the Year VI (1797-1798), six remained for only one year, three for two years, three for three years, and two for four years. It was common also for numbers recorded at the beginning of the school year to fall off as the year wore on. We may take as an example the replies of the professors of Mathematics to the questionnaire of 1799, which was issued in May of that year. The professor at Caen had had 113 pupils in the preceding fall but only 45 when he returned the questionnaire. At Saintes the number had fallen from 30 to 14. Arbogast, who had served for three years on the Committee of Public Instruction of the Convention and now taught at Strasbourg, had begun the year with 50 students, but "the number is now greatly reduced."[43]

Some of the professors were busy, while others had very little to do. In the same school one professor would have a class of over a hundred, while another had only five or six. Some could do little except lecture, since there were no assistants, all being "professors" of the same rank, ranging in age from the twenties into the seventies. At Nancy in 1799 the professor of Mathematics reported having 100 pupils, his colleague in Physics-Chemistry 15, and in General Grammar nine. At Grenoble there were 132 in Mathematics, 13 in Physics-Chemistry, and only five in General Grammar. Here the professor of General Grammar, named Gattel, a man of fifty-six in 1799 who had taught Philosophy at the College of Grenoble before the Revolution, had as one of his pupils the sixteen-year-old Henri Beyle, better known as Stendhal. Writing over 30 years later, Stendhal remembered Gattel with approval, but his account of the other professors ran from the amusing to the caustic.[44]

[43] Archives Nationales, F^{17} 1339, doss. 24.

[44] Chapters 23 and 24 of Stendhal's *Vie de Henry Brulard*, written in 1835, contain his recollections of the Central School of Grenoble, which he attended for three years. See his *Oeuvres intimes* (Paris, 1955), pp. 188-206. Except for Gattel he gives a rather negative account of his teachers, as well as of his classmates, who included both noble (or ex-noble) and peasant youths. In a self-deprecating picture of his class in Mathematics he claims that while he stood making a demonstration at the blackboard the professor chatted with two young nobles. Yet he won a prize in Mathematics, which he neglects to mention. A list probably printed in the Year VII includes his name "Henri Bayle" (*sic*) as winner of a prize copy of Euler's *Introduction to Infinitesimal Calculus*, in

The degree of success or failure of the Central Schools has long been debated by historians of French education. Creations of the National Convention in its final months, they remained as emblems of the Revolution and the Republic and of modern ideas in general, so that Catholic and conservative writers later dwelt on their faults, and those in the republican, liberal, and laic tradition, in the face of discouraging evidence, argued that they had been at least a fruitful experiment and a step in the right direction. Their defenders held that they were certainly better than the colleges of the Old Regime and might have become still better if they had not been rudely killed off by Napoleon Bonaparte in 1802. It is true that much of the objection of contemporaries to the Central Schools was political and counterrevolutionary. Bonaparte undoubtedly wished to redesign the schools for his own purposes, as he did everything else. But it is also true that some of the more successful private schools were neither vociferously Catholic nor especially reactionary, and that parents might prefer them for educational reasons. It may be that Bonaparte met a real need by insisting on still another plan. It is possible that the intellectuals of 1795 had not in fact produced a viable scheme for the schooling of male adolescents.

The law of 3 Brumaire, by purposely omitting both what Condorcet had called *écoles secondaires* and what he had called *lycées*, implied that the Central Schools should carry out the functions of both, that is, offer something to twelve-year-olds and at the same time operate at a university level. We must of course avoid anachronistic judgments. The pre-Revolutionary university colleges had admitted boys of twelve. The lower faculties of continental European (and Scottish) universities in the eighteenth century often did the same. Even at Göttingen in the 1790s, in its lower or "philosophical" faculty, some of the instruction was quite elementary. As the French began to reorganize the German Left Bank into departments of the Republic they dissolved the universities of Cologne, Bonn, Mainz, and Trier and undertook to replace their professional faculties with special schools and their philosophical faculties with Central Schools, according to the law of 3 Brumaire. The idea was that a Central School was something like the lower faculty of a university, or an improvement on it.[45]

Latin. See the Archives Nationales, AD VIII 27, *Procès-verbal de la distribution des prix décernés aux élèves de l'école centrale du département de l'Isère.*

[45] On Göttingen see the remarks on p. 122 of R. S. Turner, *The Prussian Universities and the Research Imperative, 1806 to 1848* (University Microfilms, Ann Arbor, Mich., a doctoral dissertation at Princeton University, 1973). Lacroix in his *Essai,* defending the *écoles centrales,* listed the courses taught at Jena in 1802 to show how much better the

The trouble was that the Central Schools were tilted in both an advanced and an elementary direction. The professors were ambitious to give higher instruction, but many of the students arrived, given the failures in the primary system, with little knowledge beyond rudimentary literacy. The course in Ancient Languages, meaning beginners' Latin, was designed for boys of twelve and was in fact taken by the youngest students. The course in Legislation was partly intended for those wishing to practice law and was in fact largely taken, since no public law schools existed, by young men for this professional purpose. The course in Mathematics, as we know from the professors' reports, might include anything from simple arithmetic and the metric system to conic sections and calculus. The course in General Grammar, which Daunou and other Ideologues saw as a culminating feature of the program, replacing the "philosophy" of the old colleges, was chosen by few students under the system of free electives, and the professors often found themselves teaching the elementary grammar of the French language instead.[46]

In some of the courses not only the intellectual level but the vocational needs of social classes were confused or overlapping. Natural History, which included bits of botany, zoology, geology, and mineralogy, often with field trips into the country, appealed both to boys expecting to work on the farm and to those aiming at careers in medicine. In addition to students, it attracted many adult auditors hoping to improve their knowledge of pharmacology and materia medica. The professor of Natural History at Toulouse had the unusual number of 157 in his course, of whom 84 were in the "healing arts" and about 100 were auditors.[47] The school at Besançon had a course in obstetrics, another sign that the Central Schools were attempting to replace the medical faculties of the Old Regime.

The course in Drawing illustrates the same point. One third of all course enrollments in all the Central Schools were in Drawing, which attracted pupils from the whole range of social classes present in the

---

German universities were than the French universities before the Revolution, and that the Central Schools had been meant to approach a standard set by the German universities (pp. 87 and 142-47). There is a good deal on reconstruction of the German Rhineland universities during the French period in J. Hansen *Quellen zur Geschichte des Rheinlandes im Zeitalter der französischen Revolution*, 4 vols. (Bonn, 1931-1938), vol. 4; see the index, "Zentralschulen."

[46] On General Grammar see Desirat and Horde, "La fabrique des élites," pp. 61-88; F. Brunot, *Histoire de la langue française*, 13 vols. (Paris, 1905-1979), 9:320-22 and 343-52; and professors' reports in the Archives Nationales, F17 1344² and 1339 doss. 24.

[47] Archives Nationales, F17 1339, doss. 24.

schools. One purpose of the course reflected the "ideology" of the Idéologues; it was to train the sense of sight, give practice in close observation, coordinate the hand and eye, and turn the pupil's attention to "things" instead of to words and persons. It was meant also to be vocationally useful to boys preparing for the skilled trades, who would learn to use the instruments of mechanical drawing, and to produce the floral and geometric designs necessary for cabinet makers, goldsmiths, silversmiths, stone cutters, textile designers, builders, and architects. It thus carried out the idea of *écoles secondaires destinées aux artistes et ouvriers de tous genres* found in the Paris plan of 1793, itself derived from the Bureau of Consultation and the Committee on Public Instruction. Many boys in the Central Schools did study Drawing for this purpose. Others, however, studied it as a cultural subject. From a reading of the reports of the professors of Drawing in 1799 one gains the impression that the latter purpose prevailed, that the course aimed at imparting good taste as well as manual skills, and that students were set to sketching and to copying from engravings of paintings and plaster casts of sculptures, including what were called "academies," that is, nudes.[48]

It is a curious fact that J. J. Bachelier, who had founded the Royal Free School of Design back in 1766 for working-class youths, was professor of Drawing at the Central School of the Panthéon in Paris in the later 1790s. The Free School of Design still existed, "open since thirty years ago for 1,500 boys aiming at mechanical occupations," and Bachelier was still one of its directors. We know also, from his report of 1799, that he had 180 students at the Panthéon and that his class met daily from nine in the morning until one-thirty in the afternoon, from which we can picture a large studio where a throng of pupils came and went with interruptions for morning classes in other subjects. "The models that he has his students copy," Bachelier said, speaking of himself in the third person, "are from the best ancient and modern masters as shown by engravings, to which he adds the study of casts in the antique style, which he has been obliged to borrow, being unable to obtain any from the Department."[49]

It appears that at the Panthéon, as in Central Schools elsewhere, the course in Drawing in part duplicated the work of the free schools of design and in part had a more elevated aim. The large enrollments

[48] Archives Nationales, F17 1341 B.

[49] Ibid., and p. 29 above. The existence of the Free School of Design is announced by the *Almanach national* for every year of the Revolution in only slightly changing language; the quotation is from the *Almanach* for the Year VIII, pp. 478-79.

show that it brought together boys of the working class and of the bourgeoisie. Many students, however, took no other course. These constituted a more purely artisan element within a school generally concerned with elite education. When the Central Schools were abolished the courses in Drawing in some cases continued as separate schools of design, as before the Revolution. The experiment in mixing different social classes with different needs and purposes in the same school was to this extent given up.[50]

A similar problem arose in the two science courses, Natural History and Physics-Chemistry, which included attention to practical problems and often to those of local importance, according to the climate, soils, and natural resources of a region, since Natural History was useful to agriculturalists and apothecaries, and Physics-Chemistry to persons in metallurgical and other trades. The weakness of the Central Schools, according to André Léon, was that they tried to do too much for too many people, in a lingering conflict between equalitarian ideals and a need for selectivity for higher or more theoretical levels, "whose difficult study," in the words even of the democratic Paris plan of 1793, "is not within the capacity of all men."[51]

There was another ambivalence in that while the best of the schools might give a sound instruction in the prescribed subjects, they also conveyed an ideology (in the modern sense) that could be offensive to many parents, and to the church. Thus the teaching of physics was probably good, despite shortages of scientific equipment, since 80 percent of the teachers had taught before, but physics was also praised as a cure for "superstition." The course in Legislation gave lessons in civics, the rights of man, and the principles of the constitution, but it was also meant to free the world from that "scourge of humanity," the professional lawyers. The Latin teacher at Tulle taught etymologies and conjugations, but also that "the consent of all peoples proves the existence of the Supreme Being," and that "knowledge is the food of the soul."[52] General Grammar presented an empirical philosophy derived from Condillac, but with its analysis of sensations and ideas it also undermined religion. It could also be quite absurd. The professor of the subject at Cahors had his pupils understand "that vowels are the expression of our sensations, and consonants the image of our ideas,

[50] A. Léon, *La Révolution française et l'enseignement technique* (Paris, 1968), pp. 203-205.

[51] See above, p. 161; Léon, ibid., p. 217, and Williams, "Science, Education and the French Revolution."

[52] G. Clément-Simon, *Histoire du collège de Tulle depuis son origine jusqu'à la création du Lycée (1567-1887)* (Paris, 1892), p. 367.

so that each sign of the alphabet has for them its own determinate value."[53] At Nîmes, in interviewing candidates for the professorship of History, the educational board looked for no "sterile knowledge of facts" but someone with "that enlightened philosophy . . . that considers history as a series of moral and political experiments for the use of posterity," and who would trace "the history of the human mind, the route it has followed, the obstacles that have blocked it, the social institutions of different peoples, their laws, arts, customs and manners, the influence of religious opinions and especially the progress of liberty."[54] History thus pointed out the evils of monarchy, tyranny, fanaticism, and priestcraft.

The books recommended by professors to their students show an aspiration for advanced studies together with a strong commitment of the philosophy of the Enlightenment. Of 45 professors of History who told the minister of the interior what books they used many mentioned simple chronological tables and the rather tame works of Rollin and Millot, but 25 mentioned Condillac, 15 Mably, and 10 Voltaire. They made generous use also of French translations of British writers, including Priestley, Gibbon, and Adam Smith.[55] A list of books requested for its library by the Central School at Lille suggests the tone of that establishment; it included the *Encyclopédie*; the complete works of Voltaire, Rousseau, Diderot, and Mably; the *Journal des savants*; and the memoirs of the new National Institute, Buffon, Linnaeus, and Lacépède in botany, Euler and Legendre in mathematics, and in history Gibbon's *Decline and Fall of the Roman Empire* and Dupuis's *Origine de tous les cultes*, a work that shocked contemporaries by declaring that Jesus Christ was as mythical a being as Hercules.[56]

It was thus for reasons of both philosophical tone and pedagogical methods that the Central Schools suffered from low enrollments and could with difficulty compete with private schools. Even partisans of the Republic and the Enlightenment felt the need for more structure

[53] Rouziès, *Tableau analytique des études de l'Ecole Centrale du Lot présenté au Ministre de l'Intérieur par le citoyen Rouziès, professeur de Grammaire Generale à la même école* (Paris, An VII), p. 10. All courses in the curriculum are described.

[54] Guy, "L'enseignement de l'histoire," p. 95. See also L. Trénard, "Manuels scolaires au 18ᵉ siècle et sous la Révolution," *Revue du Nord* (April-June 1973).

[55] Guy, "L'enseignement de l'histoire," p. 99.

[56] J. Peter, *L'enseignement secondaire dans le département du Nord pendant la Révolution, 1789-1802* (Lille, 1912), pp. 152-53. The ministry of the interior, recommending books to be awarded as prizes in 1798, included the works of Locke, Condillac, and Court de Gébelin for prizes in General Grammar, and those of Montesquieu, Rousseau, Holbach, Beccaria, Filangieri, and Adam Smith for those in Legislation. See the *Décade philosophique* for 20 Thermidor of the Year VI, p. 309.

and discipline in the plan of study, with more sense of direction, than the law of 3 Brumaire had provided. We must therefore turn again to plans, discussions, and reports, first to legislative debates in the Council of Five Hundred in 1798-1799, and then to a special Council on Public Instruction appointed in 1799 to advise the minister of the interior, and of which most of the members were Idéologues.

More Democrats: The Debate of the Year VII

Hardly had the law of 3 Brumaire gone into effect when proposals were made to change it, in a general feeling that the reform of 1795 needed further reform. Ginguené himself, as chief of the bureau of public instruction, observed in March 1796 that the old educational system had been destroyed and no new one yet replaced it.[57] One consequence was a frequent complaint by professors in the Central Schools that they felt no certainty for the future. In the legislative chambers, especially in the Council of the Five Hundred, during the four years of the Directory, discussions went on that repeated much of what had been said from 1792 to 1795, but which produced no results, so that, with Penelope still undoing and redoing the work of her loom, and the Directory seeming a dull interlude between the Convention and the Consulate, these discussions have received less attention than they deserve.[58] This is especially true of a debate that lasted intermittently from November 1798 to the end of April 1799, that is, through half the Year VII, which in the intelligent presentation of conflicting viewpoints and in comprehensive coverage of the whole subject, was surely one of the best that occurred during the whole Revolutionary decade.

The debates expressed a demand for further democratization and stronger national controls, and were also highly politicized. At first the matters touched on were fairly routine. Although 45 departments expressed a desire to have a professor of modern languages in their Central Schools, the Five Hundred discussed the question but took no action.[59] In the summer of 1797, by the law of 25 Messidor of the Year V, the sale of properties formerly belonging to the old colleges was discontinued. Since these properties remained in the national do-

[57] *Décade philosophique*, 10 Germinal IV, pp. 15-28.

[58] An exception must be made for M. S. Staum, who in his *Cabanis: Enlightenment and Medical Philosophy in the French Revolution* (Princeton, 1980), devotes pp. 272-81 to the debate of the Year VII.

[59] Archives Nationales, AF III 108.

main there were some who hoped that the resulting income might be used instead of tax revenues to finance an educational system. Then in September came the coup d'état of Fructidor, when under dangers real and imagined of a monarchical restoration the more positive republicans drove out the royalists and various moderates.

On the day after the coup d'état, on September 5, 1797, an old Jacobin, P. J. Audouin, obtained in the Five Hundred the creation of a Commission on Republican Institutions, to strengthen "institutions for guaranteeing the continuance of the Republic."[60] The word "institution" meant the process of instituting as well as a thing already instituted. The government therefore "instituted" stricter controls on nobles, clergy, and royalist plotters. The increased suspicion of priests caused difficulty for both private and public schools. It was at this time that the government ordered the local authorities to send inspectors into private schools, tried to ferret out unauthorized schoolbooks, demanded enforcement of the republican calendar and hence the opening of schools on Sundays and the observance of the half-holiday of the *quintidi* and holiday of the *décadi*, and required that anyone in government employment must have his child in a public school (*primaire* or *centrale*) and in the future have attended such a school himself. In March 1798 it was ordered that no one might be head of a private school unless widowed or married, in an attempt to exclude both constitutional and refractory priests and even ex-priests who had not, by marrying, made a public and irrevocable commitment to the new civil order.

The election to the legislative chambers in the spring of 1798, which under the constitution was an annual affair, produced a large number of democratically minded or "Jacobin" deputies. The government, however, having put down the Right in the preceding September, now was uneasy at the mounting influence of the Left. Raising an alarm over a return of the Terror, the "Directorials" quashed the election of about a hundred deputies, in what was called the coup d'état of Floréal in May 1798.

Quite a few democrats, however, survived the coup d'état of Floréal. After both coups there were still 140 deputies of the Left and 110 or 120 of the Right still sitting among the 750 in the Council of Five Hundred and the Council of *Anciens*.[61] It is the democrats who are of

[60] *Moniteur* for 25 Fructidor of the Year V, p. 1425, and 26 Vendémiaire of the Year VI.

[61] J. R. Suratteau, *Les élections de l'an VI et le coup d'état du 22 floréal* (Paris, 1971), pp. 445-46; Lynn Hunt et al., "The Failure of the Liberal Republic," *Journal of Modern History* (December, 1979), p. 741.

the most interest for our purposes. None had played any great role in the Revolution hitherto; only a few had been members of the Convention, and one had been a liberal noble in the Estates-General of 1789 and hence a member of the Constituent Assembly. Here again we note the rapid coming and going of characters on the Revolutionary stage. The participants in the educational debate of the Year VII, most of them elected in the Year VI, had in most cases been local administrators during the opening years of the Revolution and during the Terror; they made their speeches in the Five Hundred in the Year VII and so were reported in the national press; and after Bonaparte's coup d'état of the Year VIII they returned to private life or became officials under the Consulate and Empire. The fact that ordinary persons could express carefully thought out ideas on education in 1798-1799 of course shows that it was not only the intellectuals of Paris who concerned themselves with the subject.

Chief spokesman in these debates was Roger Martin of Toulouse. Born in 1741, he had been a professor of physics before the Revolution, and would be so again after 1800. Elected to the Five Hundred in 1795, and so a member of that body from the beginning, he was a firm but not extravagant republican, who in 1796 and 1797 made several unsuccessful attempts to get reconsideration of the educational system. He was joined in these efforts in the summer of 1798 by several newly elected colleagues of democratic views. One of these was the noble (or ex-noble) already mentioned, Heurtault de Lamerville, who like Roger Martin was a man in his fifties. He had been an army officer before the Revolution, then an administrator in the department of the Cher from 1791 to 1795. Two others were young men still in their twenties. One was Félix Bonnaire, who was teaching in an Oratorian college in 1789, then worked with Heurtault-Lamerville in the Revolutionary administration of the Cher, and later, under Bonaparte, became prefect of the Hautes-Alpes and a baron of the Empire. The other was P. J. Briot, an activist of 1793, who taught briefly at the Central School of Besançon in 1797; after his equally brief appearance on the national scene, and his refusal to accept Bonaparte, he went off to Italy, where he became involved in the underground origins of the Carbonari, and so served as a link between the French Revolution and the revolutionary movements of the following century. These three, Heurtault, Bonnaire, and Briot, diverse as they were, formed with Roger Martin the principal members of a team that produced the plan of education soon to be explained.

On June 5, 1798, Roger Martin again raised the question of education in the Five Hundred, in language showing that the revolutionary spirit was not yet extinct. Despite the brilliant conquests of the French people, he said (associated revolutionary republics were forming at this time in Holland, Switzerland, and Italy), the new order was not yet safely established. It was threatened by "a flood of clandestine teaching, an endless conspiracy against reason and liberty, in which ignorance and bad citizenship combine to corrupt the future generation and undermine the Republic at its foundations." What is needed to counter this menace, he continued, is "not a few isolated fragments of national education but one great arrangement of literary establishments, a general and complete system of public instruction combining all the parts, and in which all the parts mutually support and enlighten each other." Roger Martin's motion was seconded by Briot, who said that the Central Schools, as yet hardly organized, already harbored, along with the primary schools, various "royalists and ignorant fanatics" who were protected by "reactionary authorities." Briot also demanded "a general plan for the organization of public instruction and republican institutions."[62]

So the idea arose again of one total, comprehensive, uniform, and centralized plan, this time not primarily as a measure of rational administration, as for Rolland d'Erceville in the 1760s, nor as a means of producing a better world in the future, as for Talleyrand and Condorcet, but as a defense for an order already in existence, still threatened by enemies wishing to overturn it. The Five Hundred agreed, and enlarged and renamed two of its committees into a joint Commission on Public Instruction and Republican Institutions. Public education was all the more politicized. Where the Montagnards of 1793 had expressed doubts on control of schools at all levels by a centralized state, it was now the neo-Jacobins, proto-democrats, and most determined republicans who pressed for centralization.

The Five Hundred also requested the Executive Directory to supply information, with recommendations, on the actual state of the schools. The Directory replied in a message to the legislators in October 1798, signed by one of its members, Treilhard, who had a son at the Central School of the Panthéon. The message, while holding that minor changes in the existing system would be enough, pointed out weaknesses on which it said all were agreed. One such weakness was the void between primary and Central Schools. Since a boy in the primary schools could learn only the elements of reading, writing, and arithmetic and could

[62] *Moniteur*, 20 Prairial of the Year VI, p. 1042, for the session of 17 Prairial. Briot's word *réactionnaire* was new in French in 1798; it came into English a half-century later. See also the *Moniteur* for 8 Messidor, pp. 1123-24.

do so by the age of nine, he either had nothing to do and learned nothing for three years, until the age of twelve when he might enter a Central School, or else he went to a private school where he might be exposed to royalist and Catholic principles. To strengthen the primary schools the Directors proposed a salary for their teachers to be paid by each commune from public funds. To fill the void it proposed a higher primary school for each canton, where history, geography, geometry, drawing, and French and Latin grammar would be taught, as well as a system of prizes to encourage emulation, and competitive scholarships to pay the living costs for a few bright boys away from home, and so enable them to move up from the communal to the cantonal and then to the Central School in the chief town of the Department. Each Central School should in any case have boarding facilities to enable students from outside its town to attend. The Directors also deplored the professorial loquacity that the system of "oral courses" encouraged. "Finished lectures and learned discourses may prove the talents of the professor, but contribute only imperfectly to the progress of the pupils." They might be suitable for older students but should be banned from the Central Schools, where the pupils should have more daily practice in writing and composition. The order of the nine courses might also be rearranged, and General Grammar, having been shown to be pedagogically unsuccessful, might better be replaced by Logic.[63]

In this message from the Directors to the Five Hundred we note the acknowledgment of faults in the existing system, the absence of ideology in the sense of the Idéologues, and a continuing belief in a single-track series of schools, with no thought that the primary and higher levels should be intended for different social classes. It is evident also that the Directors, sensing the ambivalence in the Central Schools, would turn them away from the idea of a university and more toward that of a "secondary" school in the later sense.

Roger Martin and his co-workers produced the report of the Commission on Public Instruction and Republican Institutions almost simultaneously with the message from the Directory. Working independently, they agreed with much in the Directors' statement but went far beyond it. First, Roger Martin explained the plan as a whole in a speech to the Five Hundred, announcing that his colleagues would

[63] The message of the Directory was printed by the Council of Five Hundred; doubtless in the Bibliothèque Nationale, but the copy used here is at the British Library, Croker, FR 235, unnumbered item following no. 21. See also Gontard, *Enseignement primaire*, pp. 180-82.

present the particular parts of it at intervals during the following days. The whole plan was thus set forth in installments:[64]

November 9	Roger Martin	The plan as a whole
12	Heurtault-Lamerville	Primary schools
13	Bonnaire	Central schools
17	Briot	"Lycées," in Condorcet's sense
19	Cabanis	Schools of medicine
21	Hardy	The same, supporting Cabanis
22	Dulaure	Reinforcement of republican institutions
23	Leclerc	Schools of music
26	Heurtault-Lamerville	Schools of painting, sculpture, and architecture

In each case the Five Hundred heard the speaker, ordered his speech printed, and adjourned further consideration until a time when all the printed versions could have been read. When discussion took place, at intervals from January through April 1799, it revolved almost entirely about matters raised in the first four speeches listed above, and most especially on the primary schools. The ideas on medical education expressed by Cabanis and Hardy, which had been fruitlessly debated in the Year VI, also produced no results in the Year VII; one of the most significant of these ideas was that medical schools should not be kept apart as "special schools" but should be merged in the proposed "lycées" where they would benefit from the teaching of the chemical and biological sciences. As for Dulaure's speech, it simply called for strin-

---

[64] Full titles of the first four components of the plan, all under the heading Corps Legislatif: Conseil des Cinq-Cents, are as follows: *Rapport général fait par Roger Martin sur l'organisation de l'instruction publique, séance du 19 Brumaire An VII* (35 pp.); *Rapport fait, au nom des commissions de l'instruction publique et des institutions républicaines réunies, par Heurtault-Lamerville, député du Cher, sur les écoles primaires, séance du 22 Brumaire* (27 pp.); *Rapport fait par Bonnaire (du Cher) au nom des commissions . . . réunies, sur les écoles centrales, séance du 23 Brumaire* (29 pp.); *Rapport fait par Briot (du Doubs) au nom des commissions . . . réunies, sur l'organisations des lycées, 27 Brumaire* (39 pp.). These four, as well as the others listed above and about a hundred other *rapports* and *opinions* having to do with the debates in the Years VI and VII on education, are conveniently assembled in the Maclure collection of French Revolutionary materials at the University of Pennsylvania (vols. 1279, 1280, and 1281), of which microfilm copies exist in other American institutions, including Yale University. The presentation of the plan and ensuing debate can of course also be followed in the *Moniteur.*

gent enforcement of the laws against priests, private schools, and undesirables in the public schools as enacted during the preceding year. Leclerc was interested in music for its part in national festivals and the republican cult. Heurtault-Lamerville argued for schools of painting, sculpture, and architecture to a large extent for the same reason. If little came out of this canvass of the educational scene it must be remembered that the Council of Five Hundred, like the Convention before it, was beset by other questions, such as finances, the salt tax, and sale of émigré lands, and by April 1799 by the disputed elections of the Year VII, arguments over the freedom of the press, the deficit and corruption, and by military reverses, with an Austro-Russian army sweeping through Italy, threatening Switzerland, and heading for an invasion of France.

Within present limits it is possible only to note a few highlights in this plan of the Year VII. It revived the multilevel system of Condorcet. There would be an *école primaire* in every commune, paid for by a school fund to which all taxpayers contributed. Since Condorcet's word *secondaire* had become vague and controversial, the plan called schools at this level *écoles primaires renforcées*. The existing Central Schools occupied the place of Condorcet's *instituts*. The plan used his word *lycée* in the sense of a university. Roger Martin, in the opening exposition, insisted on the need of considering all these levels together, argued that the Republic could afford financially to support them all, and refuted the arguments of those who held, as many had held in 1793, that instruction above the elementary level should be left to private initiative. He allowed for the existence of private schools, as assured by the constitution, but urged the strengthening of the public system as a means of combating them.

Heurtault-Lamerville developed the argument for an improved primary system, which he said must offer, for some at least, more than the "3 Rs" to which the law of 3 Brumaire purposely confined it. There must be "reinforced primary schools" to teach such things as history, geography, grammar, land measurement, and commercial procedures. What was needed was to "bring the primary system, without denaturing it, into closer connection with the Central Schools." The proposal was "in the interest of the poor who become rich only by education, and of not separating the trunk of the tree of knowledge from its roots." In his argument for more and better primary education Heurtault-Lamerville was supported by Cabanis (among others), who differed strongly from his fellow Idéologues on this matter.[65]

---

[65] Heurtault-Lamerville, *Rapport* (see above), pp. 3-4; Staum, *Cabanis*, p. 279.

Bonnaire, reporting on the Central Schools, insisted that their low enrollments were due to political causes inspired by hatred of the Republic, but he nevertheless envisaged significant changes. He repeated the thought that the primary and Central Schools must be more closely joined. The small fee that they charged should be abolished, and scholarships should be provided for the living costs of needy pupils who could not live at home. The age requirement for all courses should be done away with, and entrance to each course should depend on an examination to test readiness for the course. Instead of a supposedly identical Central School in every department there should be two kinds: ordinary Central Schools inclining in the direction of primary education, with two teachers of Latin, Greek, and French grammar instead of one professor of Ancient Languages, and with no Physics-Chemistry taught at all, since it was impossible to teach physics to boys who knew no mathematics; and 16 more elaborate Central Schools in 16 important towns (including three in Belgium) where there should be two professors of Mathematics instead of one, and Physics-Chemistry should be taught. In all of them, General Grammar should be replaced with a course in how to think (i.e. Logic). Such a proposal was bound to offend the Idéologues. The idea of having two levels of Central Schools anticipated the distinction, made in 1802 and in the Napoleonic university, between the lower level *collèges secondaires* and the higher level *lycées*.[66]

It fell to Briot to make the case for *lycées* in Condorcet's sense of the word. He was the most radical and Jacobinical of the group, and in fact used the word "democracy" several times in his speech. What he proposed was in effect a university of the modern kind, such as France would not have for a long time but would soon develop in Germany. The trouble with the pre-Revolutionary colleges and universities, he said, was that they had been created only for teaching, so that they had been unable to engage in the improvement of knowledge (*le perfectionnement de la science*, or "research") and so could not keep up

---

[66] Bonnaire, *Rapport* (see above), *passim*. He spoke already in the accents of a Napoleonic prefect:

> However you organize education, citizen colleagues, the government must be given the means to stimulate both professors and students in the public schools; and by arousing concern for those haunts of bad citizenship and superstition, those private boarding establishments, the offspring of royalist reaction, that have sprung up all over France, you will arm the government with the authority necessary to paralyze, even to destroy, those which, remaining faithful to the system that created them, might continue to defy the Republic and its institutions. (p. 19)

with the progress of the age. The Central Schools could not serve this function; their pupils were too young. What was needed was five great advanced institutions, geographically distributed in Paris, Brussels, Dijon, Poitiers, and Toulouse. More might be added later, but they must remain few enough to preserve high quality and large enough for all subjects to be taught in the same place. Briot expressly rejected the notion of advanced special schools unconnected with each other. He thought, like Cabanis, that medicine should be taught in the proposed lycées in close proximity to the biological sciences. The study of law, despite the course in Legislation in the Central Schools, he found to be "almost entirely neglected." It would be a "singular disgrace" for France, with its constitutional liberties, to have fewer law professors than Germany. Law and jurisprudence should therefore be located in the lycées. Each *lycée*, admitting students from the Central Schools, with scholarships where necessary, should have about 30 professors, who would enjoy firm tenure "as a guarantee against envy and intrigue." They would teach law, medicine, history, literature, philosophy, mathematics, the natural sciences, and the moral and political sciences—even "anthropology, for example, which is neither the physical nor the moral science of man, but combines them both and inquires into their relationships, and is now taught with some success in the universities of Germany." All subjects should support each other. Not only, said Briot, had the Central Schools despite their faults achieved more than the old colleges had done in a hundred years, but "within five years the lycées that we ask you to organize will have done more for the sciences than all the universities and all the sorbonnes that some people pretend to regret."[67]

When discussion of the plan began, it ran into insuperable opposition. Against repeated pleas by Roger Martin, Heurtault-Lamerville, and Bonnaire, the Five Hundred refused to begin by considering the plan as a whole. Some who took this view did so because they believed primary schooling to be the most important and insisted that it be decided first. Others would hear no talk of a total plan because they wanted to preserve a sector of education free from the state. There was general agreement on the need for universal schooling, but only for rudimentary literacy, and hence only for the ages of about six to ten.

---

[67] Briot, *Rapport* (see above), passim, with the quotations respectively on pp. 6, 23, 21, and 9. Since Briot anticipated the "true" modern university this aspect of the plan of the Year VII was especially praised by Louis Liard, rector of the University of Paris and reformer of French higher education in the 1890s, in his *L'enseignement supérieur en France, 1789-1893*, 2 vols. (Paris, 1888-1894), 1:297-306.

The proposal for "reinforced primary instruction" won little support. All these views had been expressed in the Convention six years before.

Some ultra-democrats thought that the plan did not go far enough, less for pedagogical than for social reasons. As in 1793, the case for a democratization of education was damaged by the bugbear of "education in common." One of the ultras, a man with the un-French name of Sherlock, of whom nothing seems to be known, called for *éducation commune* along the lines of Lepeletier's plan of 1793, that is, the forcible removal of children from their parents so that rich and poor could be educated alike.[68] Another, J.P.F. Duplantier from Bordeaux, also demanded *éducation commune*; mere supervision over private schools was not enough, they must be suppressed, and mandatory public schools should be set up as "strong dikes against the crimes and errors of inequality."[69] A third was L. F. Sonthonax, a firebrand who had been sent to Saint-Domingue in 1792 to deal with the consequences of the slave rebellion; he had proclaimed the abolition of slavery there (the modern Haiti), recruited the blacks to assist in defense against the British, worked with Toussaint l'Ouverture, and been elected in Saint-Domingue to speak for that colony in the Five Hundred. He, too, called for *éduction commune*, to which he added the need for a national language, declaring that the West was backward because it could not communicate with the rest of France. Rich and poor should be forced to go to school together; the son belonged "less to the father than to the country"; and anyway, what would have become of the Romans if they had been taught "to regret the Tarquins and blaspheme the memory of Brutus and Scaevola"?[70]

For those who may be called liberals, including various Idéologues and the editors of the *Décade philosophique*, the plan went much too far. Like some of the Montagnards of 1793, they rejected the idea of a comprehensive system of state-controlled education. They agreed on the necessity of universal primary schooling, to be limited to the bare elements of reading, writing, arithmetic, and republican morality; and they argued that, realistically speaking, the children of the mass of the people had neither the time, the need, nor the inclination to spend more than three or four years at school. They found themselves asserting also, unlike the Montagnards, and anticipating what later hap-

[68] *Opinion de Sherlock (député de Vaucluse) sur la nécessité de rendre l'instruction publique commune à tous les enfants des Francais, séance du 24 Nivôse VII.*

[69] *Opinion de J.P.F. Duplantier (député de la Gironde) sur l'établissement des écoles primaires nationales, séance du 24 Nivôse.*

[70] *Opinion de Sonthonax sur le projet présenté par la commission d'instruction publique, relativement aux écoles primaires, séance du 1 Ventôse,* with quotation from p. 8.

pened, that the primary system should be entirely separate and self-enclosed, with no connection to the schools above it. The great error of the commission, said J. C. Bailleul, was to suppose that the primary schools were or ought to be a step toward the Central Schools; actually, they had nothing to do with each other.[71]

On April 7, 1799, Heurtault-Lamerville made a long speech attempting compromise and conciliation. He was answered by Boulay de la Meurthe, who was well to the left at this time, but who said that the primary schools would fail if they tried to do too much, that private schools should be allowed at all levels, that republican morality could not be imposed by force, that the English republic of the seventeenth century had failed because it became too extreme, that ancient Athens had had private teachers, and that Adam Smith, that "colossus of talents," had pointed out the laziness and incompetence of teachers maintained without competition by public or endowed funds. The Republic should leave things alone—*laissez-faire, voilà la grande maxime qui doit diriger le gouvernement.*[72] Bonnaire replied in defense of the plan. If left to free enterprise, he insisted, either there would be no education at all or it would be "an education in counterrevolution and fanaticism." As for Athens, anyone there "who had talked in favor of the King of the Persians would have been torn to pieces by the people."[73]

The final word was spoken by Andrieux, a well-known literary man, deputy from Paris, and collaborator in the *Décade philosophique.* After noting the fantastic cost of the commission's plan, and remarking that France already excelled in the arts and sciences without any great unified system of higher learning, and declaring that republican morality should be inculcated by everyone and not merely by schoolteachers, he called it a great error to suppose that the primary schools should lead on upward to further education. The commission was wrong, he said, in calling the primary school the "peristyle to the temple of the arts." It was no peristyle; it should be a plain small building built for utility. In a republic where 20 out of 30 million could not read, it

[71] *Motion d'ordre faite par J. C. Bailleul sur la discussion relative aux institutions républicaines, séance du 9 Germinal.* For comment on the debate in the *Décade philosophique* see its numbers for 30 Brumaire (p. 384), 10 Frimaire (p. 448), 20 Nivôse (p. 126), 20 Pluviôse (pp. 253-56), 30 Germinal (pp. 190-91), and 10 Floréal (pp. 254-55).

[72] *Moniteur* for 23 Germinal, p. 826, 851, reporting the session of 18 Germinal. Boulay's speech was apparently never printed. His unusual reference to the Cromwellian republic may be explained by the fact that he had just finished writing a book on the subject.

[73] *Moniteur* for 1 Floréal, pp. 879-80; the speech was apparently never printed.

should teach reading above all else. The bright boy, having learned to read, would then find his own way to higher things, though Andrieux did not explain how.

"There is a widely circulated idea," said Andrieux,

> and one much accredited up to a certain point, that a gap exists in our present system of instruction between the primary and Central Schools, and that this gap must be filled by the secondary schools of Condorcet or by reinforced primary schools of the present report. We are offered a system of instruction in which it seems that every Frenchman should begin in the primary school and end up in the National Institute. I confess that I am far from adopting any such idea or sharing in such a systematic notion.[74]

The debate petered out in the political crisis of the following months, with the two legislative chambers staging a counter coup d'état against the Directors, bringing on a "neo-Jacobin" revival and threats of terrorist measures, as the Russians under Suvarov moved into Switzerland and an Anglo-Russian force landed in Holland, to all of which a resolution was found in Bonaparte's coup d'état of Brumaire in November of 1799. The great educational plan of the Year VII evaporated like its predecessors. It failed to achieve the grand structure that it aimed at. Nothing was done to correct faults in the primary and Central schools on which many good republicans were in agreement.

In the general breakdown of constitutional government it seems clear that education was not to be improved by the free and open discussion of parliamentary methods. But at the same time, during this Year VII, the executive was attempting reform through administrative means, by the appointment of a special Council on Public Instruction.

AND IDÉOLOGUES: THE COUNCIL ON PUBLIC INSTRUCTION

François de Neufchâteau, minister of the interior for two months in 1797 and again for about a year in 1798-1799, was an energetic administrator in the numerous areas for which the ministry was responsible. He had a budget of 44 million francs for the Year VII, of which 17 million were for hospitals and charitable institutions, five million for public instruction, one million for the production of standard weights

---

[74] *Opinion de Andrieux (de la Seine) sur l'instruction publique dans les écoles primaires. Séance du 1 Floréal.* Printed later, in Messidor. For the quotations see p. 20. Andrieux's speech was praised in the *Décade philosophique*, to which he was a frequent contributor; see the number for 30 Germinal of the Year VII, pp. 190-91.

and measures to be sent out in introducing the new metric system, and so on for various other purposes. He busied himself with the improvement of internal waterways, draining of marshes, development of agricultural stations, and turning the Louvre into a public museum of art. He was the moving spirit in the industrial exhibition held at the Champ de Mars in September 1798, said to be the first of its kind, and of which one of the express purposes was to display manufactures that might compete with those of England. Here, in 67 arcades, were to be seen such items as steel razors, rifle-barreled guns, new escapements for clocks, new balances for the precise weighing of metals, the new typographic designs of the Didots, and cotton yarns and fabrics. "Technology," as the minister said in his opening address at the exhibition, "is in fact opening up a vast field."[75]

He turned his attention also to education. (He was himself the son of a village schoolteacher.) In September 1797 he issued a circular to all professors in the Central Schools, asking that they submit to him their *cahiers*, that is, the materials used in their courses, such as copies of their notes and lectures, their plans of study, and lists of books read both by themselves and by their students. The professors were so slow in complying with this difficult assignment that they had to be reminded of it in July 1798 and again in May and September 1799. The minister hoped also to raise the tone of the Central Schools by encouraging rivalry or emulation. Praising the old *concours général* of the pre-Revolutionary University of Paris, which he said had greatly improved the quality of students' work after its introduction in the 1740s, he proposed a similar contest to be held on a grander scale. Where the old *concours* had involved only the 10 Paris colleges, the minister now envisaged one among the hundred Central Schools of the enlarged Republic, a competition in which selected students in each school on a given day would write a paper on a set subject, determined by the national government and revealed only on the day itself, to be turned in with a code number instead of the student's name so that the awards would go without favoritism to the most inventive and best executed work. Nothing came of this idea, which is worth mentioning only as

[75] The budget for the ministry of the interior for the Year VII is itemized in the *Moniteur* for 14 Brumaire of the Year VII. The part of it relating to public instruction (plus weights and measures) is summarized in Column 3 of the Appendix to this book. A description of the industrial exhibition by a British visitor is printed in Crosland, ed., *Science in France in the Revolutionary Era* (note 10 above), pp. 132-39. For François de Neufchâteau's speech see the *Moniteur*, 5 jour complémentaire VI, and for the concluding report on the exhibition, ibid., 2 Brumaire of the Year VII.

a sign of a French taste for competitive meritocracy that both preceded and followed the Revolution.[76]

In October 1798, just as the great debate on education in the Five Hundred was beginning, François de Neufchâteau appointed a Council on Public Instruction to assist and advise him. He selected eight persons, all fellow members of the National Institute. They were given a salary of 6,000 francs a year, three times what a professor in the Central Schools received. Among them were the mathematician Lagrange and the chemist Darcet to speak for the natural sciences. Representing belles-lettres were the grammarian Domergue and an elderly man of letters named Palissot, who had written a comedy called *Les philosophes* back in 1760 that poked fun at those vehicles of the Enlightenment; but Palissot was in fact an admirer of Voltaire and published a *Génie de Voltaire* in 1806. The other four on the Council were all of the class in moral and political sciences of the Institute and in fact of its subsection on "the analysis of sensations and ideas." That is, they were Idéologues—Garat, Ginguené, Jacquemont, and Lebreton. Jacquemont was currently the head of the bureau of public instruction in the ministry, in which Garat and Ginguené had preceded him. Domergue was a professor of General Grammar at the Central School of the Quatre-Nations in Paris. Lagrange held a chair at the Bureau of Longitudes, and Darcet at the College of France. Lagrange and Garat had taught at the Ecole Normale of 1795. The Council was clearly made up of bigwigs of the educational scene. But its members and the legislators who supported Roger Martin's plan in the Council of Five Hundred, all persons of less note, seem to have operated in complete ignorance, or at least disregard, of each other's efforts.[77]

The "ideological" tone of the Council was greatly enhanced by the addition to it, in February 1799, of the founder of Ideology himself, Destutt de Tracy, also a member of the Institute in its section on the analysis of sensations and ideas. He brought with him not only a more doctrinaire insistence on a method of knowledge but a combative spirit of forcible enlightenment. His short tract on "the means of establish-

---

[76] *Lettre du ministre de l'intérieur aux professeurs et bibliothécaires des Ecoles Centrales, 10 Germinal VII*, in the *Moniteur* for 22 Germinal, pp. 322-23.

[77] For the document creating the Council on Public Instruction see the Archives Nationales, F17 1014 doss. 5. Daunou was at first appointed but declined to serve and was replaced by Ginguené. Staum, "The Class of Moral and Political Sciences," p. 372 finds that Jacquemont was not a full-fledged Idéologue. The papers of the Council on Public Instruction are in the Archives Nationales, F17 1011, 1338, and 1339. Short accounts of the Council were written in 1800 by Dumouchel, Jacquemont's successor as chief of the bureau of public instruction, and by Vincent Campenon, secretary to the Council; they are in F17 1339 doss. 25, nos. 388 and 389.

ing the moral character of a people," published a year before, had argued that law was more important than education, or rather that law was itself a means of education, operating through the channels of self-interest, pleasure, and pain to produce appropriate motivations. Nine-tenths of the population, he said, would benefit more from a reduction of taxes than from a legion of schoolteachers. He wrote also at this time, and published anonymously, an approving analysis of Dupuis's huge work on the origin of all religions. It was hardly calculated to moderate the conflicts in the schools. Dupuis's work, said Tracy, "proves that the ancient fables have never been understood, because it has not been seen that all religions are always only a cult of nature and its principal agents, the heavenly bodies, fire, and the other elements." Or again: "Christian theology, when explained by the same method, now appears, like its predecessors, to be only the cult of nature and the sun, renewed with different names and symbols." And Christ had no more historical existence than Hercules, Bacchus, and Osiris, of whom it had once been fervently believed that they were supernatural beings.[78]

The original mandate of the Council was to review the books to be used in the primary and Central schools. In adding Destutt de Tracy, the minister intended to broaden its work into a more extensive investigation. It was apparently Tracy who developed the questionnaire sent on 20 Floréal (May 1799) to all the Central Schools, which produced much of the factual information on which the description of these schools in the preceding pages is based. It was probably at the instigation of Tracy that the Council prodded the professors to send in the *cahiers* or teaching materials requested in 1797. After study of these papers Destutt de Tracy composed circular letters to some of the professors in the Central Schools, criticizing their work, telling them what the purpose of their course should be, and offering suggestions for improvement. Meanwhile the Council, which met every 10 days, labored at its final report, which was written by Destutt de Tracy and was submitted to the minister of the interior on 16 Pluviôse of the Year VIII, or February 5, 1800. By that time the Directory had expired, and Napoleon Bonaparte was the presiding genius of France.[79]

[78] *Quels sont les moyens de fonder la morale chez un peuple?* (Paris, An VI); *Analyse de l'origine de tous les cultes, par le citoyen Dupuis, et de l'abrégé qu'il a donné de cet ouvrage* (Paris, An VII), pp. 1-3, reprinted in 1804, as an anonymous counterattack on Bona-parte's attempt to make peace with the Catholic church. See Kennedy, *Destutt de Tracy*, p. 110. For Kennedy's account of the Council on Public Instruction see his pp. 84-88.

[79] The questionnaire, the circulars, and the final report of the Council were published by Tracy in his later years, as an appendix to his *Eléments de l'Idéologie; troisième partie, tome deuxième: De la Logique* (Paris, 1825), pp. 261-324. They were again reprinted by

In its review of schoolbooks submitted for approval by authors and booksellers the Council endorsed many and rejected some. One case of rejection, for example, was a three-volume work on the history of England. The report, signed by Lagrange, found the work full of unfavorable allusions to the existing regime in France, since it praised General Monk for restoring Charles II, extolled William Pitt, and approved of "reinforcement of royal authority against attacks by democracy." Another rejected work was politically harmless but was judged to be pedagogically unsuited. It was a French equivalent of a work on business English, a *Grammaire des commerçants*. The author of this work, according to the report, "has not followed the analytic method, the only one that the Council wishes to approve, because it is the only method which, by leading the pupil from the object to the sensation, and from sensation to ideas and judgment, enables him to arrive at definitions, rules and general maxims that he then understands well, because they result from his own observations." The Council, therefore, "while not pretending to require any professor or teacher to adopt any particular system," felt it its duty not to encourage "principles contrary to sound methods of teaching."[80]

Despite repeated reminders, the professors in the Central Schools responded tardily and irregularly to the request to send in their *cahiers*. The Council hoped that after study of all such materials it might standardize teaching at the highest possible levels. Taking an ambiguous stand on the practice of lecturing, it declared that the *dictée* of the Old Regime should by no means be revived; but it nevertheless expressed the hope that lectures already being given by some professors, as shown by their *cahiers*, would be of such quality as to be published as introductory textbooks. To speed up the response Destutt de Tracy wrote four circular letters in August and September 1799, over the signature of Quinette, the minister of interior who replaced François de Neufchâteau in the political crisis of that summer. They were addressed as reminders to professors who had failed to send in the materials requested two years before, but they were circulated to others as well. Only those to professors of Ancient Languages, General Grammar, History, and Legislation were actually dispatched.

These circulars, though addressed to the recusants, reflect the thinking of the Council as shaped by the *cahiers* that had been received. The

---

A. Duruy, *L'Instruction publique et la Révolution* (Paris, 1882), pp. 391-411 and 433-48.

[80] Archives Nationales, F17 1011, nos. 1561 and 1623. This carton is entirely composed of minutes of the meetings of the Council from Frimaire to Messidor of the Year VII.

professors of Ancient Languages were told that they should make their pupils more conscious of the use of words. Those of General Grammar were chided for misunderstanding the purpose of their course, instructed not to confine themselves to ordinary grammar, and advised to give the course after Ancient Languages and before History, Belles-Lettres, and Legislation, so that a bridge would be formed from language instruction to the art of reasoning as applied to these latter subjects. The professors of Legislation received the longest letter, though they had the fewest students; they were to teach moral principles as derived from nature and show how public, private, and criminal law was the embodiment of such principles. The professors of history were to teach "the march of the human mind," make sure to bring in the ancient Near East as well as Greco-Roman antiquity, and while using Millot as a basic text also have their students read Condillac, Voltaire, Adam Ferguson, and Dupuis, the last-named being valued for showing "the source of inter-connections between all superstitions."[81]

At the very time when these letters went out the Council on Public Instruction received an unexpected jolt. Quinette, an old revolutionary of 1793 (though later a Napoleonic prefect), was brought in as minister of the interior during the neodemocratic revival of the summer of 1799. He seems, like Napoleon, to have had his doubts about the Idéologues. For example, he raised questions about scholarships and aid to the talented poor to which the Council had paid no attention in its questionnaire of 20 Floréal. He pointed out that the scholarships of the old University of Paris, by which several hundred boys and young men had been brought from the provinces to study in the capital, were still concentrated in the Prytanée français (formerly Equality College and before that, Louis-le-Grand) and were still bringing youths to Paris who might better receive their scholarships in their home departments in the Central Schools. In this way, said Quinette, the quality of the Central Schools would be raised, and the Prytanée could remain as a residence hall for older students attending the "special" schools of the capital. The Council did in fact put this idea into its final report a few months later. Meanwhile, however, on October 7,

---

[81] Destutt de Tracy, *Eléments*, p. 288; Duruy, *Instruction publique*, p. 438. See Archives Nationales, F[17] 1339 doss. 11-22 for discussions in the Council in preparation for the circulars, which were printed at the time, being intended for a hundred schools. The *cahiers* sent in by professors, with accompanying materials, are in F[17] 1344[1] to 1344[31]. They provide abundant evidence for actual teaching in the Central Schools and as such have been used for the articles on General Grammar and History in the *AHRF* of 1981 mentioned in note 27 above, and on Physics-Chemistry by Williams in "Science, Education and the French Revolution," pp. 311-30.

1799, Quinette with great politeness informed the Council that its budget would be cut and the salaries of the members discontinued immediately. He also took steps to move the Council out of its quarters in the Palais des Arts (the Louvre) by issuing orders for its location elsewhere. It is evident that the demise of the Council was not due only to the decision of Bonaparte, nor was it entirely a consequence of the coup d'état of Brumaire that followed a month after Quinette's action.[82]

The members of the Council continued to work voluntarily, without salary, for several months. Digesting the *cahiers* that had been received, and the results of the questionnaire of 20 Floréal, to which the response was more favorable than to the request for *cahiers*, with at least three-quarters of the professors replying, the Council produced the final report as drafted by Destutt de Tracy and submitted it to the new minister of the interior, Lucien Bonaparte, in February 1800. The report candidly acknowledged many weaknesses on which it said that professors in the Central Schools were agreed. It noted that many schools had attempted remedies but were blocked by the provisions in the law of 3 Brumaire. It observed that these attempts had resulted in many variations from one school to another, and that experiment was commendable, but that nevertheless there was "only one single good method, one single natural order in which the studies could profitably be taken, so that a general measure should fix the duration of study in a uniform manner."[83] So we return to the idea of a central plan under a central authority.

The report announced that the primary schools were indeed important, but that nothing could be done about them in the extreme shortage of qualified teachers, who could not be produced until the Central Schools were improved. The planners worked from the top down. A young man's education should be complete by the age of twenty, they said, including his professional education in special schools, by which they meant the Polytechnique, the other technical schools, the schools of medicine, and others that they had in mind but which did not yet exist. Allowing for four years in these special schools, a youth should complete his work in the Central Schools at the age of sixteen. He should therefore enter at the age of eight or nine so as to receive a good general education before going on to his professional studies. The Central School would thus embrace elementary work. The pri-

---

[82] Quinette on the Prytanée français, Archives Nationales, F[17A] 1338 doss. 4, no. 13; on the termination of salaries, no. 15.

[83] Tracy, *Eléments*, p. 300; Duruy, *Instruction publique*, p. 395.

mary school was no longer seen as the avenue, "vestibule," or "peri-style" opening into higher levels; it was a different system, as had been said in the Five Hundred by Andrieux, who, if not exactly an Idéo-logue, was a member of the section on Grammar in the National Institute.

The one-track system envisaged in all the Revolutionary plans from Talleyrand to Roger Martin was thus abandoned. Idéologues prevailed over democrats. The two-track system of the nineteenth century was laid out: a short track for the populace and a longer track for the class of families that could afford and expect something better for their children (or at least their sons), reinforced by a few poorer boys of such exceptional promise, even at the age of nine, that the government might aid them financially in the public interest.

There were intimations also of a Napoleonic centralization. The report insisted that only slight and gradual modifications in the Central Schools were required, but in fact it called for a complete overhaul of the system. There must be a uniformity of purpose, methods, and standards throughout the country. "But it cannot be expected that all professors will reach the desired aim at the outset; we must continue to require of them to send in, at the beginning of each year, the program that they intend to teach, and at the end of the year a summary of the instruction they have given."[84]

Attached to the report was a detailed tabulation, as shown in the table that follows, that may be compared with the plan of 3 Brumaire on p. 245 above.[85] We now have a proposal for a strictly graded school, arranged in year-long grades from one to eight, with no choice of courses for the students and with each course to last for a specified length of time. Courses have prerequisites; none may be taken unless those preceding it have been successfully passed. The student enrolls in three courses at a time, no more and no less, arranged in three parallel streams of what Americans would later call the humanities and the natural and the social sciences. The humanities are strengthened by six years of study of Latin and Greek, followed by two of belles-

[84] Tracy, *Eléments*, p. 318; Duruy, *Instruction publique*, p. 408.

[85] Duruy in 1882 was unable to locate the tabulated Plan of Studies and was obliged to omit it from his reprinting of the report; but the table had been published by Tracy as an appendix to his *Observations sur le système d'instruction publique* (Paris, An IX), and in 1825 in his *Eléments*. An original manuscript copy of the table, identical with what Tracy published, is in the Ginguené papers at the Bibliothèque Nationale, Nouv. acq. no. 9193, folio 178. These papers also contain materials concerning the work of the Council on the review of books, the questionnaire, the professors' *cahiers*, and the preparation of the final report.

lettres. Mathematics goes on for four years beyond simple arithmetic and must be studied before physics and chemistry. General Grammar is now taught to eleven-year-olds, and two years of it precede the moral and political sciences. Drawing, which the report noted was being studied by sons of artisans in the Central Schools in very large numbers, is now set aside as a recreational subject, a *délassement*, to be pursued for eight years, along with physical exercise, the *arts agréables*, and modern languages, if desired, from a private teacher. The expulsion of Drawing from the heart of the program, together with the extension of Latin, was a sign that boys of artisan families should find their vocational instruction elsewhere, and that the Central Schools would be designed to serve the better educated class.

For the more advanced studies, for young men from sixteen to twenty years old, the Council expressed satisfaction with the existing *grandes*

	Proposed Plan of Study			Pupil's approximate age
Year	Languages and Literature	Physical Sciences and Mathematics	Ideological, Moral, and Political Sciences	
1	Elementary Latin and French	Elementary Arithmetic	—	9
2	Continued	Elementary Physical Geography and Natural History	Elementary Political and Historical Geography	10
3	Latin and Greek	Pure Mathematics	General Grammar	11
4	Continued	Continued	Continued	12
5	Continued	Natural History and Chemistry	Moral Sciences and Legislation	13
6	Continued	Continued	Continued	14
7	Belles-Lettres (Rhetoric)	Applied Mathematics and General Physics	History	15
8	Belles-Lettres (Ideology)	Continued	Continued	16

Note by Destutt de Tracy: Drawing is carried on during the whole eight years in time left free from other activities, from which it serves as relaxation. The same holds for the other agreeable arts, physical exercise, and modern languages that may be studied in private lessons. (Table adapted from Destutt de Tracy's appendix to his *Observations sur le système d'instruction publique*.)

écoles spéciales ou de service public. It added, however, that the moral and political sciences should be more fully developed and indeed that, at some future date, no one should hold high office in the Republic unless he had studied these sciences. It therefore proposed the establishment of a special school of moral and political sciences, to be formed by modifications in the College of France. Since the new school would be entered only upon examination and would give concluding examinations as tests for professional acceptability, the College of France would in effect be "modified" out of existence. The Council also suggested that, again at some future date, no one should be admitted to any of the *écoles spéciales ou de service public* except by producing proof of having taken the course in Legislation at a Central School. So we sense another intimation of the Napoleonic "monopoly."

The efforts of the Council on Public Instruction, like so many others, came to nothing. The Council lost its originator and protector when François de Neufchâteau left the ministry in June 1799. His successor, Quinette, took the first steps in its demotion. After Napoleon Bonaparte became First Consul in November he assigned the ministry of the interior to his brother Lucien. It was therefore to Lucien Bonaparte that the Council submitted its report in February 1800. Weeks passed, and it still received no response from the minister. A copy of the report went to the chemist Chaptal, now on Napoleon's Council of State, who replied only with a noncommital acknowledgment. At the request of Lucien Bonaparte the new chief of the bureau of public instruction, Dumouchel, prepared a short history of the Council. The former head of the extinct University of Paris gave a mildly favorable account of the Council's work but added that it had virtually ceased to meet, and indeed no longer had even a meeting place. In any case, he remarked, all its members except Domergue and Palissot now had well-paying seats in the Senate and Tribunate under the Constitution of the Year VIII. Lucien Bonaparte thereupon ordered the files and papers of the Council transferred to the bureau of public instruction. The Council was suppressed in October 1800.

Let us compare the plan of the Council on Public Instruction with the one developed by Roger Martin, Heurtault-Lamerville, Bonnaire, Briot, Cabanis, and others in the Council of Five Hundred—the plans, to be brief, of the Idéologues and the Democrats. The Democrats adhered more than the Idéologues to Condorcet's educational plan of 1792. They envisaged five great universities spread throughout France; the Idéologues favored the nascent *grandes écoles*, separate specialized establishments that were mostly in Paris. The Democrats conceived of universities as centers for the production of new knowledge; the Idéologues were more inclined to see new knowledge as the domain of the Institute and the schools as vehicles for the diffusion and application of truths already established. Showing more awareness of German universities than the Idéologues did, the Democrats would have law, medicine, and all sciences brought together in the same institution. Their plan, through Cabanis, gave serious thought to medical education, which they thought should take place in a general university setting; Cabanis, though an Idéologue, did not persuade his fellow Idéologues in this matter. The Democrats saw a single track from the primary through the Central to the advanced schools, and they proposed to enrich the primary schools for boys who would not go beyond them; the Idéologues brushed aside the problem of elementary and mass education and explicitly rejected the one-track system. For the Central Schools, both groups thought that examination rather than age should be the qualification for admission to a course; both called for more teaching of Latin and the addition of boarding facilities to the schools; but where the Democrats wished to get rid of General Grammar the Idéologues would reinforce it, and where the Democrats would keep Drawing as a useful subject the Idéologues relegated it to the status of an adornment. Finally, the Democrats wished to reduce and if possible abolish fees, and their plan included seriously considered financial projections. The plan of the Idéologues ignored finances and found fees acceptable.

The Democrats anticipated the twentieth century, the Idéologues the nineteenth. Perhaps, therefore, the plan of the Idéologues was more in the realm of the possible. There were elements in both plans that foreshadowed the rearrangements under Bonaparte in 1802. Bonaparte, if no Idéologue, was after all a member of the National Institute, in "mechanical arts," not in "moral and political sciences." His idea of modernization was not to count on people in general but to work through a highly trained, organized, and cooperative body of scientific and administrative experts.

CHAPTER 7

MODERNIZATION: COLLECTIVE POWER

THE FRENCH, after repelling the invasion of 1792 and repeatedly defeating the armies assembled against them, went on to dominate the continent of Europe for 20 years. This gross fact may be taken as another sign of modernization. While the British were more advanced in the mechanization of industry and in banking and credit, the French produced an organizational machine that for many years nothing could stop. The philosopher Hegel in 1806, looking out from his rooms at the University of Jena, where he was writing his *Phenomenology of Mind*, and watching the French army wind through the old university town with Napoleon at its head, imagined that he saw the World Soul riding on horseback. This was a Hegelian way of saying that France and Napoleon, at this particular stage in world history, represented the progressive and cutting edge in the movement both of liberty and of power.

France and Germany in 1800 had about the same population, between 25 and 30 million in each case. Germany was divided into numerous small states that worked at cross-purposes. The 30 million Frenchmen could make their weight felt collectively. In the language of the present book, they were more nationalized, politicized, and democratized than the other peoples of Europe or than they themselves had been before 1789. There was more national unity to the degree that older barriers of provincial separatism and class privilege had been overcome. There was more political effectiveness, which after 1800 now meant the ability of the government to evoke the spirit and employ the resources of the country, thanks to the "abolition of feudalism," the improvement of tax collections, and the repression of internal discord. There was even something left of democratization in the legal equality of the Napoleonic codes and in the principle of careers open to talents.

It was a source of French strength that much of all this was admired in the rest of Europe. In Belgium, Germany, Italy, and elsewhere the French found persons willing to work with them in a reordering of their own countries. Even unreconciled enemies saw something to be imitated. In Prussia, after its total collapse at the hands of Napoleon in 1806, reformers looked to France for clues. One of them, Gneisenau, a professional army officer close to the king, put down his reflections in a kind of private memorandum to himself. "One cause especially," he wrote,

"has brought France to this peak of greatness. The Revolution has awakened all the forces in the country and given each force its appropriate sphere of work. Hence have come heroes to command armies, statesmen to the highest administrative posts, and finally the greatest man produced by the French people to be their head. What endless powers lie sleeping undeveloped and unknown, in the womb of a nation!"

Why, he asked, have the royal courts not known how to tap these powers? "Why have they not chosen this means to increase their strength a thousandfold, by opening to the ordinary person [*dem gemeinen Bürgenlichen*: "burgher"? "bourgeois"? "citizen"?] those triumphal gates through which only the noble has been allowed to pass? This new era needs more than names, titles and parchments; it needs new kinds of action and power."[1]

A few sporadic statistics suggest that Gneisenau's observation was not mistaken. A list made in 1812, for example, of 56 "notables" of the department of the Orne in Normandy—that is, of persons with enough property, status, and ability to be officially regarded as important—shows that 13 of them were of the pre-Revolutionary nobility, and the other 43 were lawyers, physicians, government employees, and businessmen of the former Third Estate. Among about 20 men who served as ministers in charge of government departments from 1800 to 1814 several were nobles of the Old Regime, but the fathers of six others were an engineer, a shipowner, a textile manufacturer, a shop-

---

[1] G. Pertz, *Das Leben des Feldmarshalls Grafen Reithardt von Gneisenau*, 3 vols. (Berlin, 1864), 1:301-302. Gneisenau went on to add more specficially: "The Revolution has set the whole national strength of the French people into action, through the equalizing of different estates [*Stände*] and equal taxation of property." He published similar thoughts in a Königsberg newspaper; see P. Paret, *Yorck and the Era of Prussian Reform* (Princeton, 1966), p. 132.

keeper, a peasant, and the chief surgeon at a hospital. Of the 18 marshals of the Empire named by Napoleon from 1804 to 1813 the social origin of 11 is identified as bourgeois, 4 as popular, and 3 as of the old nobility. Of 3,600 persons granted noble titles by Napoleon about a fifth had been nobles before the Revolution, while three-fifths were bourgeois and another fifth had been born in the "popular classes."[2]

What emerged from the Revolution, and was consolidated under Napoleon, was a new elite or governing class drawn from the active elements, noble and non-noble, of the society of the Old Regime. Given their ages, most of those to whom the statistics just cited refer had in fact been educated in pre-Revolutionary schools. For Napoleon, the main purpose of his own educational program was to prepare and perpetuate a class of notables for the future—military men, administrators, judges, government servants, engineers, scientists, literary lights and to a lesser extent industrial managers—who would follow his lead in producing a modern society as he understood it. The real source of his power, with due regard to his own abilities, lay in the collective energies of the French people.

THE LAST PUBLIC DISCUSSION, 1800-1802

Bonaparte, aged 30 in 1799, was a charismatic young general who had defeated the Austrians, carried the Revolution to Italy, and supported the civilian republicans in the political crises of 1795 and 1797. Though a product of the pre-Revolutionary *écoles militaires*, he owed nothing to family background and embodied the rapid rise of unknown youthful talent that gave strength to the new order. His program now was to put an end to the Revolution while preserving the most important innovations of its first two years, and to do so by accommodating the widest possible spectrum of opinion while forcibly repressing the extremists of both left and right. For such a program he enjoyed widespread support, which declined only as his own personal ambition became more apparent. For two or three years he allowed considerable freedom for public discussion, both in the press and in the government apparatus that he set up.

At the top of this apparatus, under the constitution of the Year VIII, was a strong executive composed of three Consuls, among whom the

---

[2] For the 56 notables see L. Bergeron, *France under Napoleon*, trans. R. R. Palmer (Princeton, 1981), pp. 80-83; for the ministers, ibid., pp. 73-76, and for the marshals, ibid., pp. 65-66. For the Napoleonic nobility, ibid., p. 69, and J. Tulard, "Problèmes sociaux de la France impériale," *Revue d'histoire moderne et contemporaine* 16 (July-September 1970):656; a special issue on "La France à l'époque napoléonienne."

First Consul, Bonaparte himself, possessed all the authority. In the other branches of government there was much continuity of personnel from the previous regime, and a place was found for many of those mentioned in preceding pages as concerned with education. Most important was the Council of State, which met privately with the First Consul to draft legislation; the member of this Council charged with educational matters, following a brief tenure by Roederer, was Fourcroy, who had dealt with such problems from 1793 to 1795. There were the usual ministries, and in the ministry of the interior the chief of the bureau of public instruction was Dumouchel, who had held the same position under the Directory. Below the ministers were the prefects, one for each department, and one of whom was Félix Bonnaire, who had been in Roger Martin's group in 1798. For the passage of laws the Council of State submitted projects for enactment to the Legislative Body, of which the Abbé Grégoire and Roger Martin were members. The Legislative Body enacted or rejected a proposal only after hearing the report of the Tribunate, where free discussion took place until it was purged and largely silenced in March 1802. In the Tribunate were Ginguené, Daunou, Benjamin Constant, Jacquemont, Jard-Panvillier, and J. B. Say, though the first three were expelled in 1802. Having a dignity of its own was the Conservative Senate, designed to "conserve" the new regime and the Revolutionary changes that the regime accepted; one of its functions was to determine the membership of the two legislative chambers. In the Senate were Destutt de Tracy, Garat, Cabanis, Volney, and François de Neufchâteau, along with several leading men of science. It will be seen that the Idéologues were well represented in the new government. They had supported the coup d'état of Brumaire in the hope of securing an enlightened republic against both obstinate royalism and dissatisfied democracy.

A public airing of education took place from 1800 to 1802 in the Tribunate and in an outburst of books and tracts, eventuating in the law of Floréal of the Year X, or May 1802. After that, until the fall of Napoleon in 1814, public discussion played no part. But before examining this discussion it is well to suggest the conditions in which it took place.

One of Bonaparte's first actions was to obtain the abolition of the fading decadary cult and the whole program of national festivals. A law of December 1799, "considering it important to the public prosperity to preserve only those national festivals that have been accepted by all the French, and to leave no memory that may tend to raise divisions among friends of the Republic," suppressed all *fêtes nationales* except two—the anniversaries of July 14 and 1 Vendémiaire, which marked the fall of the Bastille and the proclamation of the Republic.[3] The date of the death of Louis XVI, for example, would no longer be celebrated as an occasion for public rejoicing. The purpose was to attract all but inveterate royalists into a new consensus. The effect was to abandon an aspect of educational policy that had been present in almost all planning since 1789. There would be no more deliberate effort to reshape adults. Public education would take place in schools and be designed for the young. It would value mental effort above republican virtue, for it would attempt to produce competent individuals rather than mold a whole people for a future society.

It was also immediately after the coup d'état that the harassment of private schools came to an end. There were a great many private schools in actual operation in 1800, mostly conducted by laypersons, with varying degrees of religious or Catholic coloration. The *Moniteur*, in its number for 1 Frimaire of the Year IX, published a list of the best and most fashionable in Paris, giving the names and addresses of 13 *pensionnats* for boys and of six for girls. Some of the best of these establishments for boys sent pupils to attend courses in the Paris Central Schools. The girls' boarding schools were very diverse; there were about 70 of them in Paris, of varying scholastic merit and ideological hue; one was run by the widow of the Girondin Brissot, another by Mme de Campan, who had been lady-in-waiting to Marie-Antoinette, and still another by Stéphanie-Louise de Bourbon-Conti, who said that she followed the methods prescribed by Rousseau. Throughout the rest of France were a few pre-Revolutionary colleges that had never closed, others that were in fact revivals or attempted revivals of pre-Revolutionary institutions, and still others that had been newly created during the Directory under the constitutional guarantee for private schools. As the private schools proliferated they offered an ever stronger competition to the Central Schools, which themselves were changing.

The *Décade philosophique*, always springing to the defense of the Central Schools, was full of reports in 1800 and 1801 on new programs adopted locally by the school of this or that department, calling for strict examinations, required attendance, and a specified number and sequence of courses to be taken over a set period of years.[4] In Paris, the three Central Schools were reorganized in 1801 by an order of the

---

[3] *Moniteur*, for 4 Nivôse of the Year VIII, p. 374, and 5 Nivôse, p. 378. The law was passed by the "lame-duck" Five Hundred and Anciens before adoption of the Constitution of the Year VIII.

[4] *Décade philosophique*, 20 Messidor of the Year VIII, pp. 73-81; 10 Fructidor of the Year VIII, pp. 405-11; 10 Frimaire of the Year IX, pp. 441-44; 30 Nivôse of the Year IX, pp. 151-59; 20 Fructidor of the Year IX, pp. 495-97; 30 Vendémiaire of the Year X, pp. 156-69.

prefect of the Seine, who probably worked with some of the professors. A strictly graded six-year program was instituted, somewhat along the lines proposed by the Council on Public Instruction the year before, and the old *concours général* of the 10 pre-Revolutionary Paris colleges was restored as an annual competition among students of the Paris Central Schools. But as the Central Schools began to meet the objections raised against them, and as religious and private schools nevertheless continued to draw most of the students, the educational future of the French people became if anything only more uncertain. There may have been no more pupils in the Central Schools in 1801 than in 1799.[5]

Since his campaigns in Italy Bonaparte had foreseen the need of a reconciliation with the pope. Recognition of the French Republic by the pope would disarm the counterrevolution, reduce the influence of émigrés and especially of the émigré bishops, alleviate the religious divisions within France, and allow Catholic teachers to take a more favorable view of the new order. The new pope, Pius VII, installed in 1800, was more willing than his predecessor to accept certain principles of the French Revolution. In France, as the excitement of the Revolution wore off and the most optimistic expectations faded, there was more willingness to accept and even idealize the Catholic tradition, as shown in the public reaction to Chateaubriand's book, *The Genius of Christianity*, which appeared in 1802. It was in April of that year that the agreement between France and the papacy, the Concordat, was promulgated with appropriate ceremonies at Notre Dame, just as debate on the educational law of Floréal was beginning in the Tribunate.

The Concordat represented a compromise in which each party had something to gain, the Republic obtaining papal recognition as a legitimate government, and the Papacy getting recognition and protection for the Catholic religion in France. Such concessions to Rome gave offense to the anticlerical and antireligious elements in French opinion. The Concordat was strongly opposed by most of the Idéologues, whose theory of knowledge and insistence on one single method of "the truth" made them the sharpest intellectual opponents of the announced truths of religion. Where the Idéologues would combat or even destroy the clergy, Bonaparte preferred to tolerate, control, and use them. Opposition in the Tribunate to his settlement with the church

[5] A. Aulard, *Paris sous le Consulat*, 4 vols. (Paris, 1903-1909), 2:614, 654, 681. See also Lanzac de Laborie, "L'enseignement secondaire au début du Consulat: Les écoles centrales," *Revue des études napoléoniennes* 12 (1917):257-86.

provided one reason for Bonaparte's decision to purge that body. After the purge in March 1802 the Tribunate accepted the Concordat by a vote of 78 to 7, and the Legislative Body by 228 to 21. In this matter, as in some others, Bonaparte's policy at this time enjoyed more public favor than the objections of the opposition.[6]

Another of the controlling conditions was financial. To the perennial question of how an educational system should be paid for, there were those who answered that its revenues should come from its own propertied endowment rather than from taxes. It was estimated in 1800 that unsold property remaining in the national domain, confiscated during the Revolution from the church and the émigrés, reached a value of between 300 and 400 million francs. The notion of drawing on church properties to pay for schools had been expressed in some of the *cahiers* of 1789, as well as by Condorcet and others as recently as Roger Martin's group in 1798-1799. Others held a similar view in 1801 and 1802. A. V. Arnault, who was Dumouchel's superior in the ministry of the interior, argued for a permanent endowment of individual schools. Roederer of the Council of State was of the same opinion. J. F. Champagne, head of the Prytanée français, made a strong argument for an endowment of education from lands in the public domain. Fourcroy, in presenting the law of Floréal of the Year X in April 1802, assumed that such an endowment would exist. In Italy, in 1802, as the French proceeded to annex the kingdom of Piedmont, converting it into six French departments, the French authorities and their Italian co-workers, intending to make the University of Turin conform to the French pattern, endowed it with landed property to be held perpetually in its own right to the value of 545,242 francs a year.[7]

In January 1801 the government of the Consulate proposed legis-

---

[6] See Irene Collins, *Napoleon and his Parliaments, 1800-1815* (London, 1979), pp. 56-67. The Tribunate before the purge also rejected the Civil Code.

[7] A. V. Arnault, *De l'administration des établissements d'instruction publique et de la réorganisation de l'enseignement* (Paris, An IX), pp. 3-6; Roederer in a letter to administrators of the Prytanée, Archives Nationales, S 6255 doss. 2; Fourcroy in *Archives parlementaires*, 2nd ser., 3:485; J. F. Champagne in *Vues sur l'organisation d'instruction publique dans les écoles destinées à l'enseignement de la jeunesse* (Paris, An VIII), pp. 86-90, or in my translation, *The School of the French Revolution* (Princeton, 1975), pp. 285-88. On Turin: *Vicissitudes de l'instruction publique en Piémont depuis l'an VII jusqu'au mois de Ventôse an XI par Brayda, Charles Botta et Giraud, anciens membres du jury d'instruction publique de la 27ᵉ division militaire* (Turin, An XI), pp. 63, 68; F. Boyer, "Les institutions universitaires en Piémont de 1800 a 1802," *Revue d'histoire moderne et contemporaine* (July-September 1970), p. 916; and D. Outram, "Education and politics in Piedmont, 1796-1814," *Historical Journal* 19 (1976):611-33.

lation to this effect for France, as part of a plan for liquidation of the national debt. For several years about five million francs a year of tax revenues had been spent on the schools. The idea was that, if this sum of five million for the schools should be obtained from the revenues of the national domain instead of from taxes, then an equal sum from taxes could be put into a sinking fund toward payment of the public debt. The government therefore proposed to set aside 180 million francs' worth of property in the national domain as a special fund (consisting of farms, forests, urban real estate, etc.), of which one quarter of the income should go to support disabled and retired soldiers and three-quarters for the support of education. The income from three-quarters of 180 million would produce about five or six million a year to serve as a permanent endowment for the schools.[8]

There was lively objection to this proposal (before the purge) in the Tribunate. It came mainly from members of the liberal and Idéologue group who were using every opportunity to assert parliamentary independence against encroachments by the executive. Some feared that the interests of government creditors, and hence the credit of the state, would be endangered if so large a proportion of the national domain should be withdrawn from the possibility of sale. In the debate the interests of public finance and of education were thoroughly intermixed. Some favored the idea of a large educational endowment but not as in the bill proposed by the government. The main speaker urging rejection was Benjamin Constant. Most of his speech had to do with public credit. He made important points, however, on education. The project, he said, did not specify whether individual schools and colleges should be endowed, and thus become financially independent, or whether the whole huge endowment would remain under control of the state, which in that case would have the power to allocate the proceeds from time to time at will. "Public instruction would then no longer depend on the legislature, that is on the nation, but on the government alone. The results might be terrible under a government

---

[8] M. Marion, *Histoire financière de la France depuis 1715*, 6 vols. (Paris, 1914-1931), 4:221-28, and his *Vente des biens nationaux pendant la Révolution* (Paris, 1908), p. 316. Marion discusses only the financial aspects of this action, and no French historian of education seems to have seen it as being of any significance, as if the whole idea of endowed education, after the Revolution, had become so foreign to French experience as to be incomprehensible. It is barely mentioned by A. Aulard, *Napoléon et le monopole universitaire* (Paris, 1911), pp. 90 and 357. A. [Marais] de Beauchamp, *Recueil de lois et règlements sur l'enseignement supérieur*, 6 vols. (Paris, 1880-1893), 1:58, mistakenly dates this law as 30 Ventôse of the Year VIII.

less enlightened and less well-intentioned than ours."[9] The Tribunate rejected the project by a vote of 56 to 30.

It then went to the Legislative Body, before which spokesmen for the government and for the Tribunate made their arguments. The government insisted that the project would both reduce the debt and strengthen education by protecting it from fluctuations in tax revenues and the vagaries of fiscal need. Benjamin Constant repeated the arguments he had made in the Tribunate. The Legislative Body, deciding against the Tribunate, adopted the proposal by a vote of 227 to 58. It became known as the law of 30 Ventôse of the Year IX.[10]

Had the law ever been carried out French education would in effect have been supported by an enormous land grant, though the question of whether individual schools or a central bureaucracy would control the income remained unclear. But the law was never applied. Nor does it seem ever to have been repealed. What seems to have happened is that the law was simply ignored and forgotten. Bonaparte, especially as the Third Coalition formed against France in 1803, had other uses for the money. He also began to present endowments to his own favorites, or to important persons that he wished to link to himself. The "endowment" of 400,000 francs a year that he awarded to his University in 1808 was an altogether different matter from what was contemplated in the law of 1801, for it was comparatively trifling in amount and represented an indemnity for lost college properties, not an allocation from the national domain as a whole. Public education in France remained financially dependent on the state, so far as it was not paid for by the students' parents.

OLD COLLEGES OR NEW CENTRAL SCHOOLS?

Meanwhile the Years VIII and IX, or roughly 1800 and 1801, saw an outburst of published writings devoted specifically to education such as had hardly been witnessed (if we rule out the printed speeches of legislative debates) since the heady days of 1789-1791. Though these writings covered many topics, at their heart lay the question of whether the *collèges* of the Old Regime or the new Central Schools offered the best model for future development. At one extreme was La Harpe, the lecturer on literature who had turned violently against the Revolution

[9] *Archives parlementaires*, 2nd ser., 2:441-48, 544-74, 594-600, 652-88, with the quotation from Constant on p. 660.

[10] J. B. Duvergier, *Collection complète des lois, décrets . . . de 1788 à 1830 inclusivement*, 30 vols., plus index (Paris, 1834-1838), 12:403.

and who eulogized the old University and its colleges as known before 1789. Inclined in this direction, but more weighty, moderate, and informed, was J. A. Chaptal, a chemist and manufacturer who became minister of the interior in November 1800. Rallied in defense of the Central Schools were not only the Idéologues and the *Décade philosophique* but at least six others, all professors in the public system, whose published views were the more significant because they arose from their own experience and observation.

Chaptal brought out his tract at the time when he became minister. It was well publicized, for it ran through eight consecutive days in the *Moniteur*, and appeared also as a book. After praise for Talleyrand, Condorcet, the Convention, and the Five Hundred Chaptal nevertheless concluded that little had been accomplished. "Almost everywhere the Central Schools are deserted." Or again: "The system of public instruction that exists today is essentially bad." The fault was not in the subjects taught but in the method of teaching and in organization. Despite their shortcomings the schools before 1789 had instilled habits of work and thought. "It may be taken as fundamental that before the Revolution the nature of public instruction required some reforms, but it cannot be denied that the method of teaching was admirable." Chaptal thought it a strong point of the former system that education "was entrusted to corporate organizations," by which he meant such groups as the Oratorians and the Doctrinaires. He admitted their weaknesses: they taught but did not invent, they became stagnant, they encouraged few doubts in their students' minds. But they took teaching seriously; they had a system in which the duties and relationships between teachers were defined; they put their pupils into classes graded by age so that the teacher knew how to present his subject; and they were economical, with teachers eating and living under the same roof.[11]

After becoming minister Chaptal launched a survey, addressed to the prefects of the hundred departments, asking them to report the number of schools and colleges in their departments before the Revolution, their assets, income, and number of teachers and students in 1789, the number of such institutions surviving or established in the Year IX, the teachers and buildings that might still be available, and the state of local opinion as to what should now be done. The prefects made inquiries of the councils of their departments and arrondissements; in short, the government was consulting the population. A vast

---

[11] J. A. Chaptal, *Rapport et projet de loi sur l'instruction publique* (Paris, An IX), with the quotations at pp. 7, 12, and 9.

mass of information thus accumulated in Paris. In some departments the Central School was said to be flourishing, in others poorly attended. In most, the need was expressed for more numerous local colleges, as before 1789. In some places the local people wanted to have a "teaching order" (like the Oratorians, etc.), and in some they wanted their colleges to be endowed with their own property and income, as in many cases before the Revolution. It is possible that some of this information was slanted, since Chaptal had made his own views known, and prefects often tried to report what they thought was pleasing to the higher authorities. The survey of the Year IX nevertheless revealed a widespread dissatisfaction and a belief that in some ways education had been better served in the last years of the Old Regime.[12]

Among those arguing for the Central Schools we may begin with Destutt de Tracy, who published two tracts on education also in the Year IX.[13] One was his *Observations on the Present System of Public Instruction*. It was really only a restatement of his report of the year before for the Council on Public Instruction, complete with a table for a system of annual grades, as explained on pages 275-76 above.

[12] Replies to the Enquête de l'An IX are in the Archives de l'Université de Paris, carton 27, and at the Archives Nationales, F^{17} 1317$^{3\text{-}8}$. E. Allain, in *L'Oeuvre scolaire de la Révolution* (Paris, 1891 [Burt Franklin reprint, New York, 1969]), pp. 349-432, attempted a statistical tabulation comparing the data for 1789 and for the Year IX, and published copious excerpts from 28 prefects, the deliberations of the general councils of nine departments, and those of the arrondissement councils in 61 departments. D. Julia and P. Pressly, in "La population scolaire en 1789," *Annales E.S.C.* 30 (November-December 1975), found the figures reported in 1801 (An IX) for numbers of colleges and students before 1789 very inaccurate, since the local authorities could not remember, or in some cases wished to exaggerate, the number for the Old Regime. Allain's tabulation therefore cannot be used, but his excerpts from verbal reports of the prefects and local councils remain valuable, though there may be some bias in his selection. Allain disapproved of the Revolutionary efforts in education, but he was a respected scholar, and his excerpts express conflicting views. Chaptal published an *Analyse de procès-verbaux des conseils généraux de départements, sessions de l'An IX* (Paris, An X), of which chap. 6, pp. 521-648, is devoted to education. BN. Lf^{136}89. Reports by members of the Council of State sent out on tours of inspection in the Year IX were published long ago by F. Rocquain, *L'Etat de la France au 18 Brumaire* (Paris, 1874); they include occasional observations on public instruction, especially those by Fourcroy, pp. 129-227.

[13] Destutt de Tracy, *Observations sur le système actuel de l'instruction publique* (Paris, An IX), and *Projet d'éléments d'idéologie à l'usage des écoles centrales* (Paris, An IX). This project was reprinted as *Eléments d'idéologie, première partie. Idéologie proprement dite* (Paris, 1804), and later in his four volumes on *Idéologie* in 1827. In 1827 Tracy could still say of his earlier work that "I frankly admit to believing that I have arrived at the truth, and that no doubt or embarrassment remains in my mind on the questions I have treated" (1:xi-xii).

The other was his *Elements of Ideology for the Use of the Central Schools*. This was more than a rear-guard defense of the course in General Grammar that so few students seemed willing to study. It urged "the teaching of the ideological, moral and political sciences, which after all are sciences like the others."[14] There were many, of course, who believed that the moral and political sciences, if sciences at all, and if equated with "ideology," were highly partisan in their content. Tracy's work was duly praised in the *Décade philosophique*, which likewise expressed frequent disagreement with the ideas it attributed to Chaptal.

The six professors had more to say that was relevant to practical questions. All defended the Central Schools, but only on condition of sweeping changes, so that, like Tracy and the Council of Public Instruction of 1799, they virtually called for a new system. One of these writers was J. F. Champagne, head of the Prytanée, formerly Equality College, and before that Louis-le-Grand. One was Sylvestre Lacroix, member of the Institute and professor of Mathematics at the Central School of the Quatre-Nations in Paris. Another was Etienne Barruel, also professor at the Quatre-Nations, and an examiner for the Ecole Polytechnique. A fourth was Dellard, professor of physics at the Central School of the Seine-et-Oise, and a fifth was Dutens of the Roads and Bridges. To these may be added Biot of the College of France, who a little later, in 1803, published a history of the sciences in France during the Revolution in which he discussed the Central Schools.[15]

All these writers deplored the inadequacy of primary schools, in numbers and range of studies, and noted the gap between them and the Central Schools. As Dutens said: "Our system of public education is like a ladder from which the lower rungs are missing. One sees well enough from the middle to the top, but how do you get to the first rung?"[16] Here are some of the ideas on which they mostly agreed:

[14] Tracy, *Projet . . . des écoles centrales*, p. 12.

[15] Champagne, *Vues*, as in note 7 above. S. F. Lacroix, *Discours sur l'instruction publique prononcé à la distribution des prix des Ecoles Centrales du Département de la Seine le 29 thermidor An VIII* (Paris, An VIII), and see also his more extensive *Essai sur l'enseignement général et sur celui des mathématiques en particulier* (Paris, An XIV-1806). E. Barruel, *Observations sur l'instruction publique et particulièrement sur les écoles centrales* (Paris, An VIII). A. J. Dellard, *Observations sur les écoles centrales* (Paris, An IX). J. Dutens, *Des moyens de nationaliser l'instruction et sa doctrine* (Paris, An VIII). J. B. Biot, *Histoire générale des sciences pendant la Révolution française* (Paris, An XI, 1803). Arnauld, in the work cited in note 7 above, expressed many of the same ideas as these six professors. P. L. Lacretelle, in his *Idée sommaire d'un grand travail sur la nécessité, l'objet et les avantages de l'instruction . . .* (Paris, An VIII), was as fatuous as in his tract on education of 1791—see pp. 89-90 above.

[16] As quoted in a review in the *Journal de Paris*, 22 Messidor of the Year VIII, p. 1405. This work of Dutens is the only one of those surveyed here that I have not seen.

There should be a level called "secondary" between the primary and Central Schools. Primary and secondary schools, designed for all, should be free and paid for by the state, or at least strongly subsidized by it. (Chaptal was of the same opinion.) As for the Central Schools, their great fault was that they attempted an instruction that was over the heads of the pupils, considering their age. There should be more than one teacher of Latin. There should be boarding facilities so that out-of-town pupils could attend. With one in each of a hundred departments, the Central Schools were unreasonbly distributed without regard to population. There were too many if they were conceived of as places of advanced study and too few if they were meant for students beginning at the age of twelve. Not every department needed or could support the nine professors and the librarian required by the law of 3 Brumaire. About a dozen or so of the existing Central Schools should therefore be retained and developed as places of relatively higher studies. The remaining ones, greatly increased in number, but each with fewer than nine professors, should provide a more modest level of instruction and be better articulated with elementary schools. The famous "courses" as given in the Central Schools, being suitable for older students, might be retained in the more advanced institutions, but for pupils of younger age there should be annually graded "classes."

The writers whose ideas we are attempting to summarize differed with Destutt de Tracy and most of the Idéologues in important ways. Not only did they want schools paid for by the public treasury. They did not share the explicit distinction made by Destutt de Tracy, Andrieux, and others who envisaged a "two-track" system, with schools for the populace on the one hand and for a more highly educated minority on the other. To use Dutens' word, they thought that all pupils should at least begin on the same ladder. Or as Lacroix said, the government should indeed offer different kinds of instruction, including preparation for business and the skilled trades as well as the sciences, "but these forms of knowledge should be grafted on to a principal trunk, so that the pupil on leaving this trunk may attach himself to the branch whose fruits are best suited to his tastes and needs."[17] He added that this was what all enlightened persons before the Revolution had desired. But Lacroix was no complete equalitarian:

> To try to spread all the sciences equally, and make everyone equally educated, is as chimerical as to try to bring on an equality of fortunes; but if excessive wealth alongside absolute destitution is a sign of bad government, of which it constantly adds to the vices, it would

[17] Lacroix, *Discours*, p. 21.

be at least useless to have many isolated learned persons among a mass of people plunged in deep ignorance, and it might become harmful by giving credit to some dangerous opinions. There must be a gradation of minds with respect to culture, as there is of conditions with respect to fortune. It is the intermediate segments that join the extremes and give strength to the whole.[18]

It is worth a moment also to quote Etienne Barruel. As professor of physics and examiner for the Polytechnique Barruel must have been acquainted with Fourcroy, who remained close to the Polytechnique and was the chief author, along with Bonaparte himself, of the law of Floréal of the Year X. Barruel's *Observations* was an exceptionally broadly conceived and balanced work. "It is not enough," he said, "to have analyzed the rights of man and meditated on the principles of the social system . . . it is necessary also to understand the art of teaching."[19] There was too much freedom, uncertainty, and confusion of ages in the Central Schools; it was laughable at the recent distribution of prizes in Paris to see a man of twenty-eight and a boy of twelve competing for the same award. Yet the Central Schools should be improved, not abolished. Barruel then made most of the points noted above. In addition, he called for a ministry of public instruction that would coordinate the levels of instruction from the primary up through the special schools, and also attend to the education of girls. More "emulation" would be good for both students and teachers. There should be scholarships and student aid, awarded for merit, with precautions to keep out the rich, and with relief of war veterans obtained in some other way. For teachers, there should be a career pattern laid out, with a known course of promotion, fixed salaries, and retirement pensions. Something like the academic degrees of the old University should be restored. And there should be a system of inspection for the maintenance of standards, with visitors to inspect the Central Schools and professors in the Central Schools to inspect the schools below them.

The point in surveying these details, at the cost of some repetition, is to lay a basis for judging the system introduced by Napoleon Bonaparte. Did he impose his own views and crush a promising and progressive educational experiment, as liberal critics have generally said, or did he go along with a wave of changing opinion, while doubtless also supposing that his reorganization would strengthen the country, and so consolidate his own position?

[18] Ibid., p. 20.
[19] Barruel, *Observations*, p. 10.

THE LAW OF 11 FLORÉAL OF THE YEAR X

The Council of State divided itself into sections each of which worked with one of the ministries. The section assigned to the ministry of the interior considered educational policy on many occasions from 1800 to 1802. Fourcroy and Roederer were members of this section, as was A. C. Thibaudeau, who like Fourcroy had been a member of the National Convention and who remained more attached than Fourcroy to the republican and democratic ideas of 1793. Bonaparte himself often sat in on these discussions. Meeting privately, the Council was the one place where the First Consul accepted and even invited a free expression of conflicting opinions. We have the recollections of Roederer and Thibaudeau as evidence of what happened.[20]

Bonaparte agreed with Chaptal that the Central Schools had been unsuccessful, with a few exceptions including the three Central Schools of Paris, which he thought were doing well, especially since, as already noted, they were currently being reorganized by the prefect of the Seine. Bonaparte's most distinctive contribution at this time was his notion of a number of "lycées" to be populated with a large number of students enjoying government scholarships for board, room, and tuition. Many observers had proposed that about 20 of the Central Schools should be built up to a high level of study and be organized as boarding schools while continuing also to accommodate day pupils. Bonaparte carried this idea further than anyone else. He appropriated the high-sounding word *lycée* for the institution he had in mind, and he thought in terms of thousands of scholarships. A new word in French at the time, *lycée* since the 1780s had meant a private place where public lectures were offered for a fee. Then it had been used, by Condorcet in 1792 and by Roger Martin and Briot as recently as 1799, to mean in effect a university, of which there need be only a few, devoted to the highest study of all the sciences, literature, and the arts. Bonaparte's *lycée* was for adolescent and general education, after which the student would go for advanced instruction to one of the "special" schools. He also proposed far more scholarships than anyone

[20] A. C. Thibaudeau, *Mémoires sur le Consulat, 1799-1804, par un ancien Conseiller d'Etat* (Paris, 1827); *Oeuvres du comte P. L. Roederer,* 8 vols. (Paris, 1853-1859), 3:397-403 and 436-38. The work of Pelet de la Lozère, *Opinions de Napoléon ... par un membre de son Conseil d'Etat* (Paris, 1833), contains nothing on education before the year 1806. For the years 1801 and 1802 see also L. Liard, *L'enseignement supérieur en France, 1789-1893,* 2 vols. (Paris, 1894), 2:14-32, and L. Grimaud, *Histoire de la liberté de l'enseignement en France,* 6 vols. (Paris, 1944-1947), 3:167ff.

else, with appointments to be made by the First Consul. As it turned out in the law of Floréal the number was 6,400.

In previous plans, as in the thought of the six professors whose writings of the Years VIII and IX have just been surveyed, scholarships were to be awarded on competitive grounds for scholastic merit or talent. Some had stressed the use of scholarships for poor youths of limited means or proposed that talented boys of more affluent families should hold honorary scholarships only. Bonaparte's idea was different. He certainly wanted to recruit talent, but he supposed that he would find quite enough of it among families of at least moderate property. Many year later, at St. Helena, he tried to associate himself with the more democratic ideas of the Revolution. "In fact," he said in 1819 to his British doctor, Barry O'Meara, "the Imperial Government was a kind of republic. Called to the head of it by the voice of the nation, my maxim was, *la carrière ouverte aux talents*, without distinction of birth or fortune, and this system of equality is the reason why your oligarchy hate me so much."[21] It is true that many in the British and European upper classes thought of Napoleon as a crowned Jacobin. But actually, in 1801 and 1802, his idea of careers open to talent was likely to mean that the record of a young man or his family during the Revolution, whether royalist or republican, and whether they had emigrated or remained in France, need not stand in the way of employment and advancement in the public service.

It was not to encourage bright boys from needy homes that Bonaparte called for a generous program of scholarships. Since it was a main complaint against the Central Schools that they did not attract enough students to develop successfully or justify their cost, Bonaparte meant to use the scholarships as a way, in effect, of buying students, or as Fourcroy said, of assuring that the lycées would not be peopled only by professors. From the beginning, Bonaparte thought of his scholarship program as flexible and temporary. As soon as the lycées had enough paying students the program might be discontinued. Meanwhile the program would be a kind of pump-priming or pedagogical Keynesianism; scholarships would be fed into a lycée that was

[21] Barry O'Meara, *Napoleon in exile: or a voice from St. Helena*, 2 vols. (London, 1822), 1:405, under date March 3, 1817. O'Meara italicized the phrase *carrière ouverte aux talents* while leaving it in French. He naturally published in English, but his conversations with Napoleon had been in French, of which he kept careful notes. The French translation, *Napoléon dans l'exil, ou Echo de Sainte-Hélène*, 2 vols. (Paris, 1822), 1:430, is identical in meaning at this point. The common idea that Napoleon favored the "career open to talents" is shown by the inclusion of a few words of this passage in Bartlett's *Familiar Quotations*.

short of students and taken away from one that had drawn enough paying students to cover its costs, with changes from year to year, until all lycées could carry themselves financially so that no more scholarships would be required. As Bonaparte wrote to Roederer: "A lycée in the last analysis is only a simple college. . . . The state scholarships are only a subsidy for the formation of colleges."[22]

Objections to Bonaparte's ideas were raised in the Council. It was said that the First Consul could not possibly appoint 6,000 scholars with any accuracy or equity, that in trying to do so he would stir up unfavorable comment on himself, and that the scholarships should be awarded by open examination, "so as to induce ordinary citizens and people with money to establish secondary schools at their own expense." Bonaparte listened carefully, according to Thibaudeau, and replied by talking for more than an hour. It would of course not be the First Consul personally who selected the scholars, he said, but the State. In any case the Council did not understand the politics of the question. It would be one function of the scholarships to reward families that had served the State, or were still serving it, in various military and civilian capacities. Did the Council desire rich enemies of the French Revolution to infiltrate the schools? Not all scholarships should depend on examinations, since examinations told very little about a boy of ten or twelve, whose future prospects did not become apparent until after the age of puberty. Both sets of ideas, those of Bonaparte and those of the Council, were blended in the legislation that was finally agreed on.[23]

It was Fourcroy, for the Council, who submitted the resulting plan to the Legislative Body on 30 Germinal or April 20, 1802, in a long speech explaining the reasons and expectations underlying its detailed provisions.[24] The plan rescinded and replaced the law of 3 Brumaire of the Year IV. Like that law, and like so many plans since Talleyrand's, the new plan envisaged a multilevel structure of schools called *primaires*, *secondaires*, *lycées*, and *écoles speciales*. Provision of primary schools was left to the decision of local governments. Both local governments and private persons were urged to set up intermediate schools, which, however, would qualify as *secondaires* only when authorized by the central government after meeting certain criteria. The lycées stood well above the secondary schools in rank; not only was their instruc-

---

[22] Roederer, *Oeuvres*, 3:436-38; a memo from Bonaparte dated Floréal of the Year X. The same idea of a temporary program was again expressed in Napoleon's "note" cited in note 39 below.

[23] Thibaudeau, *Mémoires*, pp. 127-32.

[24] *Archives parlementaires*, 2nd ser., 3:476-85.

tion more thorough, but their professors were civil servants salaried by the State, they could be promoted from a lesser to a greater lycée, and they could look forward to retirement pensions. They would also be supervised by a corps of traveling inspectors, who would visit them at least annually, shield them from interference by the local governments, and assist in the selecting of teaching personnel by drawing on a national pool, where the Central Schools had been dependent on local influence and local talent. The special schools were defined to mean those already existing (such as the Polytechnique), new medical schools to be added to the three already in operation, 10 law schools (it was now that the public teaching of law was revived, defunct since the disappearance of the pre-Revolutionary law faculties), and schools for various sciences and fine arts, somewhat as in the law of 3 Brumaire (pp. 233-34 above) with the addition of modern languages. Each or several of the special schools should be located *près d'un lycée*, meaning "near" or vaguely affiliated with it, and should be supervised by the administrative board of the lycée—a somewhat amorphous concept, suggesting that each lycée, or at least the town in which it was located, was to be a kind of university center with a concentration of higher and professional studies. Actually, none of the special schools in the sciences and fine arts was established.

Fourcroy offered the proposal in a spirit of compromise. It would combine, he said, the best features of the old universities and colleges with the best features of the Central Schools, while correcting the inadequacies of both. Through its scholarship program it would please those who desired a generous funding by the State, but it would also satisfy those "who think with [Adam] Smith that instruction should be left to private initiative."[25] It did not really abolish or repudiate the Central Schools. It merely recognized that only a certain number of them were large or flourishing; these would be elevated into lycées, and the others made into *écoles secondaires*, somewhat as many friends of the Central Schools had in fact recommended. To reassure those who feared the Catholic clergy it was provided that the heads of lycées must be married men, or men who had been married; but no such requirement was laid down for the professors, who therefore might in some cases be members or ex-members of the clergy.

A boy might enter a lycée as early as the age of nine and would follow a required course of six annual grades, running in each year in two parallel streams of language and literature and of mathematics and science. The arrangement thus closely reflected the plan of Destutt de

[25] Ibid., p. 480.

Tracy, the Idéologues, and the Council on Public Instruction of 1799 (p. 276 above), with the notable omission of a third stream of "ideological, moral and political sciences." Since the lycée could be entered at the age of nine (though not all would do so), it was obviously not designed to follow on the *écoles secondaires* but to be a separate track, and in this respect also the plan coincided with the one drawn up by Tracy and the Council on Public Instruction. It was more liberal, however, in not totally separating the two tracks, for it provided that a boy in an *école secondaire*, by winning a scholarship, might transfer to a lycée and so work his way up to one of the special schools and a fruitful later career.

The scholarships, indeed, as Fourcroy said, were the key to the whole system. There should be 6,400 *élèves nationaux* whose tuition and living costs in lycées and special schools were paid by the government; of these, 2,400 were to be selected by the government from among the sons of military men and civil servants, and 4,000 would come from the *écoles secondaires* after a competitive examination, with the government having the right to choose one of two candidates so presented by the school in each case. Different views expressed in the Council of State on the award of scholarships were thus compromised. For Fourcroy himself, the precedent that he mentioned was that of the Ecole Polytechnique, where serious competitive tests had been used since 1794.

The scholarships were the key because, in the first place, by supplying to one school as many as 150 scholars at 700 francs a year paid by the State they made possible the immediate establishment of lycées as good-sized institutions until enough paying students came in. In the second place, the scholarships were designed to encourage the formation of "secondary" schools in the new sense of the word, or the conversion of private schools to secondary status, since only the recognized secondary schools would have the right to have pupils compete for scholarships in the lycées. In addition, to encourage emulation in the secondary schools, prizes would be awarded to those of their teachers who had the most pupils admitted to lycées. Third, completion of studies at a lycée would be necessary for admission to one of the special schools, a provision that repeated, *mutatis mutandis*, a demand often made by republicans at the time of the Convention and the Directory. Finally, the existence of such a tightly interlocking public system, with attractive scholarships, was intended to reward friends of the government, to make new friends, and to draw families away from patronage of private schools, some of which were incompetent, some ephemeral, some frivolous, some inclined to undue religiosity or royalism, and some even tinged by the old Jacobinism.

The proposal was debated for several days in the Tribunate, which, though purged a few weeks before, still produced a variety of critical opinion.[26] A democratic opposition was voiced by P. F. Duchesne, who had been active in the Revolution at Grenoble. What the state should pay for, he thought, was elementary education, to combat the illiteracy that impeded economic progress; he therefore objected to the 4,000 competitive scholarships in the lycées and would use the money instead for primary schools. He noted that the government provided for no scholarships in the secondary schools, so that a really poor boy could never get far enough to compete for one in the lycées. In short, he told the Tribunes, "you must choose between the interest of a few families that are privileged in fact, if not in law, and of a huge population that will remain without education if this proposal is accepted."[27] More conservative views were expressed by Siméon, who said that many poor families would not send their children to a primary school even if it was free, and by Carrion-Nisas, who feared that ancient languages would be neglected and thought that a corporate and celibate teaching body, like the old Oratory, was much to be preferred. The strongest speech in favor of the proposal came from Jacquemont, who had been head of public instruction in the interior ministry for a short time under the Directory and one of the Idéologue members of the Council on Public Instruction in 1799. The proposal, said Jacquemont, did in fact correct many weaknesses in the Central Schools, in which the professors had had no security of tenure, assurance for the future, or protection against the disputes and intrigues of local boards; it also filled a gap that all acknowledged by encouraging the creation of secondary schools. The Tribunate approved the proposal by a vote of 80 to 9, and it passed the Legislative Body exactly as submitted by the Council of State, becoming law on 11 Floréal of the Year X, or May 1, 1802.

For a while the law of Floréal met with general satisfaction. It was accepted as an improvement on what had gone before. The lycées became a permanent and distinctive feature of the French educational system. The law gave no such assurance of *liberté de l'enseignement* as the constitution of 1795 had done, but private schools were tolerated and remained active. It remained to be seen what Bonaparte's future attitude to these schools would be, how he would use or abuse the

[26] Ibid., pp. 493-98, 519-42.
[27] Ibid., p. 533.

scholarships in the lycées, how in general he would comport himself—he had the Senate make him Consul for life only three months after the Floréal law, and Emperor of the French in 1804.

THE NAPOLEONIC LYCÉES

The law specified no number of lycées to be established, but Bonaparte in a first flush of enthusiasm thought that it might be as many as 400. There were two ways, he wrote to Roederer, in which lycées could be formed at once. One was for the government to approach the towns, promising to "grant" them a lycée on certain conditions, namely, that they have a suitable place to put it (such as a former college) and that they provide from their local revenues for the costs of furniture, maintenance, beds, tables, and kitchen equipment. The towns would readily agree, he supposed, and the larger ones would soon supply a full complement of paying students. The other way was to force the best existing colleges, "such as Juilly, Sorèze, Tournon, etc.," to come into the system by the threat of competition. The head of such a college should be brought to Paris and told that his establishment was about to fail, since "six national lycées are going to be set up in your neighborhood," but that of course the government wished to preserve so distinguished an institution, and would do so by converting it into a lycée, of which the head might remain as principal.[28]

As it turned out, it was not so easy to produce lycées. There were only 36 of them within the pre-Revolutionary borders of France at the end of the Napoleonic regime in 1814, and most of them were established between 1802 and 1806.[29] Most of the stronger Central Schools were soon converted into lycées, with the rest becoming "secondary" schools under the Floréal law. Any school having at least three teachers and 50 pupils could apply for recognition as "secondary," and a great many existing private establishments chose to do so, so that by 1806 there were reported to be 747 secondary schools within the French Empire.[30] Since the Empire then included Belgium, the German Left

[28] See note 22 above.

[29] France, Ministère de l'Instruction publique, *Statistique de l'enseignement secondaire en 1865* (Paris, 1868), pp. 1-21, lists all lycées in existence in 1865, with dates of their foundation and brief histories of the buildings that they occupied.

[30] Fourcroy's report of 1806 in *Archives parlementaires*, 2nd ser., 9:78. On the procedures of conversion of existing schools into *écoles secondaires* and lycées see the *Instruc-*

Bank of the Rhine, and the former Italian kingdom of Piedmont, the number within the pre-Revolutionary French borders may have been about 600. Half of them (370) were now classified as *écoles secondaires municipales* ("the old colleges under another name," as Fourcroy said, and soon to be renamed *collèges communaux*); they drew financial and other support from the towns, though their teachers were appointed by the minister of the interior. The other half (377) were called *écoles secondaires particulières*; they were private schools operated as their own enterprises by their heads. The municipal schools were said in 1806 to have 22,490 pupils, the private schools 27,710. Both kinds had the right to have their pupils compete for scholarships in the lycées. Below them, too small to qualify as secondary but above the primary level, the government knew of 4,500 other private schools with some 25,000 pupils. There was no town in the Empire, according to Fourcroy, that lacked an adequate school.

With only 36 lycées, it may seem that their significance should not be exaggerated. They were nevertheless the cynosure of the system. The public secondary schools were supposed to resemble them on a smaller scale; they taught the same subjects, though to a less advanced point, and the municipal secondary schools and the lycées were subject to much the same regulations as laid down by the national government.[31] A large secondary school with as many as eight teachers (a lycée had to have nine) was likely to be much like a lycée, except that its patronage was more local and that it would have no national scholarships.

What then were the lycées like? There has been less recent study of education in the Napoleonic years than for the Old Regime, the Revolution, or the nineteenth century, so that it is difficult to give a solid answer to this question. The issues are blurred by the partisanship of later writers, who, echoing Napoleon's own contemporaries, and whether

---

tion du conseiller d'état [Fourcroy] *chargé de la surveillance de l'instruction publique, aux inspecteurs généraux . . . chargés de l'organisation des Lycées*, 13 Brumaire of the Year XI, and the *Arrêté relatif aux maisons d'éducation tenues par des particuliers, et qui sont susceptibles d'être erigées en écoles secondaires*, 19 Vendemiaire of the Year XII, in *Recueil de lois et règlements concernant l'instruction publique depuis l'édit de Henri IV en 1598 jusqu'à ce jour*, 8 vols. (Paris, 1814-1827), 2:289-303 and 3:4-5.

[31] The regulations of 1803 for lycées are in ibid., 2:304-11 and 418-37, and for *écoles secondaires communales*, ibid., 3:6-17. They include plans of study and lists of approved books as well as organizational rules. There is much on the lycées in Aulard, *Napoléon et le monopole universitaire*. We are especially well informed on the lycée (and other schools) at Lyon, thanks to L. Trénard *Lyon de l'Encyclopédie au Préromantisme*, 2 vols. (Paris, 1958), 2:619-49, and S. Charléty, *Histoire de l'enseignement secondaire dans le Rhône de 1789 à 1800* (Paris, 1901).

conservative-royalist or liberal-republican, have portrayed his lycées as somber barracks, excessively militarized, with incompetents as teachers and ruffians for students, and with humane learning sacrificed to mathematics and science.

In a way, there was nothing very new about the Napoleonic lycées. Of the 36, only four were housed in buildings built as recently as the eighteenth century; all the others were in colleges or former abbeys and convents dating as far back as 1550 or before, many of them having once been Jesuit. Buildings, of course, had a longer useful life when neither plumbing nor wiring was required, in the absence of running water, good light, and central heating. Nor were the teachers newcomers, except for the youngest; many were carried over from the Central Schools, many had taught in the old colleges, and many were of the clergy or ex-clergy, of the kind willing to accept the changes since 1789, and hence disliked by sympathizers with the Old Regime.

The plan of study was said by its advocates to combine the best features of the pre-Revolutionary colleges, by which was meant a strictly ordered sequence of studies, and of the Revolutionary plans and the Central Schools by which was meant more attention to modern subjects than in the colleges before 1789. The following table allows easy

Year	Languages and Literature	Mathematics and Sciences
I	Elementary Latin and French; some history and geography	Elementary arithmetic
II	Continued	Arithmetic continued; elementary natural history
III	Continued	Elementary geometry; astronomy
IV	Latin and French authors	Algebra, chemistry; mineralogy
V	Continued	Algebra and elementary calculus; map study and cartography
VI	—	Differential and integral calculus; mechanics; physics, electricity, and optics
VII*	Philosophy*	

*Added in 1809. "Philosophy" included not only metaphysical and moral philosophy but also physics, chemistry, and advanced mathematics.

comparison with the arrangements at the Central Schools (p. 245) and as proposed in 1799 by Destutt de Tracy and the Council on Public Instruction (p. 276).[32] It will be seen that this new program for the lycées, adopted in 1802, departed widely from that in the Central Schools, but followed quite closely the recommendations of the Council on Public Instruction. If the new plan virtually reversed the original idea for the Central Schools, it showed continuity with the proposals by which these schools would have been reformed if the republican Idéologues had had their way. That is, it extended the study of Latin and literature and of mathematics and science over the whole series of years at school, with each year graded according to the student's age, and with no elective courses or other options. The Drawing, General Grammar, and Legislation of the Central Schools disappeared. The moral and political sciences urged by the Idéologues found no place in the lycées—nor, at first, did their proposal for Greek. The main subjects were Latin and Mathematics. The new plan, with elementary teaching left to the hazards of local governments and the Brothers of the Christian Schools, and with its concentration on Latin and mathematics, confirmed the preference of the Idéologues for a two-track system, with the directing elements of society receiving a special and more demanding education apart from the rest of the population.

The pattern for each lycée was to have an executive head, the *proviseur*, who was also a professor, and four whose titles were professors of Latin, and four known as professors of Mathematics. The professors of Latin taught French and some history and geography, those of Mathematics taught the sciences. When compared with the colleges of the Old Regime it appears that the lycées gave a more continuous and greater attention to mathematics and the sciences. Their renewed emphasis on Latin revived the pre-Revolutionary practice. It was often asked, then and later, what so much concentration on Latin had to do with the needs of a modern society. The answer usually given was that the training of the mind and the formation of taste were desirable under modern conditions, to which Fourcroy added (he was of course

[32] *The Statistique de l'enseignement secondaire* (note 29 above) contains a large tabulation following p. 441 showing plans of study, by student year, for 1802 as well as for 1789 and several other years up to 1865. Victor Duruy, minister of public instruction in the 1860s, also explains the program of 1802 in his introduction to the *Statistique*, pp. xvi-xix. See also Lanzac de Laborie, "L'enseignement secondaire pendant la période napoléonienne: Fondation et régime primitif des lycées, 1802-1814," *Revue de Paris* 6 (1924):292-324. There has been little study of Napoleonic schools in the past half-century, but a notable exception is June K. Burton, *Napoleon and Clio: Historical writing, teaching and thinking during the First Empire* (Durham, N.C., 1979).

a scientist himself) that it was by a knowledge of classical antiquity that Europe had overcome the barbarism of the Middle Ages.

As the years passed there was more of a tendency to revive the pre-Revolutionary plans of study. In 1809 the early years at the lycée were designated as Grammar, the intermediate years as the Humanities culminating in Rhetoric, and a year was added called Philosophy, in which physics and mathematics were included. A second year of Philosophy was introduced a little later. This nomenclature simply reflected the French educational tradition. The books prescribed for Philosophy ran from Plato and Aristotle through Bacon and Descartes to Locke and Condillac. The subject was no longer taught in Latin, as in the colleges before 1789, nor was it ever thereafter taught in Latin except for a few years in the 1820s when the educational die-hards vainly attempted a come-back. In general, although Napoleon preferred the scientific subjects, his aides in the educational apparatus were grounded in the French literary culture, and in the minutiae of curricular planning, some class hours were lost to the sciences and given to the humanities. Napoleon himself strongly favored the teaching of history, especially modern history of a kind to show the need and merits of the Fourth Dynasty, as he liked to call his regime, setting up as successor to the Merovingians, Carolingians, and Capetians. But much ancient history was still also studied.

The lycées differed from the Central Schools in that they were residential institutions, having boarders who either paid their own way or held scholarships (the *pensionnaires* and *boursiers*, both called *internes*), but they also had many day pupils (*externes*) who either lived at home or attended classes at the lycée while living in nearby private boarding schools. They differed also from the Central Schools in that no adult auditors sat in their classes. These facts, plus the fact that all students took the same subjects, meant that the lycées had a more intensive school atmosphere or "spirit" than their predecessors. It is not easy to say what this atmosphere was.

It was military and regimented. Discipline was strict, but corporal punishment was forbidden—a Revolutionary reform that proved permanent in France, and that distinguished it from the practice in the schools of England and other countries. By the regulations, often repeated, the students wore a uniform of blue cloth with yellow buttons on which the name of the lycée was inscribed, were organized in squads under student sergeants and corporals, and marched in formation at the sound of a drum from class to class and to the study halls, dining halls, dormitories, and "recreations." Undoubtedly this is what happened. The difficulty in visualizing the reality arises from the fact that the day students were expressly forbidden to wear the uniform or to take part in the study halls, recess periods, or excursions from the school. They could only attend the professors' classes, at the close of which they had to depart from the school. The number of such day students was large. Two of the four Paris lycées had day students only. For France as a whole, in 1813, there were 8,356 day students and only 6,136 residential students in the 36 lycées.[33] Similar regulations for wearing the uniform and quasi-military organization applied to the municipal colleges, with the same exclusion of day students, and in the municipal colleges the proportion of day students was even higher, with 19,730 day pupils and 9,829 residential pupils reported for 1813. The martial atmosphere must have been much diluted by the constant coming and going of so many boys and young men who were allowed no part in it. In addition, there is uncertainty as to how much of this martial atmosphere should be attributed to Napoleon. We have seen how a vogue for military airs in the colleges had arisen as far back as the 1760s.[34] After Napoleon's fall, during the first Restoration, in September 1814, much the same regulations were reissued, still requiring the uniform and marching in formation, and with the same exclusion of day students.[35] In any case there were in the lycées and municipal colleges two kinds of students, with the day students figuring as second-class citizens.

The residential school was the ideal because it gave *l'éducation* as well as *l'instruction*; that is, it aimed at the formation of character, which for Napoleon meant the habits and incentives that would be useful to him in the public service. It was to produce such schools that the 6,400 scholarships of the law of Floréal were introduced. And it was Napoleon's hope that a rising number of residential students whose families paid their expenses would make the scholarship program less necessary. This hope was not realized. In 1813 there were only 2,209 paying residential students in the lycées and 3,500 who enjoyed scholarships.[36] Not only was a figure of 3,500 far less than 6,400, but even

[33] See p. 319 below. These figures, like those also given here for the municipal colleges, are from the *Statistique* published in 1868 (note 29 above). Duruy, as minister in the 1860s, drew for his retrospective figures beginning with 1809 on the work done under his predecessor Villemain. Indeed, all enrollment figures for the First Empire, as given by Aulard, Grimaud, and others, seem to derive from Villemain. On the uncertainties and errors in Villemain's retrospective statistics for the years 1809-1814, see Julia and Pressly, "La population scolaire," pp. 1539-47.

[34] See above, pp. 27-28.

[35] *Recueil de lois et règlements depuis l'édit de Henri IV . . . ,*, 5:498, 504.

[36] Figures are from the *Statistique*, note 29 above. The figure of 2,209 given here for *pensionnaires* does not include 427 *demi-pensionnaires* who are included as residential

of the 3,500 only 2,199 were financed by the national treasury, the rest having been transferred by 1813 to the local governments and paid for by them as *bourses communales*. The national scholarships had also been diluted, many of them having become three-quarters or half-scholarships, because with the disappointing number of paying students it was necessary to multiply the number of state students without corresponding increase of expense. As to who received·the state scholarships we have data only for the year 1806. At that time, in all the lycées, including those of Brussels, Mainz, and Turin, there were 3,923 students holding national scholarships. Of these, 1,378 were the sons of military personnel, 1,301 the sons of civilian government servants, 361 of judges, and 883 of "simple private persons." Only these 883 owed their scholarships to competition in the secondary schools. The rest, while including many who were scholastically qualified and some whose parents had only modest incomes, owed their scholarships to selection by the minister of the interior in recognition of their fathers' service to the state.[37]

Napoleon, in short, used the lycées and the scholarships to reward his supporters and to educate young men who would be loyal and useful to himself. The lycées were stepping stones to the higher professional and military schools that he saw as pillars of his system. They were in fact patronized by families that were friendly to him, or who in general shared in the innovative and patriotic spirit that had arisen since 1789. It was mainly for this reason that others avoided them. Some complained that the lycées were irreligious, though Napoleon had introduced chaplains and religious exercises to offset this objection, while allowing non-Catholic students to be excused. Some complained that the professors in the lycées were a dubious lot, with ex-monks, married ex-priests, freethinkers, pretended intellectuals, dullards, and pedants all mixed together; but since such criticisms came from disgruntled elements, from *idéologues* to *dévots*, it is hard to know what to make of them. More understandable was the dislike of many parents for the military atmosphere of the lycées. The lycées were also expensive for those without scholarships. For some parents, the mere fact that they were run by the government was enough to make them

---

students on p. 304 above and p. 319 below. The *demi-pensionnaires* apparently took their meals, wore the uniform, spent the day at the school, and participated in its activities; they were counted as *internes*.

[37] Fourcroy's report, *Archives parlementaires*, 9:83. Fourcroy noted that many of the 883 who won competitive scholarships were in fact the sons of military or other government personnel; he wished to emphasize the importance of the lycées to the government.

distasteful. For others, the extreme emphasis on Latin and mathematics seemed irrelevant to their son's future careers, and for some the study of Latin and mathematics was simply too difficult. It could not be said in France, either then or for long afterward, that the public schools were too easy.

In any case, the failure of the lycées, and to a lesser extent of the municipal colleges and so of the whole public secondary system, to attract as many students as seemed necessary, and hence the strong competition from the private schools, was the main reason for the next step, the creation of the Imperial University.

THE IMPERIAL UNIVERSITY

It was an old and common idea among progressive thinkers, heard at least since the 1760s, that France should have a nationally uniform system of education, providing the same advantages equally to all parts of the country, under a supervision that would assure good quality everywhere. All had also argued that education should fortify the regime that they had in mind: the monarchy before the Revolution, the constitutional regime contemplated in the Talleyrand report, and the republic in the plans of 1793 and in the laws of 1795 and 1802. As one fairly obscure writer had said in 1768, the state must rest on the "union of minds and hearts among its citizens. Uniformity of teaching and education is the surest way to establish it."[38] Many writers and commentators whose ideas we have surveyed, and the authors of the Talleyrand plan, the Condorcet plan, the Paris plan of 1793, and the laws of 3 Brumaire of the Year IV and 11 Floréal of the Year X, had envisaged an elaborate system in which the lower schools prepared for the higher, and the higher oversaw the operations of the lower, with various levels and specialties carefully fitted together in one great pyramid of education.

None, however, had put anything definite at the summit of the pyramid. None had provided the degree of regulation needed to achieve and maintain such a system. This was provided by Napoleon in his Imperial University. It is not quite correct to say that he simply carried on the centralizing tendencies of the Revolution. What he carried on was a set of goals that implicitly required a high degree of centralization; what he added was the central authority that had been missing. He went further than many liked, but the fact that his University so

[38] J. A. Borrelly; see above p. 59.

long survived him suggests that it was thought to serve a desirable purpose.

Many voices had also called for a "teaching order," a *corps enseignant* or *corporation*, by which they had in mind, not the Jesuits expelled in 1762, but something like the Oratorians and the Doctrinaires whose orders were suppressed in 1792, that is, bodies of professional teachers who took no religious vows and who had become secularized well before 1789. The weaknesses of the Central Schools made the idea of a firmer organization more appealing. Some of the local governments, in replying to the prefects' inquiries in 1801, expressed a desire for such a teaching order, as did Chaptal when he became minister of the interior. What was wanted was a system in which properly qualified men, after receiving some training in their youth, would be given the incentives to make teaching a lifetime career.

As the first lycées were organized in 1803 and 1804, and the number of residential students who paid their own fees proved to be disappointing, both the Council of State and the minister of the interior proposed raising the fee so as to cover the expense. Napoleon strongly disagreed.[39] In effect, he said that the government instead of raising the price should find more customers, that is, students. For this purpose more central control was called for; the state councillor in charge of education (Fourcroy) should undertake *une grande surveillance*, visit lycées throughout the country, and maintain frequent contact with them by correspondence. The Emperor threw in a few afterthoughts in this memorandum of February 1805. "Perhaps it will soon be time to take up the question of forming a teaching body." In this connection he mentioned the Jesuits, though all he admired in them was their organization, "with their general, their provincials, etc.," and their system of ranks. A teaching body should provide the ground for a spirit of emulation, or constructive competition, by which one began by teaching in the lowest classes, then might rise by merit to the higher, and then become administrative head of the school. For the same reason, marriage should be forbidden to the youngest teachers; they should see marriage as a goal to be attained after establishing themselves professionally and being ready to support a family, "as in other civil careers." Teachers should also take pride in their occupation. The Emperor would honor those who distinguished themselves. "The world will sense the importance of a teaching corporation when it sees a man who after being a student in a lycée is then called by his talents to

[39] "Note sur les lycées," dated 27 Pluviôse of the Year XIII (February 16, 1805), in *Correspondance de Napoléon I*, 32 vols. (Paris, 1858-1869), 10:180-84, no. 8328.

teach in his turn, advancing from grade to grade, and finding himself toward the end of his career in the highest ranks of the state."

Of all political questions, said the Emperor, this was perhaps the most important. And he closed with a remark that his republican predecessors might have made. "There will be no fixed political state without a teaching body with fixed principles. So long as one does not learn from childhood whether to be republican or monarchist, Catholic or irreligious, etc., the State will not form a nation; it will rest on vague and uncertain foundations; it will be constantly exposed to changes and disorders."

Or again, we catch a glimpse of what Napoleon was aiming at in words spoken in the Council of State in March 1806.[40] He wanted to control opinion. For what purpose? It was in part military. "Military fanaticism is the only kind that is of any use to me—one needs it to get killed." But it was also in defense of the Revolution.

> My principal aim in establishing a teaching body is to have a means of directing political and moral opinions. This institution will be a guarantee against reestablishment of the monks—I shall no longer be pestered with that question—otherwise they will be reestablished some day or other. As for myself, I would rather entrust public education to a religious order than to leave it as it is; but I want neither one.

During these discussions of 1805 and 1806 the terms "teaching body" and "university" came to be used interchangeably and to refer not only to the public schools but also to controls over the private schools from whose competition the public system was suffering. There was much disagreement among the Emperor's advisors. Champagny, who had succeeded Chaptal as minister of the interior, repeated all the fears expressed in 1793 of a sluggish and self-serving centralized bureaucracy. Portalis, the minister of religious affairs, defended the private schools and the right of parents to send their children where they wished. Both opposed a strong central educational power. The opposite view prevailed, no doubt because Napoleon wished it so, but for reasons expressed by Fontanes, who was then president of the Legislative Body. Far from being a Jacobin, Fontanes had been a very tepid republican; he was known for his religious sympathies; he had taught Belles-Lettres in the Central Schools, and he was a polished speaker who could please the Emperor without offensive flattery. He said that

---

[40] Pelet de la Lozère, *Opinions de Napoléon . . . par un membre de son Conseil d'Etat* (Paris, 1833), p. 167.

the views of Champagny and Portalis would be valid "in a homogeneous society living with old traditions." But such was not now the case. "In the aftermath of a Revolution, as we emerge from anarchy and are in the presence of hostile parties, there must be in teaching as in all else a unity of views and of government. France needs, at least for a while, a single University and the University needs a single head."[41] The Emperor concurred. A brief law was submitted to the Legislative Body, approved without debate by the Tribunate (which was soon thereafter abolished), and duly enacted. Fourcroy presented the law in a long speech that was in fact the last reasoned discussion of education until after the collapse of the Empire.[42] The law of 1806 stated, as its first article:

"1. There shall be formed under the name of the Imperial University a body exclusively charged with teaching and education in the whole Empire."

The word "exclusively" implied what came to be called the *droit exclusif* or *monopole universitaire*, or that all teachers public and private were to be in some sense members of the new University. A second article provided that teachers would have certain civil obligations, and a third that a more detailed organization would soon be announced. This came in 1808 with the decree (not a "law," for the formalities of action by the Legislative Body were now dispensed with) by which the Imperial University was created. The decree mapped out a vast structure in 144 articles.[43]

The first point to be made is that the Imperial University was not a university at all in the sense then usual in Europe, or in France before the Revolution. A second point is that it excluded the highest French institutions of learning, such as the College of France and the Museum of Natural History, as well as the Polytechnique and the engineering and military schools. It thus continued the dichotomy set up in 1795

---

[41] E. Rendu, *M. Ambroise Rendu et l'Université de France* (Paris, 1861), p. 33. Ambroise Rendu worked in the University under Fontanes and later under the Restoration; his recollections and papers were published by his son Eugène and are a principal source (used by Aulard, *Napoléon et le monopole universitaire*, pp. 145-64) for this immediate background to the law of 1806.

[42] *Archives parlementaires*, 9:401-406. See also Fourcroy's long report to the Emperor, ibid., pp. 77-89.

[43] Beauchamp, *Recueil des lois et règlements*, 1:171-88. (This is not to be confused with the *Recueil* cited in note 30 above, where, however, the same decree may be found.) On the decree of 1808 and its application see Aulard, *Napoléon et le monopole universitaire*, pp. 141-370; and Lanzac de Laborie, 'La haute administration de l'enseignement sous le Consulat et l'Empire: Roederer, Fourcroy, Fontanes," *Revue des études napoléoniennes* 10 (1916):186-219.

by Fourcroy's law of 30 Vendémiaire and Daunou's law of 3 Brumaire of the Year IV, and laid the way for the future dichotomy between *université* and *grandes écoles*. A third point is that it applied not merely to France but to the whole French Empire, which by 1810 came to have 130 departments ranging from Rome on the Tiber to Lübeck on the Baltic Sea, and that its influence was felt in the associated states of the Grand Empire, as at the university of Padua in the Kingdom of Italy and at Göttingen in the Kingdom of Westphalia. This influence was of course cut short by Napoleon's fall in 1814.

At the head of the University was a Grand Master (the word *maître* meant also a teacher), a position to which Napoleon appointed Fontanes. Fourcroy, who had worked on education since 1794, died soon after, a disappointed man. Advising the Grand Master was a University Council, a mixture of intellectual luminaries and senior officers of the University. The whole Empire was divided into educational districts called "academies," each in charge of a rector, each with his council. At both the central and the academy levels there were inspectors who visited, reported on, and assisted the teaching establishments. Within each academy there might be "faculties," designed to give advanced instruction, and of which there were five kinds, each with its dean— sciences, letters, law, medicine, and theology. The faculties had no connection with each other, and those in the same town did not constitute a localized university; they were more like the special schools envisaged in various plans since the Talleyrand report, none of which had come into existence except for law and medicine. In any case very few academies had more than two or three of the five faculties.

Hierarchically below the faculties were the schools that it was the real business of the Imperial University to control. These included two kinds of public schools, the lycées and the "secondary" schools now renamed communal colleges; and the two kinds of private schools, of which the higher kind were now called simply *institutions*, and the lower kind for younger boys were designated as *pensions*. In the public system the teachers, called "professors," enjoyed the status of civil servants; they were selected, trained, appointed, transferred, promoted, paid on a salary scale determined by the state, and pensioned in old age. In the private system each school had to be authorized by the minister of the interior, who also had to approve its appointments. All were subject to visits by the inspectors and supervision by the rectors. For completeness, it may be added that primary schools were briefly mentioned in the decree of 1808, and in principle belonged to the University, but that they in fact received little official attention. The main business of the rectors and inspectors was to assure the quality of instruction and inform themselves (and the Grand Master) on the political attitudes of teachers in the lycées, communal colleges, *institutions*, and *pensions*.

A fifth kind of "secondary" school, the *petits séminaires* or junior seminaries, made the task of supervision more difficult. Under the Concordat the bishops were allowed to set up seminaries for the training of priests. Before the Revolution it had been customary for a youth aiming at the priesthood to attend an ordinary college, along with others, before going to a seminary. Many, including Fourcroy and Napoleon himself, thought that this practice should continue. But now, as the bishops argued, the state schools were so imbued with free-thinking, atheism, or simply religious neutralism that it was necessary to have religious schools for boys before the age at which they would proceed to higher theological studies. Junior seminaries thus multiplied throughout France, available to boys and young men up to the age of eighteen or so. Many families who had no intention for their sons to enter the priesthood sent them to the junior seminaries for ordinary schooling, preferring their religious sponsorship and atmosphere, and often their lower cost, to either the public schools or the other private schools, many of which were conducted by laymen.

An innovation of the University was the reintroduction of academic degrees, which had disappeared in the Revolution. Those for law and medicine had been revived in 1802, along with the organization of schools for those subjects, and had been made prerequisite to the practice of those two professions. The decree of 1808 framed a more comprehensive system of degrees as an apparatus for regulation. Students in a lycée after their years of Rhetoric and Philosophy, and after passing an examination, earned the bachelor's degree, the *baccalauréat ès arts*, which thus resembled the *maîtrise ès arts* of the colleges of the Old Regime. Once having this degree in letters, they might after further examination obtain the *baccalauréat ès sciences*. Further study in one of the faculties led to an intermediate degree, the *licence*, and to the highest degree, the *doctorat*. The degrees in law and medicine were becoming well established, but there was little call for those in theology, since the clergy disliked theological education in institutions operated by the state. A degree in letters or science was required of all teachers, in both private and public schools, but it was made easy to obtain for men currently active. The old *maîtrise ès arts* was ruled to be equivalent to the bachelor's degree, and *agrégés* of the former University of Paris—as well as professors at the College of France, the Museum, and the Polytechnique—could become doctors of sciences or of letters virtually upon request. Men who had taught in the abol-

ished religious congregations, by which were meant Oratorians, Doctrinaires, Benedictines, and so forth, or in the *écoles militaires* before
the Revolution, if they could prove 10 years of teaching experience,
were allowed to take degrees in the University without examination,
according to their status in 1809: those teaching in the more elementary classes became bachelors, those in the intermediate classes *licenciés*,
and professors of Rhetoric and Philosophy became automatically doctors of letters or of sciences. No purge of the schools was intended.
The purpose of the government was not to freeze teachers out but to
compel them to come in.[44]

The bachelor's degree was the key to the whole system. It was awarded
only after examination "on whatever is taught in the higher classes of
the lycées." The examination itself, very simple by later standards, was
a half-hour's oral response to questions posed by three judges. Before
taking it the candidate had to produce evidence of having studied
Rhetoric and Philosophy for two years in a lycée or "in a school where
this twofold instruction has been formally authorized," which might
mean an *institution* or even a junior seminary. The baccalaureate was
thus a mechanism for making the instruction in private schools conform to the public system. It was also a prerequisite for admission to
the higher faculties and special schools, and hence for entrance into
the professions, as well as for certain appointments in the civil service.
The purpose of course was to induce more students to enter the lycées,
to control the private establishments, and to promote uniformity, or
at least lay a common foundation for the directing class of notables,
administrators, and experts on whose competence and dedication
Napoleon relied to build his empire.[45]

The faculties of letters and of science conducted the examinations
for the baccalaureate so that the higher bodies in the hierarchy had a
means of control over the lower. In practice the hierarchy was indis-
tinct, since many professors in these two faculties, especially outside
Paris, were simply professors of Rhetoric or Mathematics or Philosophy in the local lycée, who acted as professors in the faculties also. In
Paris the faculties of letters and of science were staffed by men who
were simultaneously professors in the Paris lycées or at the College of
France, the Museum, the Polytechnique, the Bureau of Longitudes,
and so forth. The main function of the faculties of letters and science

[44] For the award of degrees according to prior degrees on teaching experience see the
general orders of May 12 and 23, 1809, in Beauchamp, *Recueil des lois et règlements*,
1:218-19.
[45] For the examination see ibid., 1:174, 224, 250.

(those of law and medicine were more professional) was to act as guardians of the gate by examining, passing, or failing the candidates for the bachelor's degree.

For the preparation of teachers in the lycées an Ecole Normale was authorized in 1808 and opened in 1810. It resembled the Ecole Normale of 1795 in nothing but name. The inspectors chose 134 bright youngsters in the lycées, by competitive examination, but only 50 appeared at the opening of the school. They had to be at least seventeen years old, were financed by the government, and were exempted from military service in return for a promise to serve in the University for at least 10 years. They were housed in the upper floors of the old Plessis College, which had been incorporated into the Imperial Lycée (formerly Louis-le-Grand), and since the lower floors of Plessis College also housed the Paris faculties of letters and of science we can see the modesty of the operation. Students took a two-year course, in which after the first year they might be examined for the baccalaureate, so that the first year overlapped with the work of the lycée; after one more year they might obtain the *licence*. Instruction was both by lecture and by question and discussion sessions, in which the students were encouraged to learn how to present material in their future classes. About three-quarters aimed at teaching letters, largely Latin, and a quarter at the sciences, largely mathematics and physics. A separate channel for teacher preparation was created by revival of the *agrégation* of the Old Regime, to which any graduate of a lycée could aspire by study in one of the faculties, without attending the Ecole Normale. It was several years before either channel could produce significant results. Both show, however, a serious intent on the part of the government to produce a body of professional teachers. It was teaching, not "research," that was emphasized. The mission of schools for adolescents was to transmit knowledge, not to criticize, renovate, or dispute it. It remained also, more for Fontanes and his subordinates than for Napoleon, the cultivation of literary style and aesthetic taste.[46]

Financially the University was self-supporting. It had an income of its own that was enough to cover its expenses. Napoleon presented it with a *dotation*, or guaranteed endowment, of 400,000 francs a year, to be paid by the national treasury, as a replacement for the income-producing properties of the 10 former Paris colleges lost in the Revolution; and he also conveyed to the University all property that had

---

[46] *Centenaire de l'Ecole Normale* (Paris, 1895), pp. 212-13; Duruy's introduction to *Statistique l'enseignement secondaire*, pp. cxxiii-cxxvi; Aulard, *Napoléon et le monopole universitaire*, pp. 344-53. On the *agregation* see pp. 62-63 above.

belonged to colleges and universities throughout the Empire that had been confiscated but had not been sold to private persons or was not assigned to other public uses. Very little such property was left, if we may judge by the fact that the income from its own domain that figured in the University budget for 1812 was only 45,000 francs. Nor was the endowment of 400,000 francs very munificent, being much less than had been contemplated in the abortive law of 1801, or than the endowed income of French colleges before the Revolution. Since the annual income of the University in Napoleon's time was about 2,600,000 francs it is evident that it came mostly from other sources.[47]

By far the most important was the University fee, or *retribution universitaire*, which produced about 1,800,000 francs a year. It had to be paid to the University both by the public lycées and communal colleges and by the private *institutions* and *pensions*. The head of each such establishment took the amount that he himself charged to parents for his *pensionnaires* (i.e. for board, room, and tuition), multiplied it by the number of his students including scholarship holders and day students, and remitted one-twentieth of the total every year to the University. In addition he had to pay a smaller sum every 10 years in order to stay in the system. This financial burden on the member schools was the chief cause of objection to the University and seems to have aroused more complaint than any interference in their internal operations, choice of teachers, or tone and content of courses of study.

Most of the income of the University went for what may be called overhead. The salaries, expenses, and offices of the Grand Master, the University Council, and the inspectors-general consumed over 900,000 francs in 1812, and the rectors, deans, and inspectors of the regional academies took another 650,000. The only items in the budget of 1812 containing funds that reached teachers and students were 113,000 francs for the Ecole Normale and about 550,000 for the various faculties. In addition, outside the University budget, and paid directly to the lycées from the national treasury, was a sum of 1,200,000 francs for scholarships. In general, it is clear that the University was a system by which, although public schools also contributed, the private schools were made to pay for the public authority that was set up to supervise them. This, of course, meant that the parents of private as well as public school students carried the cost. At a time when the financing of schools by general taxation was out of the question, in other coun-

---

[47] For this and the following two paragraphs see the Appendix below, and the tables in C. Jourdain, *Le budget de l'instruction publique . . . depuis la fondation de l'Université Impériale jusqu'à nos jours* (Paris, 1857), pp. 294-99, and his explanations throughout the book.

tries as well as in France, there was a certain ingenuity and even justice in the arrangement. Though loudly protested against, the *retribution universitaire* lasted right through the Restoration and was not abolished until 1844.

It was the parents who paid for education at the secondary level in both the public and the private schools, except in so far as their sons could obtain scholarships, and except for subventions by some of the towns. The state was not inactive, however; indeed its budget for public instruction in 1812 was larger than that of the University.[48] Within a total of 3,100,000 francs it designated 1,200,000 for scholarships in the lycées, as just noted. All the rest went to higher learning: some to the faculties of law and medicine, which lived mainly on their own fees; and some to the Institute, the College of France, the Museum of Natural History, the Bureau of Longitudes, the School of Oriental Languages, and the great libraries of Paris that had become public property during the Revolution.

MONOPOLY AND COMPETITION

Napoleon said later at St. Helena that the University was one of his greatest achievements, but he was never satisfied with it during the six years between its founding and the date of his abdication. He continued to be irritated at the prosperity of the private schools. As he said in a note of 1810, it would be best if eventually there were no private schools at all; they were too transient, they came and went, disappearing with the death of their heads, or passing into other hands; whereas the University was an undying corporation, composed of men who shared in a common training and a common outlook, whose official status and secure tenure made them impervious to intellectual fashions and parental demands, and who would reproduce themselves generation after generation. The University was to be a stable force, "a guarantee against pernicious and subversive social theories on one side or another," by which he apparently meant, without saying so, both the Catholicism of "monks" and the liberalism of Idéologues.[49] He always insisted that his University was not antireligious, with priests among its teachers and chaplains in its schools; and he called his regime "liberal," meaning that it was more modern, enlightened, and efficient

[48] For the state budget, see ibid., pp. 300-301.
[49] This note of 1810 was published by Arthur Chuquet in the *Revue internationale de l'enseignement* 62 (1911):230-31. Chuquet was uncertain whether it was addressed to the Council of State.

than others, and more fair to the formerly unprivileged classes. He could not see why anyone should disagree with him.

The private schools were very numerous; there were 50 *institutions* in Paris in 1810, and 81 classified as *pensions*, not to mention primary schools, and the girls' schools that Napoleon deliberately excluded from the University. Many of them were very small, some were as large as the best lycées. Most were under lay auspices, though like the public schools they might have priests among their teachers. Opposition to them was not a mere conflict between church and state. Or rather, the conflict between religious and secular influences might be found throughout the University in schools of any type, so that Napoleon had his doubts even on the spirit within his lycées. Especially troublesome were the junior seminaries, the *petits séminaires*, which were not so transient as other private schools because they were maintained by the bishops in each diocese. There was reason to suppose, especially when the Pope was brought in captivity to France in 1809, that the junior seminaries were not inspiring their pupils with wholehearted loyalty to the regime. The government blamed them also for teaching almost no science or mathematics. With their lower fees, or sometimes free instruction, and probably also with their easier studies, they were attractive to many families to whom the official system had little to offer. Hence they had many pupils who had no intention of entering the priesthood.

Napoleon urged Fontanes as Grand Master to look more closely into all such matters, but Fontanes and the University Council were more tolerant than the Emperor of the existing variations and more disinclined to stir up unnecessary opposition. Dissatisfied, Napoleon then turned to his minister of police, who sent a circular to the prefects of the departments. Some prefects failed to reply, some tried to excuse themselves by saying that with the founding of an independent University the schools were outside their jurisdiction, and some responded only with reassuring generalizations. Many reported, however, after careful inquiry, that the spirit in the schools was good, that their teachers were "devoted to the government," used approved books, and taught the glories of the Fourth Dynasty. A few viewed the situation with alarm. They cited the cases of towns where the lycée or college withered away while its competitors flourished. The more anticlerical prefects denounced the junior seminaries as haunts of superstition and backwardness.[50]

[50] C. Schmidt, *La réforme de l'Université Impériale en 1811* (Paris, 1905). Most of this book consists of the text of relevant inquiries and the replies of the prefects. Aulard, *Napoléon et le monopole universitaire*, chap. 7, draws heavily on the work of Schmidt, who was his student.

It is not easy to weigh in Napoleon's mind the motivations that led to what followed. His whole system reflected the notion that everything should be rationally managed and organized. It was an idealization of bureaucracy, on the premise that the government knew best and that the best men served in the government. The University was set up outside the government, and Napoleon seems really to have believed that it should be shielded from political pressures, but it was nevertheless an arm of the state and the state represented the public interest. There was a fear of anything not known to the authorities or anything on which reports could not be readily obtained. There was a willingness to repress enemies of the regime. But the regime had few identifiable dangerous enemies. Even the modern writer who has most closely studied the French private schools of this period, and who was altogether hostile to the *monopole universitaire*, concludes that the private schools and even the junior seminaries were giving support to the Empire, that they were less harassed than under the Directory, and that there was more objection to the University during the Restoration than there had been in Napoleon's time.[51] Disaffection with Napoleon increased as the wars kept recurring on ever more distant battlefields, but it remained latent and passive; opponents of the regime proclaimed their adherence while waiting for it to collapse under its own overextension.

In any case Napoleon in 1811 embarked on a program really to crush the private schools. He especially wanted to strengthen his lycées, of which there were still only 36. By a long edict of November 1811 he ordered the number to be increased immediately to 100, with enough communal colleges to be converted into lycées to achieve this figure. Of the private schools, the *institutions* and *pensions* located in towns having a lycée or college were ordered to send their pupils to classes in that lycée or college; that is, they would be reduced to the status of boarding houses or tutoring schools, with the private schoolmasters allowed only to assist pupils with their lessons. This provision only renewed attempts that had been unenforceable throughout the Old Regime, since a similar provision had occurred in Henry IV's statute of 1598 for the University of Paris, and it echoed attempts made by the Parlement of Paris in the 1780s. In addition, by the decree of 1811 the heads of *institutions* and *pensions* were forbidden to take boarding students over nine years old so long as vacancies existed in the college or lycée of the same town. The decree was especially harsh on the junior seminaries. It reaffirmed the powers of the University over them, limited their number to one in each department,

[51] Grimaud, *Histoire de la liberté de l'enseignement*, 4:407-20.

and ordered the closing of all except those located in towns having a college or lycée, to which it required that their students be sent for their classes, where they would be clearly marked out by having to wear ecclesiastical costume.[52]

A frantic series of further efforts followed the decree of 1811. In March 1812 the Emperor ordered the Paris lycées to be enlarged to accommodate more boarders. As a curious example of his taste for imperial grandeur he projected a vast Palais de l'Université to be built along the Seine, "a series of buildings" to house the Grand Master, the Ecole Normale, the retirement home for superannuated professors, and halls for the annual prize-giving ceremonies, all to be surrounded by spacious gardens but with nothing for ordinary classrooms, professors' studies, or student living quarters. It must be built at once, said the Emperor; only one stone was ever laid. Even during the invasion of Russia he could not take his mind off the subject. At Vitebsk, in July 1812, he dictated a letter ordering students in private as well as in public schools to wear a uniform of blue cloth, "indigo pastel," with suitable accessories. Barely returned from Russia, he forbade private schools to hold any public exercises in towns having a college or lycée. In April 1813 he required them, if they posted public announcements of their programs, to print the posters in yellow letters on a black background and to keep the announced programs absolutely unchanged. In Germany, from his headquarters on the day after the battle of Dresden, on August 29, 1813, he again demanded the formation of more lycées in 18 French towns, which he named, and in three others in his Empire—at Cologne, Trier, and Cuneo (near Genoa)—as well as the immediate conversion into lycées of two of France's most eminent private schools, Juilly and Sorèze.[53]

[52] For the text of the decree of 1811 see Beauchamp, *Recueil des lois et règlements*, 1:319-40, and the *Recueil de lois et règlements* (Paris, 1814-1827), 4:298-335. The decree even reached out to the primary schools (articles 107-108), declaring that the University would take measures to improve the teaching of reading, writing, and arithmetic; that the Brothers of the Christian Schools would be "certified and encouraged" by the Grand Master; and that the heads of their congregation would be made members of the University, an honor that surely implied an increased vigilance over them. The reader will observe that nothing is said in the present pages on elementary schooling in these years, but one may refer to M. Gontard, *L'Enseignement primaire en France de la Révolution à la loi Guizot (1789-1833)* (Paris, 1959), and to P. Zind, *Les nouvelles congrégations des Frères enseignants en France de 1800 à 1830*, 3 vols. (Lyon, 1969).

[53] For letters and orders enforcing the decree of 1811 see *Recueil de lois et règlements* (Paris, 1814-1827), 4:336-43; the relevant passages in Schmidt, Aulard, and Grimaud; and J. Quicherat, *Histoire de Sante-Barbe, collège, communauté, institution*, 3 vols. (Paris, 1860-1864), 3:122-28. Sainte-Barbe was a leading *institution* or private school in Paris, having originated more as an offshoot of the Prytanée français than from the pre-Revolutionary Sainte-Barbe from which it took its name.

All this outburst produced only mixed results. At Napoleon's abdication in April 1814 there were still only 36 lycées within the old French borders, and those in the rest of the Empire were no longer subject to the Imperial University, which was henceforth called the University of France. There is evidence, however, that the campaign to force private school students to attend classes in the lycées had some effect. We find the evidence in a statistical report submitted by the minister of the interior to the Legislative Body in February 1813.[54] From this it appears that, in all the lycées of the Empire, the number of boarding students rose only from 6,800 to 8,000 between 1809 and the school year 1812-1813, or about 18 percent, while the number of day students rose from 2,700 to 10,000 for an increase of 260 percent. That most of these day students came from private schools is shown by other figures pertaining only to France within its old borders. These are seemingly more exact though not altogether reliable, and they have the advantage of being broken down into more meaningful categories, as in the table that follows.[55] It will be seen that the number of day students coming from private schools quadrupled, while

Students	1809	1813	Percentage of change
Residential			
National scholarship holders	3,880	2,199	− 43
Communal scholarship holders	319	1,301	+ 308
Total scholarship holders	4,199	3,500	− 17
Self-financed	1,728	2,636	+ 53
Total	5,927	6,136	+ 4
Day			
Living at home or with relatives	2,188	4,620	+ 111
Coming from private schools	953	3,736	+ 292
Total	3,141	8,356	+ 166
Total students	9,068	14,492	+ 60

Note: Table shows numbers of students in the 36 lycées within pre-Revolutionary French borders.

[54] "Exposé de la situation de l'Empire," reprinted in *Archives parlementaires*, 11:245.

[55] *Statistique de l'enseignement secondaire*, p. 74. The figures are subject to doubt (see note 33 above), but the present inferences depend on the relative size of the categories, not on the exactness of the numbers. The self-financed residential students in the table are the *pensionnaires* of Duruy's statistics, with whom 427 *demi-pensionnaires* are here included. The students living at home or with relatives are *externes libres*; the students coming from private schools are *externes appartenant à des établissements libres*.

the number of residential students remained virtually unchanged, and the number of scholarship holders actually declined. But even a quadrupling of these day students represented a minority of the relevant enrollment in private schools, so that the same figures show a desultory enforcement. The Empire was not ruthlessly repressive or "totalitarian" in a way that later times were to know.

Historians have differed over the meaning to be attached to the Napoleonic "monopoly." Alphonse Aulard, writing in 1911, concluded that the attempts at monopoly had been ineffectual, and saw in Fontanes a kind of crypto-royalist and mild Catholic who as Grand Master discreetly blocked the implementation of the Emperor's wishes, so that in reality there never was any monopoly. Louis Grimaud, a scholarly lawyer outside the French university system, and apparently a Catholic writing in the 1940s, concluded that the monopoly had been real enough, since private schools could not exist without authorization by the state and were damaged by the efforts made to subordinate them to the public system. He conceded, however, that the private schools were less troubled even at the end of the Empire than during the Revolution and under the Directory. It is in part a matter of definition. In one sense there was a monopoly, in another sense there was not. There was a trend toward monopoly, and if the Empire had lasted longer, and if competition had been less strong, the monopoly might have been realized. Even so, it would not have been due only to Napoleon's ambition. Nor was it only a consequence of the Revolution. The contending forces were of long standing. It may be recalled that when C. F. Lamoignon of the Parlement of Paris, in 1783, had urged a uniform system of education under the state, his cousin Lamoignon de Malesherbes had warned against monopoly and favored competition.[56]

The Higher Spheres

Napoleon's University, so far as it was more than an administrative machine, was essentially a teaching establishment, consisting of lycées and secondary schools and of higher facilities whose main activity was to give instruction. Its faculties of law, medicine, and theology were meant for the training of practicing lawyers, physicians, and priests. Professors in the faculties of sciences and of letters were indeed enjoined to keep abreast of new discoveries in their subjects, "so that

[56] See above, p. 78.

teaching may always be abreast of acquired knowledge," but it would be only by luck or exception if they were to make any further discoveries of their own.[57] Their function, like that of the professional faculties, was to transmit the most reliable acquired knowledge to the oncoming generation. In addition, they certified the results by the award of degrees. In this there was much of the spirit of the Enlightenment, a belief that many old errors had been corrected by new truths recently found, so that the most urgent problem was to put the new knowledge to work. There was little of the idea expressed at this same time by Wilhelm von Humboldt, and presumably incorporated into the University of Berlin founded in 1810: that both the professor in teaching and the student in learning should be engaged in exploring the unknown, since a spirit of inquiry was the mark of a truly educated mind. That teaching and research should go together was a new and German idea, destined eventually for possibly excessive triumphs. The French idea was that teaching and research should both excel, but be carried on in at least relative separation. It took another 80 years for the "German" idea to pervade France.

Higher learning, understood as the active pursuit of new knowledge, therefore went on beyond or above the University. An exception may be made for the faculties of medicine, which benefited also from the schools of pharmacy. Medicine was the closest of the faculties to actual science. The Revolutionary changes, codified under Napoleon, had brought medicine and surgery together and both into more habitual contact with reorganized hospitals. Medicine, therefore, not yet closely joined with biological research since the pathological effects of microorganisms were unknown, took advantage of the new opportunities to observe disease among numerous patients who were now assembled and classified in hospital wards. Medical progress came to rely on statistical study, by which correlations of symptoms could be observed, or the successive phases of an affliction could be traced, or the probabilities in the use of a given treatment or drug could be estimated. There were also statistical surveys of the relation of disease to weather, water supply, poverty, or housing, which proved useful when cholera became epidemic about 1830. During the Revolutionary and Napoleonic years the recurring wars, with their casualties, made possible the testing and even the improvement of the surgeon's arts.[58]

In the absence of "graduate students," a social role yet to be invented, and with the lycées corresponding to English and American

[57] Beauchamp, *Recueil des lois et règlements*, 1:249.
[58] On medical schools see the references in chap. 5, n. 36 above.

colleges, the faculties of sciences and of letters had only few and very occasional students, except those at the Ecole Normale in Paris. Their professors found themselves often addressing audiences of interested adults, somewhat like professors in the Central Schools before 1802, or as in the lyceums that grew up in the United States at this time. It was a practice that inhibited specialized research, but it promoted qualities for which French learning was once famous, such as clarity, order, a pleasing style, and an avoidance of pedantry. In the sciences it also promoted a fairly high level of popularization. In literature, or what was called belles-lettres, it was not even supposed that new knowledge was possible or especially relevant. Napoleon once remarked that a professor of literature could have little to say that a fourteen-year-old boy did not know. Professors of the subject gave polished talks on the well-known classics, and their publications usually consisted of textbooks, edited works, translations, commentaries, anthologies, and *morceaux choisis* from Latin, Greek, and French authors.

It was only in Paris in the early years of the University that the faculties of science and of letters were of importance. Even in Paris they were shadowy bodies. At the end of the Empire the Paris faculty of sciences consisted of nine professors, of whom two were also professors in the Paris lycées, three in the College of France, three in the Museum of Natural History, and three in the Ecole Polytechnique (including two who were also in the College of France). They made a distinguished roster, but as a faculty they added no scientific strength to what existed before. The faculty of letters was somewhat larger, with 12 professors, since there were more examinations to be held for the baccalaureate in letters than in the sciences and more students at the Ecole Normale requiring attention. Of the 12, two were from the College of France and three from the Paris lycées. Among the others, holding no other appointment, were the philosophers Laromiguière and Royer-Collard and the youthful Guizot, who made his debut by lecturing on modern history. The faculty of letters thus added a small increment to the Paris intellectual scene. But to a large extent both faculties were staffed by men whose base was outside the University and who simply gave it a part of their time, thus earning a supplement to their salaries.[59]

---

[59] On the personnel of the faculties of sciences and of letters see the *Almanach impérial* for 1813, pp. 857-58. In general, also L. Liard, *L'enseignement supérieur*, 2:65-124; and Aulard, *Napoléon et le monopole universitaire*, pp. 315-55. Liard and Aulard were both active in reform of French higher education at the turn of the century, hoping to create modern research universities, and so they viewed the Napoleonic arrangements with strong disfavor.

It is a paradox that in this golden age of French science an Emperor who actually admired the sciences did so little to advance them. Perhaps he did not need to. He drew on men educated before the Revolution. He maintained the great learned establishments that had been reshaped by the National Convention. He reorganized the Institute, suppressing its class in moral and political sciences, without much harm to individual members, who were simply transferred to other classes; and in fact the Institute won marks of his favor, as when it received the quarters it has ever since occupied, moving into the building vacated by the old College and Central School of the Quatre-Nations. The college, renamed the Lycée Bonaparte, was transferred to a new neighborhood on the right bank of the Seine. Members of the Institute (who again became "academicians" in 1815) also received from Napoleon the dress uniforms in which they have since held their formal sessions under the dome of the one-time college chapel, built in memory of Cardinal Mazarin.

The College of France was again briefly threatened, as during the Revolution, by another proposal that never was realized. The bureaus of the ministry of the interior developed a project for a "special school of literature and history" to be located in the College, or even to replace it. The Emperor sent back his comments in a moment of leisure during his campaign of 1807 in eastern Europe.[60] The regime was fast becoming more sycophantic, and someone had suggested the appointment of an imperial poet and an imperial historiographer. Napoleon rejected both. An official poet, he said, would become an object of ridicule. An official historian would never be trusted. "It is generally accepted that a historian is a judge who should be the voice of posterity, and that so many qualities and perfections are required of him that it is hard to see how a history can be written on command."[61]

He continued with a little essay on the meaning of "special schools" as projected in the law of Floréal of 1802. They all, he said, represented studies above the lycées. Cases in point were the new schools of law, where the new legal codes were explained, and the schools of medicine, where one learned how to attend the sick. The engineering and military schools were obvious examples, as was the Bureau of Longitudes, which he thought was in effect an advanced school of mathematics. But as for the advanced study of literature, if it meant dwelling on the beauties of language, he dismissed it as useless. "A professor of belles-lettres may be entertaining, if he is witty, and in-

---

[60] *Correspondance de Napoléon I*, 32 vols. (Paris, 1859-1869), 15:121-37, nos. 12415 and 12416; A. Lefranc, *Histoire du Collège de France* (Paris, 1893), pp. 314-28.

[61] *Correspondance de Napoléon I*, 15:122.

teresting, if he has the art; but he develops no new principle or new ideas ... he only teaches you what you learned in college; and he himself if he professed for forty years would know no more on the last day than in the first year."[62] Even so, he accepted professors of belles-lettres as harmless. There was, however, another meaning of literature (as indeed there then was in both French and English), since it might include history and geography. These were factual subjects on which instruction was possible.

For geography he proposed the creation of four chairs, one each for Europe, Asia, Africa, and the Americas. As for history, he said that he himself had wasted much time reading books that proved to be useless. There should be instruction in critical bibliography and historiography so that students could learn where to go to find out what they wanted to know. There should be more attention to recent history. It was absurd that a French youth in 1807 could more easily learn about the Punic Wars than about the War of American Independence concluded in 1783. Chairs were especially needed in the history of law and of military operations. Granted that the historian was a judge, what Napoleon wanted was "facts," somewhat like Ranke's *wie es eigentlichen gewesen war*. All told, said the Emperor, a "real special school of literature" must have 20 or 30 professorships.

Nothing came of this idea, and the College of France survived as it had been since the Revolution, and indeed since 1772. Still with 19 chairs, it was in fact flourishing. Between 100 and 200 auditors (students and others) flocked to its courses in physics, chemistry, medicine, anatomy, and natural history, the last named being taught by the eminent Georges Cuvier. Almost as many attended lectures on Latin poetry and French literature. A hundred went to hear "the law of nations" expounded. Naturally only a few studied Hebrew, Arabic, Persian, or Turkish, but from 25 to 30 heard Lalande, Mauduit, and Biot on pure and applied mathematics. These were large numbers for Europe at that time for such advanced study.[63]

The Museum of Natural History at the old Jardin des Plantes was little changed since its reorganization in 1793. Its staff consisted of 13 regular professors and 12 younger *aides-naturalistes* who were lodged on the grounds, as well as four professional painters whose work in the era before photography was indispensable to natural history. The professors were an eminent group: Cuvier in comparative anatomy; Lamarck in invertebrate zoology; Lacépède and Geoffroy Saint-Hilaire

[62] Ibid., p. 131.
[63] The figures are from Fourcroy's report of 1806, *Archives parlementaires*, 9:84.

in the zoology of quadrupeds, reptiles, and fish; Vauquelin in chemistry; Jussieu in botany; and Haüy in mineralogy. There seems to be no record of the number of their students or others who studied with them. All are memorialized in the street names of Paris near the Jardin des Plantes, except for Haüy, whose name even the French may find it difficult to pronounce.[64]

The Ecole Polytechnique underwent significant changes during the Napoleonic years. A knowledge of Latin was added to the admission requirements, with ensuing debate on whether this signified simply a reactionary step, or a good test of scholastic aptitude, or a desire to attract a more high-toned student body. Until 1805 students at the Polytechnique received a cash stipend from the state and made their own living arrangements outside the school. In 1805 the school was militarized, or at least converted to a residential school under strict discipline, with students required to pay a *pension* for room and board, except for a fund of about 30,000 francs a year for scholarships. These were awarded on a basis of combined need and merit, being intended only for those who were both impecunious and stood among the 30 highest on the admissions examinations, by which about 150 a year were admitted. With a two-year program there were usually about 300 students in residence, for whom new quarters were found in the old Navarre college, one of the 10 colleges of the pre-Revolutionary faculty of arts. The school was also transferred from the ministry of the interior to the war department. In the years from 1795 to 1808 about a third of those completing the work had gone into civilian careers, either within the government or outside it—the Roads and Bridges, Mines, Geographical Engineers, public instruction, civil administration, and a few into commerce and manufacturing. That is, during these years two-thirds had gone into the artillery, military engineering, and other branches of the armed forces. After 1808, under pressure from Napoleon and the war department, and against protests from the school, the number of graduates entering the artillery, military engineering, and infantry reached almost 100 percent, and many of them died or disappeared in the campaigns of 1812 and 1813.[65]

The school had a distinguished faculty of about 14, including several

---

[64] *Almanach impérial*, 1813, p. 871.

[65] Fourcroy in *Archives parlementaires*, 9:84-85, and Lacuée's report, as governor of the Polytechnique, ibid., pp. 89-93. A. Fourcy, *Histoire de l'Ecole Polytechnique* (Paris, 1828), gives details on the curriculum, scholarships, militarization, and location of the school, pp. 250-76, and in an appendix he lists the names and subsequent fate or careers for each annual entering class. There is a summary of occupations entered by all graduates of the school from 1795 to 1808 in Archives Nationales, AF IV, 1040, no. 54.

members of the Institute and of the College of France. A. M. Ampère, after whom the measure of electrical current is named, taught at the Polytechnique for many years. Laplace, Lagrange, Fourcroy, and Berthollet also appeared there at various times. Among those still present as professors in 1813, and whose names have occurred in previous pages of this book, we find Hassenfratz, who had been an outspoken Montagnard in 1793; Etienne Barruel, an examiner for the school who became its librarian; and Monge and Guyton-Morveau, who both served as its director. The plan of study continued to emphasize higher mathematics and pure physics, with successive diversions to more practical subjects as the military demands increased. The Ecole Polytechnique in Napoleon's time, despite or perhaps because of the wars, was the most famous school of the physical and engineering sciences in the world; it served as a model for others established in neighboring countries, and some 30 years later its graduates were building railways throughout Continental Europe.[66]

Outside these institutions supported by the state there were private groups contributing to the sciences, as had been usual under the Old Regime. There was in particular the Society of Arcueil, which by 1806 was sufficiently organized to maintain its own laboratories and publish its memoirs. Arcueil was a village about five miles from Paris where Laplace and Berthollet each had a commodious country house. It was here that the laboratories were situated. Another active participant was Chaptal, chemist, manufacturer, minister of the interior for four years, and a man of considerable private means. They financed their experiments and publications with their own money, which indeed was hardly independent from the state, since all three were members of the Senate with salaries of 25,000 francs a year, five times that of even a well-paid professor. Other scientific notables such as Monge, Biot, Gay-Lussac, and Arago were drawn into the group. Many were busy in the public system, at the Institute, the College of France, or the Polytechnique, but they carried on important work at Arcueil, on such matters as the expansion of gases and the velocity of sound, and they took pains to bring in promising younger men also, thus becoming a kind of private "special school" of the sciences.[67]

Mainly, however, the impact of the Revolutionary and Napoleonic years upon science was to make it a public enterprise, publicly recog-

[66] *Almanach impérial*, 1813, pp. 251-52. The impact of the Polytechnique and its graduates may be seen in R. Cameron, *France and the economic development of Europe, 1800-1914* (Princeton, 1961), pp. 50-63 and passim.

[67] M. Crosland, *The Society of Arcueil: A view of French science in the time of Napoleon I* (London, 1967), esp. pp. 232-76.

nized, honored, and subsidized, in a way that had indeed begun under Louis XIV but had proceeded only piecemeal during the Old Regime. Science became a profession in which men without inherited fortune could make a living. The wealthy and the noble could of course take part if they were serious, but gentlemen amateurs were excluded. The state provided salaries and stability of tenure in the higher scientific establishments, and for the lycées it prescribed the level of salaries that were for the most part paid ultimately by the parents. Science was systematically taught to teenagers, and a young man wishing to make a career of it could find an opening with some chance of promotion, since below the constellation of famous names there were numerous well-defined positions as laboratory assistant, or demonstrator, or preparator, or *aide-naturaliste*. In all these respects, according to Maurice Crosland of the University of Leeds, England in about 1850 was only where France had been in the 1780s.[68]

A similar pattern was imprinted on the more purely teaching institutions. It was ordered that appointment to the faculties should be by open competition, publicized in advance, and with provision that no relative of a candidate could be among the judges. If favoritism and nepotism were not wholly done away with, the meritocratic principle was firmly asserted. Under the watchful eyes of inspectors and rectors, beginning teachers were in fact as time passed promoted to higher teaching positions, and a very few could become inspectors and rectors themselves. Or they might move on into other kinds of work. An example is provided by the entering class of 1811 at the Ecole Normale, 24 scholarship boys of modest ambitions born between 1789 and 1793. In 1840, when they were about fifty years old, over half were still in the University, including two professors at the Sorbonne and one who was the rector at Metz. The others included a departmental prefect and several others in the civil service, a successful merchant, and an historian, Augustin Thierry.[69]

Beyond the sphere of science and teaching were other realms of art and learning. At the Louvre, the Archives, and the Bibliothèque Nationale (Impériale from 1804 to 1814) the basic nationalizations of art objects, manuscripts, and books made during the Revolution were organized and consolidated. To some extent they were enlarged by similar items brought from other countries by the victorious French.

[68] Crosland, "The development of a professional career in science in France," *Minerva* 13 (1975):38-57; R. Fox, "Scientific enterprise and patronage of research in France, 1800-1870," *Minerva* 11 (1973):442-73; R. Fox and G. Weicz, *Organization of science and technology in France, 1808-1914* (Cambridge, Eng., 1980).

[69] A Tudesq, *Les grands notables de France, 1840-1849*, 2 vols. (Paris, 1964), 1:351.

At the Imperial Conservatory of Music and Declamation, with over 300 students, there were in 1813 25 professors of voice and orchestral instruments in its section on music, and in the section on declamation, which meant the theatrical arts, there was a professor of dance and three of acting, including the famous actor, Talma.[70] Architecture, painting, and sculpture were combined in the Ecole des Beaux-Arts. Among the learned and cultural enterprises that were subsidized was the *Description d'Egypte*, a work in 21 magnificent folio volumes of text, maps, and colored engravings, which arose from the French expedition to Egypt in 1798 and long remained a main source for the nineteenth-century study of Egypt, both ancient and modern.

So "modernization" went forward on many fronts. Most of the higher schools drew some of their students from other parts of the Continent. France, or rather Paris, was the cultural capital of Europe more indisputably than in the days of the Sun King.

[70] *Almanach impérial*, 1813, pp. 875-78.

CONCLUDING REFLECTIONS

WITH THE RESTORATION of the Bourbons in 1814, and the return of royalists of various persuasions from moderates to extremists, there arose a cry to do away with all the works of the Revolution and Empire, including the University. Napoleon's educational system, they said, was despotic, militarized, and irreligious. It was the liberals, fearing worse, who came to its defense. Guizot, for example, argued that Bonaparte had perverted his own program, using it to reward soldiers and create dependents, especially by handing out scholarships to a rather poor class of people. But Guizot also thought that the University should be preserved, since a centralized state control over public instruction would maintain high quality, uniform standards, and a true "national education"—such as had been called for since the 1760s.[1]

Another defender of the University was Ambroise Rendu, who had been an inspector-general and member of the University Council under Napoleon and a moderating influence in its affairs. He found that one argument against the University was simply that it was new. It was not new at all, Rendu insisted. It was not even a creation of Bonaparte's. Its real origin went back to the reform of the University of Turin in 1771 by Charles-Emmanuel III of Piedmont. "In a word," said Rendu, "the University of France is only a copy, on a larger scale, of a model already old, the University of Turin."[2] To show that the University of France was old was meant to reassure conservatives; and it should have been gratifying to royalists also, since both Louis XVIII, now the reigning king of France, and his brother, the future Charles X, back in the 1770s, had married granddaughters of Charles-Emmanuel III.

Rendu therefore published a tract showing in parallel columns the resemblances between the University of Turin of the 1770s and the University of France of 1808. His comparison revealed that, as in

---

[1] Guizot, *Essai sur l'histoire et sur l'état actuel de l'instruction publique en France* (Paris, 1816), passim, e.g., pp. 57-58.

[2] A. Rendu, *Premier supplément aux observations sur le discours prononcé à la Chambre des Députés dans la séance du 31 janvier 1816 concernant l'instruction publique et l'éducation* (Paris, 1816), pp. 2-3.

France, there had been a central authority in Turin, composed of a single head with his council, which had powers of appointment and inspection over all the subordinate colleges in the kingdom; that the University of Turin had faculties awarding the degree of bachelor, *licencié*, and doctor; that it enjoyed a guaranteed income from the government of 300,000 francs a year; that it awarded competitive scholarships by examination; and that the University possessed the *droit exclusif* or monopoly, since no one was allowed to teach the arts and sciences, as taught in the University, except by special permission. There were a few points on which Rendu remained silent, or conceded that the parallel was inexact. For example, he neglected to point out that the University of Turin had been endowed with properties of its own, that its faculty of philosophy (corresponding to the new French faculties of sciences and of letters) had given no degree except the old *maîtrise ès arts*, and that its scholarship arrangements in a Collegio di Nobili had been for young nobles only and concentrated in the city of Turin. In France, the disendowment of individual colleges, the distribution of scholarships in lycées throughout the country, the disregard for noble status, the Ecole Normale for the preparation of teachers, and the higher degrees in sciences and in letters were innovations.

How Bonaparte could have learned anything from the University of Turin is also unclear. The Piedmontese government had closed it in 1792 for fear of revolutionary disturbance. It remained closed for several years. In 1799, when monarchist forces briefly prevailed during the War of the Second Coalition, they had used the University of Turin as a barracks and its Academy of Sciences as a prison. When the French returned in 1800, they and their Italian republican collaborators reopened the university. It is true that they largely carried on the structures set up in the 1770s. But if a parallel between the University of France and the University of Turin was to be found, it might have been found as well in the reformed and republican University of Turin of 1802. In any case, other European countries of the Old Regime could have furnished similar parallels for centralized state control. And in fact the University of Turin, whether in its monarchical or republican phase, far from being a model for Napoleon, was denatured and weakened by its absorption into the Imperial University after 1808.[3]

---

[3] On the University of Turin in these years see the sources cited in chap. 7, n. 7 above. Also: N. Bianchi, *Storia della monarchia piemontese*, 3 vols. (Turin, 1879), 3:69-72, 488-95, and *La Università di Torino nel 1900: Anno 496ᵉ della fondazione* (Turin, 1900), pp. 34-38. On precedents in various monarchies of the Old Regime see p. 38 of the present book. On relations between the universities of France and Turin see also *Archives parlementaries*, 9:94-96, and [G. Cuvier] *Université Impériale: Rapports*

Rendu's exercise was therefore somewhat pointless, except for its immediate purpose of persuading a stubborn opposition. It was also unnecessary, since during the very weeks when he was writing it, in March 1816, Louis XVIII decided to retain the University of France, while putting it under a new Commission on Public Instruction, of which Rendu became a member. "Thus," as he hastily added at the end of his tract, "the two great principles of *unity* in government and public education, and of *uniformity* in teaching, are again consecrated by the express will of an enlightened prince."[4] The University survived because all French governments in the following century, however otherwise disparate, valued the unity and uniformity that it might lend to their regimes.

Rendu's effort nevertheless illustrates, on the specific matter of education, a problem that has long existed in interpretation of the French Revolution as a whole. It is the problem of continuity and change. To what extent did the Revolution carry on developments that had preceded it, and to what extent did it represent a repudiation of the past or a radical new departure? Continuity and change are of course not logical opposites. A rapid change may simply accelerate a continuing process.

In a few words, to summarize the preceding chapters, various moves toward greater national unity in education were gaining momentum during the Old Regime and became more insistent and more widely participated in by the politicization of the Revolution, one aspect of which was a drive toward democracy in the sense of equality, which was blocked and superseded by other concerns of the Enlightenment, notably a belief in progress and a desire for efficiency, for the training of qualified experts, and for a process of modernization. All these trends were present throughout and remained so in later times; they simply varied in strength at any given moment. Religion survived, but the church as an organized body exercising public authority was pushed to the sidelines. Centralization of control, though often warned against, always prevailed because it followed from the demand for "unity and uniformity," to be achieved not at the lowest common denominator but as a means of high-level standardization, and for equity between the regions of France. This abstract pattern may be seen not only in education but also in other matters affected by the Revolution, such as law, taxation, civil administration, and the army.

---

sur les établissements d'instruction publique dans les départements au-delà des Alpes, faits en 1809 et 1810 par MM. Cuvier . . . (Paris, 1810 or 1811).

[4] Rendu, *Premier supplément*, p. 56. Italics in the original.

In apology for the title of the present book it must be admitted as doubtful whether humanity had been improved. Yet the title is not merely ironic. Of course the dreams of Helvétius and Rousseau had not come true. Of course the excited visions of 1793 had failed to materialize. But the conditions of living for many human beings had been improved by the Revolution, which, by dissolving the old privileged bodies and interest groups, made it possible to effect changes that more peaceable reformers had called for in vain. The chief immediate beneficiaries were undoubtedly those who acquired property from the Revolutionary confiscations. Not only did the state prevail over the church; the former church properties passed into private hands, at various social levels from the affluent and the middle classes down through a few artisans and shopkeepers in the towns and on into the more prosperous peasantry. These were also the people who were most concerned with education and from whose ranks the directing elements in French society were recruited. For the mass of the population, at the level of elementary schooling, very little had changed; the rate of basic literacy in 1820, as already noted, stood about where it might have been expected without the Revolution, on a curve that had been rising since the time of Louis XIV, and probably before. For those who could get beyond elementary schooling, the families of property owners, government employees, professional people, managers of businesses, scientific researchers, and artists, and for such formerly disadvantaged types as Protestants, Jews, and freethinkers, there now existed a public system of education, nationally uniform, religiously neutral, open to youthful talent, at all levels up to the highest and most specialized, and including libraries and art galleries that now belonged to the "nation."

The French Revolution not only produced educational and cultural institutions of a modern kind. Nor did it only, as is often said, provide a deplorable though brief example of the use of virtue and terror to reconstruct the human race. It offered a forum where such luminaries as Talleyrand and Condorcet, and many more ordinary and now forgotten people, some of whom were professors and teachers themselves and some of whom moved in and out of the Revolutionary assemblies, could address themselves thoughtfully to concrete problems of education, aiming both at short-run solutions and at larger objectives. Most of the problems and objectives are still with us today.

APPENDIX

EXPENDITURES OF THE CENTRAL GOVERNMENT FOR PUBLIC INSTRUCTION, HIGHER LEARNING, AND THE ARTS 1789-1812

THE FOLLOWING TABLE is so arranged that items on the same horizontal line refer to the same institution or function under changing names for the four years 1789, 1794-1795, 1798-1799, and 1812. The use of the table is not to give exact data but only to show continuities and relative magnitudes.

Figures are for expenditures of the central government only; that is, they exclude those made by local governments, as for colleges before the Revolution, Central Schools under the Directory, and secondary schools and lycées under the Empire. A blank means that the institution did not exist at the time indicated; a question mark means that the institution or function existed but that the amount spent is not known to the present author. Values are expressed in livres for 1789 and 1794-1795, in francs for 1798-1799 and 1812, but the change in name of the monetary unit involved no significant change in value. How much the Convention allowed for inflation in authorizing these expenditures for 1794-1795 cannot be known. Considering that some items are omitted, and in view of the items queried, the totals for each date should be somewhat higher. The Imperial University in 1812 was financially self-supporting from the fees it levied, so that its only receipts from the central government were the sums shown for scholarships in the lycées and for the law and medical faculties. The figures for the University and for the Ecole Normale (then part of the University) are given here only for the record and are not included in the total expenditures of the central government for 1812.

For 1789 the source is the speech and accompanying tabulations submitted to the Constituent Assembly on January 29, 1790, by the chairman of its committee on finance, the Marquis de Montesquiou. The purpose was to list actual expenditures with a view to possible economies. See *Archives parlementaires*, 1st ser. (Paris, 1880), 11:378-84. See also the *Aperçu général des réductions sur la dépense publique* as

1 Monarchy 1789		2 Convention, An III 1794-1795	
UNIVERSITY OF PARIS			
Faculty of Theology	9,450		
Faculty of Law	5,600		
Faculty of Medicine	3,600	School of Health, Paris	502,964
		School of Health, Strasbourg, Montpellier	317,348
ADOLESCENT EDUCATION			
College of Louis-le-Grand	378,000	Equality College (Louis-le-Grand)	380,940
and nine other colleges		Nine other Paris colleges	251,368
of Faculty of Arts		Central Schools	27,924
		Society of French Youth	244,286
		Vocational School at Liancourt	55,196
		Orphans' School at Popincourt	39,179
Free School of Design	?	Free School of Design	15,600
SCIENTIFIC AND TECHNICAL			
Academy of Sciences	93,158		
Society of Medicine	36,200		
School of Surgery	7,500	School of Surgery	15,805
College of France	39,900	College of France	88,494
Jardin des Plantes	129,000	Museum of Natural History	410,893
Observatory	17,380	Bureau of Longitudes	25,481
School of Engineering	?	School of Public Works	?
School of Roads and Bridges	?	School of Roads and Bridges	?
		Weights and Measures (metric)	281,892
		Inventions and Discoveries	273,073
CULTURE AND THE ARTS			
French Academy	25,400		
Academy of Inscriptions	43,608		
Academy of Painting, etc.	?		
Schools of Painting	?	Schools of Painting and Sculpture	40,371
Schools of Music	?	Schools of Music	178,691
Art Collections	?	Conservatory of Art	267,900
		Preservation of National Monuments	850,828
School of art at Rome	?		
Turkish and Arabic at Louis-le-Grand	?		
LIBRARIES			
Bibliothèque du Roi	150,000	Bibliothèque Nationale	189,816
		Other Paris libraries	88,493
		Cataloguing	39,128
AWARDS, SUBSCRIPTIONS, SUBSIDIES, FOR WRITERS, ETC. AND LEARNED PROJECTS	198,150	NATIONAL AWARDS	2,475,904
MISCELLANEOUS			
		National Festivals	410,893
		Ecole Normale	1,884,648
		Primary Schools	262,014
TOTALS			
Monarchy	1,136,946	Convention	9,619,129

Note. For an explanation of the ? see the preceding text of the Appendix.

3 Directory An VII 1798-1799		4 Empire 1812	
		[IMPERIAL UNIVERSITY]	[2,358,328]
		Faculties of Law	50,000
School of Health, Paris	266,972	Faculties of Medicine	250,000
Schools of Health, Strasbourg, Montpellier	229,232		
Prytanée français	119,082	Lycées (scholarships)	1,200,000
Reorganization of Schools	100,000		
Vocational school at Liancourt	354,000	Vocational school at Châlons	250,000 *
Free School of Design	20,000	Free School of Design	37,000 *
National Institute	400,000	National Institute	440,000
College of France	99,829	College of France	128,000
Museum of Natural History	419,578	Museum of Natural History	300,000
Bureau of Longitudes	110,533	Bureau of Longitudes	120,000
Ecole Polytechnique	394,133	Ecole Polytechnique	250,000 *
School of Roads and Bridges	72,000	School of Roads and Bridges	?
Weights and Measures (metric)	1,120,000		
Conservatoire des Arts et Métiers	119,800	Conservatoire des Arts et Métiers	?
National Institute, as above	—	National Institute, as above	—
Schools of Painting and Sculpture	80,188	Schools of Painting and Sculpture	95,000 **
Schools of Music	309,496	Conservatory of Music	106,000 **
The Louvre	312,410	The Louvre	?
School of art at Rome	34,950	School of art at Rome	80,000 **
School of Oriental Languages	23,000	School of Oriental Languages	40,000
Bibliothèque Nationale	149,413	Bibliothèque Impériale	200,000
Other Paris libraries	97,880	Other Paris libraries	115,000
Books	76,270		
NATIONAL AWARDS, ETC.	200,000	AWARDS AND SUBSCRIPTIONS	270,000
National Festivals	400,000	[Ecole Normale]	[113,012]
Directory	5,508,766	Empire	3,931,000

Note. For an explanation of the * and the ** see the preceding text of the Appendix. Bracketed items in column 4 of the table have been excluded from the total, and the number of francs given there for Ecole Normale has been included in the number for Imperial University at the top.

printed in Paris in 1790, and *Extrait raisonné des rapports du comité des finances sur toutes les parties de la dépense publique* (Paris, 1790).

The figures given here for the Year III are rearranged from figures in the large foldout table in J. Guillaume, *Procès-verbaux du Comité de l'Instruction publique de la Convention Nationale*, vol. 6, following p. 948. This table is the final report of the Executive Commission on Public Instruction (on which see above, pp. 209-10) at the time of its dissolution at the close of the Convention. Dated 1 Frimaire IV and signed by Ginguené, it gives figures for the years II, III, and IV; but it includes only five months of the Year II, since the Commission began operating on 1 Floréal II, and the Year IV was still mainly in the future on 1 Frimaire IV. Hence it seems best to present here only the figures for the Year III. The data are for payments ordered by the Commission, but to what extent they were actually paid under conditions of the time cannot be known. The Commission's table records the laws and decrees of the Revolutionary Assemblies authorizing each payment, with dates of the authorizations, mostly 1793 and the Year II, but with a few going back as far as 1790. Hence the figures for the Year III mainly illustrate the program of the Convention at the height of the Revolution in 1793-1794.

The source for the Year VII is the *Moniteur* for 14 Brumaire VII, where the budget adopted for the ministry of the interior was published. As a budget, it shows expected and authorized rather than actual expenditures, and so reflects policies and intentions at a time when many payments were in arrears.

For 1812, see C. Jourdain, *Le budget de l'Instruction publique et des établissements scientifiques et littéraires* (Paris, 1857), p. 300. Jourdain, an official in the Ministry of Public Instruction during the Second Empire, included only institutions under jurisdiction of that ministry in the 1850s. The present table is therefore supplemented by other items. Those marked with an asterisk are from a document of 1808 published by A. Aulard, *Napoléon Iᵉ et le monopole universitaire* (Paris, 1911), p. 138. Those marked with a double asterisk are from documents of 1806 reprinted in the *Archives parlementaires*, 9:86 and 97. It is likely that these figures for 1808 and 1806 were not very different in 1812.

INDEX

academies (pre-Revolutionary), 32-34; during Revolution, 99, 162, 174, 175, 234
Academy of Sciences, Royal, 33, 49n, 151, 162, 207, 214, 234
adult education, 129, 175, 180, 187, 190-97, 244, 283. *See* festivals
agrégation (1766), 63-64, 94, 219, 311; (1808), 313
Aix-en-Provence, Central School, 248, 251
d'Alembert, 17, 23, 43, 49, 51, 210
Alexander I of Russia, 38
Allain, E., 289
Amis de la Patrie, section des, 159
Ampère, 326
Andrieux, 267-68, 291
Angers, College of, 60, 109; Central School, 249
Aquinas, Thomas, 19
Arago, 326
Arbogast, 104, 166-69, 222, 251
architecture, 192
Archives, National, 173, 327
Arcueil, Society of, 326-27
Aristotle, 16, 17, 19, 40, 303
army, 184-85, 206, 325
Arnauld, *instituteur*, 91
Arnault, A. V., 285, 290n
Artillery School, 229
Athénée, 152
Audouin, P. J., 258
Audra, Abbé, 51
Audrein, Y. M., 90, 92, 93, 104
Auger, 90, 92, 141
Aulard, A., 320, 322n, 336
Autun, College of, 172
Avallon, College of, 21-22
Avignon, 195

Babeuf, 138, 144-46
baccalauréat, 311-12
Bachelier, J. J., 29, 89n, 254
Bacon, Francis, 210, 303
Bailey, C. R., 22n, 65
Bailleul, 267
Baker, Keith, 130n, 225n
Bancal des Issarts, 133
Barère, 186-87, 201, 222
Barruel, E., 290, 292, 326
Baudeau, Abbé, 54, 57-58, 59, 140
Beauvais College, 17, 46
Beaux-Arts, Ecole des, 328
Benedictines, 15, 50n, 66-68, 110-12, 142, 312. *See* Sorèze
Berlin, University of, 321
Bernardin de Saint-Pierre, 215, 217, 220, 224
Berthollet, 152, 154, 171, 215, 326
Besançon, 183; Central School at, 246, 248, 259
Bibliothèque de l'Arsénal, 173, 315
Bibliothèque Mazarine, 173, 315
Bibliothèque Nationale (Royale, Impériale), 34, 99, 173, 315, 327
Bien, D. D., 66n, 67n
biens nationaux (for support of schools), 114-20, 285-87, 313-14. *See* endowments
bilingual schooling, 185-90
Biot, 205, 290, 326
blacks, 83, 187, 266
Boissy d'Anglas, 196, 199, 219, 222, 227, 233
Bonaparte, Jérome, 242
Bonaparte, Josephine, 143
Bonaparte, Lucien, 274, 277
Bonaparte, Napoleon, 81, 82, 210, 240, 242, 252, 278; during Consulate, 281-

Bonaparte, Napoleon (*cont.*)
85, 293-95, 299; during Empire, on
lycées, 299-306; on Imperial University, 306-20; on higher schools, 322-
24; University of Turin, 329-30
Bon Conseil, section du, 160
Bonn, 252
Bonnaire, Félix, 259, 262, 264, 277, 282
books, confiscation of, 118, 172. *See* Bi-
bliothèque Nationale
Borrelly, 55, 59, 306n
Bougainville, 216
Boulay de la Meurthe, 267
Bouloiseau, M., 54n, 94n
Bouquier plan and law, 170, 179-83,
190, 198, 226
Bourbon-Conti, Stéphanie Louise de,
283
Bourdon, L.J.J.L. de la Crosnière, 91,
92, 99; known also as Léonard Bour-
don, 137, 141, 142-44, 163, 222
Bourdon de l'Oise, 169
Bourges, University of, 19, 60
bourses, see scholarships
Breck, Samuel, 68-69, 111
Brienne (*école militaire*), 66
Brienne, Loménie de, 23, 51
Briot, P. J., 259-60, 264-65, 277, 293
Brisson, 49n, 246
Brissot, 81, 99
Brissot, Mme, 283
Brongniart, 173
Brothers of the Christian Schools (Frères
de la Doctrine chrétienne), 108, 241,
302, 318n
Brumaire, law of 3 Brumaire Year IV,
167, 230-36, 252, 274, 295, 306, 310
Buache, 215, 217
budgets, 32, 174, 268, 313-15. *See* Ap-
pendix
Buffon, 256
Buonarroti, P., 145
bureaucracy, 77, 87, 135-36, 169, 308,
317. *See* centralization
Bureau de Consultation des Arts et Mé-
tiers, 151, 152, 153, 164-67, 207, 234
Bureau des Brevets et Inventions, 151
Bureau of Longitudes, 173, 315, 323
Burke, Edmund, 84, 102

Cabanis, 89, 222, 234, 262, 278, 282
cahiers (1789), 12, 86-88
Cahors, University of, 44; Central
School of, 255-56
Calas, Jean, 48
calendar, republican, 160, 192, 197, 241.
See *décadi*, festivals
Calonne, 23, 24
Cambon, 115
Cambridge University, 20n, 38, 39
Campan, Mme de, 283
Camus, A. G., 89n
Carbonari, 259
Carcassonne, Central School, 248
Carnot, Lazare, 104, 185
carrière ouverte aux talents, 294. *See* tal-
ents, meritocracy, scholarships
Carrion-Nisas, 298
Carroll, Charles, 19
Cassini, J. D., 173
catechisms, republican, 125, 239-40
Catherine II, 12, 21, 24
Central Schools (*écoles centrales*), 117,
167, 208, 212, 226, 231, 242-56,
261, 264, 269, 272-78, 283-84, 287-
92, 298, 299
centralization, 38-39, 77-78, 91-92, 199,
244-45, 260, 264n, 274-75, 292, 296,
306; in Napoleonic University, 306-
20. *See* "national education," and the
various plans under Rolland d'Erce-
ville, Poitiers, Talleyrand, Condorcet,
Brumaire Year IV, Floréal Year X
Chabot, 169
Champagne, J. F., 90, 115n, 171, 207-
208, 234, 285, 290
Champagny, 308
Chappotin, 112
Chaptal, 277, 288-89, 291, 307, 326
Charles III of Spain, 38
Charles X, 329
Charles-Emmanuel III of Piedmont, 329
Chartier, R., 39n, 53, 86n
Chateaubriand, 284
Chénier, M. J., 224
Cheverus, Jean, 68
Chisick, H., 21n
Choiseul, 27
Choquart, Abbé, 27

church, relation to state on education. Before Revolution, 9, 40, 45-48, 69, 72-77; during Revolution, 86-87, 102-103, 124-25, 180, 236-38; under Napoleon, 284, 311, 315-16, 332. *See* clergy as teachers, religious neutralism, *congrégations séculières*, Jesuits, Oratorians, Doctrinaires

Cicero, 7, 16, 26, 217

Citoyennes Révolutionnaires Républicaines, 150

Civil Constitution of the Clergy, 102, 187

Clément de Ris, 209

clergy as teachers, pre-Revolutionary, 3-4, 16, 49-50, 55-56, 74-75, 125; during Revolution, 87, 99-100, 103, 135, 158, 180, 216, 247, 258; under Napoleon, 296, 301, 305, 308, 311, 315. See *congrégations séculières*, religious neutralism

Coffin, Charles, 46-47

Colbert, 33, 41

collèges, pre-Revolutionary, 12-26, 40-42, 64-65, 71-72; during Revolution, 79-80, 92, 103-19, 133, 137, 161, 163-64, 170-72, 198, 214; under Napoleon, 287-89, 300. See *écoles militaires, collèges communaux*

collèges communaux, 300, 304, 310. See *secondaires, écoles*

College of France (Collège Royal), 34-35, 55, 99, 173, 277, 290, 309, 315, 322-24

Cologne, 252, 318

Columbia College, New York, 191

Commissions. *See* Public Instruction, Public Works, Eleven

Committees. *See* Public Instruction, Public Safety

Commune des Arts, 131, 151

Compère, M. M., 41n, 86n, 243n, 247

Concordat, 284, 311

concours général, 24, 79, 94, 104, 269, 284

Condillac, 17, 25, 54, 225, 255, 256, 273, 303

Condorcet, 17, 23, 32n, 104, 124-25, 131, 225-26

Condorcet, Mme, 223

Condorcet plan, 82-83, 124-29, 146, 165, 169, 211, 226, 230, 233, 277, 306

congrégations séculières, 15, 106-108, 135, 247. *See* Oratorians, Doctrinaires

Conservatory of Arts and Trades (Conservatoire des Arts et Métiers), 207, 235

Conservatory of Music, 174, 328

Conspiracy of Equals (1796), 138, 145

Constant, B., 224, 282, 286

constitution (in connection with education), 56, 81-82, 227, 230-31

corporal punishment, 103, 303

corps enseignant, 307-308

Council of State (Napoleonic), 282, 293, 307-308

councils. *See by subject designation*, e.g., Public Instruction, etc.

Coupé de l'Oise, 163, 169

Courdin, J., 90

cours révolutionnaires, 190, 197-207

Crevier, J.B.L., 55, 56, 58, 140

Crosland, M., 229n, 327

Crouzet, 164n, 210, 214

Cuneo, 318

Cuvier, Georges, 246, 324

Danton, 140, 181

Darcet, 152, 270

Daubenton, 215, 217, 224

Daunou, 90, 93, 107, 135-37, 222, 225, 227, 233, 234, 282

Daunou plan, 82, 178. *See* Brumaire, law of 3 Brumaire Year IV

David, J. L., 131, 150, 173

Décade philosophique, 223, 225, 266, 283, 288, 290

décadi, 193, 239, 258. *See* calendar, republican

Dechristianization, 180-81

Degranthe, 90, 93, 104

degrees (academic), 14, 31; disappearance in Revolution, 105; under Napoleon, 292, 311-12

Dellard, 290

democracy, meaning of, 121-22, 146-47, 158, 186, 188, 213, 219, 277-78,

democracy (*cont.*)
298. *See* equality (in schools)
Design, Royal Free School of, 29, 174.
See Drawing
Desmoulins, C., 99
Destutt de Tracy, 4-5, 222, 224, 234, 270-78, 282, 289, 291, 297, 302
dictée, 17, 272
Diderot, 12, 21, 23, 24, 27, 54, 56, 210, 235, 256
Dijon, University of, 23, 44
"Directorials," 225, 258
Doctrinaires (Pères de la Doctrine chrétienne), 15, 25, 45, 50-51, 66, 106, 108, 247, 288, 307, 312
Domergue, 223, 246, 270
Dommanget, M., 146
Drawing (*dessin*), teaching of, 29, 167-68, 249-50, 255, 276, 302. *See* Design
Dresden, 318
droit exclusif, 309, 330
Duchesne, P. F., 298
Ducos, J. F., 133
Dufourny, 79, 162, 164-65, 181, 200, 222
Dugas, 185
Duhem, 188-89
Dulaure, 262
Dumouchel, 30n, 93, 103, 210, 230, 277, 282, 285
Dumouriez, 134
Duplantier, 266
Dupont de Nemours, 12, 54, 72, 165
Dupuis, C. F., 183, 256, 271, 273
Durand-Maillane, 131
Duruy, A., 117n, 275n
Duruy, V., 302n
Dutens, 290

écoles. See under subject designation, e.g., Polytechnique, Normale, *primaires, secondaires*, etc. *See also* schools, Central Schools
écoles centrales. See Central Schools
écoles d'application, 229
Ecole de Mars, 201
écoles militaires, 28, 66-69, 110, 140, 142, 175, 201, 242, 281, 312
éducation commune, 92, 133, 137-46, 154-56, 188, 194, 266

éducation nationale. See national education
Egypt, 210, 328
elementary education, pre-Revolutionary, 9-12, 41; in Revolutionary constitutions, 81, 84, 137, 227, 231; in Talleyrand plan, 96; disruption, 105; in Condorcet plan, 125, 128-29; during Revolution, 140-41, 179-83, 236-41; in Central Schools, 253; in debate of Year VII, 263, 266-68; for Idéologues, 274-75; under Napoleon, 298, 302, 310, 318n, 332. See *primaires, écoles*; Bouquier plan; *éducation commune*
Eleven, Commission of, 227-28
Elizabeth, Queen, 39
Elliot, Sir Gilbert, 27
émulation, 24-25, 79, 94, 292, 297, 307
Encyclopédie, 17, 43, 44, 51, 256
endowments (for education), 8, 44-45, 73, 92, 102; loss of endowments, 114-20, 134; views on endowments, 257-58, 285-87; under Napoleon, 313-14. *See* scholarships, mortmain, *fondations*
Engineers, School of Military, 229. *See* Mézières, Polytechnique
Epinal, College of, 118
equality (in schools), 24, 58-59, 67, 87; in Talleyrand plan, 95; in Condorcet plan, 124, 128-29, 132-33, 136; in Lepeletier plan, 141; for Babeuf, 145-46; in Paris plan of 1793, 162, 168-69; in other plans, 226, 255; under Napoleon, 291-92, 294. *See* scholarships, *éducation commune*
Equality College (Collège de l'Egalite), 171-72, 174, 176, 207-208, 248. *See* Louis-le-Grand
Essarts, des, 33
Eton College, 14
examinations, 40, 63, 69, 87, 98, 203-207, 229, 243, 278, 295, 297, 312-13
Eyrard, F., 76n

Fabre d'Eglantine, 169
Ferguson, Adam, 273
Ferlus, 111
Ferry school laws, 185
festivals (*fêtes révolutionnaires*), 81, 132, 135, 154, 163, 175, 184, 190, 193-96, 231, 232, 282-83

fêtes décadaires, 193-94, 282
fêtes nationales. See festivals
financial aid. *See* endowments, scholarships, budget, *instruction gratuite, biens nationaux*
Finistère, section, 157
Fleury, cardinal, 46
Floréal Year X, law of, 295-98, 306, 323
fondations, 44, 117. *See* endowments, scholarships
Fontaine de Fréville, 77n, 91
Fontanes, J.P.L., 246, 308, 310, 313, 316, 320
Fouché, 107, 117
Fourcroy, 36; in National Convention, 152, 165, 170, 173, 198, 200, 203-204, 206, 222, 224, 227-28, 229, 233; under Napoleon, 282, 285, 293, 295-97, 300, 307, 310, 326
Francis I, 34
François de Neufchâteau, 268-72, 282
Frederick the Great, 12
Furet, F., 9n

Garat, 36, 164, 171, 209-11, 214, 215, 217, 218, 222, 234, 270, 282
Garnier, Abbé, 35, 55
Garrelon, 111-12
Gattel, 251
Gay-Lussac, 326
Genlis, Mme de, 52
Geoffroy de Saint-Hilaire, 173, 324
Geographers, School of, 229, 325
Gibbon, 256
Gillispie, C. C., 32n, 151n
Ginguené, 209, 222-23, 230, 234, 257, 270, 282, 336
girls' schools. *See* women's education
Girondins, 130, 132
Gneisenau, 280
Godechot, J., 82n
Gohier, 164
Gosse, Abbé, 29
Göttingen, University of, 100, 252, 310
graded classes (annual grades), 14, 40, 67, 242, 275, 296, 301-302
grandes écoles, 226, 277
Gray Sisters, 108
Grégoire, Abbé, 137, 161, 186-87, 222, 234, 238, 282

Grenoble, 182; Central School, 251
Grimaud, L., 237n, 320
Guéroult, 90n, 246
Guillaume, J., 105n, 108n, 123n, 146, 179n, 225n, 336
Guizot, 123, 322, 329
Gustav III of Sweden, 38
Guyard, Mme, 95
Guyton de Morveau, 53, 58-59, 140, 152, 169, 198, 200, 224, 326

Haffner, Isaac, 100-101, 105
Hahn, R., 33n, 130n, 151n, 233n
Harcourt College, 25n
Hardy, 262
Harrigan, P., 50n, 107n
Hassenfratz, J. H., 152-54, 165, 181, 200, 222, 326
Haute-Marne, Central School, 250
Haüy, 215, 224, 325
Health, Schools of (Ecoles de Santé), 205-207. *See* medicine, teaching of
Hébert, 100, 181, 184
Hébertism, 156n, 157n
Hegel, 279
Helvétius, 3-4, 21, 23, 54, 103, 223, 240
Helvétius, Mme, 223
Henry IV, 40, 61, 317
Heurtault-Lamerville, 259, 262, 263, 265, 267, 277
History, teaching of, 18, 256, 273, 303, 324
Humbolt, W. von, 85, 321
Hume, David, 27, 136
Hyslop, B., 87n

idéologie, 156, 222-23, 290
Idéologues, 4, 167, 209, 222-24, 240, 263, 270-78, 284, 286, 298, 302, 305
Institute, National (1795), 167, 223-24, 231, 232-35, 270, 277-78, 315, 323
Institute, National, in Talleyrand plan, 98-99
instituts (in Condorcet's sense), 126-27, 161, 166, 171, 179, 211
instruction gratuite, 43, 59, 88, 97n, 114, 119, 125, 227, 244, 291

Jacobins, 78, 79, 103, 137, 142-43, 161,

Jacobins (*cont.*) 165, 188, 199, 213, 258, 268

Jacquemont, 270, 282, 298

Jansenism, 45-46

Jardin des Plantes (du Roi, Royal), 34, 99, 168, 173, 324. *See* Museum of Natural History

Jard-Panvillier, 183, 282

Jefferson, Thomas, 54n, 187

Jesuit colleges, 13, 15, 41, 75, 307; dissolution, 47, 60

Jesus Christ, 256, 271

jeunes de langue, 43, 174. *See* Oriental languages

Jews, 38, 99, 187, 332. *See* religious neutralism

Joseph II, 38

Josephists, 108

Jourdain, C., 30n, 39n, 336

Juilly College, 21, 299, 318

Julia, D., 9n, 41n, 53n, 86n, 114n, 185n, 228n, 235, 304n

Jullien, Marc-Antoine, 26

Jussieu, 152, 173, 325

Kennedy, Emmet, 222n, 237n

Kennedy, Michael, 104n

Labène, J. G., 141

La Caille, 17, 49n

Lacépède, 104, 224, 256, 324

La Chabaussière, 210, 239

La Chalotais, Caradeuc de, 53, 55, 56, 58, 59, 123, 237

Lacour, 90, 93

Lacretelle, P. L., 89-90, 290

Lacroix, Sylvestre, 210, 246, 250, 252n, 290, 291

La Flèche College, 21, 49, 66

La Fontainerie, 53n

Lagrange, 164, 171, 215, 224, 270, 272, 326

La Harpe, J. F., 36, 84, 152, 215, 217, 220, 287

laissez-faire, 267

Lakanal, 106, 135-37, 161, 189, 210, 212-13, 218, 222, 227, 234

Lalande, 224

Lamarck, 173, 224

Lamoignon, C. F., 78. *See* Malesherbes

language, national, 11, 96, 183-90, 200, 266

langue d'oc, 184, 185

Laplace, 215, 224, 326

Laromiguière, 106, 322

Latin quarter, 29, 42, 94, 157

Lavoisier, 23, 132n, 151, 165-66

law, teaching of, 31, 41, 98, 105-106, 265, 273, 278, 412, 414

Lazarists, 108

Leblanc, Nicolas, 148, 164-65

Lebon, 107

Lebreton, 210, 234, 270

Leclerc, J. B., 133

Leclerc, J. T., 156

Legendre, 17, 210

Legrand, Abbé Louis, 24, 114

Leith, J., 53n, 190n

Lemonnier, 49n

Léon, André, 255

Lepeletier, Félix, 137-38, 144-45, 181, 222

Lepeletier, Michel, 20, 138-39, 141, 163

Lepeletier plan, 20, 138-39, 141, 143, 145, 154, 155, 226, 266

levée en masse, 109, 160

Liard, L., 322n

liberté de l'enseignement, 95-96, 135-36, 180, 227, 230, 236, 263; under Napoleon, 298, 316-20. *See* "private" schools

Lille, schools at, 28, 136; Central School, 249, 256

Linnaeus, 256

literacy, 10-12, 105, 202, 208, 230-31, 332. *See* elementary education

Locke, 5, 17, 19, 210, 303

Louis XIV, 9, 12, 15, 33, 41

Louis XVI, 72, 82, 134, 283

Louis XVIII, 329, 331

Louis-le-Grand, College of, 5, 19, 21, 43, 54, 62-63, 80, 113, 117, 171-72, 176, 313. *See* Equality College, Prytanée français

Louis-Philippe, 52, 143

Louvre, 34, 173, 269, 327

Lozère, 162

Lycée des Arts (1781, *républicain* after 1792), 35, 131, 152, 210, 242

Lycée des Arts (1792-1798), 131, 152,

165, 234-35

lycées (in Condorcet's sense, for higher education), 126-28, 133, 161, 166, 168, 179, 211, 232, 264-65, 293

lycées (Napoleonic), 293-306, 312-13, 317-20

Lyon, colleges at, 109-10, 118-19; Central School at, 246

Mably, 25, 54-55, 256

Maggiolo line, 10-11, 105

Mahérault, 164n, 210, 214

Maintenon, Mme de, 175

Mainz, 252

Major, J. F., 90, 93, 141

Malesherbes, Lamoignon de, 78

Marat, 100, 138, 142, 156

Maréchal, Sylvain, 196

Maria Theresa, 38, 70

Marie-Antoinette, 283

Marmontel, 33, 247

Mars, School of, 201

Martin, Roger, 115, 259-63, 265, 270, 275, 277, 282, 293

Masuyer, J.B.C., 133

mathematics, teaching of, 17, 51, 167-68, 250-51, 253, 276, 302

Mathieu, J. B., 193-94

Mathiez, A., 197

Mazarin, cardinal, 42, 114, 323

Mazarin College, 17, 42. See Quatre-Nations

Medicine, Faculty of (pre-Revolutionary), 33, 161, 173, 205-206. See universities

Medicine, Royal Society of, 33, 44

medicine, teaching of, 31, 41, 98, 168, 206-208, 253, 262, 265, 278, 310, 321. See Health, Schools of

Mentelle, 215, 217

Mercier, 19, 36, 49, 224

meritocracy, 138, 229, 269-70, 327. See talents, examinations, scholarships, equality

messageries, 40, 43

metric system, 176, 268-69

Mézières (school of engineering), 44, 174, 200, 202

Michigan, University of, 32

military atmosphere in schools, 27-28,

67, 201-202, 303-304

Millin, 210

Millot, 18, 256, 273

Mines, School of, 44, 174, 229, 325

Minimes, 66

Mirabeau, 81, 88-89

Mittié, 159

Monge, 164, 200, 215, 224, 326

monopole universitaire, 236, 309, 315, 320. See centralization

Montgolfier, 18

Montmartre, faubourg, 159

Montpellier (town), 183

Montpellier, faculty of medicine, 173, 206

moral and political sciences, 127, 168, 233-34, 276-77, 290, 323

More, Hannah, 12

Morellet, 247

mortmain, 44-45

Mouret, Mme, 87n

Museum of Natural History, 213, 309, 315, 322, 324, 325. See Jardin des Plantes

Nancy, Central School, 251

Nantes, Edict of, 40

Nantes, University of, 44

Napoleon. See Bonaparte

National Commission on Education (Poland), 38

"national education," 52-61, 70-74, 87, 90-91, 158, 329. See plans under Rolland, Poitiers, Talleyrand, Condorcet, Lepeletier, Paris, Brumaire IV, Roger Martin, Council on Public Instruction, Floréal X, University (Napoleonic)

national language. See language, national

National Society of Arts and Sciences (in Condorcet plan), 126-28, 131. See Institute, National (1795)

Navarre, Père, 55, 56

Navarre College, 18, 103-104, 325

New York, University of the State of (1784), 39

Nimes, Central School, 256

Nollet, 18, 49n

Nord, department of the, 249

Normale, Ecole (1795), 201-202, 208-19, 226, 232

Normale, Ecole (1808), 219, 313, 322, 327
"notables," 280, 312

oath (civil), 102-103, 108-12
Observatoire, section de l', 157
Observatory, 34, 168, 173. *See* Bureau of Longitudes
O'Meara, Barry, 294
Oratorians, 15, 18, 25, 45, 50, 66, 106-10, 115, 247, 288, 307, 312
Oriental Languages, School of, 174, 315
Orléans, University of, 60
Oxford University, 20n, 38, 39
Ozouf, Mona, 197

Palissot, 270
Panthéon, Central School of the, 248, 254
Panthéon-français, section du, 157-58, 183
Paris, Commune of, 147-49, 161
Paris, Department of, 79, 147-48, 161-65, 208
Paris, plan of September 15, 1793, 146, 160-69, 226, 255, 306
Paris, sections of, 122, 148-50, 155-60, 200, 219
Paris, University of. *See* University of Paris
Parker, H. T., 9n
Parlement of Paris, 41, 47, 60-62, 70, 241, 317
patois, 11, 184, 185, 187-88
Pau, University of, 44
Pellicier, Abbé, 62
Pension Militaire, 27
periodical press, 83-84, 99-100, 184
Perpignan, University of, 44
Peter the Great, 71
Petit, M. E., 169-70
petites écoles. See elementary education
petits séminaires, 311, 312, 316, 317-18
Peyrard, F., 164, 165
pharmacy, 34, 44, 174
Philosophy (as highest class in a college), 14, 17-18, 25, 40, 51, 301, 303
physics, teaching of, 18, 51, 250, 276, 301-302, 325-26
Pinel, 207

Pius VII, 284, 316
Plessis College (Paris), 171, 313
Poitiers, University of, 28, 60, 72-74, 108
Poland, 38, 52, 59, 78
Polytechnique, Ecole, 202, 228-29, 290, 309, 322, 325-26. *See* Public Works, School of
Pombal, 38
Pont-à-Mousson, 44
Pontlevoy, College of, 111-12, 210
Ponts et Chaussées. *See* Roads and Bridges
Portalis, 308
Prades, Abbé de, 51
Prairial, insurrection of (1795), 219
Priestley, 256
Prieur de la Côte-d'Or, 200, 222, 228, 229
primaires, écoles, 96, 125, 134, 143, 161, 166, 179-83, 211-12, 231, 236-40, 260-61, 263, 267-68, 274-75, 290, 295, 310, 318n. *See* elementary education
Princeton College, 17
"private" schools, pre-Revolutionary, 8, 26-30, 57, 61; during Revolution, 111-12, 131, 133, 135-36, 170, 179-80, 236-42, 258, 267; under Napoleon, 283, 295, 297-98, 300, 308, 312, 314-20. See *liberté de l'enseignement*
Proyart, Abbé, 28, 29, 76
Prudhomme, 100
Prussian General Code (1794), 12
Prytanée français, 21n, 119, 248, 273, 290
Public Instruction, Commission on (Commission of Six, 1793), 137, 161, 163-64; (Commission of Nine, 1793), 169
Public Instruction and Republican Institutions, Commission on (1797-1798), 82, 258, 260, 262-67
Public Instruction, Commission on (1816), 331
Public Instruction, Committee on (Legislative Assembly), 82, 124; (National Convention), 123, 134-35, 165-67, 187-89, 193-94, 210, 227-28

Public Instruction, Council on (1798-1800), 5, 270-78, 284, 289, 297, 298, 302

Public Instruction, Executive Commission on (1794-1795), 198, 209-10, 226, 230, 336

Public Instruction, "ministry" of, 137n, 209

Public Safety, Committee of, 134, 161, 178, 181, 186, 191, 194, 197-98

"public" schools, meaning of, 8, 12, 41, 52ff., 58, 114, 135, 236-42. See *collèges*, "national education"

Public Works, Executive Commission on (1794-1795), 198, 202

Public Works, School of (1794), 198, 202-205, 208, 228. *See* Ecole Polytechnique

Quatremère de Quincy, 104

Quatre-Nations (Mazarin College), 42, 173; Central School of the, 248, 290, 323. *See* Mazarin College

Quicherat, J., 318n

Quinette, 272, 274

Quintilian, 7

Rabaud Saint-Etienne, 132

ratio educationis (of Maria-Theresa), 38, 71

Raymond de Varennes, 89

Reason, cult of, 1793, 160

Reims, University of, 60

religious neutralism in schools, 27, 68, 99-100, 124-25, 239, 243, 305, 311, 332

Rendu, A., 309n, 329-31

Rennes, College of, 118

retribution universitaire, 314-15

Richard, Gabriel, 31-32

Rigolet de Juvigny, 30

Rivard, D. F., 17, 55, 62

Roads and Bridges (school of), 44, 174, 202, 229, 290, 325

Robespierre, 20, 21, 23, 26, 122, 130, 137-38, 140, 142, 163, 181, 193-95, 226

Roederer, 282, 285, 293, 295, 299

Rohan, 23

Rolland d'Erceville, 53-54, 55-56, 58,

60, 62, 70-72, 78, 260

Rollin, Charles, 7, 19, 24, 25, 46, 140, 256

Romme, Gilbert, 104, 124, 130, 133, 169, 189, 218, 219

Rousseau, 30, 48, 52, 81, 102, 193, 210, 256, 283

Royer-Collard, 322

Rühl, 163

Sabourain, 109

Saint-André, Jeanbon, 132

Saint-Antoine, faubourg, 159

Saint-Cyr (girls' school), 175

Sainte-Barbe, College of, 318n

Sainte-Marthe, College of, 27-28, 108-109

Saint-Just, 81

Saint-Malo, 195

Saint-Omer College, 19

Saint-Sulpice, 31

saltpeter, etc., school of, 200

sans-culottes, 6, 122, 139, 148-49, 153, 160, 168. *See* Paris, sections of

Sans-culottes, section des, 147, 156, 157, 160

Savoure, pension, 242

Say, J. B., 223, 282

scholarships, pre-Revolutionary, 14, 21, 59, 62, 63, 66, 73, 116; during Revolution, 92, 110, 116, 134, 136, 170, 176, 207-208, 273; in Talleyrand plan, 97, 101; in Condorcet plan, 129; in other Revolutionary plans, 136, 212, 232, 264; under Napoleon, 293-98, 304-305, 314, 319, 325, 327. *See* endowments, talents

School of Mars (Ecole de Mars), 201

schools. *See under subject designation*, e.g., Public Works, Roads and Bridges, Mines, "public," "private"

science sociale, 127

secondaires, écoles, 125, 167, 179, 199, 209, 212, 231, 254, 268; under Napoleon, 295-97, 300, 310

secondary education, 8, 13, 73, 140, 161, 167, 236, 242, 310-15. See *collèges*, Talleyrand plan, Condorcet plan, Central Schools, *écoles secondaires*, lycées, *petits séminaires*

sections. *See* Paris, sections of

Seine-et-Oise, Central School, 290

Serieys, A., 158

Shapiro, G., 86n

Sherlock, 266

Sicard, 215

Sieyès, Abbé, 134-36, 153, 234

Sieyès-Daunou-Lakanal plan, 135-37, 153, 163

Siméon, 298

Smith, Adam, 44, 59, 223, 256, 267, 296

Snyders, G., 13n

Soboul, Albert, 147n, 149, 155

social mobility, 23, 52, 57-59, 86n, 229, 280-81. *See* scholarships, meritocracy

Société d'Histoire naturelle, 131

Société du Point central des arts et métiers, 151

Société philomatique, 131

Société royale d'émulation, 142

sociétés populaires, 149-50, 161, 179, 184, 190, 200

Society of French Youth (Société de la jeunesse française), 143, 175

Sonthonax, 266

Sorbonne, 31, 46, 51, 105

Sorèze, College of, 27, 67, 110-11, 172, 249, 299, 318

Sparta, 56, 157, 160

"special" schools, 232, 252, 265, 274, 277, 293; under law of Floréal, 295-96, 297, 312, 323-24

Staël, Mme de, 224, 236

Stendahl, 251

Strasbourg, University of, 100-101, 105, 173, 206; Central School, 249, 251; *gymnase protestant*, 249

Strogonov, 104

Suard, 247

Supreme Being, cult of, 193-97

Surgery, College of, 34, 44, 206

Taine, 84

talents, 59, 71, 79, 87, 93; in Talleyrand plan, 96; in Condorcet plan, 128; for Mittié, 159; in Paris plan of 1793, 162; for Polytechnique, etc., 229; under Napoleon, 294. *See* scholarships, social mobility

Talleyrand, 23, 75, 76, 224, 234

Talleyrand plan, 20, 82, 83, 90n, 94-101, 180, 306

Talma, 328

Tarn, Central School, 249

Taton, R., 16n

teacher training. See *agrégation*, Ecole Normale

Terror, 121, 160, 196

Thermidorians, 209, 224

Thibaudeau, A. C., 170, 293, 295

Thiébaut, Dieudonné, 55

Thierry, A., 327

Thouin, 214

Tocqueville, 23

Tournon, College of, 68, 299

Toussaint l'Ouverture, 266

"track" system (as between primary and secondary), 140, 168-69, 212-13, 231, 261, 267, 275, 278, 291, 297, 302

Tracy. *See* Destutt de Tracy

Treihard, 260

Trénard, L., 51n, 110n

Trier, 252, 318

Tuileries, section des, 156

Turgot, 23, 44, 51, 54, 72, 124

Turin, University of, 38, 285, 330

Unigenitus, 45-46

United States of America, 114n, 154

universities, pre-Revolutionary, 12, 14-15, 30-32, 39-43, 70-73; during Revolution, 85, 98, 100-101, 126, 162, 164, 264-65, 277-78; German, 85, 100, 252, 252n, 265, 321; European, 38-39

University (Napoleonic), 70, 73, 306-22, 329

University of Paris, 14, 20-21, 28, 39-40, 46-47, 60-61, 70, 269, 317; during Revolution, 79-80, 115, 119, 161

Vandermonde, 215

Vauquelin, 325

veterinary schools, 44, 174

Vicq d'Azyr, 33, 152, 154

Vienne, College of, 115

Vignery, J. R., 155n

Viguerie, J. de, 22n, 50n, 106n

Villemain, 304n

Villier, J., 90
Vitebsk, 318
Volney, 215, 234, 282
Voltaire, 21, 23, 33, 48, 49, 256, 270, 273

Westminster Abbey, 191
West Point Military Academy, 229
Witherspoon, John, 17

women's education, 9, 45, 56, 57, 175, 241, 242, 283, 292, 316; in Revolutionary plans, 81, 89, 93, 95, 97-98, 100, 125, 150, 160, 167, 171, 231, 242, 292, 316. *See* elementary education
Worcester, Mass., 18

Ysabeau, 107

Library of Congress Cataloging in Publication Data

Palmer, R. R. (Robert Roswell), 1909-
The improvement of humanity.

Includes index.
1. Education—France—History—18th century.
2. France—History—Revolution, 1789-1799—Education
and the revolution.   I. Title.
LA691.5.P35   1985   370′.944   84-15048
ISBN 0-691-05434-7